CW00969461

Dürrenmatt

By the same author

The theatre of Friedrich Dürrenmatt (Oswald Wolff, London and New York, 1980)

Dürrenmatt

Reinterpretation in Retrospect

Kenneth S. Whitton

OSWALD WOLFF BOOKS

BERG

New York / Oxford / Munich

Distributed exclusively in the US and Canada by
St. Martin's Press, New York

First published in 1990 by
Berg Publishers Limited
– Editorial Offices –
165 Taber Avenue, Providence R.I. 02906, USA
150 Cowley Road, Oxford OX4 1JJ, UK
Westermühlstraße 26, 8000 München 5, FRG

© Kenneth S. Whitton 1990

All rights reserved.
No part of this publication may be reproduced
in any form or by any means without the permission
of Berg Publishers Limited.

Library of Congress Cataloging-in-Publication Data
Whitton, Kenneth S.
Dürrenmatt: reinterpretation in retrospect / Kenneth S. Whitton.
p. cm.
"Oswald Wolff books."
Includes bibliographical references.
ISBN 0–85496–650–1
1. Dürrenmatt, Friedrich—Criticism and interpretation.
I. Title.
PT2607.U493Z948   1990   89–17885
832'.914—dc20   CIP

British Library Cataloguing in Publication Data
Whitton, Kenneth S. (Kenneth Stuart) 1925–
Dürrenmatt: reinterpretation in retrospect.
1. German literature. Swiss writers. Dürrenmatt, Friedrich
I. Title
838'.91409

ISBN 0–85496–650–1

Printed in Great Britain by
Billing & Sons Ltd, Worcester

For Marjory, Kirsty and Kenneth

Contents

Contents

Foreword

The present study will complement my previous book, *The theatre of Friedrich Dürrenmatt* (London and New York, 1980). There I dealt, as the title indicates, almost exclusively with Dürrenmatt's stage-plays, referring only where appropriate to his theoretical and other writings. In this volume, I examine in detail all Dürrenmatt's narrative works – stories, novels and radio-plays – and the most important essays, speeches and lectures which have appeared in published form since 1947.

I have thus been able to look back over more than forty years of his writings and to take the opportunity to consider my own interpretations garnered over these years and some of the 'traditional' interpretations of Dürrenmatt's works in the light of more recent critiques, and especially in the light of Dürrenmatt's own assessment of his life and career, as he too has been recently 'recollecting in tranquillity'.

Since I understand that the Swiss Embassy has kindly provided most institutions with the dtb (detebe) (Diogenes Taschenbuch) edition of Dürrenmatt's collected works, the *Werkausgabe* (Diogenes Verlag AG, Zurich) of 1980, I have decided to take these thirty volumes as the source of all my quotations (unless otherwise indicated). The volumes are therefore identified as WA1 etc. (cf. pages 234–44) below.

I should like to thank my publisher, Dr Marion Berghahn, for her patience and encouragement, my editors, Chris Bessant and Justin Dyer, the Librarian, Miss Grace Hudson and the counterstaff of the J.B. Priestley Library, University of Bradford, for their unfailing courtesy and assistance, and Friedrich Dürrenmatt and his wife, Charlotte Kerr, for their gracious hospitality during my visit in July 1988.

A final word of thanks goes to my wife for her support and understanding during the trying days of preparation of the book: 'Dann ist Vergangenheit beständig . . .'.

Kenneth S. Whitton
Leeds/Bradford
1988–9

–1–

Friedrich Dürrenmatt

Denn alle Schuld rächt sich auf Erden.
(Goethe)

Friedrich Dürrenmatt, born on 5 January 1921 in the little village of Konolfingen in the Emmental, not far from the Swiss capital Berne, has shared with his countryman, Max Frisch (born 1911), the distinction of being among the leading authors in the German language in the post-war years. His *oeuvre* contains almost every genre of writing available – plays, poems, radio-plays, novels and short stories, essays, television, film and operatic scripts and libretti, along with theoretical and philosophical treatises – and he is, in addition, a not inconsiderable painter and sketcher, with a number of exhibitions to his credit.

Now in his late sixties, Dürrenmatt stands a Protean figure in the world of European literature and culture, 'oftmals verlacht und dennoch [dir] trotzend' to paraphrase one of his own favourite dramatic characters, Graf Bodo von Übelohe-Zabernsee, in the play *Die Ehe des Herrn Mississippi* – in some ways a lonely, isolated figure, in others an important representative of a very Swiss, humanist, enlightened, libertarian conscience.

An attempt was made early to prove that Dürrenmatt was 'the child of his father', a Protestant clergyman, and that most of his works were written under the influence of a strong Christian faith, but even the most enthusiastic proponent of this belief has felt obliged to recant in recent years. If any further indication were needed that the theory no longer held water, it was given to me by Dürrenmatt himself when I visited him in his home in Neuchâtel in July 1988, and he expressed such obvious amazement that his son Peter (born in 1947) should have become a clergyman! (It must, however, be added that the son has shown that *he* is 'the child of his father' by his active involvement in anti-war demonstrations, and a subsequent four-month prison sentence in Neuchâtel in 1973 as a conscientious objector.)

Dürrenmatt was the son of Reinhold Dürrenmatt, a kindly, earnest and scholarly parson who read the Old Testament in

Hebrew, and the New Testament in Greek and Latin, every day. He had been a popular and caring minister till his retirement, his house open to all comers, his mind to all religions and sects. Dürrenmatt vividly remembers the negro Modidihn who was invited to dinner 'und aß Reis mit Tomatensoße. Er war bekehrt, aber dennoch fürchtete ich mich.' (WA26, 17). This is only one of the themes which he picks up again in his *Stoffe I–III* (A1/2) after having first touched on them in the early essays 'Vom Anfang her' (1957) and 'Dokument' (1965) (both now in WA26). What he does not stress in these early works, however, is the resentment which he obviously felt towards his father, and which has clearly remained a major factor in his personal development. In one sense, he is grateful to his father for his having introduced him to so many literary, biblical and classical themes – above all, to the theme which, as we shall see, has dominated Dürrenmatt's thinking in recent years, Theseus and the Minotaur: 'Am liebsten jedoch erzählte mein Vater vom königlichen Theseus, wie er die Räuber Prokrustes und Pityokamptes besiegte, und vom Labyrinth des Minos, von Dädalus erbaut, [um] den ungefügen Minotaurus gefangenzuhalten' (A1, 23).

The parents had been childless for twelve years, and the father was forty when Friedrich ('Fritz') was born; the age-gap in these authoritarian family circumstances proved too great. The young Fritz seemed more attracted to the memory of his grandfather Ulrich (1849–1908) who, 'klein, gebückt, bärtig, bebrillt, mit scharfen Augen', had been a much more worldly figure than Dürrenmatt's father, since he had been politically active, had published his own newspaper and had even 'done time' (ten days) for one of the scurrilous poems printed in each number of his *Berner Volkszeitung*. It should, however, be added that the grandfather showed few signs of Swiss 'humanism' and egalitarianism. In Dürrenmatt's own words, he was a man, 'der den Freisinn, den Sozialismus und die Juden haßte' (A2, 13).

Stoffe I–III makes very clear how lonely and cut off from his fellows the young Dürrenmatt felt. He admits that this was due in part to his being 'the son of the manse' – 'eine bestimmte Stellung', he writes (A2, 22) – but also in part to the growing gulf between him and his parents, and to his rich imagination which enabled him to people the peaceful Swiss landscape with the bloodthirsty heroes of Ancient Greece and Rome, an interest not shared by his schoolfriends. This strain of individuality in his character is mirrored not only in his works, where 'der große Einzelne' is a constant theme, but also in his private life where, although on occasion a convivial and even kindly host, he prefers to keep himself to himself, and lives now, with his second wife, in his isolated eyrie in the Chemin du Pertuis-du-Sault high above Neuchâtel in French-speaking Switzerland.

Nor were his relations with his mother Hulda (née Zimmermann), who ruled the Dürrenmatt household, much more satisfactory. Although Dürrenmatt tried to look after his mother in her old age, his feelings of guilt at his neglect are vividly expressed in the introduction to the story 'Mondfinsternis': 'Es quält mich noch jetzt, ihr gegenüber kein nachsichtigerer Sohn gewesen zu sein' (A2, 18). Her strong Christian evangelical belief in the power of faith – she stressed continually in later years how all of Dürrenmatt's literary successes were due solely to the grace of God – eventually sickened the son who writes of the 'Mauer aus Glauben' which he felt was lowering over him. These pages in 'Mondfinsternis' (now in *Stoffe II–III*) (e.g. 15–19) alone show how unwise it is to portray the later Dürrenmatt (of, say, 1970 on) in the same terms as the Dürrenmatt of *Es steht geschrieben* and *Der Blinde* of 1947–8. The feelings of personal (Calvinistic) guilt which are a, if not *the*, major theme in Dürrenmatt's work, are made nowhere clearer than in his pathetic description of his father's death in an old people's home on 6 February 1965, nine days after his eighty-fourth birthday, and of his mother's in 1977 at the age of almost eighty-nine.

Stoffe I–III gives a much truer picture of those early years than anything so far published by, or on Dürrenmatt. An older (and wiser?) man looks back on the source of his 'materials', his 'themes': 'Gleichzeitigkeit sagt nichts aus. Das Ferne rückt erst mit der Zeit näher. Die Wirklichkeit weitet sich nur allmählich aus. Zwar geschieht nichts ohne den Hintergrund, wo die Ursachen dafür liegen, daß wir denken und schreiben, aber dieser Hintergrund ist gestaffelt wie eine Landschaft' (A1, 57). Although most of the biographically orientated books and articles on Friedrich Dürrenmatt have been bound to mention these early experiences, none has been able to realise the profound influence that was exerted by that early isolation, an isolation compounded of his position as the pastor's son and the quite different social stratum into which this forced him, his own very different literary and artistic interests, the growing disagreement with his parents, particularly his father, and even, when the family moved from village life in Konolfingen to the capital Berne in October 1935, his difficulties in repressing his own native *Landberndeutsch* for the *Stadtberndeutsch* of the Freies Gymnasium there. (The Berne dialect 'Miuchmäuchterli', 'a milk jar', plays a part in his detective novels, e.g. in *Der Verdacht* (WA19, 200)). In retrospect, it seems almost perverse that Dürrenmatt deliberately placed himself in an identical position when on 1 March 1952 he moved to Neuchâtel where, for thirty-seven years, he has felt himself a stranger, still speaking 'ein unmögliches Französisch'. As he writes in *Versuche* (1988), by calling the town Neuchâtel and not Neuenburg 'halte ich sie höflich auf Distanz, sie ist mir nie ganz vertraut geworden' (A6, 18). His 'fragment', 'Zur Dramaturgie der Schweiz' (1968–1970), also makes his views on the peculiar position of the 'Welschschweizer' very clear: 'er weiß nicht, weshalb er eigentlich Schweizer ist, ja, er ist manchmal dem Franzosen gegenüber leicht geniert, Schweizer zu sein' (WA28, 74).

Again in retrospect, we see that Dürrenmatt has always lived in a 'labyrinth' – indeed, when the family moved to Berne that 'Labyrinth [wurde] Wirklichkeit' (A1, 49), for his subsequent early career is a struggle against forces which attempt to rob him of his individuality. He reacted strongly, for example, against the attempted inculcation of pre-war Goethean ideals by the Freies Gymnasium's Rektor in Berne – 'während überall die goethischen Ideale zusammenkrachten' (A1, 53) – and against the senseless shoe-cleaning which was his lot during his time in the Rekrutenschule in the summer of 1942 before his poor eyesight released him from further military service. Indeed, there are grounds for maintaining that his decision to give up university studies showed that here too he was in a world foreign to his temperament. He studied in Berne before service in the recruits' school (1941–2), then, after one *Wintersemester* in Zurich under the 'hochpathetischen' Professor Emil Staiger (1942–3), he studied six more *Semester* under Professor Herbertz for philosophy and Fritz Strich and Emil Ermatinger for Germanistik in Berne (autumn 1943 to June 1946). It was here that his intense dislike of the world of 'Germanistik' originated (cf. A2, 121–2; WA1, 293).

Dürrenmatt's continual mention of a proposed doctoral dissertation on 'Kierkegaard und das Tragische' reads well but, in the light of his own admission that he was a 'ziemlich verbummelter Student' (WA27, 125) who had an inferiority complex because he had studied ten *Semester* 'ohne akademischen Abschluß', one rather doubts his expressed good intentions (cf. WA27, 37). Not that everything that he studied was anathema to him. He read Plato, Aristotle, Aristophanes, Kant, Schopenhauer and Nietzsche, while Wieland and Lessing were his favourite German classical authors. However, the major theme of his studies was philosophy and not 'literature'.[1]

No, it seems rather that Dürrenmatt's nocturnal sessions with the Expressionist-influenced painter Walter Jonas were much more seminal. Here, he claims, he first heard the names Kafka, Jünger, Heym, Trakl and Büchner, and was able, almost for the first time, to free himself from the bonds of convention, to enter a non-academic, non-priestly, non-authoritarian milieu and to develop his two major interests, painting and writing.

It should not be forgotten that Dürrenmatt had another 'chip' to carry on his shoulder: he was at that time extremely stout, indeed he has never been particularly healthy.[2] The diabetes which has dogged him for most of his life must have contributed to that feeling of 'other-ness' which is so marked a feature of his personality. It tires him quickly – 'Kämpfen Sie 25 Jahre gegen die Müdigkeit, die Ihnen Zucker im Blut macht', he said dispassionately to Heinz Ludwig Arnold in 1975 when the latter suggested that Dürrenmatt's writings were a sort of defence against despair (F1, 66) – and we shall be examining the effect of the disease on his development and his work in later chapters.

To all appearances, Dürrenmatt found happiness with his actress wife Lotti Geißler. She was playing in an Ibsen piece in the Stadttheater in Basle and had had a part in the Swiss film *Vreneli vom Thurnsee* at the time. They married in the Registry Office in Berne on 11 October 1946; the next day, the religious ceremony, conducted by Dürrenmatt's father, took place in Ligerz on the Bielersee (Lake Bienne) where Frau Lotti's mother lived. On 14 October they moved to Basle where their son Peter was born on 6 August 1947. Then on 17 July 1948 they moved to the 'Festi', a house above Ligerz overlooking the Bielersee, where they stayed until the final move on 1 March 1952 to nearby Neuchâtel.

Their three children, Peter, Barbara (born on 19 September 1949) and Ruth (born on 6 October 1950) have lived very much their own lives, and Dürrenmatt did tell me during my visit in 1988 that he no longer understood his children – but that is a state of affairs not unique to celebrated authors! The couple's early financial tribulations are, as we shall see, closely connected with the production of the author's early works, but the move to Neuchâtel in 1952, and the later affluence of the 1960s and 1970s, led to a rather grand life-style, most obviously visible in Dürrenmatt's magnificent and authoritative wine-cellar.

Frau Lotti's death on 16 January 1983 was a severe blow to Dürrenmatt; a man who needs a good deal of attention, both physical and organisational, he was greatly helped by the ministrations of an understanding wife. He plunged back into the world that he knew best, the world of work, wrote his first play for six years, *Achterloo* (1983), and travelled to Greece and South America. Then on 8 May 1984 he remarried. Charlotte Kerr, a Munich journalist, actress and film-maker, had met Dürrenmatt after the production of *Achterloo* in Zurich in October 1983, and in the jointly written book *Rollenspiele* (1986) (A4) she describes how they worked together on a new version of the play *Achterloo III* (which then became *Achterloo IV* and was produced in the rococo theatre in the castle at Schwetzingen in the Black Forest in 1988). She then embarked on a four-hour film on Dürrenmatt's life and career, *Porträt eines Planeten: Von und mit Friedrich Dürrenmatt* (F10), which was shown on the SDR III programme on 26 December 1984. The film is based on Dürrenmatt's cataclysmic drawings and is, in essence, a conversation with Frau Kerr in their house in Neuchâtel and neighbouring places. It is particularly interesting for Dürrenmatt's reminiscences which are sometimes more vivid here than in their written form in *Stoffe I–III* and *Rollenspiele*.

My conversation with Dürrenmatt and his wife in their beautiful home in July 1988 centred on those themes which we both felt had dominated his writings during nearly fifty years. He, now sixty-eight, was keen to look back over his long and undoubtedly chequered career and to point out what he saw as his successes and failures. I, having studied his works for almost forty years, was keen to see whether my plan to 'reinterpret' these works 'in retrospect' was capable of fulfillment. The following chapters, which lay much more weight than is usual on the 'prose-works' as opposed to the more celebrated plays, will perhaps give an answer.

–2–

The Early Narrative Works

There has been much conjecture and debate among Dürrenmatt scholars about the genesis of these early works. Peter Spycher's detailed survey of the narrative prose points out that, although Dürrenmatt indicated that the *Novellen* were written 'zwischen den Jahren 1943–1946', and could or should be seen as the 'Vorfeld' to the dramas of 1947 onwards, some of the works (e.g. 'Der Tunnel' and 'Der Hund') were written much later (in 1951/2), while Dürrenmatt made clear that he worked on 'Die Stadt' till 1952 (cf. C46, 31). Spycher, of course, is here considering the volume *Die Stadt (Frühe Prosa)* (1952). However, volume 18 of the *Werkausgabe* excludes 'Der Hund' and 'Der Tunnel' which are now to be found in WA20; volume 18 includes 'Die Wurst', 'Der Sohn', 'Der Alte' and 'Aus den Papieren eines Wärters'. The latter piece gives the title to the volume, an interesting decision made either by the author or by the editor, Thomas Bodmer, since it seems to underline the claim made by Armin Arnold among others that many of these stories have a Kafkaesque provenance (cf. C2, 10), although I mentioned in my previous book *The theatre of Friedrich Dürrenmatt* (1980) that Dürrenmatt had assured me in 1969 that he only read Kafka 'much later' and that 'Die Stadt' in particular 'von Platon kommt', (B23, 18, note 13).

Dürrenmatt's own testimony in *Rollenspiele*, as related by Charlotte Kerr, is exact. On Christmas Eve 1942 Dürrenmatt was studying philosophy, and was painting, in Zurich, 'wilde, expressionistische Bilder'. In the evenings he would discuss literature, 'Kafka, Musil, Büchner', with the painter Walter Jonas who encouraged him to start writing.[1] After a night's drinking session, Dürrenmatt meant to go home for Christmas. Stumping through the snow, he came on Georg Büchner's gravestone – '1813–1837' – and is reminded of the grandmother's tale in *Woyzeck*, 'eine poetische Weltbeschreibung'. Back in the bar behind the Café Odeon in Niederdorf, he ordered the cheapest drink possible, 'Vermouth mit Gin', and wrote his very first story, 'Weihnacht'. 'Er sieht den Weg vor sich,' writes Frau Kerr. 'Er wird Schriftsteller' (A4, 50–1).

I have never had any doubts that these stories are an essential part of the Dürrenmatt *oeuvre*; one need only consider his vast output of paintings and sketches to realise that apocalyptic visions, catastrophic happenings, grotesqueries and obscenities have dominated his thinking since these earliest days. As he reminisces, it is this type of happening which forces its way back into his mind: the butcher in Konolfingen cutting up bloody meat – Dürrenmatt remembers 'wie das Blut aus den großen Tieren schoß' – the vegetable-seller dividing up a lettuce with his handless arm, the children playing in an empty grave till just before the burial-party arrived, and the frightening vision of the all-devastating Flood, 'Gottes Zorn'. Truly, as Dürrenmatt wrote originally in his essay 'Dokument' (1965), 'das Grausen blieb, das mich erfaßte' (WA26, 13). It is difficult, therefore, for me to agree with commentators such as Hans Bänziger who wrote at the end of his discussion of the early stories, 'Was bleibt? Ein starker Eindruck und die Genugtuung, Dürrenmatt später auf einem anderen Posten antreten zu sehen' (C7, 142–3), or Murray Peppard, who thought that 'Dürrenmatt's early prose can now be seen as a dead end' (B18, 24), an opinion with which Timo Tiusanen concurred (B22, 41–2).[2] Gerhard Knapp's judgement 'daß in ihnen bereits die Grundlagen des späteren Schaffens vorhanden sind' (C29, 15), and Armin Arnold's belief 'daß diesen ersten Arbeiten etwas Echtes und Ursprüngliches anhaftet' (C2, 9), are much closer to my own point of view.

* * *

As we have seen, 'Weihnacht' (now in WA18, 9–12) was written during Dürrenmatt's first *Semester* of study at the University of Zurich in 1942–3. Full of good bourgeois, anti-parental and anti-Christian invective, he hurled his challenge to God in a poem written for a *Buch einer Nacht* during that exciting time with Jonas in his studio:

> Im Spiegel ruht die Welt.
>   Sie hat Kopfweh.
> In der Mitte sitzt Gott.
>   Er schläft.
> Sein Haar ist weißes Licht.
>   Um seinen Hals windet sich eine Schlange.
>   Sie würgt.
> Gott ist erstickt (cf. Wyrsch, E49, 23).

Jonas added sketches to the book. Dürrenmatt comments on the period, 'Es galt gegen die Welt an sich zu protestieren, Gott an sich zu attackieren' (A2, 129). There was a feeling of emptiness in the young man, isolated from his home, from his university course with these pointless 'strukturellen Untersuchungen' of works of literature, and, not least, from his country, standing helplessly neutral in the middle of a world conflagration. 'Weihnacht', 'a short, short, revealing story' (Diller), expresses that mental and physical ice-cold isolation. The prose-poem contains twenty-eight sentences and 122 words:

> Es war Weihnacht. Ich ging über die weite Ebene. Der Schnee war wie Glas. Es war kalt. Die Luft war tot. Keine Bewegung, kein Ton. Der Horizont war rund. Der Himmel schwarz. Die Sterne gestorben. Der Mond gestern zu Grabe getragen. Die Sonne nicht aufgegangen. Ich schrie. Ich hörte mich nicht. Ich schrie wieder. Ich sah einen Körper auf dem Schnee liegen. Es war das Christkind. Die Glieder weiß und starr. Der Heiligenschein eine gelbe gefrorene Scheibe. Ich nahm das Kind in die Hände. Ich bewegte seine Arme auf und ab. Ich hatte Hunger. Ich aß den Heiligenschein. Er schmeckte wie altes Brot. Ich biß ihm den Kopf ab. Alter Marzipan. Ich ging weiter.

Students of Dürrenmatt will recognise familiar themes here which reappear in later works: the guilty wish to startle, to *épater le bourgeois* (in Molière's phrase), and the gratuitous blasphemies, but also the remarkable plasticity of language which easily allows a picture to form in the mind's eye of a young man, full of personal guilt, attacking a dying God in a Swiss-cold, unfeeling world.

'Weihnacht' was followed by a longer story, 'Der Folterknecht', written at the beginning of 1943 (13–19), a horror story of Man's punishment on earth. Again there is an economy of language, with sentences of three, four and six words: 'Die Stunden kriechen'; 'Die Luft ist siedendes Blei'. It is the story of a pact made between a dandy, with money, a wife and two children, and a torturer, 'der letzte der Menschen', to change their roles for two years. The torturer enjoys his two years with the dandy's sensual wife – 'Sie umarmt ihn. Er fährt ihr über die Brust' (17) – in a cruel and violent company. When he returns after two years, the dandy fails to keep the appointment. Disgusted, the torturer returns to the sleeping woman and murders her: 'Er hebt die Fackel. Feuer gießt sich über weißes Fleisch' (18). He is condemned to be tortured to death, this time by the former dandy – who now reveals himself as God. The world is a torture-chamber, and it has been abandoned by God, the *deus absconditus* of Protestantism, appalled by the sins of the world.

It is perhaps a little fanciful to think of this 'Folterkammer' as the torture-chamber depicted by Max Frisch in his famous diary-entry of late 1946, 'Drei Entwürfe eines Briefs', where he wrote of the Swiss during the war, 'Wir wohnten am Rande einer Folterkammer, wir hörten die Schreie, aber wir waren es nicht selber, die schrien' (C17, 632). Nevertheless, the mutual choice of the theme and the word is interesting. Interesting too is the strong sexual symbolism of the piece: the hungry woman, the mention of 'Brust', 'Haut' and 'Fleisch', and the colour red – the fire, the torture-chamber, the blood, the wine ('altes Blut') and a 'red eye' is mentioned (17)! According to the section 'Der Rebell' in *Stoffe II–III*, Dürrenmatt had his first sexual experience – with a French girl – at this time, but the dominating impression is again of a lonely young man tortured by feelings of guilt, hotly challenging the authoritarian God of his childhood (cf. A2, 128–9).

The third work of Dürrenmatt's literary apprenticeship, 'Die Wurst', written in the winter of 1942–3, was not published until 1978 (in the *Lesebuch*, A9, 19–23) and was known to Dürrenmatt researchers through Lotti Dürrenmatt's reminiscences in Wyrsch's *Die Dürrenmatt-Story* where, we learn, the story was originally – and more eccentrically – titled 'Die Zungenwurst' (E49, 23).[3] I would claim that this is our first sight of that very Dürrenmattian sense of the comic with which the literary world was soon to become so familiar. (The story is now in WA18, 21–5).

The man who kills his wife and makes her into a sausage – 'verwurstet sie'! – is brought to trial. While the trial proceeds, the judge, 'der höchste Richter', looks avidly at the red, steaming, juicy sausage. The man is condemned – 'Der Tod öffnet sein Maul' (25) – and his last perverse wish, to eat the sausage, is granted. But 'der höchste Richter sieht auf den Teller. Die Wurst ist weg' (25). The condemned man and everyone else look, horrified, at the judge. 'Die Welt wird ein ungeheures Fragezeichen' (25)!

The style is once again one of short, sharp sentences of rarely more than six words, leaping *sprunghaft* from point to point, while the *topos* is, of course, as old as literature itself: the jealous Medea serving up his own children as a stew to Jason or, in Shakespeare's *Titus Andronicus* (of which Dürrenmatt later made a 're-version' for Düsseldorf in 1970), Saturninus being served a meat pasty of Tamora's two sons.

As in 'Der Folterknecht' there is a strong sexual element in this story, an element which I believe is not met with again in Dürrenmatt's work until the late 1970s. The symbolic colour red appears again in the prosecutor's 'Glatze', the sausage and the accused's lips ('getrocknetes Blut'). However, the overriding artistic element here is the 'grotesque', that 'demonic made ludicrous' as L.B. Jennings accurately describes it (in B15; cf. B23, 96, note 52): the awe-inspiring, fearful 'höchste Richter', sitting in absolute judgement ('wie Gott') over the miserable, trembling, accused man ('ein Floh'), is made ludicrous by his despatch of the human sausage.[4]

The fourth and last short story of 1942–3 is 'Der Sohn', first published in the *Lesebuch* in 1978 (A9, 15–18) and now in WA18, 27–30. A famous surgeon suddenly gives up his wealthy practice to seek a wife. After visiting many brothels, he marries an eighteen-year-old beauty, the daughter of a rich industrialist, then, after the birth of their son, brutally leaves her to die ('unter heftigen Blutungen'). He brings his son up in a villa, fifty kilometres from the town. The upbringing is strange – 'derart, daß er stets nackt mit ihm lebte' (29) – and the boy's every wish is granted. The boy has no human contact until, when he is fifteen, his father procures him the lowliest prostitutes, whereupon the son runs away – 'nackt, wie er geschaffen' (30) – to return twenty-four hours later, pursued by the police for having killed an innocent man. The pair defend the villa with machine-guns against the police until it goes up in flames. The son, wounded in the shoulder, accuses the father – 'er habe ihn zu einer Bestie gemacht' (30) – whereupon the father, 'ohne mit der Wimper zu zucken', shoots him down.

The writing here seems more assured and 'professional': the 'Hochfrequenzstil' of the earlier stories gives way to a more flowing and fluent prose. Some of the elements that we have already noted reappear – the sexual and the gratuitously cruel, for example – but there is no grotesque here since there is no humour. As in 'Der Folterknecht', the sense of retribution is strong.[5] It does not need the psychiatrist's couch to decide that the 'Vater–Sohn–Konflikt' theme, so beloved of the German Naturalists and Expressionists, can be traced back to Dürrenmatt's own personal conflict at the time. It does, however, underline the strong sense of having been wronged which appears in Dürrenmatt's later reminiscences of his childhood. Heinrich Goertz, one of Dürrenmatt's latest German commentators, seems to query this. 'Lastet die Autorität seines Vaters auf Friedrich Dürrenmatt so stark?' he asks (C18, 19). I feel certain now that it does and did, and indeed I have given the discussion of these juvenile, unpublished pieces more space than they are normally allotted because of the early appearance in them of major Dürrenmattian themes and concerns.

* * *

There were physical as well as mental problems, Dürrenmatt writes in *Stoffe*. The severe illness that he suffered in the spring of 1943 brought abdominal pains and constant vomiting – an infectious hepatitis – and, although he did finish his 'Komödie' (q.v.) in Eison, a 'Nest' in Wallis, in the summer of that year, he writes, 'Ich stand im Leeren, ein Schriftsteller ohne Fähigkeit zu schreiben' (A2, 130; WA1, 293–4).

Dürrenmatt's first *published* work, 'Der Alte', appeared in a Berne daily paper *Der Bund* (No. 12) on 25 March 1945 (and is now in WA18, 31–9).[6] The date is perhaps significant for the warlike theme. A small country is invaded by a mighty force; only in the villages is there resistance, and this is soon overcome. A deep hatred grows up against the unknown 'old man' who is oppressing the villagers, and a young married woman is deputed to visit him: 'so fand dieser Haß den Weg zu einer Gestalt, die ganz im Hintergrunde war' (34). She finds him in an old-fashioned, small ('Swiss') room, surrounded by old books and 'Büsten der Denker', poring over a map. She has come to kill him, but his unconcern lames her and she gives her gun up to him helplessly. As he says, 'Es gibt nichts Unbedeutenderes als den Tod' (38). *Nothing* moves him, in fact – he is the nihilist supreme. When he returns the gun to the woman, a gesture 'wie alle Dinge, deren Wesen im Absurden liegt' (39), she shoots him, feeling the hate, the author writes, that men sometimes feel for God.

'Die Wurst' and 'Der Folterknecht' had introduced the Dürrenmattian theme of 'judging' and 'to-be-judged'; here, in the light perhaps of political circumstances in which the possibility of Switzerland's being invaded by Nazi Germany was not a remote one, the cruelty of what Dürrenmatt was later to call the 'Mächtigen' *vis-à-vis* the victims, or 'Opfer', was shown. Although Dürrenmatt himself has often been portrayed as a nihilist at this time – and even although he had a sign 'Friedrich Dürrenmatt, nihilistischer Dichter' on his door in Zurich – only later does he begin to draw characters who could be stereotyped as nihilists. Here, however, retribution is dealt to the 'men in power' and the sympathy is with the 'Opfer', the victims, the 'Volk' – although the old man's indifference would seem to suggest that he knows that his 'power' will not die with him.

Dürrenmatt, unlike his older countryman, Max Frisch, had had no experience of 'real' army service, and therefore, apart from his remarks on his Rekrutenschule (above, 4) did not and could not comment personally on the war, as Frisch did in *Blätter aus dem Brotsack* (1940) and *Dienstbüchlein* (1974). However, he could not but be aware, firstly, of the war raging around him and, secondly, of the importance for German literature of neutral Switzerland. There, for example, were held the premières of Brecht's *Mutter Courage* (on 19 September 1940), *Der gute Mensch von Sezuan* (on 4 February 1943) and *Leben des Galilei* (on 9 September 1943), all in the Schauspielhaus in Zurich. (Dürrenmatt, otherwise a not very enthusiastic theatre-goer, he tells us, went to see *Der gute Mensch von Sezuan* at Walter Jonas's suggestion, and it has remained his favourite Brecht play (A2, 126; WA1, 293–4)).

When I suggested to Dürrenmatt during our conversation that Goethe's 'Denn alle Schuld rächt sich auf Erden' had often seemed to me a good motto for his own work, he smiled and did not disagree.[7] Almost all of these early stories circle around the theme of guilt and retribution, and we have seen that the young author himself was tortured with personal doubts at this time. His next two stories 'Das Bild des Sisyphos' (1945) (now in WA18, 41–56) and 'Der Theaterdirektor' (WA18, 57–69) were both written in 1945 and first published in 1952; both have guilt and retribution as their theme.

'Das Bild des Sisyphos' does concern a *picture* about Sisyphus, but has no other connection with Albert Camus's famous Kafka-orientated essay 'Le mythe de Sisyphe' (1942). The narrator, Dürrenmatt himself, on a visit to a village in the Suisse Romande watches a group of children alternately building and knocking down a house of cards, and he is involuntarily reminded of the fate of a man whom he had known years ago, a latter-day Sisyphus who rose only to fall. The man, known as 'Rotmantel' because of his 'Vorliebe für die rote Farbe' (45) – the symbolic 'red' plays its part here too! – had become rich and powerful by 'ein verstecktes Verbrechen'. He had once owned a Hieronymus Bosch painting of Sisyphus – 'ein loderndes Feuermeer' (46) of red – whose hellish agonies, the narrator feels, parody and intensify his own 'Schuld des Verdammten'. The story is of the man's desperate attempts to buy the painting back from the rich banker who now owns it. This is his 'Sisyphus task' (cf. Dürrenmatt's 1946 painting).

The narrator's illness, and the subsequent continuation of the story by his doctor, lends the narrative the quality of a feverish dream, for the ensuing scenes flash before our eyes like a speeded-up film. The struggle for the picture between the rich banker, almost a parody of a Swiss 'type', and Rotmantel, whose power 'ihre Wurzel im Bösen selber hatte' (51), ends in victory for the latter. But when the narrator visits him later, he finds the man just as one would find a 'zottigen Minotaurus', in a labyrinth-like attic room, grotesquely lit by the flickering red light of a fire, and destroyed like the children's house of cards.

Why? Retribution has come to the man, for his crime had been to fake the Bosch picture when he was a poor young painter and to sell it to make a fortune, 'um aus nichts etwas zu machen' (55). In so doing, and this is his retribution, he had betrayed his God-given talent and his art: *Ex nihilo nihil*. He throws the fake Bosch on to the fire, himself to perish later, Spycher suggests, as his house burns down (C46, 65). This is a most powerful short story, containing many scenes which betray both the prentice painter and – I agree here with Elisabeth Brock-Sulzer (C12, 286) – the future 'Theatermann' with an eye for a telling 'scene'. For me, however, its main and present interest is the development of the theme of guilt and retribution, presented to us here in visual terms where colours (red, above all), furniture, clothes and odours represent emotions and beliefs.

'Der Theaterdirektor' (WA18, 57–69) might be seen as a typical product of 1945, since it tells of a powerful theatre manager 'dem die Stadt erliegen sollte' (59), after it had taken him first as a joke. Could this be a Hitler-parallel? Certainly the parallel becomes closer as the story of the seduction of an audience by ever-more revolutionary and frightening productions proceeds, and it becomes clear 'daß ihm von Anfang an das Theater nur als Mittel diente, jene Macht zu erlangen, die sich später als rohe Herrschaft der schrecklichen Gewalt enthüllen sollte' (62). The similarity between the manager's new theatrical style, where 'eine Tragödie in eine Komödie verwandelt wurde, während sich ein Lustspiel zu einer Tragödie verfälschte' (62), and Dürrenmatt's later theatrical technique was remarked upon in my previous book (B23, 32), but the point here is the sense of growing confusion, fear and unrest in the audience(s) as the manager uses his productions to rape their minds: 'den Menschen zu vergewaltigen und in den Bann einer reinen Willkür zu ziehen' (65). The audience is then personified by the manager's promotion of a young, not-too-gifted classical actress whose unskilled talents are first praised and then reviled by the public because she does not, and will not, follow the manager's directions to the letter. We realise that the manager has chosen her as his revenge on the town, while the town has been seduced 'auf die Freiheit zu verzichten und sich dem Bösen zu ergeben, denn Schuld und Sühne gibt es nur in der Freiheit' (67). This prefigures interestingly the people of Güllen in *Der Besuch der alten Dame*, 'eine Gemeinde, die langsam der Versuchung nachgibt' (WA5, 144).

Under the roaring approval of the 'Menge', the actress is hauled up on a *Strafkolonie*-like contraption which 'einem ungeheuren und überirdischen Insekt zu gleichen schien', and which first slashes off her clothes and then, to cries of 'Töte sie!', beheads her (68). We are told that the audience streams out of the theatre to start 'the revolution', but as the last lines of the story make clear it is the revolution of a 'new day', of a 'new order', directed not by the town, but by its dictator, the theatre manager.

Thus we *do* see the Hitler-parallel, written at a time when Germany was reaping the harvest of its 'sins' for having succumbed to 'evil' by denying that love of freedom and 'commonsense' which Armin Arnold saw represented by the brave young actress (C2, 15). Certainly, the dictatorial figure of the Theaterdirektor must have been conceived at about the same time as the charismatic figure of Johann Bockelson in Dürrenmatt's first play, *Es steht geschrieben*, written between July 1945 and March 1946, a figure who becomes even more like the Theaterdirektor in the revised version, *Die Wiedertäufer*, of 1966.[8]

We have seen that Dürrenmatt found Berne a 'labyrinth' when he moved from Konolfingen in 1935. He has never conquered his dislike of towns and was not enamoured of his first married home at Sankt Albanvorstadt 30, in Basle's patrician quarter. The next story that we consider tells once again of mobs and over-filled town milieux, of frightening visions, dreams – and murders.

'Die Falle' (WA18, 71–95) was written in 1946, published as Dürrenmatt's first book (*Der Nihilist*) by the Holunderpresse, Horgen, Zurich, in 1950 and then incorporated into *Die Stadt* in 1952. It is Dürrenmatt's longest story to date (twenty-two pages) and shows a growing command both of language and of narrative technique. He returns to the 'Ich-Erzähler' format and to his by now favoured 'Rahmenerzählung', a story within a story, a popular nineteenth-century narrative device.

The story is the nihilist's life as related to the author-narrator. None of the characters in these early stories has a name – if we except 'Rotmantel'! – but we are told of *this* character: 'Ihn besiegte der Tod, der zu ihm gehörte' (76). And Death dogs him. A man is mysteriously shot in a field and, as the nihilist stands over the body, he is approached by the dead man's unconcerned wife and is asked why he is there. 'Ich will mich töten.' 'Wozu?' 'Weil ich den Tod liebe.' 'Du bist ein Henker?' the wife asks, the first mention of a favourite Dürrenmatt theme (80). The woman seems to be the 'opposition' to the 'absolute', as we also noticed in 'Der Theaterdirektor'.

The nihilist accompanies the woman, 'den Menschen . . ., mit dem er sterben wollte' (82) to her house where, after making love to her, he sinks into a dream which is in essence a vision of the end of the world, of mankind descending into a darkness at the end of which is 'ein riesiger Feuersee' (84). As the mob of mankind sweep down past the nihilist, he decides to claw his way back into 'Life' and finds himself fighting back 'through the Ages', past the Middle Ages, Rome and Greece, then past people dressed in furs and skins – 'So zog die Menschheit an ihm vorbei, hinab in die Tiefe' (87) – until he finds himself alone: 'Er stand im Leeren' (87). Strangely enough, this is the phrase which Dürrenmatt used in *Stoffe* to describe his own state of mind at this time of his life (above, 12). The dream's solution is to plunge him back into the abyss with the others as he cries, 'Gnade, wo ist Gnade, ohne Antwort an ihrem [i.e. der Menschheit] Antlitz' (90).

The dream is therefore his death-wish. On waking, he shoots the woman and flees through the wintry village, for he has discovered that, like most men, he has fear of his *own* death. 'Ich will leben,' he cries (92), now 'ein Mensch wie jedermann, ein Mensch mit einer Stellung, der heiratete, der Kinder hatte, ein Haus, ein Automobil, eine Geliebte' (94). When he finishes his story, he walks the narrator to an empty factory to take leave of him, and the narrator finds that he has walked into a trap, or 'Falle'. The point of the rambling story has been the nihilist's wish to kill *him*, the man who knew 'das Geheimnis seiner Verzweiflung' (95). But since the nihilist knew that he had already committed one crime which had robbed him of his humanity, his retribution is to shoot himself.

Many interpretations of the story are to be found in the various studies of Dürrenmatt; however, Tiusanen's off-hand comment, 'The storytellers just walk around, get engaged in strange undertakings and see macabre nightmares or visions', seems a little harsh (B22, 33–4) 'Die Falle' on the one hand shows the burgeoning confidence of the coming writer – the juvenile 'baroqueness' has to be taken on board with the striking images and scene-painting – and, on the other hand, for our retrospective purposes, does give an insight into the author's developing thematic concerns.

One of these was mentioned for the first time in 'Die Falle' when the nihilist begged for God's grace, 'Gnade'. Given the circumstances of the time, 1946, when the world was striving to come to terms with the consequences of the defeat of a major evil, Nazism, where traditional belief in a benevolent God had been gravely undermined – and that this young Swiss author was known to be the son of a clergyman – it is not surprising that his first commentators approached his early works from a religious point of view.

Some find his works consonant with a deep religious conviction and a concern with God's grace (e.g. D13, 23; E6, 12); others are equally certain that he was the nihilist of his story, although Brock-Sulzer always believed that he changed the title to 'Die Falle' to avoid that very charge (C12, 292)! Whatever view is held of his belief, it is undeniable that Dürrenmatt at this time *was* enmeshed in a web of doubt. The works of these years, 1946–9, all centre round religious belief and motifs. One of the first, the very first on a biblical theme, is the short story 'Pilatus' (WA18, 97–115) which went through many, much longer, versions before the final one of 1946.[9]

We noted in our discussion of 'Die Falle' the first mention of the executioner, 'der Henker', and the 'Pilatus' story takes up the theme in that it represents Pontius Pilate as the guilt-ridden executioner of God-made-Man, although again the main character has no name in the story, only in the title. The motto placed before the story is 'Denen aber draußen widerfährt alles durch Gleichnisse, auf daß sie mit sehenden Augen sehen und doch nicht erkennen und mit hörenden Ohren hören und doch nicht verstehen' ('but unto them that are without, all these things are done in parables; that seeing, they may see and not perceive; and hearing, they may hear and not understand', Mark iv, 11–12). Significantly, Dürrenmatt omitted the closing words, 'lest at any time they should be converted and their sins should be forgiven them' (98). From this motto, then, we understand that Pilatus recognises from the outset 'daß der Mensch', brought before him in chains by the mob, 'niemand anders war als ein Gott' (99); the Roman's incomprehension of the possibility of such an occurrence, and his consequent horror at its significance, 'weil er die Wahrheit wußte, ohne sie zu verstehen' (112), is the crux of the parable-like story. Pilatus knows that the God has come to kill him. Although Dürrenmatt has skilfully blended here the four Gospel versions, Pilate's sceptical 'What is truth?' (in John xviii, 38) and his central statement, 'Der Abgrund zwischen Mensch und Gott war unendlich gewesen, und nun, da der Gott diesen Abgrund überbrückt hatte und Mensch geworden war, mußte er an Gott zu Grunde gehen und an ihm zerschmettern, wie einer, den die Welle an eine Klippe schleudert' (104), points to the more detailed description of the Christ–Pilate relationship given in John xviii–xix.

Here Dürrenmatt discusses, as Emil Weber rightly states, the problem 'des absoluten Paradoxes des menschgewordenen Gottes' (E48, 37), and the possible/probable theme of his planned dissertation *Kierkegaard und das Tragische*. This, Dürrenmatt wrote in his letter to Walther Muschg, is the true 'Tragödie der Antike' and indeed of philosophy itself: that these doubting and questioning thoughts have prevented Pilate 'wie ein Kind zu sein', since 'whosoever shall not receive the kingdom of God as a little child, he shall not enter therein' (Mark x, 15). Only if Pilate had believed *like a child* could the 'tragedy' have been avoided. But instead he called for a bowl of water, 'in der er zum Zeichen seiner Unschuld die Hände wusch' (112), and became a 'Henker'.[10]

In the light of all that Dürrenmatt has written since 1946, I believe that this story, 'Pilatus', is the first to adumbrate his love of the paradox. This is the greatest paradox of all: that 'the Son of God died; it is to be believed because it is absurd. And He was buried and rose again; the fact is certain because it is impossible', the *credo quia absurdum* of Tertullian's *De carne Christi*. With Kierkegaard, this paradox leads Man into despair, but then (for some) out of it, to Faith (cf. Diller, D11, 134–5).[11]

The 1952 volume *Die Stadt (Frühe Prosa)* ended with the story 'Pilatus' even though, chronologically, 'Die Stadt' was the later story (1947). Armin Arnold wondered if Dürrenmatt had arranged this order so that there would be 'ein ganz bestimmtes Ordnungsprinzip', i.e. to begin with Christ's birth ('Weihnacht') and end with his death (C2, 19). Maybe. Volume 18 of the *Werkausgabe*, however, finishes with 'Die Stadt', followed by 'Aus den Papieren eines Wärters', which Dürrenmatt's end-note of 1980 tells us is the 1952 rewriting of 'Die Stadt', a theme 'dem ich damals nicht gewachsen war' and which he finished 'zwanzig Jahre später' (= 30/40?) in *Stoffe I*, in the section titled 'Der Winterkrieg in Tibet', A1, 95–190.

Most of Dürrenmatt's commentators, like me, have chosen to tackle his work chronologically, perhaps because of the richness of the material and the 'enormous corpus' of secondary literature to which it has become impossible to refer other than selectively (Daniel Keel's bibliography in WA30 has over a thousand titles, and there are many more). The author himself, however, feels that one should discuss his work differently: 'Schriftsteller sollten einander nach ihren Urstrukturen, Urmotiven und Urbildern zugeordnet werden, nicht chronologisch' (A1, 78). I hoped that we might be able to kill two birds with one stone.

* * *

An examination of Dürrenmatt's sketches and paintings, both in his house where they decorate every wall and in the volumes *Bilder und Zeichnungen* (A8) and *Oeuvres graphiques* (A12), show that one of these *Urmotive* is the labyrinth (cf. above, 4). From his earliest days to the present, Dürrenmatt has never ceased using this as a symbol of his (or Man's) incomprehension of the world around him. 'I am a stranger afraid/ In a world I never made', wrote A.E. Housman – this is the theme of 'Die Stadt' (WA18, 117–47) and its successors: 'Die Welt ist ein ungeheures Fragezeichen', to paraphrase that sentence in 'Die Wurst' (above, 10). Whether one calls this story 'Kafkaesque' to give it a provenance is really immaterial. Dürrenmatt always insists that the theme is from Plato's 'Höhlengleichnis' ('Cave Allegory') in his *Republic* (*Politeia*) (Book VII), where the incarcerated sit in a cave which has one opening. They are chained, neck and legs, so that they cannot move and can only see ahead. Between them and the fire is a path with a wall, along which people carry all sorts of barrels and containers. All the prisoners can see are the shadows of these people on the wall, so that they must believe that these are real. If they could turn their heads, they would see that the shadows are but an illusion. The state's task, therefore, is to lead men from the world of illusion ('Schein') to that of reality ('Sein'), to the 'wahre Wesen des Schönen, Gerechten und Guten' (C38, 211–12).[12]

'Die Stadt' is told, again, in the first person of a hungry young painter. After describing his own absurd ('sinnloses') life and his room in the eastern suburb whose walls he had decorated from top to bottom – as Lotti Dürrenmatt tells us that her husband did to their first room (E49, 23)! – he pictures a labyrinthine town full of strange, mysterious and unnamed people. An executioner 'in einem roten Mantel und einer gelben Maske' (123–4) – Dürrenmatt's 'hellish' colours – represents the dictatorial, bureaucratic nature of the town's government. The rebellion which breaks out against it collapses, ridiculously, when the rebels come up against the town madman whose screaming – 'die Sprache jener Dinge war, die uns stumm umgeben und uns schweigend vernichten' (131) – drives the rebels back to the town, trampling over those who had fallen by the wayside. This ends Part I. In Part II the narrator enters the service of the town authorities as a guard. It looks as if one could assume that Dürrenmatt's 'Stadt' is his own town of Berne, with its river near the icy mountains, its cathedral and, above all, its 'niedrigen Lauben' or covered arcades. But it is an 'unidyllic' Berne, one which was to become a mental and physical labyrinth for Dürrenmatt in the years 1939–45. And it is to a labyrinth that the narrator is led to meet 'drei alte Weiber' (the Parcae?), playing cards, drinking tea from Chinese cups and wearing light summer clothes, 'schlampig und von einem grellen Rot' (133). A young girl assigns him a narrow niche in the wall of a long corridor opposite a 'prisoner'. He feels proud to be occupying 'eine Schlüsselstellung', guarding 'Gefangene, Verbrecher, Rebellen' (137). But soon the question arises: who are the guards and who are the prisoners? This is the Platonic question, 'Sein oder Schein', which the narrator tries to puzzle out by logical thinking. But thinking is useless here: he must *believe* that he is a guard, that he is *free* – Kierkegaard's 'pathetischer Sprung' from the 'Gefängnis des Denkens' to the 'Freiheit des Glaubens', the 'leap into Faith'. As in 'Pilatus', to believe this one must believe 'like a child', but 'Die Stadt' does not finish there – in fact, it does not finish at all: 'Doch kam mir an diesem Punkt meiner Überlegungen die entscheidende Idee (die kopernikanische Wendung gleichsam): Ich mußte die Anordnung der Wärter anders denken: Ich mußte . . .' (147).

I shall return later to Sydney Donald's interesting attempt to trace the Minotaur/labyrinth theme through Dürrenmatt's work (D14). For the moment, I should like only to draw attention to his comment that the 'few, brief references' to freedom in 'Die Stadt' 'serve merely to enhance the *irony* of whether the narrator's freedom is real or illusory' (my italics, 209). The point is of some interest since I spent so much time in *The theatre of Friedrich Dürrenmatt* tracing the sources of Dürrenmattian humour. Humour is in short supply in these stories, but the ironically baroque motto to 'Die Stadt' might indicate that the most Dürrenmattian trait is about to break through: 'Aus den Papieren eines Wärters, herausgegeben von einem Hilfsbibliothekar der Stadtbibliothek, die den Anfang eines im großen Brande verloren gegangenen fünfzehnbändigen Werkes bildeten, das den Titel trug: Versuch zu einem Grundriß' – which most non-Germanic Germanists will recognise as the *Urwitz* about German academics, a breed regularly mocked by Dürrenmatt. So, as we shall see on many occasions later, freedom, irony and humour are closely linked in Dürrenmatt's mind.

'Die Stadt' is therefore the unfinished fragment of a novel, undertaken like so many of the works of this period to earn money. (Comfortably-off professorial literary critics often mention this fact with some surprise, as if writers should write 'for art's sake'!) Yet the theme was never far from the author's mind, and he took it up again in 1952. 'Aus den Papieren eines Wärters' (which now ends WA18, 149–93) starts from the less dramatic motto 'Die hinterlassenen Papiere eines Wärters, herausgegeben von einem Hilfsbibliothekar der Stadtbibliothek' (150), but contains a good deal of the substance of 'Die Stadt'. The author, 'ohne Glauben' (151), describes the town in more despairing terms. Just as Kafka's Landvermesser fails to penetrate the secrets of the Castle, so too Dürrenmatt's narrator finds the town, firstly, a jungle-puzzle – 'Wie sollten wir aber je Einblick in die Entwicklung der Stadt erlangen können, wenn uns der Einblick in ihre Ordnung verwehrt ist?' (152) – then its reality simply as 'Hell': 'wer hätte mehr Wirklichkeit als die Hölle, wer mehr Gerechtigkeit, und wer ist so ohne Gnade wie sie?' The town is much more decrepit than in 'Die Stadt', even more 'unidyllic'. The tenement buildings are 'baufällig' and 'verwahrlost' (153), and the attitude towards people more bitter and contemptuous: 'Auch fing ich an, die Menschen zu haßen [*sic*], weil ich sie verachten lernte' (156). Such contempt for the town and its complacent inhabitants leads the narrator to contemplate a crime, indeed a murder, albeit a 'sinnloser Mord' because, as he says later, 'in dieser Welt hatte nur noch das Verbrechen einen Sinn' (165). The victim is to be one of the town's officials who lives in a 'dreckigen Mietskaserne' nearby. Yet before he can commit the crime, he receives an invitation to visit the administration where, to his surprise, this very official offers him an army post because of his previous active service against bandits.

The long conversation between them (163–85) reflects not only Dürrenmatt's growing interest in the theme of 'those in power' ('die Mächtigen') over the weak and the victims ('die Opfer'), but also the Swiss guilt at their non-participation in the recent world wars for Freedom. It is the official who insists that the only hope for the world is the individual who will work and fight for Freedom. Dürrenmatt's narrator is made to deny this by eagerly seizing the opportunity of having 'Macht über Menschen' (183) and volunteering to take part in the war still raging in Tibet. The official's last words remind the narrator, however, that 'Die Türe [*sic*] ist offen', that he (Man) can always renounce his lust for power.

As in 'Die Stadt', Part II of this story (186–93) leads the narrator to report to the three old women – this time drinking tea out of *Japanese* cups! – where he is given a uniform and taken down into the labyrinthine bowels of the earth. Now, however, he is clearly a 'Wärter'; there are no niches, no question of 'Who-is-where?', no Kafkaesque ponderings, but a realistic meeting with his former army commandant who addresses him as 'Hänschen' and points to a naked, bearded man hanging by his hands with a heavy stone round his feet. Why is he there? 'Weil der Schweinehund sich einbildete, er sei kein Wärter.' And what did he think he was? 'Ein Gefangener,' says the commandant (193).

Thus there *are* still questions, and in 1951–2, amongst all his other work, Dürrenmatt was still forced 'eine Welt der Sinnlosigkeit darzustellen, in der ein Sinn gesucht wird, den es nicht gibt, ohne den sie jedoch nicht ausgehalten werden kann', his private labyrinth, his 'endloser Alptraum', which was soon to become a 'Weltlabyrinth' (cf. A1, 75). The Existentialist *angoisse* of Sartre and Camus, the now perceived horrors of the concentration camps, the fear of the atom bomb, the growing bureaucratisation and anonymity of society all played their part in explaining the 'colouring' of the theme. Dürrenmatt was not satisfied with his treatment and we shall study the development of the theme in later pages (below, 86).

* * *

I turn now to the last of the prose works contained in that early volume *Die Stadt*. It is generally felt that the last two works, 'Der Hund' (1951) and 'Der Tunnel' (1951) should be separated from the *very* early narrative works; possibly for this reason they are now to be found in WA20 with an even later story, 'Die Panne' (1956). By 1951–2 Dürrenmatt was an established author, with three plays, a number of radio-plays and, above all, two detective novels to his name. 'Der Hund' and 'Der Tunnel' thus belong to the second phase of his career.

'Der Hund' (WA20, 9–18), like 'Pilatus', is a parable. It tells of an old and ragged man who, accompanied by a dog, 'ein riesiges und entsetzliches Tier' (11), calmly reads from the Bible to a few people outside the town hall. The narrator is fascinated by him and accepts his invitation to his cellar-dwelling where he finds a girl in a dark-blue dress, the old man's daughter. The man had been a rich industrialist who had then 'found the Truth' and had left his family to proclaim It to the world. (How often Dürrenmatt portrays these 'rich industrialists' who give up their ill-gotten gains!)

The huge dog has prevented anyone from visiting them, but the girl calmly announces that the narrator and she will now be married and that she will be protected from the animal. The narrator then describes with feeling their love-nights – 'wir lagen Leib an Leib, immer wieder ineinander versinkend' (15) – but he can never make the girl leave the room to go for walks or to the theatre, 'wo sich entscheidende Dinge vorbereiteten' (16). One day the girl asks the narrator to kill the dog, which is now lying in front of the cellar preventing the old man from going out. Setting out under a sky 'von einem tiefen, bedrohlichen Rot' (17), they fight their way through the crowds and traffic only to arrive too late: the old man lies 'vom Hunde zerfetzt' (incidentally, we are never told where they actually came from!). The narrator loses track of the girl until, three days later, he hears footsteps and looks out to see the girl calmly walking down the street with the huge dog, 'sanft und lautlos wie ein Lamm' (18).

A slight story, 'Der Hund' shows nevertheless Dürrenmatt's growing mastery of the craft of the born story-teller: one wants to know what is going to happen; one's mind is arrested by the powerful images and the evocative language. Bearing in mind Dürrenmatt's earlier experience with dogs (cf. note 9), we can see this beast as the incarnation of Evil which prevents the proclamation of the Truth, but is then overcome by the pure love of the girl for another human being. Weber's religious exegesis seems rather far-fetched, but his final quotation from Dürrenmatt's later *Prosakomödie, Grieche sucht Griechin* (1955), does convince: 'Die Hoffnung, ein Sinn sei hinter all dem Unsinn, hinter all diesen Schrecken, vermögen nur jene zu bewahren, die dennoch *lieben*' (my italics, E48, 29–30; WA21, 149).

The last work to be considered in this chapter might be taken to be a masterpiece to judge from the number of anthologies of short stories, in many languages, in which it has appeared, and from the number of full-scale studies written on it (cf. the Bibliography in WA30, 492, 1986 edition, for example). 'Der Tunnel' (now in WA20, 19–34), attracted keen critical attention from the outset, since it was so obviously an autobiographical sketch of an author who was one of the leading young names in German literature after the war. Like his 'Ich-Erzähler', Dürrenmatt had been 'ein Vierundzwanzigjähriger' in 1945, he too was 'fett', and his published works made much of the 'Schreckliche hinter den Kulissen' (21). It was well known too that he smoked Ormond Brasil 10 cigars, and that, as a student, he had regularly made the weekend 'zweistündige Bahnfahrt' from Berne, where he was living with his parents, to Zurich (although these towns are not named in the story) by the 17.50 train, arriving at 19.27.

The story's enduring popularity shows, however, that it had, and has, many other claims for nomination as a small masterpiece. Karl Moritz's comment that because the train deviates from normalcy Dürrenmatt is anxious to show that our world is menaced by mechanisation is undeniably valid, but somewhat trite (quoted in B22, 38). There is so much more to this eerie tale. The process is from normality to terror – from the normality of an Emmental summer's evening with a cloudless sky, of a full train (all but in the first-class section) through which the young man has to battle to find a whole bench-seat in a third-class compartment, of the red-haired(!) girl quietly reading a novel and a fat man, 'noch dicker als er'(!)(22), playing chess opposite him, to the entering of the tunnel on time as usual. Then come the first signs of unease 'als der Tunnel kam, der ihm länger als sonst zu dauern schien' (22), a tunnel normally so short that the reading lights were never switched on. But to practised readers of horror stories, little signs lead to great events: the narrator goes out into the corridor 'in welchem ein hochgewachsener Mann in einem hellen Regenmantel auf und ab ging, ein schwarzes Halstuch umgeschlagen' (23–4). A *black* scarf!

And from now on, normality yields to concern, concern to panic, panic to terror. True, 'kein Land besitz[e] so viele Tunnel wie die Schweiz' (24), as the chess player says, but even that, and the guileless, typically phlegmatic (and rather stupid) English tourist tapping his English pipe on the window and unwittingly believing that he is passing through the Simplon tunnel, cannot pacify the young man, and he makes his way to the front of the train to find that the driver has already jumped off and that only the guard is left in control. The guard answers the young man's panic-stricken comment that there is no such tunnel on this route with: 'Nichts beweist, daß am Tunnel etwas nicht in Ordnung ist, außer natürlich, daß er nicht aufhört' (28) – the 'ludicrous made demonic' with a vengeance. (In passing, it is interesting to note that the only tunnel of any length between Zurich and Berne is the Aarau tunnel just before Olten, which takes about twenty seconds to traverse. There is a much longer tunnel, taking about forty-five seconds, between Berne and Neuchâtel, after Roßhausen.)

As the train rushes 'downward', the guard/conductor asks the 'merciless' young man, 'Was sollen wir tun?' (34). The answer to the Kantian question in the original version is 'Nichts'. Then follow ten lines describing his 'gespensterhafte Heiterkeit', before he repeats, 'Nichts. Gott ließ uns fallen, und so stürzen wir denn auf ihn zu' (34). The theological, indeed teleological, answer has attracted most of the critical attention from those who wished to read deep religious significance into these early works, and for whom the young man's 'fall' was not into Hell, but into the arms of a loving, caring God, a perfectly acceptable Christian interpretation. Hans Mayer, who writes of Dürrenmatt's 'Theologie ohne Gott', claims that the end indeed declares God's presence, but that He is shown to be useless for our modern condition (E31, 483–4).

Looking at Dürrenmatt's work from the vantage-point of 1989

and considering what we now know of his life in those days, Mayer's negative view would seem to be the likelier one. Dürrenmatt's own revision (in 1978) for the *Werkausgabe* omitted the last sentence, so that the story now finishes with the repetition of the young man's 'Nichts', which seems to indicate that there is, and will be, nothing to be done; God has no part to play.

It is not the least difficult of the tasks of a commentator on Dürrenmatt to decide when and where he ceased to have even a conventional religious belief; it is now plain, however, that it was indeed much earlier than most critics claim. He does seem to have shared Kafka's view in his third *Oktavheft*: 'Wir sind, mit irdisch befleckten Augen gesehen, in der Situation von Eisenbahnreisenden, die in einem langen Tunnel verunglückt sind'.

* * *

Although there are various points of view about the importance of these early narrative works, and I have quoted a few of them, I am of the opinion that, seen from the distance of forty years, they do represent views and themes to which Dürrenmatt has remained peculiarly faithful. The accents have changed, but the substance has *not* changed. He saw the stories in 1952 as a 'Vorfeld' to the dramas of the 1950s, and then as an attempt, 'mit sich selbst etwas auszufechten, oder, wie ich vielleicht besser, nachträglich, sage, einen Kampf zu führen, der nur dann einen Sinn haben kann, wenn man ihn verlor', as he wrote in the 'Anmerkung I' to volume 18 (197). It is always assumed that this 'battle' was between painting and literature, and that literature certainly won the battle in 1945. But since he stopped writing seriously for the theatre from about 1976, when 'ich mich im Theater ins Abseits gespielt hatte' (WA25, 164), and turned to essays and theoretical works, he has returned even more intensively to painting. I believe that he now perceives in these early works *Urmotive* and *Urstrukturen* which have never left him. All credit, then, to Elisabeth Brock-Sulzer who, twenty years ago, wrote, 'Wer aber näher in diese frühen Texte hineinhorcht, entdeckt in ihnen schon einen sehr großen Teil der späteren Themen' (C13, 21). The search for these *Urmotive* and *Urstrukturen* is now our task.

−3−

Trivialliteratur or 'Philosophical Thrillers'?

The Detective Novels

It was Professor Leonard Forster, late of the Schröder Chair of German at the University of Cambridge, who in 1961 reported Dürrenmatt's opinion of his work on his detective novels as that of a *Sonntagsromancier* (B11, 9). Critical opinion of these works has varied widely, and wildly, over the years: from agreement with the author to regard them as rather slight works, suitable for study at Leaving Certificate level 'because the language is so easy', as a first-year student said to me; then to their treatment as full-blown novels, suitable for philosophical investigation for doctoral theses and even for 'deconstruction'; then to what I believe they should be seen as now, namely proof that Dürrenmatt was in his early years what he is undeniably now, a master story-teller-plus. That 'plus' is what I wish to examine at the end of this chapter.[1]

Although I have chosen to devote this book mainly to a study of Dürrenmatt's prose writings, I can clearly not fail at least to take notice of his stage-works, with which of course he made his name in those early days. His first play, *Es steht geschrieben*, which caused a memorable scandal in the Schauspielhaus in Zurich at its première on 19 April 1947, contained a good deal of that baroque writing which we have noted in the early stories. The lewdness of the 'Tanz auf dem Dach'-scene (WA1, 135–41), Jan Bockelson's 'Ich hüpfe mit dem Bäuchlein und wackle mit dem Ärschlein' (138) and Knipperdollinck's caressing of the phallic wood blended ill, thought the audience, with the religious ambience of the play. Kurt Hirschfeld, then Deputy Director of the theatre, reported, 'Und doch ertrugen nicht alle Leute das Ungewohnte, die Ballung von Bildern'; one reviewer felt that he had experienced the 'noch reichlich chaotischen und sehr zuchtlosen Pubertätsfieber[n] eines sicher sehr hoch begabten Anfängers' (E49, 23–4). But it was a *succès de scandale* which heralded for most theatregoers the arrival of a new and promising author.[2]

Thus we find the play of interest here because of the use of themes known to us now from the early stories; the obsession with death, with war, with torture, with executioners (*Henker/Opfer*), with power-seeking, unhinged individuals pursuing evil ways, with guilt and retribution, and with grotesque and blasphemous language – and all, of course, an underlining of the young author's own religious doubts of the time, seen too in the second drama, *Der Blinde*, première on 10 January 1948 in Basle.

Two basic misconceptions have been made about Dürrenmatt. The early commentators, trying perhaps to make this jovial, critic-baiting neutral Swiss less of a nihilistic 'bear' than was claimed, strove to show the 'basic optimism' in his work, to show that his main characters did receive 'Grace', did 'win' at the end of the day. Then the pendulum swung to the other extreme and he was made out to be a 'cultural pessimist', dooming the world to a cataclysmic end. The truth would seem to lie, as it often does, in the middle: Dürrenmatt is a *realist* who cannot see an easy way out, an easy answer to the problems that our world has set itself, but believes that, while protesting against the misuse of power, the stupidity of governments and the loss of individual freedom, one must go on living one's own life as best one can. (The verb *bestehen*, to endure, dominated his early vocabulary.) 'Il faut cultiver notre jardin' indeed, and 'mit Humor' if possible! 'Ohne Humor,' he said to me during my visit in 1969, 'sollte man nicht schreiben' – and he has kept his word.

Although I noted in my earlier book that it was the *Komödien*, his third and fourth plays, *Romulus der Große* (première in Basle on 25 April 1949) and *Die Ehe des Herrn Mississippi* (première in Munich on 26 March 1952), which brought Dürrenmatt his first real taste of fame and success in Europe, it was strangely enough the 'pot-boilers', these detective novels, written at about the same time, which have ensured his enduring popularity in many countries. The genre had been very popular in the 1930s with many translations of Wallace, Christie, Sayers *et al*. In 1950 Radio Beromünster broadcast a police series, *Inspektor Wäckerli*, about a police-chief and a hoodlum, Döbeli, which gained high listening figures, had the same effect as the later 'Durbridge serials' and made the '*Krimi*' a best-selling genre in Switzerland (cf. too the magazine *Kriminalspiegel*).

Dürrenmatt, with two small children and a sick wife, and in severe financial difficulties having just lost his temporary income as a sketch-writer for the Cabaret Cornichon in Zurich, was now living on the meagre fees paid to theatre reviewers by the Zurich paper *Die Weltwoche*. The story of how he wrote to six publishers offering six different novels, and received six advances, was first told by Curt Rieß in *Esquire* in May 1961 – although this could not have happened in 1951 as Rieß claimed since, as we shall see, the first instalment of the first novel appeared in 1950.[3]

The *Schweizerische Beobachter* offered Dürrenmatt an advance of 500 francs (about £40 at that time) which his wife thought he had stolen, and he started work on *Der Richter und sein Henker*. The story appeared in fortnightly instalments in the *Beobachter* from Jahrgang 24, No. 23 (15 December 1950) to Jahrgang 25, No. 6 (31 March 1951). Peter Spycher notes that there were many alterations to the *Beobachter* version when the book appeared in 1952 (C46, 387). It is now in WA19, 9–117.

It is one of the tricks of Fate, therefore, that this novel, written under 'inartistic' circumstances, and moreover one of the most 'Swiss' works that Dürrenmatt has ever written, should by the 1980s have sold well over a million copies throughout the world and, with *Der Besuch der alten Dame*, ensured that the author is a very rich man. 'Ich habe es nie bereut, und ich habe auch nie abgeleugnet, daß ich diese Dinge geschrieben habe, um Geld zu verdienen,' he told Horst Bienek in 1962 (F3, 108).

Just why *Der Richter und sein Henker* should have attained such world-wide popularity is indeed a difficult question to answer. It clearly has not got the transatlantic punch of a Raymond Chandler or a Dashiell Hammett, the British elegance of an Agatha Christie or a Dorothy L. Sayers, or the sex-and-violence of the more modern schools. Nor can the reason really be the philosophical depths which many a Germanist has found in it. And it is most certainly not because of the elegant use of the German language, since so many critics, much less kindly disposed towards Dürrenmatt than his friend Elisabeth Brock-Sulzer, have echoed her words: 'Die Feinde von Dürrenmatts Kunst finden ja nicht selten Gelegenheit, ihm Fehler anzukreiden, eben Helvetismen.' She cites as but one example his predilection for using the accusative instead of the nominative case after the verb 'werden': 'Er wird ein*en* Schlosser' (C12, 238–9)!

The story is probably well known. The locale is the Swiss countryside in November 1948, between Berne and Ligerz on Lake Bienne (the Bielersee), the place where the Dürrenmatts were then living and which plays a major role in the plot. A Berne police lieutenant, Ulrich Schmied, is found shot dead in a blue Mercedes. Kommissär Bärlach, the Berne police superintendent, suffering terminally from cancer, had made a wager forty years ago in

Turkey with an immoral murderer, Gastmann, that he would destroy him one day, and he now sees an opportunity of doing so. He details another of his lieutenants, Tschanz, to pursue Gastmann, and when Tschanz finally 'proves' Gastmann guilty of Schmied's murder he kills him. Bärlach then reveals that he has only 'used' Tschanz as an 'executioner', since he had known all along that Tschanz himself was the murderer of Schmied, of whom he had been professionally jealous.

The attraction and the popularity of the story might lie first of all in its unorthodoxy. One is not asking here 'Who–dun–it?' but *why* was it done? Elizabeth Boa agrees with this and suggests indeed that we should borrow Tzvetan Todorav's distinction between the 'whodunit', i.e. the 'thriller', and the 'novel of suspense', into which category this novel would then fall (D4, 40–6). There are, of course, deeper questions of public and private morality, as well as of the nature of Evil which we have seen Dürrenmatt discuss already.[4]

Ira Tschimmel follows this line of enquiry by establishing three central themes in the novel which seem well worth pursuing: 'die Unvollkommenheit des menschlichen Geistes'; 'die Ambivalenz des Zufalls'; and 'die Realisierung von Gerechtigkeit und Recht' (E43, 180). He does not, however, in my opinion, stress sufficiently the enormous importance of the comical elements in the work, the satire on Switzerland, on Swiss police and on political bureaucracy for example, which, by contrast and expectation, deepens the mystery and eeriness of the novel for many Europeans.

The treatment of *Zufall* (Chance) has long been considered one of the major *Urmotive* in Dürrenmatt's work. He uses the word a great deal, nowhere more famously than in the '21 Punkte zu den Physikern' where he wrote some years later, 'Je planmäßiger die Menschen vorgehen, desto wirksamer vermag sie der Zufall zu treffen' (*Punkt* 8) (WA7, 91). Bärlach believes too that such a 'rule' makes it certain that he would eventually destroy Gastmann because 'human imperfectibility' would be bound to lead to an error. Gastmann himself expounds Bärlach's belief 'daß die menschliche Unvollkommenheit, die Tatsache, daß wir die Handlungsweise anderer nie mit Sicherheit vorauszusagen, und daß wir ferner den Zufall, der in alles hineinspielt, nicht in unsere Überlegung einzubauen vermögen, der Grund sei, der die meisten Verbrechen zwangsläufig zutage fördern müsse', and then refutes it by claiming that that very 'Verworrenheit der menschlichen Beziehungen' would enable crimes to be committed that could *not* be solved (68).

The charm of their arguments is that both men, the 'good' and the 'evil', are shown to be acting *ir*rationally against the pedantic rationality of Dr(!) Lucius Lutz, the 'Untersuchungsrichter' and Bärlach's 'Chef', who *does* believe in the 'Baconian [view] of a procedure that starts from firmly established facts and builds on this sure foundation a structure of verified knowledge', as A.M. Wright notes (D47, 64).[5]

The plot of the novel develops too in a most unorthodox manner, since the detective seems to take little interest in the case. He never looks at police reports and ignores both the shot corpse and his chief's protestations. Dürrenmatt himself even appears in the role of the 'writer' who knew Gastmann well and whose conversation with Bärlach (in chapter xiii) is more important than some commentators have granted (76–84). The writer knows Gastmann primarily as a good cook, but nevertheless sees in him the pure nihilist that he is, 'weil er das Gute ebenso aus einer Laune, aus einem Einfall tut wie das Schlechte, welches ich ihm zutraue' (82). Therefore Gastmann can do either good or evil – *Chance* will decide. Evil is the expression of Gastmann's freedom, the 'Freiheit des Nichts', the freedom to do as he wishes. This is the key to the book, the explanation of Gastmann's murderous career over forty years and of Bärlach's relentless pursuit of him. Just as they are both acting against Lutz, so strangely enough they both want their own freedom to act as individuals – and we realise that they are indeed the two sides of Dürrenmatt's own character, the Faustian 'zwei Seelen': 'Zwei Seelen wohnen, ach! in meiner Brust,/Die eine will sich von der anderen trennen'.

Here too the Good will triumph, but in a rather negative way for, as far as we know from this novel, the police chief has only one year to live. Bärlach seems to be looking in at himself as he looks down at the dead Gastmann: 'Bärlach stand immer noch gebückt, und das fahle Licht der Zelle lag auf seinem Gesicht und auf seinen Händen, umspielte auch die Leiche, für beide geltend, für beide erschaffen, beide versöhnend' (108).

Meanwhile the executioner, 'der Henker', Tschanz, seems at first not to have been judged as Gastmann was. Although he too has to endure a 'Gericht' of a sort, that is a 'meal' not a 'trial', and a gargantuan Dürrenmattian meal it is too, he is allowed to go free. Bärlach is happy 'daß ich *einen* richtete' (116). But the last page tells us that justice, retribution overtook Tschanz also as his car is crushed by a train.

Günther Waldmann, and others, claim that the crime story is a typical work of the *Aufklärung* (Enlightenment) in that, the detective 'clears the affair up' in a rational and logical way, usually before a gathering in the library, in court or in the lawyer's office (E47, 45 ff.). The detective – Poirot, Maigret, Miss Marples *et al.* – is omniscient and omnipotent, and in some films omnipresent as well. Dürrenmatt's Bärlach and his methods in this first novel *begin* to mirror rather that post-war world of uncertainties, of doubts, of *Angst*, where nothing is finished, solutions are not offered, problems are not solved. *Chance* leads to the detection of the criminal and the crime.

Jan Knopf, in his 1976 book on Dürrenmatt, quotes the French philosopher and biologist Jacques Monod on 'le hasard', Chance, in a German translation: 'Der reine Zufall, nichts als der Zufall, die absolute, blinde Freiheit als Grundlage des wunderbaren Gebäudes der Evolution – diese zentrale Erkenntnis der modernen Biologie ist heute nicht mehr nur eine unter anderen möglichen oder wenigstens denkbaren Hypothesen; sie ist die einzig vorstellbare, da sie allein sich mit den Beobachtungen und Erfahrungstatsachen deckt.' Knopf agrees that Dürrenmatt employs Chance in his works to demonstrate 'die Ohnmacht des Menschen und seiner Vernunft' (C31, 46–7).

In another field, the German scientist Werner Heisenberg had enunciated the 'uncertainty principle' in quantum mathematics which states that 'the product of the uncertainties of our knowledge of the values of conjugate variables is always greater than Planck's constant'. This 'Ohnmacht des Erkennens', the operation of *Zufall*, lies at the heart of so much modern art. Bärlach, with his physical infirmities, his (for Swiss eyes and ears) inefficient, antediluvian police methods and his coarse, gargantuan appetite, is on the way to becoming one of the anti-heroic detectives of the 1960s and 1970s in shabby overcoats and 'gumshoes', operating on a financial shoe-string from seedy hotel rooms. In *Der Richter und sein Henker*, however, we are only 'on the way' to this (e)state: Bärlach *does* find a solution to the 'crime'; indeed one could say that it is a fairly typical crime-story ending in that 'good' triumphs and the 'guilty' meets his retribution. Dr Leah's contention that 'being an artist, [Dürrenmatt] is driven to find patterns that he would criticise in the conventional detective story as being over-logical, over-exaggerated, unnatural and improbable in the ease and clarity of their solution' holds perhaps for this story (D27, 67). We shall have to see if it holds for the others. (It should be admitted too that the first version, the printed original text, had a good many linguistic mistakes and textual *non sequiturs*, most of which have been corrected for the WA. (cf. Spycher, C46, 386, note 3).)

To return then to my question above (28), it seems that the

enduring appeal of *Der Richter und sein Henker* is due to three factors. Firstly, it appeals to young students of German literature because the language is reasonably uncomplicated, it is a good story in itself and it has what so many German books to be studied so significantly lack, a sense of humour. The burial scene, in particular, is found to be very funny. Secondly, it has sufficient philosophical depth – although that 'philosophical' is an adjective that had to be used most circumspectly in Dürrenmatt's presence twenty years ago! – and, in conjunction with the theoretical approach to 'Trivialliteratur' so popular at the moment with certain German(ic) academics, is sufficiently unorthodox in its structure to form a 'suitable case for treatment' at academic levels. Thirdly, its unusual position as a *Swiss* crime story set in a picturesque part of a country widely regarded as a tourist paradise and not as a hot-bed of crime, has led to popularisation among a still wider audience first through a TV version (in 1957 with Hans Gottschalk), and then through the film version in 1978 made by Maximilian Schell, in which Dürrenmatt himself appeared as the 'uncomfortable' writer, 'Friedrich'. Dürrenmatt is continually amazed by the attention paid to this little tale, especially by solemn academics, but always hopes that, after reading this novel, readers will then turn to the more serious essays and narrative works of his more mature years.[6]

* * *

Apart from the success of *Der Richter und sein Henker*, 1950 was an important year for Friedrich Dürrenmatt in another way, for it was in that year that a hospital visit confirmed the illness – diabetes – from which he was to suffer all his life. It has meant constant treatment, care and attention, but has not involved extensive hospitalisation, or any reduction in mental powers. At sixty-seven (in July 1988), he had never looked fitter or better, and one gasped to see him pedalling wildly on his health bicycle – while watching children's television – in Charlotte Kerr's 1984 film.

The popularity of *Der Richter und sein Henker* led the *Schweizerische Beobachter* to commission another novel *Der Verdacht* in instalments from Dürrenmatt. Whether he ever seriously thought of a series à la Sayers, Christie or Simenon is doubtful, particularly as the third novel, *Das Versprechen* (1957), not only has a differently named main detective, but is provocatively sub-titled *Requiem auf den Kriminalroman*.

If it had not realised the fact before 1958, the sub-title of *Das Versprechen* brought home to the general reading public that

Dürrenmatt was mocking a literary genre – and not for the last time. 'Pot-boilers' or not, these three novels have now been accepted as valid statements of a literary attitude of their times, statements of doubt about hitherto generally accepted social norms, about the place of 'literature' in a modern technological society – indeed in what Brecht called the 'wissenschaftliche Zeitalter' – and about attitudes to the values and standards of past ages. It was what was later to be called, fashionably, 'deconstruction'. Dürrenmatt's mocking of these values was also seen at this time in his play *Romulus der Große* (1949) when he makes Romulus say, 'Ich kenne die letzten Worte meiner Feldherren, bevor sie in germanische Gefangenschaft fallen: Solange noch eine Ader in uns lebt, gibt keiner nach' (WA2, 27), which then drew from the vitriolic pen of a Swiss patriot the comment: 'Mag er in seiner Komödie Bubenbergs Wort: "So lang in uns eine Ader lebt, gibt keiner nach!" mit vielen andern ins Lächerliche ziehen – der das Wort sprach, überdauerte im Geist Generationen von Nihilisten. Er wird auch Dürrenmatts *Romulus* überdauern' (A.H. Schwengeler in *Der Bund*, 18 January 1951, cf. C34, 29).

Der Verdacht, Dürrenmatt's second novel, appeared like the first in fortnightly instalments in the *Schweizerische Beobachter* from Jahrgang 25, No. 17 (15 September 1951) to Jahrgang 26, No. 4 (29 February 1952). The book version, with many alterations, appeared in 1953 and is now in WA19, 119–265. According to Peter Wyrsch, Dürrenmatt started writing his first two novels just after his first version of *Die Ehe des Herrn Mississippi* was finished, in early 1950. Like the first novel, *Der Verdacht* too is set in Dürrenmatt's own geographical parish, Berne and its environs. Superintendent (Hans) Bärlach is again the main character, and when the novel opens he is lying in bed, 'anfangs November 1948', in the Salemspital (where Dürrenmatt's own father was chaplain), reading a 1945 number of *Life* magazine. The 'Life' is both symbolical and parodistic, since new readers learn (and old readers know) that Bärlach is suffering from a 'hoffnungslose Krankheit' (123), but he has also had a heart attack which is to delay the operation by two weeks.

Bärlach believes that a picture in *Life* of a Nazi doctor, Nehle, operating without anaesthetics on a patient in the concentration camp of Stutthof reminds him, and his own doctor Hungertobel, of the distinguished owner of the Sonnenstein clinic on the Zürich-berg in Zurich, Fritz Emmenberger. The latter had gone to Germany, then to Chile, in 1932, and had returned to Switzerland in 1945, where he had made his fortune by using concentration camp methods to terrify his patients into leaving him their money. Terminally ill though he is – and indeed also retired – Bärlach, the personification of 'the Good', who believes that 'Man [lasse] die großen Schurken laufen und [stecke] die kleinen ein' (136), cannot help being forced 'in *dieser* Welt zu bestehen und für eine andere, bessere, zu kämpfen, zu kämpfen auch mit diesem seinem jammervollen Leib, an welchem der Krebs fraß' (164). This is especially so after he has been visited by the 'riesenhaften Juden' Gulliver, who, a modern Asahuerus, had been operated on by Nehle in 1943 and whose terrible story shows us again how guilty the neutral Swiss Dürrenmatt felt about having stood outside the 'Folterkammer' of the world (above, 9).

Bärlach's battle for justice is now to be fought on his enemy's territory, for he asks his doctor to have him admitted to Emmenberger's clinic under the guise of a rich Swiss businessman, 'Blaise Kramer'. To the doctor's protest, 'Es hat keinen Sinn', Bärlach replies, 'Die Gerechtigkeit hat immer Sinn' (177). This 'act of stupidity' might well be seen, as Ira Tschimmel sees it, as proof of Dürrenmatt's 'Absicht, daß er dem gattungstraditionellen Bild vom Detektiv als dem vollkommenen Logiker ein Ende bereiten will' (E43, 182).

Bärlach is prepared to put his theory to the test by allowing himself to be operated on by Emmenberger. Only three people know that he is in the clinic: Gulliver, Hungertobel and the eccentric journalist Fortschig, whose Christian names, Ulrich (that of Dürrenmatt's cantankerous grandfather) and Friedrich (Dürrenmatt's own), suggest why so many of his views about the Switzerland of 1950–2 echo Dürrenmatt's. Chance intervenes once again, however, and once again in the form of a newspaper photo – ironically in *Der Bund* – showing Bärlach's retirement ceremony.

Nor is Emmenberger surprised by *his* chance unmasking: 'Ein indizienloses Verbrechen ist in dieser Welt des Zufalls unmöglich' he says (242), and adds later, 'aus Zufall wird man recht und aus Zufall schlecht' (248). Now supported by his 34–year-old nihilistic mistress, Dr Edith Marlok, the first of Dürrenmatt's many female 'grotesques', Emmenberger will operate on Bärlach in eight and a half hours' time at 7 a.m. But the giant Jew Gulliver, both 'judge' and 'executioner' here, intervenes, poisons Emmenberger 'nach dem Gesetze Mosis' – we are reminded of Herr Mississippi's iron credo of justice – and leaves the Don Quixote-like superintendent with the oft-quoted words: 'Wir können als einzelne die Welt nicht retten . . . Wir können nur im einzelnen helfen, nicht im gesamten . . . So sollen wir die Welt nicht zu retten suchen, sondern zu bestehen, das einzige wahrhafte Abenteuer, das uns in dieser späten Zeit noch bleibt' (264).[7]

Bearing in mind all the time that we are dealing with a story written in instalments for a magazine, and not with a refined Iris Murdoch-like novel, it is useful nevertheless to note how Dürrenmatt's *Urmotive* and *Urstrukturen* are developing. The story is clearly strongly influenced by the age: Gulliver is the personification of the maltreatment of the Jews by the Nazis – the film *Nacht und Nebel* on the atrocities of the Holocaust was circulating in Europe at the time – and Dürrenmatt's 'use' of the character as retribution for Nazi guilt is a model for later 'judges' and 'executioners'. (If the 'labyrinth' theme is not touched on as such, we note that the grotesque dwarf, whom Gulliver befriended in Stutthof, is called *Minotaurus*!)

Bärlach's and Fortschig's attacks on Swiss complacency and, literally, other-worldliness mirror Dürrenmatt's growing dissatisfaction with the atmosphere of the larger Swiss towns. He makes Bärlach reflect on his arrival in Zurich, 'Zurich war ihm sonst nicht recht sympathisch, vierhunderttausend Schweizer auf einem Fleck fand er etwas übertrieben' (193) – a nice jibe – and he was soon to leave German-speaking Switzerland for Neuchâtel.

The deliberate choice of the name Emmenberger with its Swiss connotation of Dürrenmatt's own home district of *Emmen*tal, well known for its fanatical religious sects ('Überhaupt wurde im Dorfe viel bekehrt', he writes of Konolfingen in *Stoffe* (A1, 18)), allows Dürrenmatt to contrast that type of fanaticism, in its own way just as dangerous, Dürrenmatt suggests, with the fanatical *un*-belief of Emmenberger 'daß mir meine Existenz das Recht gibt, zu tun, was ich will' (251). Such a hatred of fanaticism runs like a thread through Dürrenmatt's works: many of the characters in his plays – Jan Matthisson, Mississippi, Ämilian, Nebukadnezzar, right through to Cardinal Richelieu in *Achterloo* – are accused of that inflexibility which, in the last resort, makes 'fools' (*Narren*) of them by bringing their schemes to nought, but not without their first having wreaked havoc among their fellow human beings. Richelieu in *Achterloo* says, 'Was ihn [den Menschen] verteufelte, war unser Hang *zum Absoluten*' (my italics, A10, 87).

Thus P.B. Gontrum's summary of *Der Verdacht* as 'an allegory of the modern world in which a representative of humanitarian principles seeks to call to justice a man who is the embodiment of a particular aspect of our modern understanding of evil' could be *mutatis mutandis* a not unfair description of Dürrenmatt and his 'philosophy' in the immediate post-war years (D19, 88). How such a writer could be called a 'nihilist' is difficult to comprehend at this remove, and Dürrenmatt might be correct when he says that those who write this about him are in fact only mirroring their *own* nihilism (in the 'Anhang' to *Die Wiedertäufer* in WA10, 134).[8]

The Bärlach of *Der Verdacht* is not the Bärlach of *Der Richter und sein Henker*: where the latter solved the murder by a type of logical thinking and showed clear signs of that omniscience of which I wrote above, this Bärlach works *intuitively*; Dürrenmatt seems to compensate for Bärlach's weak physical state by allowing him to follow active intuitive mental processes. Although the detecting *methods* are different, Bärlach's *situation* is not unlike that of the television detective Perry Mason, who solves his cases from a wheelchair. Both detectives effect a striking contrast between physical weakness and mental strength. Dürrenmatt sees Bärlach's intuitive methods nevertheless as profoundly 'scientific'. Years later, in February 1979, giving a lecture on Albert Einstein in Zurich, Durrenmatt stressed how the great physicist's thinking was based on intuition: 'Die Verbindung dieser Sinnen–Erlebnisse zu den durch die Regeln der Logik verbundenen Begriffen und Sätzen sei *rein intuitiv*, nicht selbst logischer Natur' (my italics, WA27, 161, cf. D47, 66 and below, 198).

In addition, Bärlach is *brave* – and the concept of the 'mutige Mensch' was soon to be enshrined in Dürrenmattian theory by the publication of his 'Theaterprobleme' in 1954–6. He too will decide 'die Welt zu bestehen, in der wir oft leben wie Gulliver unter den Riesen. Auch der nimmt Distanz, auch der tritt einen Schritt zurück, der seinen Gegner einschätzen will, der sich bereit macht, mit ihm zu kämpfen oder ihm zu entgehen' (WA24, 63). As William Gillis wrote, 'If man wants justice, he must pursue it, but more often than not the certain attainment of it is something he must leave to Heaven' (D18, 13)!

Heinrich Bodensieck's general article on Dürrenmatt's three stories (E10) shows that Dürrenmatt criticism is fairly generally agreed that *Der Verdacht* is the weakest of the three: we read of Gulliver as the 'papiernen Juden', that Bärlach is not a 'vorbildlicher Held' but a 'Moralist', and that the story is 'gruselig-gräßlich'. The latest book on the author, that of Heinrich Goertz (1987), is likewise cool towards the second novel, finding the plot 'gewalt-sam konstruiert' (C18, 37). As *The Quarry* in E.R. Morreale's 1962 translation, it has had a fairly successful run, but has not (yet) reached the apogee of a film version.

* * *

The last of these early detective novels, *Das Versprechen* (1957) (WA22, 9–163), actually started life as a film script. The title of the Swiss Präsens Co. film was an extraordinarily clumsy one: *Es geschah am hellichten Tag*; in the 'Nachwort' to WA22, Dürrenmatt himself has to write of the film, 'der leider den Titel . . . führt'. He relates there how the Polish producer Lazar Wechsler asked him for a film script on the theme of sexual crimes against children, to serve as a warning to parents. The Hungarian director Ladislao Vajda and he then turned the script into the novel, even though the novel went in another direction, 'jenseits des Pädagogischen', and became a criticism of 'einer der typischsten Gestalten des neunzehnten Jahrhunderts', the detective (203). Hence the sub-title, *Requiem auf den Kriminalroman*. One must recall here once again the 'Theater-probleme' (see below, 162). This celebrated essay on the theory of modern drama ends with that provocative question, 'Wie besteht der Künstler in einer Welt der Bildung, der Alphabeten?', and a *possible* answer is suggested: 'Vielleicht am besten, indem er Kriminalromane schreibt, Kunst da tut, wo sie niemand vermutet' (WA24, 71–2).

I have suggested already that German critics seem to take crime stories, 'thrillers', much more seriously than Anglo-Saxons, who have traditionally bought them 'to read on the train'. However, with the flood of Anglo-Saxon literature – albeit usually in trans-lation – all over post-war German-speaking countries, and the emigration of so many Germanic scholars to North America, the crime story/*Detektivroman*/*Kriminalroman*/'*Krimi*' has been elevated to the status of a huge, new scholarly theme, much of it linked to the more general theme of 'Trivialliteratur', still a curious genre for Anglo-Saxon scholars. Ulrich Schulz-Buschhaus's formidable *Formen und Ideologien des Kriminalromans: Ein gattungsgeschichtlicher Essay* (C43) is a widely quoted source for theoretical material.

One of the major problems for Germanic students of the crime story is, of course, the language, and one cannot but feel that many of the essays and books relating to the theme are written with the German translation of the English, and particularly of the Ameri-can, book as source. This obviously cannot hope to render the flavours of Brooklyn American or country-house English, so often an integral element of the story: one thinks of the effect of Poirot's broken English, of Philip Marlowe's clipped Americanese or Lord Peter Wimsey's affected, upper-class Oxbridge drawl. A great deal of the writer's intended effect must be lost.[9]

The film *Es geschah am hellichten Tag* – with Heinz Rühmann as Matthäi, Michel Simon as von Gunten and Gerd Fröbe (of

Goldfinger fame) as the murderer – was, in fact, quite a good one; perhaps slightly too moralistic and pedagogic, but it *was* a Swiss film after all, made for a pedagogic purpose. Like most films of the time and of the genre it has what Germans insist on calling 'ein Happy End', that is the detective finds the murderer and confirms the chocolate-box image of Switzerland which not only Dürrenmatt among Swiss intellectuals dislikes so much. The film, which appeared outside Switzerland in 1959 as *Assault in broad daylight*, contained a good deal of 'local colour', pretty scenes of Chur and Zurich and appearances by Professor Emil Staiger and Dürrenmatt himself. When watching it, one remembers Dürrenmatt's own comment on Swiss films: 'Die Legende unserer Tugenden erstickt die Möglichkeit, die vielleicht in unsern Lastern läge' (in WA26, 72–3)!

When Dürrenmatt came to write the novel, however, he reverted to the attitude expressed in 'Theaterprobleme' and the style of *Der Verdacht*. This detective would *not* find all the right clues and apprehend the murderer, but would be a 'coureur d'idéals qui trébuche sur la réalité', Bergson's Don Quixote-like figure, whose 'expectations' outreach his 'réalisation', and whose efforts therefore appear 'comic' – although, as we shall see, there is a *darker* comic in this story. Dürrenmatt uses this figure continuously from now on, built as it is into the theoretical schema of 'Theaterprobleme'.[10]

Dürrenmatt's Inspektor Matthäi, 'a brilliant Sherlock Holmes figure' in the film (Forster, B11, 10), becomes a disgruntled, albeit scholarly, detective ('er hatte als Basler in Basel doktoriert' in Law (20)) in the novel, and is called, significantly, by his colleagues 'Matthäi am Letzten', that is, a man from whom there is no escaping. It is therefore his intelligence above all which is praised, so that his subsequent fall from grace is all the more effective.

Once again Dürrenmatt is the 'Ich-Erzähler', and once again he uses the form beloved of these nineteenth-century *Novellen*-authors, the 'Rahmenerzählung', a further parodistic device incidentally, a mocking of his Swiss forebears, Keller, Meyer and particularly his fellow Emmentaler, Jeremias Gotthelf, whose works tend to praise his native region. Dürrenmatt even parodies himself in the 'framework'-story by pretending that he had just given an unsuccessful lecture in Chur, a little town in Graubünden in East Switzerland – a lecture, indeed, on how to write a *Kriminal-roman*! It was unsuccessful partly because he had been in competition with his own *bête noire* from his student days in Zurich, Professor Emil Staiger, who had been lecturing 'über den späten Goethe' (11)! Accepting a lift back to Zurich from a chance meeting with a Dr H., a former superintendent of the Zurich police, he is told the strange story of the former policeman, Dr Matthäi, at whose garage they had just pulled in for petrol.

A hawker, von Gunten, reports the finding – 'ganz zufällig' – of the body of a little girl, Gritli Moser, in the woods near the fictional village of Mägendorf, and he is himself immediately suspected of the murder. Matthäi (then fifty years old) 'promises' the parents that he will find the murderer. Von Gunten, a simple man, is eventually so bewildered by the constant cross-questioning that he confesses to the murder and then hangs himself, making his guilt seem obvious. 'Die Gerechtigkeit hatte gesiegt', all believe (71). Matthäi, however, has never been convinced of von Gunten's guilt, and he gives up a planned flight to take up a new post in Jordan to return to what his police colleagues believe to be useless, indeed harmful, enquiries. This is a plot device well known to filmgoers, where the 'cop' 'hands in his badge' to pursue his own unshakeable theories. ('You're fired, Matt' and 'Sie sind nicht mehr bei uns, Herr Doktor Matthäi' (75) would seem to be a good illustration of the point about the comparable 'language' of American and German(ic) 'thrillers' mentioned above!)

Two further child murders, one in Schwyz and one in Sankt Gallen, have convinced Matthäi that a child murderer is still on the loose somewhere. To the background of the unpleasant Swiss *Föhn*, which renders so many Continentals moody and restless, Matthäi changes his character completely. He begins to drink heavily and to smoke, and 'dazu die fixe Idee, einen Mörder suchen zu wollen, den man schon gefunden habe' (90); he becomes indeed 'lächerlich', but is still convinced that the murderer will return along the same road to 'the scene of the crime'. He buys a petrol station on this road from Chur to Zurich, and sets up with a housekeeper – Frau Heller, a former prostitute known to him from his early days – and a little girl, Annemarie, who looks like the murdered Gritli and who is to serve as the 'Köder', the bait for the murderer.

The days and the weeks pass 'im absurden grausamen Warten' (122), and then, at last, Matthäi finds sufficient 'proof' to convince the police that it would be worthwhile to wait in hiding in the woods to try to trap the murderer. But nothing happens, and eventually Matthäi, Dr H. and the policemen begin to argue among themselves: 'die Situation war peinlich und grotesk, wir waren alle verlegen und kamen uns lächerlich vor; das Ganze war nichts weiter als eine lausige, hundserbärmliche *Komödie*' (my italics, 134), the word which Dürrenmatt was to use to describe almost all his plays from 1956 on and the major element of which Otto Rommel believed to be 'die Bitterkeit der Ohnmacht' (cf. E36, 273). This would certainly describe the psychological scenario in this novel.

The narrator, Dr H., then shows his listener how 'Chance' thwarted Matthäi's careful, albeit unorthodox planning. 'Unser Verstand erhellt die Welt nur notdürftig,' Dr H. says to Dürrenmatt. 'In der Zwielichtzone seiner Grenze siedelt sich alles Paradoxe an' (145). Dr H. had been called to visit a rich 89-year-old lady, Frau Schrott, now dying in the Catholic hospital in Zurich, who told him the strange story of her second marriage at fifty-five to her 23-year-old chauffeur, Albert ('Albertchen selig'). At the age of forty he had begun to act strangely, coming home one day covered with blood to confess shortly afterwards to the murder of the girl in Sankt Gallen, and later to the others. To protect her own position, particularly *vis-à-vis* her older, widowed and jealous sister, Frau Schrott had spoken to no one about the events. She related how 'Albertchen' had found another little girl, just like Gritli Moser, had set off to murder her and had been killed in a car crash on the way. The old lady's 'confession' 'solved' the crime, but Matthäi was left a broken man in his petrol station, where he 'verkam, versoff, verblödete' (141).

Leonard Forster makes rather too much of the character of Frau Schrott. She is hardly a 'grotesque monster' (B11, 12) of the metal of a Claire Zachanassian (in *Der Besuch der alten Dame*) or of a Dr Mathilde von Zahnd (in *Die Physiker*), but she is undeniably 'the criminal' in the story, since her silence allowed the weak-minded husband to commit another two crimes and to attempt a fourth. That Matthäi will never know of the existence of this woman nor of her deranged husband makes even greater mock not only of his elaborate planning and exaggerated personal and professional sacrifice, but also of traditional police methods, for only the chance telephone call to Dr H. asking him to visit the dying Frau Schrott in hospital 'solves' the crimes.[11]

Yet Professor Forster is correct in labelling Matthäi a 'fanatic'. Although he shares many of the characteristics of a Bärlach, there are substantial differences between the two detectives, not just because Bärlach 'succeeds', albeit with a 'little help from his friends', in *Der Verdacht*, but because his situation is never truly 'grotesque', that is 'ludicrously demonic'. There *is* something both laughable yet eerie about Matthäi's situation, a half-crazed, drink-sodden man, fallen from reasonably 'high estate', waiting patiently but ludicrously on the chance passing of the murderer. Hebbel's description of tragicomedy seems pertinent to our feelings as we read of Matthäi's plight: 'Man mögte vor Grausen erstarren, doch die Lachmuskeln zucken zugleich; man mögte sich durch ein Gelächter von dem ganzen unheimlichen Eindruck befreien, doch ein Frösteln beschleicht uns wieder, ehe es uns das gelingt' (C20, 379).

What Dürrenmatt does here is exactly what he did in his *Alten Dame* of the previous year (1956), where Alfred Ill's situation is as painfully comical as Matthäi's. This allows us 'das Tragische aus der Komödie heraus erzielen, hervorbringen als einen schrecklichen Moment, als einen sich öffnenden Abgrund' ('Theaterprobleme', WA24, 63). Dürrenmatt's growing narrative skill has therefore allowed Matthäi to be fleshed out as a real character – the serious, contemporary nature of the theme helps a good deal here too – and Matthäi's actions have a crazy rationality about them which the visit to the psychiatrist only underlines. Dr Locher, the doctor whom he visits, can sense that Matthäi will eventually lose his 'reason' by following 'den Wahnsinn als Methode' (101). (David Rock suggests, however, that Matthäi was simply 'unfortunate' since 'he is actually correct in his unorthodox calculations', but Rock seems to underplay the 'madness' of Matthäi's actions, which is brought out by the psychiatrist (D34, 25).) I would suggest, indeed, that Matthäi is one of Dürrenmatt's most successful literary creations, and that he could be advanced as an argument against those critics who find that Dürrenmatt presents only 'one-dimensional' characters. It may well be that *Das Versprechen* also proves Dürrenmatt's status as a novelist, still much less recognised than his status as a playwright.

This is shown too in his growing skill as a narrative and descriptive writer. He follows a great Swiss tradition of descriptive writing, of course, and some of the pages of *Das Versprechen* are among the best that he has written in this genre. His skilful use of 'the pathetic fallacy', where throughout the story the rain, wind, fog, mist and ice intensify the atmosphere of despair and gloom which Dürrenmatt likes to contrast with the 'allzu solide[n] Gefüge unseres Landes', and where the *Föhn* serves as an eerie background to disturbed human mental conditions: 'Die unnatürliche, schwere Wärme machte die Menschen böse, reizbar, ungeduldig' (34). This is an important element in the story, as are his descriptions of the fateful wood (128–30), as the police and little Annemarie wait in vain for the murderer to appear: 'Es wurde fünf; die ersten Schatten, dann die Dämmerung, das Verblassen, das Stumpfwerden all der leuchtenden Farben' (129).

Apart from the difficulty of realising that all the conversations would have been held in Swiss German, *Schwyzerdütsch*, one is also conscious of the importance of the 'Symbolik' in the novel, Dürrenmatt's instinctive feeling for associations which, of all the critics, only Spycher and Forster seem to reciprocate. Spycher's careful analysis of the background to the plot shows how 'regional' much of this novel really is, how Dürrenmatt manages to incorporate into the plot the names of well-known local personalities – the Zurich families, Hottinger and Stüssi, for example – and places – almost all the streets, towns, wines and cheeses are factual. The village of Mägendorf, central to the story, is curiously fictional, seeming to lie near the Zurich international airport of Kloten which is some thirteen kilometres east of Zurich (cf. C46, 316–18). Indeed, this is the only Swiss work of Dürrenmatt which has one of its locales in the eastern area of Switzerland, Graubünden (Grisons); most are set in the large towns, Zurich, Basle or Berne. The coat of arms of Graubünden, the *Steinbock* or ibex, is only one of the many symbols which play a central role in the plot, since little Gritli's drawing (cf. in Forster, B11, 64) attempts to reproduce the ibex which she noted on the Graubünden registration plate of her murderer, the man who had given her the chocolate truffles which looked like 'Igel' (hedgehogs). Later, little Annemarie was to receive similar truffles from *her* would-be murderer (125 ff.).

But the novel is much more than just a Swiss-based *Heimatroman*. Although we must grant that the translation naturally fails to reproduce the Helvetic flavour, wit and suspense of the original, those who read German and know something of Swiss mores will sense here an attempt by an author to use the particular to illustrate the general. As we look back on Dürrenmatt's work from a distance of thirty years, we can say that *Das Versprechen* is also much more than a '*Krimi*', even than a '*Requiem*' on a '*Krimi*'; it is a novel which *uses* the 'thriller'-scheme to make important statements about the world and the way in which people live – and die. Matthäi's world is light-years away from that of the 'cops' of Chicago, the 'flics' of Paris and the 'Bill' of London, but his own persona too seems to us to be vastly different from that of most of the other detectives with whom he has been compared. Armin Arnold writes of *Das Versprechen*, 'Was die Behandlung des Themas betrifft, so ist die Inspiration wieder bei Simenon zu suchen' and suggests the latter's *Maigret tend un piège* (E3, 192). But would Dürrenmatt not have had to spend most of his time reading nothing but crime novels to have managed to steal all of these themes? Since he continually asserts that he does not read modern literature and since his own literary output is so prodigious, we must take leave to doubt that these 'Inspirationen' are other than . . . *Zufall!*[12] Matthäi is Dürrenmatt's own man, a type developed from his Bärlach, both making a parodistic attack on the concepts of 'hero' and 'the heroic'. We know now from Dürrenmatt's later writings how suspicious he had become of Swiss 'sabre-rattling' – what even his grandfather Ulrich had called 'Säbelraßlerei' (cf. C22, 237) – at an early age. His *Romulus der Große* showed his dislike of, even contempt for, the ethos of Empire and autocratic rule – omniscience and omnipotence worried the young writer – and all three detective novels, and particularly *Das Versprechen*, set out to satirise, to 'take down' in Alexander Bain's useful phrase, those who still believed that human reason and reasoning could solve problems, great or small – a fine job of 'deconstruction'.[13]

For this reason *Das Versprechen*, the best of the three novels, is not only Dürrenmatt's 'Requiem auf den Kriminalroman', but his rather ambitious requiem on human reason altogether. Some commentators have deemed this to be a pessimistic strain in the author, but one must consider that, in all three novels, sin and guilt are punished and justice is done, and, moreover, is *seen* to be done. We *know* that Gastmann has been shot dead, that Tschanz, a murderer, was killed in a car crash, that Emmenberger was poisoned and that 'Albertchen selig' also dies in a car crash on the way to *do* evil. Thus 'die verlorene Weltordnung wird . . . wieder hergestellt', and to achieve that in his works has always been one of Dürrenmatt's 'Hauptanliegen', as he wrote in 'Theaterprobleme'. 'Denn alle Schuld rächt sich auf Erden', to quote our Goethe motto again.

* * *

Justice (*Gerechtigkeit*) and Chance (*Zufall*) are thus two of the major Dürrenmattian *Urmotive* presented in these three novels. They are themes, or *a* theme, 'Justice-achieved-through-Chance', which he was never to abandon for, only a few pages into his 1985 novel *Justiz*, we read: 'Die Gerechtigkeit läßt sich nur noch durch ein Verbrechen wiederherstellen' (A3, 11), and we realise that the old theme has received a new twist. Many commentators writing during the Dürrenmatt 'boom' in the 1960s and 1970s averred that we had seen his last *Kriminalroman* with *Das Versprechen*. Elisabeth Brock-Sulzer, one of the few to consider Dürrenmatt a 'Meister des Romans', knew in 1960 that he was even then planning another novel, *Justiz*. She was sure that, given the less hectic circumstances of his life, this novel would appear 'mit reicherer Versträhnung der

Materie' (C12, 259). We shall see (cf. 91, below).

By 1957 Dürrenmatt had behind him, of course, his literary masterpiece *Der Besuch der alten Dame* (première in Zurich on 29 January 1956) and its attendant critical and financial successes. He was ready to descend on the literary world as a 'leuchtender Meteor', to paraphrase his Bockelson in *Es steht geschrieben*. It is therefore, in one way, difficult to treat the three crime stories as a group, since the first two were conceived as magazine serials then converted, with many alterations, into novels, while the third started life as a film-script and, likewise with many alterations, was then developed ('weiterentwickelt') into a novel. In addition, Dürrenmatt's personal circumstances altered considerably between 1949 and 1957; from struggling artist to European lion indeed.

Yet, in another way, it is quite justifiable to take them as three representatives of a genre which, at the time, seemed to have been written *suae aetatis* only. It was assumed that they had been written solely for money and not from any deep creative urge; academic critics like Bänziger will always see them as 'Nebenprodukte' (cf. 'Die Menge stürzte sich auf solche Nebenprodukte' (C7, 164)), while the anti-Dürrenmatt GDR critic Jan Knopf believed that Dürrenmatt had found 'daß die hochgepriesene westliche Freiheit ohne die nötigen finanziellen Mittel oft nur ein Fetisch ist' (C31, 42). Others, like Gerhard Knapp, write that 'Ästhetisch wie welt-anschaulich sind die Detektivromane höchst aufschlußreich für den jeweiligen Standort des Autors' (C29, 29). I believe that, in retrospect, they and the early stories are that and much more: they contain the seeds, the themes, the motifs of much of Dürrenmatt's later work. This is not to suggest a 'grand design' here – artistic creation just does not work like that – but it would in my view be a grave mistake for later scholars to ignore these early narrative works.

The *Prosakomödien*

In his 1965 book on Dürrenmatt's dramas, Urs Jenny wrote, 'Dürrenmatts Neigung, um nicht zu sagen Methode, stets von einem Extrem ins andere zu fallen, bildet sich auch in der Zick-zack-Linie seines Schaffens ab' (C24, 24). It is not quite certain whether this was meant to be taken as a compliment to a Protean author or as an insult to a 'jack-of-all-trades-and-master-of-none'. Dürrenmatt was quite happy to take it neutrally with a shrug of the shoulders when I put the question to him in 1988: 'Ach was, man muß immer mal was anders machen.'

The comment was relevant when his play *Ein Engel kommt nach Babylon* was produced in Munich on 22 December 1953. It had been written earlier in that year and followed the dark baroque galli-maufry of *Die Ehe des Herrn Mississippi* (première in Munich on 26 March 1952). As he wrote in the programme-note for the *Engel*, 'Das neue Stück sollte denn auch in sich geschlossen, streng gradli-nig und farbig sein.' 'Colourful' it certainly was, depicting the world of Nebuchadnezzar, (or 'Nebuchadrezzar', as modern schol-arship seems to have it), of Babylon in the sixth century BC. Here too Dürrenmatt picked an old and favourite theme, the Tower of Babel, about which he had tried to write a drama in 1948. After writing three acts, some 150 pages, and with another six or seven acts planned, he had given up the project and handed it to his wife Lotti to be burned. This, *Der Turmbau zu Babel* (cf. WA4, 128–33), was Dürrenmatt's first (but not last) literary catastrophe – he calls it 'ein etwas dunkles Kapitel bei mir' in Charlotte Kerr's 1984 film.

It is curious that he considers his second catastrophe to have been the première of *Ein Engel kommt nach Babylon* in Munich. In *Stoffe* he gives a graphic description of what befell him and his family on that occasion. Before the rehearsals Dürrenmatt fell ill with a sinus inflammation. Then he found that the producer, Hans Schweikart, wanted to produce the play as a satire à la Wedekind or Sternheim. Finally his wife fell seriously ill with a lung embolism on the eve of the première. The production itself was more or less a flop, 'ein Achtungserfolg' Dürrenmatt called it, but added, 'das Schlimmste, was passieren konnte'. What was not known until the appearance of *Stoffe* in 1980 was *how* badly Dürrenmatt himself felt about this. We read on pages 58–9 of *Stoffe II–III* that he now felt himself to be 'in Feindesland' on the stage: 'Durch Zufall kam mein Ruhm zustande, durch Zufall der Abbau des Ruhms. Als Dramatiker bin ich ein unvermeidliches Mißverständnis' (A2, 59–60). And all this before the fame, success and financial profits which flowed his way after the *Alte Dame* and *Die Physiker*. Most scholars had been prepared to accept that Dürrenmatt had lost interest in playwriting after a series of failures beginning perhaps with *Der Mitmacher* (première on 8 March 1973, in Zurich); it was fascinating to read that his disenchantment went back as far as 1953 when, he says, he decided never to write another play. Yet he started work immedi-ately, if not on another play then on his 'Theaterprobleme', his theory of *Komödie*, which is still widely recognised as an authori-tative statement on modern dramatic theory.[14]

The 'Zusammenbruch', as he calls the failure of *Engel*, led directly to the writing of his next prose work, *Grieche sucht Griechin* (1955) (WA21). A Bavarian film director wanted to make a film with Dürrenmatt, who flew to Paris to discuss the proposition and, despite sensing the 'Unsinn des Unternehmens', began the story on his return to Neuchâtel. 'Mir schwebte auf einmal mit *Grieche sucht Griechin* etwas durchaus Bizarres, rein in der Sprache Angesiedeltes vor, irgend etwas wie in einem Brentano-Märchen' (A2, 61).

All in all, therefore, this *Prosakomödie* would seem to occupy an important position in the Dürrenmatt *oeuvre*. It is set in a peculiar French–Swiss–German metropolis, with palaces, churches and bridges, all on the banks of a large river. One would hazard a guess at Paris because of Dürrenmatt's discussions there, but names like 'Madame Bieler', 'Spätzle', 'Schränzle' and 'Emil-Kappeler-Straße' sound most un-Parisian. Although mention is made of a Swiss Embassy, one is inclined to settle for an imaginary town in French-speaking Switzerland where there are so many German names and influences, an area to which, Dürrenmatt says, he fled in 1952 'vor der deutschschweizerischen Kultur' (cf. *Versuche*, A6, 33).

Directly and indirectly, there are many bitter and satirical attacks on people and institutions in *Grieche sucht Griechin*: the institutionalised Church satirised as the 'Altneupresbyterianische Kirche'; big business in the person of 'Petit-Paysan' which is what Dürrenmatt calls a 'versteckten Namen', namely a French form of the Swiss-German 'Bührle', 'little peasant', and the name of one of Zurich's largest armaments manufacturers; the English in the persons of 'Mr and Mrs Weeman' – the only way to distinguish them, the narrator writes, is that *he* smokes a pipe! – and in general, the 'Establishment' and its hypocritical behaviour, public and private.

The story is of the turning-point in the life of a naïve, patriotic 'little man' who works in the forceps division of Petit-Paysan's huge machine factory which also manufactures armaments. He rejoices in the 'versteckten' name of Arnolph Archilochos which, if pronounced in the Swiss–German manner, is as near the obscene 'Arschloch' as one can get and which betrays also his Swiss–Greek descent. Arnolph, forty-five years old, believes implicitly in 'the Good' of Man and is exploited by all and sundry. He has erected a pantheon of the great and the good whom he worships by means of photographs placed above the bar of his favourite 'local', Chez Auguste. No. 1 is the President; No. 2 is Bishop Moser of the Altneupresbyterianische Kirche; No. 3 is his boss, Petit-Paysan; No. 4 is Passap, a wild, 'palindromic' painter who paints 'dreieckige Vierecke' which Archilochos praises as 'das richtige Leben'; No. 5 is Bob Forster-Monroe, the American Ambassador; No. 6 is

Maître Dutour, a leading lawyer in the 'City'; No. 7 is Hercule Wagner, Rektor of the university; and No. 8 is his unemployed brother Bibi (the Latin source of the name proves to be accurate since he counts on Arnolph to support him in drink, and his family generally).

Arnolph's work in Petit-Paysan's labyrinthine, Kafkaesque 'Maschinenfabrik', 'nur Zickzackgänge ermöglichend' (20), is as a 'Buchhalter', more correctly an 'Unterbuchhalter' or 'vielleicht noch genauer: Der Unterbuchhalter eines Unterbuchhalters'. There is no lower position. One day, however, his friendly bar-keeper suggests that he should look for a wife and, as the result of his advertisement in *Le Soir*, 'Grieche sucht Griechin', he meets his beautiful 31-year-old countrywoman, Chloë Saloniki. The friendship ripens. Chloë, an *émigrée* from a disorderly family in Crete, is now a maid to an English family (the Weemans) who become Nos. 9 and 10 in Arnolph's 'Weltordnung'. Chloë, a second cousin to Kurrubi in *Ein Engel kommt nach Babylon* – she too could only see the good in fellow human beings – turns out to have been (out of pure goodness!) the mistress of the President, Petit-Paysan, the Bishop *and* the revolutionary Fahrcks – again, a typical Dürrenmattian name, and probably a compound of Marx and Farner, the Swiss communist writer to whom Dürrenmatt paid such a glowing tribute in his 'Sätze aus Amerika' in 1970 (cf. WA28, 86).

Archilochos, unaware of Chloë's 'past', is amazed at the attention that is now paid to him, in cars, on the street with these various characters, but above all in his job at Petit-Paysan's where one day, after being led through labyrinthine corridors to room 'OB9GZ fünfter südöstlicher Korridor' (50 ff.), he finally meets Petit-Paysan himself who, after a series of comical misunderstandings of Arnolph's Greek name – 'Anaximander', 'Agesilaos', 'Aristipp', 'Artaxerxes' and 'Anaxagoras' (60–7) – informs the startled little man that he is to be appointed 'Generaldirektor' of the firm: 'Ihre Ernennung stellt einen schöpferischen Akt dar, eine Tat des schöpferischen Sozialismus, den wir dem unschöpferischen Kommunismus entgegenstellen *müssen*' (66). The year is 1955; the cold war in Europe is the hot war in the Far East, the Korean War has just ended (1953), and Swiss armament factories are doing a booming trade.

It takes some little time for the penny to drop for Archilochos, during which time the reader is treated to swingeing attacks on the hypocrisy and rottenness of Western civilisation, from the worldly, cigar-smoking Bishop, 'Sündige tapfer, sagte Luther' (78), via the obscenities of the way-out painter Passap who paints Chloë naked and glories in her 'so prächtigem Fleisch' (93), to the embarrassed Maître Dufour who hands over the Weemans' rococo castle to Chloë and Arnolph as 'ein Akt der reinsten Nächstenliebe', and prepares the guest-list for their wedding from those 'who knew Chloë well'! It is over half-way through the story – indeed, it is at his wedding – before Archilochos realises what has happened. In true Dürrenmattian fashion, 'Er erbleichte, taumelte. Schweiß floß über sein Gesicht. "Ich habe eine Kurtisane geheiratet"', he cries 'wie ein tödlich verwundetes Tier' (129), and he runs off, determined to take revenge on a cruel world.

The remainder of the 'plot' of this *Komödie* is the progress of Arnolph's gradual realisation that *true* love is a gift of Heaven – 'die Gnade', as the old President says to him. It is 'die Liebe, wenn Sie an diese Liebe glauben, oder das Böse, wenn Sie an diese Liebe nicht glauben' (149), and only those who truly love can make sense of an absurd world. Calming words, but when Arnolph returns to his castle to find his layabout brother drunk, his mistress ensconced there, and still no Chloë, his rage mounts and in an orgy of destruction he lays the whole building waste. And so to the (first) ending: 'Er [Archilochos] stierte aus verschwollenen Augen vor sich hin, blutverkrustet, den Hochzeitsfrack zerfetzt, mit heraushängendem Futter, die Brille verloren' (154).

There then follows ending No. 2, what Dürrenmatt calls 'das Ende für Leihbibliotheken'. Archilochos sets sail for Greece. Since the very first sentences of the novel read, 'Es regnete stundenlang, nächtelang, tagelang, wochenlang' (11), and there are constant references to the miserable Swiss weather, Archilochos is given a good reason to leave the unfriendly North to seek the warmth and friendship of the 'homeland' that he has never seen. There, during an archaeological 'dig' on the Peloponnese, he unearths . . . Chloë! She holds a little lecture to show how paradoxically 'blind' his love had been. When he discovered the 'truth' about her at the wedding, the 'scales had fallen from his eyes', that is, in his rage he had lost the 'spectacles' (see above) which had made his world so rosy, and now 'die Liebe deiner Blindheit mußte zerstört werden um der Liebe willen, die sieht und die allein zählt' (159).

This is my favourite Dürrenmatt story; there is a wealth of dramatic invention, colour, wit, savage satire, impressive and clever use of language, and, beyond all the satire and savagery, a true sense of the power of Love. Dürrenmatt called it 'Gnade', grace, at this time, but we can see from our vantage-point of retrospect that he was writing about a supreme emotion which enables us to exist, to endure a world without any obvious meaning

('Die Welt bestehen'). This Love Duet, between a Parsifal-like 'pure fool', (a *reiner Tor*, in medieval terms) and the clichéd prostitute with 'a heart of gold', is played out against a background of twentieth-century hypocrisy, vulgarity and crudity, portrayed in the same way as Dürrenmatt portrayed his modern Babylon in *Ein Engel kommt nach Babylon*: 'ein Gewirr von Palästen, Hochhäusern und Hütten, das sich im gelben Sand der Wüste verliert, prächtig und dreckig zugleich, von Millionen bewohnt' (WA4, 13). There too the story is of a love which was blind but which 'sees' at the end, as Akki and Kurrubi bravely depart for a land 'voll neuer Verfolgung, voll neuer Verheißung und voll von neuen Gesängen' (123).

Although the translation *Once a Greek* . . . by Richard and Clara Winston (1965) was hailed by the *New York Times* as the most entertaining story of the season (10 July 1965), Rolf Thiele's subsequent film (1967) with Heinz Rühmann, the superb comic, as Archilochos, and Irina Demick as Chloë made little impression on cinemagoers. Armin Arnold's comment, 'Der Roman enthält Wahrheiten und Einsichten von tiefem Ernst, die aber alle von einer Schicht einzigartigen Humors überzogen sind' (E3, 192), would seem to be a fair summing-up of what Timo Tiusanen called 'both a hilarious satire and a sentimental novel of entertainment' (B22, 148). It certainly deserves its sobriquet of 'prose' *Komödie* since it has all the ingredients for a successful stage production.

* * *

Dürrenmatt scholars know that it is practically impossible to follow this author's work chronologically: many works were composed at the same time as others, many over a number of years, many exist in several versions, many are, in fact, continuations of themes originally presented in quite different narrative or dramatic forms. As our study proceeds, we shall find that many now famous works in a particular Dürrenmattian genre had their origin in a completely and sometimes surprisingly different literary field.

A literary problem which troubled Dürrenmatt researchers over many years was the chronological order of composition of the four versions of our next work, *Die Panne*. For years now *Die Panne* (with *Der Besuch der alten Dame*, *Die Physiker* and *Der Richter und sein Henker*) has been among the most frequently studied works of Dürrenmatt; it figures on the list of 'prescribed texts' of most British Leaving Certificate (Advanced Level) boards and, to judge from the number of published studies on the book in German, must appear on Germanic and American lists as well. A word first of all, then, on its chronology, now finally established by the appearance of the *Werkausgabe* in 1980.

The plot was conceived in 1955, contemporaneously with *Griech sucht Griechin* and *Der Besuch der alten Dame*, but as Dürrenmatt confided to H.L. Arnold in 1976, the first conception was as 'one of the ten' (actually eight) radio-plays which he wrote, again for financial reasons, in these years (cf. Chapter 4 below). However, the *Erzählung* was first *published* by the Verlag der Arche in Zurich in 1956, the *Hörspiel* (also by Arche) in 1961, having been broadcast, as we shall see, by Bayerischer Rundfunk on 17 January 1956. It was then converted to a television play in 1957, and finally, to date anyway, the material reappeared as a *Komödie* in a production by the Egon Karter touring theatre in Wilhelmsbad/Hanau on 13 September 1979 (this version now in WA16). It would therefore be fair to say that we are dealing here with a work which *must* contain some of the *Urmotive* and *Urstrukturen* that we are examining.

Although Dürrenmatt said as early as 1952 that the only places to observe world events and to be able to comment on them seriously were 'Punkte' which 'hinter dem Mond liegen' (WA26, 32), as an avid watcher of television and reader of newspapers he is easily able to keep abreast of all that is happening in world politics from his eyrie in Neuchâtel. His regular visits to his 'local', the Rocher, and 'mine host', Hans Liechti, just a quarter of an hour or so down the road from his house, but also the increasing number of journeys all over the world that he has made since those early, rather monastic years with a young family in Neuchâtel, have made Dürrenmatt less the regional author that he was once considered to be, certainly in comparison with his compatriot Max Frisch, who left Switzerland to live abroad. Since the early 1960s Dürrenmatt has visited the USSR (1964 and 1967), the USA (1959 and 1969), Israel (1974), Wales (1976), the USA (for four months in 1981), Greece, then South America (1983–4) and Egypt (1985), as well, of course, as undertaking various shorter journeys here and there to receive medals, prizes and honorary degrees.

I mention this because contemporary world events clearly lie behind the writing of the plot of this *Prosakomödie*, as I should like to call it since its construction has so much in common with *Griech sucht Griechin* and, of course, it did actually become a *Komödie* on the stage.

'Die Panne' is defined in Wahrig's *Deutsches Wörterbuch* as 'Betriebsstörung (bes. an Fahrzeugen . . .)' and 'Störung im Arbeitslauf', and both definitions are relevant to the plot of Dürrenmatt's story, as we shall see. But 'Die Panne' is given a rather wider definition in the author's own introduction to the 1956 book version (now in WA20, 35–94). Having commented bitterly on the modern author's need to deliver 'Literatur, alles in allem', that is, 'Geständnisse', 'Wahrhaftigkeit', 'höhere Werte', 'Moralien, brauchbare Sentenzen', 'bald Christentum, bald gängige Verzweiflung', but then 'sei der Mund zu halten, weder zu kommentieren noch zu schwatzen' (38), he suggests that there might be no more room for story-telling, only for scientific reports on amazing technological developments, or trivial comments on world personalities in the illustrated magazines. But a writer wants, nay *needs*, to write about his own and others' private experiences too 'ohne Zusammenhang mit dem Weltganzen, mit dem Ablauf der Dinge und Undinge, mit dem Abspulen der Notwendigkeiten' (38–9). Yet, here too, the same laws obtain; Chance can take a hand in private experiences, just as chance events can cause tragedies on the world scale: 'Das Schicksal hat die Bühne verlassen, auf der gespielt wird, um hinter den Kulissen zu lauern, außerhalb der gültigen Dramaturgie, im Vordergrund wird alles zum Unfall, die Krankheiten, die Krisen' (39).

The Greek concept of 'iron Fate', life ruled by the gods in an ordered society, has given way to the modern concept of Chance in an amoral, illogically constructed universe where 'Weltuntergang' can occur 'aus technischem Kurzschluß'. The author is thinking certainly of events in 1955 such as the USSR's creation of the Warsaw Pact as a rival to NATO after Stalin's death in 1953, bringing with it the increasing possibility of world conflict. The 'finger on the button' – 'die Möglichkeit, daß . . . ein Taster falsch reagiert' (39) – became a symbol for the possibility of a global inferno. The private individual can be led into his or her own private inferno by a similar chance mishap. 'In diese Welt der Pannen führt unser Weg', writes the author, and the way leads past everyday artefacts, 'Bally-Schuhe, Studebaker, Eiscreme [*sic*] (39), where there are still perhaps possible plots for writers to develop, where 'Pech sich ohne Absicht ins Allgemeine weitet' and where, as we saw in *Das Versprechen*, the particular can become the general. This, then, is 'eine noch mögliche Geschichte'.

The 'particular' is once again Switzerland, and the main character is a 45-year-old salesman, Alfredo Traps, this time with an Italian–Swiss rather than a French–Swiss Christian name, but with a very German–Swiss surname. Dürrenmatt told me, 'Das ist natürlich von "hineintrappen", hineinfallen; Traps ist ein erfundener

Name, aber direkt aus, "hineintrappen". Es ist ein *sehr* versteckt erfundener Name! Ein Trappi ist einer, der immer Unfälle hat' (F22) (see above). His 'Unfall' or 'Panne' occurs at six in the evening when his red(!) Studebaker develops a blockage in the petrol pipe and the train journey to home, to his wife and four children, though short, would be too complicated to undertake. He seeks overnight accommodation in the little village, not without the hope 'irgendein Abenteuer zu erleben' (41). Dürrenmatt thus establishes early on a 'type', alas generally understood, of an outwardly respectable commercial traveller, eleven years married but with hidden sexual desires. He finds accommodation in a villa owned by four grotesque old men, dressed in old-fashioned frock coats 'wie ungeheure Raben' (44). We then find that all four were originally connected with the law: the host, aged eighty-seven, was a judge; Zorn, aged eighty-six, was a state prosecutor; Kummer aged eighty-two, was a lawyer; while the profession of Pilet, aged seventy-seven, is revealed dramatically only later. (The bowler hat which he wears gives a little clue to those who know something of stage or film comedy – is there something of the clown figure here (cf. E8, 206)?)

After a typical Dürrenmattian meal (47–8), washed down with typical Dürrenmattian choice wines served by the silent house-keeper, Madame Simone, the four ask Traps to join them in their evening game: 'Es besteht darin, daß wir des Abends unsere alten Berufe spielen' (45). Traps, presented as a typical driving, am-bitious, 'modern' businessman, will humour the old fogies. All four have their own roles to play, of course; the one role not yet taken is that of 'the accused'. 'Would Traps . . . .?' The unwitting Traps: '. . . es sei ihm eine Ehre, den verwaisten Posten eines Angeklagten anzunehmen' (47).

As the 'trial' continues, we realise that it is modern society which is before the bar of the court, in the dock. Traps, none too intelligent, fond of an amatory adventure or two, has to admit that it was his dalliance with the sensual wife of his 52-year-old col-league, Gygax, which caused the latter's heart attack.[15] 'Es geht hart zu im Geschäftsleben, wie du mir, so ich dir,' Traps boastfully assures the 'court', 'wer da ein Gentleman sein will, bitte schön, kommt um' (56). Despite the frantic warnings of his 'counsel', Herr Kummer, Traps has 'confessed' to a 'crime' which, first to his amazement, later to his apparent joy, carries the ultimate sentence – which can be carried out by the fourth old man, Herr Pilet, who, we now learn, was the former executioner.

The strange action takes place against the intermittent servings of noble wines, excursions with Kummer to the verandah to cool off and explanations of how these bizarre proceedings had their origin: 'Der Staatsanwalt lag im Sterben, bei unserem Gastfreund vermutete man Magenkrebs, Pilet litt an einem Diabetes, mir machte der Blutdruck zu schaffen,' says Kummer, but then the game was proposed and 'es wurde unser Gesundbrunnen, dieses Spiel' (61).[16]

Traps' and the twentieth century's moral indifference is graphically registered as the now drunken 'common man' realises that his guilt is about to be 'punished', albeit in the most unusual manner possible, not by a civil or a criminal court, but by the strictest force of moral judgement of bygone days. The reason for the advanced ages of the four protagonists becomes clear: they have reintroduced into this amoral age 'das Gesetz Mosis', just as Florestan Mississippi had wanted to do in Dürrenmatt's contemporaneous play, the iron law of necessity of the Old Testament: 'eye for eye, tooth for tooth, hand for hand, foot for foot' (Exodus xxi, 24), because, as the prosecutor Zorn says, 'Herr Gygax ist systematisch ermordet worden.' The particular becomes the general – modern society has murdered morals.

Thus, Gygax's death now becomes the symbol of the death of the twentieth century. However Traps, Zorn says, is not a true criminal but only an 'Opfer der Epoche' (87) which has lost all its guiding stars, its true morality. Only a chance meeting has enabled these four old legal dinosaurs – 'eine groteske, schrullige, pensionierte Gerechtigkeit' (91) – to judge the world from which they have fled, and Alfredo is condemned to death amid drunken applause. 'Dank, lieber Richter, Dank!' gulps Alfredo with crocodile tears, unaware of the true significance of the evening, but still revelling at being accepted as a 'Meisterspieler'. More drinking follows and Traps eventually goes up to bed by dawn-light, 'glücklich, wunschlos wie noch nie in seinem Kleinbürgerleben' (93) . . . but, when the old men go up to his bedroom, they find the 'victim' hanged, by the window: 'Alfredo, mein guter Alfredo! Was hast du dir denn um Gotteswillen gedacht? Du verteufelst uns ja den schönsten Herrenabend!' (94)

Die Panne undoubtedly deserves its enormous popularity; no one could wish for a more engaging and twisting plot, while the various scenarios probably account for its appeal to such wide audiences. As is usually the case with Dürrenmatt, there is much beneath the surface and many of the specialist studies listed in the Bibliography have examined these layers: from the symbolism of the names – Zorn, Kummer, Pilet (from French *piler*, to crush!), Alfredo's firm Hephaiston (from *Hephaistos* whose wife Aphrodite

committed adultery with Ares) and the real or invented names of
Germanic characters (cf. here particularly the studies of Bänziger
(C7) and Mayer (C36)) – to the relationship with Dürrenmatt's
contemporaneous utterances on tragedy and comedy (cf. Tiusanen
in B22). It is also taken as a well-nigh perfect example of the
Dürrenmattian 'grotesque': the four strange old men, the 'comic',
frightening meals – again 'Gerichte' in two senses – the similarly
eerie yet somehow ridiculous ambience, all these tally with the
many theories about the grotesque in Dürrenmatt's works, which
Reinhold Grimm in an early article had called their 'Grundstruktur'
(E18, 91). In the 'Anmerkung zur Komödie' Dürrenmatt wrote,
'Das Groteske ist eine äußerste Stilisierung, ein plötzliches Bildhaftmachen und gerade darum fähig, Zeitfragen, mehr noch, die
Gegenwart aufzunehmen, ohne Tendenz oder Reportage zu sein'
(WA24, 24–5). This, it seems, was his aim in *Die Panne*: by means
of these grotesque old men, with their anachronistic judicial procedures, to bring the twentieth century to court, to present in a
vivid, picturesque and accurate fashion the amoral, immoral world
of his day. Dürrenmatt *is* a moralist, above all – a realistic moralist
who deals out remorseless judgement and punishment to his erring
flawed 'heroes'. Although Alfredo seems to be sentenced to a
'comic' death by the four old men, he had suddenly realised earlier
that the 'Spiel' was about to become 'Wirklichkeit': 'Das Spiel
droht in die Wirklichkeit umzu kippen' (64). As he staggers upstairs, he is driven by his own sense of guilt to take his life and thus
achieve some sort of atonement for that guilt. 'Justice-achieved-
through-Chance' would seem to describe this character as well. It is
in this way that we can call *Die Panne* an *Urmotif* of Dürrenmatt: his
subsequent workings of the theme of the *Prosakomödie* (cf. 69 and
150 below) show how fascinated he has been by the moral problems of guilt and atonement, of sin and retribution.

True Trivia

This chapter closes with accounts of three short pieces of prose
writing which belong chronologically to the period with which we
have been dealing, but only loosely to the thematic substance, and
certainly not to the same artistic category: 'Nachrichten über den
Stand des Zeitungswesens in der Steinzeit' (WA21, 187–93),
'Aufenthalt in einer kleinen Stadt (Fragment)' (WA22, 186–200)
and 'Mister X macht Ferien' (WA21, 165–84).

The first piece, written in 1949 when Dürrenmatt was writing literary reviews for the Berne paper *Die Nation* and then for the Zurich *Weltwoche*, gives a rather heavy-handed account of the 'invention' of newspapers in the Stone Age. It contains some typical Dürrenmattian wit – 'Die Carbonalzeitung, unser ältestes Blatt, erschien alle hundert Jahre' (188) – and some typical 'Kalauer': 'Extraausgaben – wie etwa jene anläßlich der Entstehung der Alpen' (189). There are political jokes about the 'Fortschrittspartei' and the 'Alt-Konservativen', and the piece ends with the disappearance of all newspapers when the 'state' is invented, which turns all international newspapers into 'Lokalblätter' which then die out for want of support.

'Aufenthalt in einer kleinen Stadt' has something of the Kafkaesque spirit of 'Der Tunnel' about it. A played-out banker, Bertram de Schangnau (a village in the Emmental, a few miles south-east of Dürrenmatt's Konolfingen) comes to Yverdon, 'wo Pestalozzi gelebt habe', at the south-west end of the lake of Neuchâtel, to look for a job. By chance, he alights from the train between Solothurn and Grenchen in a town called Konigen, and there his adventures begin. A bomb is pressed into his hand and, as the clock strikes ten, he throws it (why?) into the town's ancient tower, the 'Stöpsel'. In Chapter 2, 'Im Coiffeurladen', he has found a room at a hotel (the Wilhelm Tell!) and thinks back to the English girl with whom he had just spent a few pleasant nights, but then he has to go to the barber's to borrow some money. In comes the town architect, furious that the town's most sacred monument has been destroyed, and we now see that the story is an 'attack' on Swiss local patriotism – hence the local names and references. Then, in 'Im Gespräch mit einem Anfänger', Schangnau meets Yvette Bein, a ten-year-old girl who takes him to her father, who has orders to kill Schangnau (why?) but cannot do it. In the last chapter, 'Erstes Telefongespräch', Schangnau decides to telephone his wife, but still has no money. And there this 1953 fragment ends. Armin Arnold writes that the 'ausgefallenen Namen [setzen] die Lachmuskeln in Bewegung' (E3, 195). My own remained motionless as I read this juvenile prose. It is presumably meant to be a preliminary sketch for the colour and fantasy of *Grieche sucht Griechin* and *its* provenance perhaps proves that *Grieche* is indeed set in the Neuchâtel region.

'Mister X macht Ferien' (1957) features the Devil (Mister X) and Mister U as God. The trivial story is of a visit by the Devil to his master, probably built up on the old saying, 'Ein X für ein U machen', to hoodwink, to bamboozle someone. The Devil wants to take a holiday – among the nuns of St Cecilia convent in Ck.

God is horrified that the Devil should want to go for a holiday 'in den einzigen Ort dort unten, wo man meine Gebote hält' (169)! The rest of the world 'drohe nach und nach zum Teufel zu gehen', we are told! God, who has the look of a Lutheran clergyman, gives the Devil permission but watches him through his ancient telescope. However, when the Devil is told by God to return to his job, evil and corruption break out again. The Devil goes 'up' to earth, swindles some Swiss bankers and, with the proceeds, buys the nuns the most beautiful gowns, perfumes – and brassières! The town gangsters, with 1950 French film names such as Coucou le Lilas, Pipi le Lis, Bébé la Rose and May MacMay, and nuns like 'Henriette vom abgeschnittenen Busen der Heiligen Agathe', come together and, under the Devil's charming chaperonship, peace breaks out: 'Das Gute bricht in die Welt hinein' (183). But when God orders the Devil to return to work, the normal world recommences its normal ways. Dürrenmatt only lightly sketches in the last few lines and gives little indication how he would have continued.

These three trivial sketches show how Dürrenmatt's mind was working at three different epochs: the first (*c.* 1949), when he was a newspaper columnist, intent on making mock of a tedious task; the second (*c.* 1953), a preparation for a longer work which would combine Swiss particularism with a more generally applicable theme; and the third (*c.* 1957), possibly a play on the thought that you can hoodwink anyone with a little bit of ingenuity – but it also has within it the seeds of another Dürrenmatt play or story on the theme of Good and Evil in the world. All three stories seem to lack the spark to set off another major theme, but it is instructive to consider three trivia beside two masterpieces. It does show that the term 'Trivialliteratur' has to be considered very carefully by non-German scholars, since it is clear that it cannot be accurately translated as 'trivial literature', as it sometimes is.

–4–

The Radio-Plays

In a world dominated by the 'flickering screen' of television, where so much information is gained from the ubiquitous 'box', and radio, for the vast majority of late-twentieth-century listeners anyway, is regarded mainly as a purveyor of non-stop pop music, it is easy to forget how important radio was between 1930 and 1950, when it and the daily newspaper fought for dominance in the struggle to supply information – and culture. It was, however, particularly after the end of the Second World War, when newspaper and paper for books were in short supply and/or rationed, the film industry was still recovering from the ravages of war and television was a growing infant, that radio in Britain really came into its own as purveyor of 'news and views'. The situation was, of course, much worse in devastated continental Europe, yet, after the return of *émigrés* (or POWs, or concentration camp victims) to Germany, attempts were quickly made to re-establish pre-war radio services, although the occupying powers were in no hurry to allow Germans back into control.

The first prize to be awarded for a radio-play (*Hörspiel* or *Funkspiel*) was given to Oscar Wessel by Norddeutscher Rundfunk in 1947, and that encouraged younger writers to try their fortune in the revived medium. The absence of books, and the difficulty of mounting lavish play productions, led to what was called a 'gathering of respected intellectuals in the "Funkhäuser"' (Martyn Bond, D5, 92). The *Hörspiel* which most older people associate with this period, of course, is the 26-year-old Wolfgang Borchert's *Draußen vor der Tür*, broadcast on 13 February 1947 and staged in 1948, but this was, in fact, something of a 'false start'. It was the 1950s that saw the blossoming of the new art-form, and some of Dürrenmatt's contributions in that period were certainly ranked among the best – although hardly of the generally high standard of the contributions of writers such as Günther Eich, Ingeborg Bachmann, Heinrich Böll or Wolfgang Hildesheimer.

In another of Martyn Bond's articles on the German *Hörspiel*, he quotes W. Flemming's reasons for the popularity of the genre. In it 'wird also eine Suggestion ausgeübt, und nicht eine Illusion, wie auf der Bühne erzeugt. Es verlagert sich alles weit eher in das Innere, weil ja das Ohr überhaupt das nach innen leitende Sinnesorgan ist im Gegensatz zum Auge mit seiner extravertierten Gerichtetheit' (D6, 49; E15).

I feel sure that this is an accurate statement, but I am equally certain that such elevated thoughts were far from the minds of the hungry and cold Germans trying to make a living in 1947–9 – and certainly far from the thoughts of the 25-year-old Dürrenmatt when he wrote his first radio-play, *Der Doppelgänger*, in 1946. Since something approaching 160 *Hörspiele* were published after the war, and some 180 were broadcast per year after 1945, this was clearly by far the most, indeed the only, lucrative art-form of the period. In an article in the Zurich *Weltwoche* (12 December 1958; now in WA17, 155–7) Dürrenmatt wrote, 'So verdanke ich dem Hörspiel viel, auch Geld; die deutschen Sender zahlen anständig', and since critics did not take radio-plays seriously, 'so läßt sich gerade in ihnen ungestört oft das Wesentlichste tun oder doch vorbereiten' (157).

Der Doppelgänger (Ein Spiel) (WA1, 295–326) was his first venture in the field. Written in 1946 in Berne just after *Es steht geschrieben* and before he finished his studies on 20 June 1946, the author described it (in 1980) as 'ein Werk, das, ganz in meiner von Kierkegaard ausgelösten religiösen Dialektik verhaftet, sich in den christlichen Paradoxien herumhetzt, im Versuch, das Problem der Prädestination darzustellen' (325). It was turned down by Radio Bern in 1946 and was not broadcast until 1961, by NDR and Bavarian Radio, later being recast as an opera by Jiri Smutny which had its première in 1975. In the 'Anmerkung', Dürrenmatt says that he still finds *Der Doppelgänger* 'bemerkenswert' and writes that it is 'mehr ein Motivknäuel als ein Werk; die Jugend liebt es, gordische Knoten zu knüpfen' – though not to 'lösen' (326)!

The play begins with a Faust-like *Vorspiel auf dem Theater* between the 'Schriftsteller' and the 'Regisseur' about the former's proposed play, 'eine dunkle Geschichte' set in a rococo castle. The subject is a man (= 'Everyman') and his double ('Der Doppelgänger'), the figure beloved by Romantics from Heine's and Schubert's to Robert Louis Stevenson's Jekyll and Hyde. The Doppelgänger wakes the man to tell him that he has been sentenced to death, for a murder committed by the double. 'Das hohe Gericht' has decided that 'Der Mann' must accept the guilt. 'Der Mann', now called Pedro, protests – Kafka-like – his innocence and incomprehension, but is told that he is about to kill another person. He is then confronted with a beautiful woman, Inez, kisses her and is ordered by her to kill her husband, who is, of course, the Doppelgänger, now Diego. (There are constant, and often quite humorous interjections from, and arguments between, writer and director which successfully 'alienate' the action, but also cleverly heighten the tension).

Inez has asked Pedro to poison her husband Diego – but he shoots *her* instead. Why? Diego says, 'Das Weib mußte sterben, denn es war der Grund des Verbrechens, das ich begangen habe' (316), that is Pedro was the unwitting 'Henker', the tool of Diego's plan. But Diego unknowingly drinks the poisoned glass and dies. Thus, Pedro has murdered 'without killing', his unjust destiny which he must now accept. 'Nur wer seine Ungerechtigkeit annimmt, findet seine Gerechtigkeit, und nur wer ihm erliegt, findet seine Gnade' (322).

In its 'Hochfrequenzstil' and theological content, *Der Doppelgänger* obviously belongs to that corpus of 'early prose' that we have just examined. Dürrenmatt himself connects it with 'Der Folterknecht', *Der Blinde* and *Ein Engel kommt nach Babylon*: 'Ein Stoff ruft stets einen Gegenstoff hervor,' he wrote (326). The central theme, the Lutheran–Calvinistic concept – 'Forbear to judge, for we are sinners all', as Shakespeare has it in *Henry VI*, Part II, III. iii. 31) – the concept of 'Grace', is met again in the two early dramas *Es steht geschrieben* and *Der Blinde*, while the *Richter–Henker* theme bulks large, as we have seen, in the two detective novels of 1950–1, and later.

The *NDR Hörspielheft* of 1965 called 1951 the 'zweite Geburtsstunde des Hörspiels' (D6, 96); Norddeutscher Rundfunk (the radio station's early name) broadcast forty-five hours of radio drama in 1949, and 130 in 1951, and since Süddeutscher Rundfunk, for example, was paying some DM 1,000 per script, it was a favoured medium for imaginative, and hungry, writers.[1] It was Radio Bern, however, which broadcast Dürrenmatt's second radio play, *Der Prozeß um des Esels Schatten* (now in WA8, 119–72), on 5 April 1951, the only one of his *Hörspiele* to go out first on Swiss radio. (The book version appeared in 1956 with the sub-title *Nach Wieland – aber nicht sehr* – which subtly gave the flavour of this delightfully anachronistic work.)

As we shall see again, Wieland and Lessing have remained Dürrenmatt's favourite classical authors – 'Ich lese die Klassiker am liebsten,' he says to Charlotte Kerr in her film – but here Wieland's *Geschichte der Abderiten (Eine sehr wahrscheinliche Geschichte)* (1774) is turned on its head. The inhabitants of ancient Abdera in Thrace were noted for their stupidity, and Wieland used them to caricature eighteenth-century German provincial life. Building a fountain but supplying no water, and purchasing a Venus by Praxiteles but placing it so high on a pedestal that no one could see it, were typical gaffes. But the best example came in Part IV, the case of the Ass's shadow. A dentist, Struthion, hires an ass to carry him to a neighbouring town. In the heat of the day, he sits down to rest – in the shadow of the ass – and is taken to court by the driver Anthrax because the ass and not the shadow was hired! The town is divided into the 'Party of the Asses' and the 'Party of the Shadows' – but at the end the poor, innocent ass is slaughtered by *both* parties.

In Dürrenmatt's version, Abdera becomes not only Berne in Switzerland, but any town with a stuffy provincial tradition (for example, Schilda in the Federal Republic). We must bear in mind too, as always with Dürrenmatt, the political and economic circumstances of the period. The Korean War which had started in 1950 was still being hotly contested and many left-wingers sided with the North Koreans against the USA-supported South, against big business and capitalism. (Picasso's wonderful *Massacre in Korea* was but one of the contemporary artistic reactions.) Switzerland's complacent post-war bourgeoisie now looked even more complacent in 1950–1 to those young Swiss who still felt a deep-seated sense of guilt at having avoided the war on the one hand, and a desire to leave Switzerland to share the excitement of the rebuilding of the Old World on the other. Dürrenmatt had already made a reputation as a controversial author with his *Es steht geschrieben* and his anti-Swiss, anti-war play *Romulus der Große* (1949); all credit to Radio Bern, therefore, that it took the risk of offending its public with this radio-play.

The story-line remains as in Wieland. Abdera (*bei* Dürrenmatt) is, says Struthion the dentist, 'eine Katastrophe! Zehntausend Einwohner . . . Kurz gesagt: Alles tiefste Provinz' (121). Struthion, who comes from Megara (Zurich?), is then portrayed as a rich capitalist; Anthrax, the donkey driver, as a 'Proletarier'. The action follows the original but, come the court case, the *echt*-Dürrenmatt patina appears. We now have a true class-comedy with many wonderfully comic lines, particularly when the hypocritical church, the time-serving politicians and the greedy armaments manufacturers are satirised: for example, the rich attend the Jasonentempel; the poor, the Latonatempel where the 'Oberpriester' Strobylus keeps a dancing girl, Telesia, the 'heilige Jungfrau', who dances to him in a 'durchsichtige[s] Kleid aus Kos' (146). The 'class' element is most strongly represented by the blustering, vulgar, obscene Tiphys, whose language takes the story anachronistically into the twentieth century. He listens to the story about the ass from his brother, Mastax: 'Ich höre zu. Gucke ihn an. Spucke aus. Schneuze die Nase. Schweige' (142). Tiphys is a true grotesque, funny but menacing, to whom Dürrenmatt significantly gives a number of class-conscious poems to sing. (In the original printed version (Arche 1956), the 'Lied des Tiphys' was by Brecht. Dürrenmatt supplied his own, more bitter, song for the 1980 *Werkausgabe*.) Tiphys later becomes the figure of 'Gerechtigkeit' sent to judge the stupid and the selfish embroiled in a stupid and selfish argument. At the end of Dürrenmatt's version, it is not the ass which is destroyed but the whole town. One man from each temple bribes Tiphys to set the *other* temple alight – and Abdera goes up in a senseless blaze.

Tiphys, about to sail away – the naturalistic 'Bote aus der Ferne' who 'solves the problem' – says, 'Ich wurde der Feuerhauch, der eure Vergänglichkeit sengte, die Gerechtigkeit, die über diese Stadt kam, und immer wieder kommen wird, ich wurde die Hölle eurer Taten, die ihr selbst begangen, die ihr selbst in euren Träumen herbeiwünschtet' (170), and it is an 'old lady' who 'comes back' in another, more famous play of Dürrenmatt!

Max Frisch used the same concept in his much more popular radio-play (*Herr*) *Biedermann und die Brandstifter* (1953): the hot embers of the West's possible destruction lie already in its own institutions. It only needs a fanatic to fan them into flames. And at the end of Dürrenmatt's play, the ass comes to ask the sad little question: 'War ich in dieser Geschichte der Esel?' – and Dürrenmatt has it printed in italics (172)! It was a question which Dürrenmatt was to ask again and again in many plays (and, as we shall see in Chapter 7, in many essays too), a question which execrates human cupidity and stupidity, especially in his own country, which he puts on trial so often and so willingly. Berne, as we have seen, figures prominently in the detective novels too: in the *après-ski*, Toblerone-loving culture of Switzerland, Dürrenmatt seems to find mirrored much of Western civilisation's *malaise*.

In one of the few scholarly articles on the radio–plays, Renate Usmiani asserts that 'Dürrenmatt hat, meiner Ansicht nach, im Hörspiel seine höchste Potenz erreicht', and she goes on to claim that, apart from the *Alte Dame* and the *Physiker* plays, they 'seine besser bekannten Bühnenstücke . . . an künstlerischem Wert übertreffen' (E44, 125–6).[2] This is a very big claim indeed, and one with which it is difficult to agree entirely, if only because the two media are so different. A stage play has so many more dimensions than a radio-play. The latter depends more, perhaps solely, on the imagination of the listener; a stage play can achieve a goal by bombarding the audience with a greater number of artistic impressions. It is instructive, therefore, to compare the stage or opera version of a *Hörspiel* with the original, and that can be done with several Dürrenmatt works, for example *Herkules und der Stall des Augias*, *Die Panne*, *Abendstunde im Spätherbst* and *Nächtliches Gespräch mit einem verachteten Menschen*.

The last-named is the next work to be considered. Written in 1951 and now to be found in WA17, 9–32, it was broadcast by Bavarian Radio in 1952 and produced as a play, *Nächtlicher Besuch*, by Hans Schweikart at the Münchner Kammerspiele. Schweikart had produced *Die Ehe des Herrn Mississippi* there on 26 March and, although Gerhard Knapp *inter alia* describes Schweikart's successful production as Dürrenmatt's 'endgültige Anerkennung als einer der wichtigsten Bühnenautoren deutscher Sprache' (C29, 50), in retrospect Dürrenmatt recalls rather his dejection after the performance, a disappointment with the theatre which was to increase, as we have seen, after *Ein Engel kommt nach Babylon* in 1953 (cf. *Versuche*, A6, 16). *Nächtliches Gespräch* was well received too, however, and was (like *Der Doppelgänger*) made into a 'Kurzoper' (under that shortened title) by Jiri Smutny and produced in Stuttgart in December 1968. There was also a memorable television version in English with Alec Guinness and John Gielgud.

The play takes up a theme which was not only on Dürrenmatt's mind during these early post-war years: Karl Kraus, who before his death in 1936 had satirically replaced the idyllic conception of the 'heilen Welt' of Goethean Weimar – 'Das Land der Dichter und Denker' – with his own bitter Austrian description of the Third Reich constructed by his countryman, Adolf Hitler – 'Das Land der Richter und Henker' – had given Dürrenmatt and others an idea to play with as the balance-sheet on the Holocaust began to be drawn up in these years, and one saw other similar tyrannies developing again in various parts of the world. Since the sub-title of the radio-play is *Ein Kurs für Zeitgenossen*, we are invited to draw parallels.

Nächtliches Gespräch is a nocturnal conversation between a man, a writer, and his 'executioner', and it is clear that he lives in a totalitarian society since his son is in a concentration camp, his friends have been persecuted and 'der Staat schloß mich in das Gefängnis seiner Ächtung ein' (15). With the Holocaust in mind, as well as the deaths of millions of other innocent people, many of whom seemed to have died without a struggle or a protest, the executioner ('Der Andere') remembers times past when dying was noble: 'Da war Verbrechen in ihrem Handeln und Gerechtigkeit in meinem Henken, die Rechnung war klar und ging auf. Sie starben einen gesunden Tod' (20). But now? Now people 'krepieren', not 'sterben' – the age of any heroic action is past and, as Dürrenmatt was to put it in a memorable phrase later in 'Theaterprobleme', we now have actions and plays 'die von Weltmetzgern inszeniert und von Hackmaschinen ausgeführt werden' (WA24, 59). Peter Johnson was absolutely correct with his suggestion that this radio-play is a 'moderne ars moriendi' (D25, 270).

The author protests that one should be able to die as one wishes, 'brav', but the executioner assures him that that is no longer possible – either people die 'wie Tiere', or they die *humbly*. Therefore, when the writer makes a Kafkaesque gesture and shouts for help from the window, there is no answer – just 'Stille' (23). And the final message must be the Christian one: 'Blessed are the meek: for they shall inherit the earth' (Matthew V, 5). '[E]in Sieg, der größer ist, als je ein Sieg eines Mächtigen war,' says the executioner, for it is now a 'meaningful' death (29). Here Dürrenmatt is developing the themes of the 'mutigen Menschen', which he adumbrates in 'Theaterprobleme' and of the 'Mächtigen' versus the 'Opfer', which were to dominate his later work.

Is it a pessimistic view of the world, or a realistic one? Looked at from the late 1980s, when Europe has survived over forty years without a major war, and when peace overtures suggest that we might even live another forty years without one, it will probably be seen by younger readers as pessimistic; looked at as the aftermath of a world conflagration, with some eleven million innocent victims slaughtered by the Nazis, and another twenty million rumoured to have perished in Stalin's pre-war holocausts, and with signs of a growing totalitarian attitude in some of the new Eastern bloc countries, it was probably a realistic assessment of the world situation. Western audiences certainly took it to be an indictment of a growing menace, and now, having just incurred *dis*favour with the patriots for his scurrilous assault on 'heroic values' in his *Romulus*, Dürrenmatt found himself attacked for his 'ignoble pessimism' – clear signs that he was well on the way to becoming his own favourite figure, 'Der große Einzelne' (the writer as 'his own man', doing 'his own thing'!).

* * *

To those who lived in, or visited, Germany in the years immediately after the Second World War, one of the most common and tragic sights was the cripple, often without arms or legs, begging by the street-side. The 'soldier-home-from-the-war' was, of course, not only a common shared reality, but it soon also became the theme of plays, books and films, as the whole new industry of 'Heimkehrerliteratur', so generously examined by academics, sprang up.

Although Dürrenmatt in Switzerland stood, in one way, outside this thematic possibility, in another way he had to be part of it since, as he once said to me, and he has repeated it to many others, 'für den Schriftsteller ist die Schweiz ein sehr guter Arbeitstisch, aber ich lebe nicht von der Schweiz, sie ist viel zu klein' (F22). His work had to be conceived with German sales in mind at a time when finance was more important to him than it is now.

In one of his later articles for *Die Weltwoche* (2 April 1953), Dürrenmatt wrote wittily about the leading comic figure of the Viennese Volkstheater, Joseph Anton Stranitzky (1676–1727), one of those 'Hanswurst'-figures 'die zwar immer Pech hat, aber immer gerade noch einmal davonkommt' (now in WA24, 27–30), a fore-runner of Brecht's 'verprügelten Helden' and Dürrenmatt's own 'mutigen Menschen'. The title of his next *Hörspiel, Stranitzky und der Nationalheld*, (WA17, 33–75) would certainly remind theatre-goers of the Viennese actor-playwright, just as the name of one of the leading characters, Baldur von Moeve, is not too far distant from that of Hitler's infamous Youth Leader, Baldur von Schirach. NWR (Hamburg) broadcast the play on 9 November 1952, by which time the Dürrenmatt family had moved (on 1 March) to Neuchâtel. Now, with three children under five years old, money had become a first priority for the writer.

The macabre humour which was gradually being understood as a central component of the Dürrenmattian style is most obvious here. The piece is again a satire on 'heroics', on 'hero-worshipping' and on idols with feet of clay, whether they be football stars, athletes, film stars or politicians. The source, according to Dürrenmatt himself, was the death in 1952 of just such a type, Eva Duarte-Perón, the glamorous wife of the Argentinian President who, as Larousse delicately puts it, 'exerça une grande influence politique et sociale'. She achieved even greater posthumous 'pop' fame as the eponymous heroine of Andrew Lloyd-Webber's musi-cal *Evita* (1978).

Stranitzky, legless from the war, is wheeled around in a chair by his friend Anton who has been blinded. Stranitzky is a former football star who remembers *ad nauseam*, but not always accurately, the goals he scored when he was a player. Anton, 'two metres tall', is a former deep-sea diver. Both are fiercely patriotic despite their appalling injuries and support their national hero, the head of the state, Baldur von Moeve. (Brock-Sulzer rather spoils the 'in-joke' by having the name spelled 'von Möve' in her book.) The two invalids hear on the radio that von Moeve is suffering from leprosy in his big toe, incurred in Abyssinia: 'Er betrat barfuß, nach der Sitte des Landes, eine Hütte und ist davon aussätzig geworden' (38)! They believe that, although as invalids they had 'nichts zu sagen' in the political world, now that von Moeve is an invalid himself he will listen to them – and 'Der Moeve muß mit uns eine Regierung bilden' (39). But when they visit and get to know the 'Nationalhelden', the scales fall from their eyes as they realise that their idol is a selfish, conceited fool who looks back not only to his own glorious 'martial past' – 'ich stand unerbittlich bei [the battle of] Saint Plinplin' (53) – but worse, in his 'agony', treasures the memories of the Weimarian 'heile Welt': 'Junger Mann,' he says to Stranitzky, 'ich leide. Frau Sorge sucht mich heim, die Goethe so trefflich in seinem Faust, zweiter Teil, beschrieb, den ich schon in Finsterwalde las und jetzt zum zwölften Mal' (53). Disillusioned, they seek refuge in the waters of the town's canal. Their bodies are never found. The 'Nationalheld' returns 'rosig und wohlbeleibt' from his convalescence on the Riviera and takes up the reigns of government again. But just as he is being welcomed back, 'zwei riesenhafte Wasserleichen' – Stranitzky and Anton – are seen in the water, 'und der Beinlose hatte seine trotzige Faust gegen den Nationalhelden gereckt' (75).

The bitter-witty dialogue, the outrageously named characters (J.P. Whiteblacke, his fiancée, Molly Wally, the Prinzessin von Teuffelen *et al.*) and the use of 'classical' motifs to contrast with the contemporary absurdities (Mozartstraße, Schubert's quartet *Der Tod und das Mädchen*, Chopin's Funeral March) give a richly comic tapestry which, with the 'in-jokes' about Switzerland in the 1950s, makes this probably Dürrenmatt's best radio-play, and one which should be resurrected for performance.

* * *

'[N]un gerade der *Herkules* . . . das hat der Schweizer gar nicht so gemocht,' Dürrenmatt said to me in 1969, and the barrage of negative criticism from the press after the production of the stage-play *Herkules und der Stall des Augias* in Zurich on 20 March 1963 could certainly be so summed up. The stage-play had many fore-bears: there is the so-called *Ur-Herkules* which Dürrenmatt described in the Schauspielhaus programme for 1962/3 as having been written 'vor zehn Jahren' and which probably went back to a sketch for the Cabaret Cornichon, writes Wyrsch (E49, 24); then there is a *Schwyzerdütsch* version *Herchules un dä Auchiasstall*, the radio-play itself and a version on record, all voices being read by Dürrenmatt himself (DGG 643013) (1957).

The radio-play (in WA8, 175–226) was written in 1954, and was first broadcast by NWR (Hamburg), then on 20 October by Radio Bern. (It and the later play version are interestingly bracketed with *Der Prozeß um des Esels Schatten* in volume 8 as 'Griechische Stücke'!) However, the theme, the satirised 'classics', that is, the great tragedies, was to become one of Dürrenmatt's favourites. He showed in his 'Anmerkung zur Komödie' (1952) how relevant he found Aristophanes' comedies to our modern situation; they were like 'Geschosse', he wrote, 'welche . . . die Gegenwart ins Komische umgestalten' (WA24, 21); and his Herkules, like his Baldur von Moeve in *Stranitzky*, is a 'Versager', a man who talks but cannot deliver, making a satirical contrast with the heroic Hercules of Greek mythology. The latter, it should be remembered, became a lampooned figure even in the Middle Ages, often portrayed as a gluttonous buffoon, as he was too in Aristophanes' *The Birds*. Dürrenmatt, too, makes him complain that he is often taken for 'einen ewig betrunkenen Kraftmeier' (183). (The Hercules myth and its relevance to Dürrenmatt is interestingly discussed by Ernst Gallati (E16).)

The 'joke' of the plot is when Augias, the King (or rather the Swiss-like 'Präsi'!) of Elis, misunderstands a reference to Herkules as the 'Säuberer Griechenlands'; he thought that it referred to *physical* cleansing – but Herkules was a *moral* cleanser! We hear of the whole action through Polybios, Herkules's much-battered secretary, the butt of most of Herkules's wrath when things go wrong, as they frequently do. The satire on the Classics is broad – too broad for some – yet it depends on some knowledge of the characters' original roles in Greek history and/or mythology. The very first words of the *Hörspiel*, Polybios's 'Nach der Erzählung des guten alten Gustav Schwab', reveal the name of the author of *Die schönsten Sagen des klassischen Altertums* (C44). This is the book to which Dürrenmatt constantly refers throughout his career, and which, I would assume, is the source of much of his seemingly extensive knowledge of the Greek classics.

Polybios attempts to convince us that Schwab's version of the Fifth Labour, namely that Hercules cleaned out the Augean stables for King Eurystheus in one day, was an *under*statement. The first four labours had, in fact, been disasters; nothing had gone right, and Polybios leads us to believe that the great reputation has been built up by a series of propagandistic eulogies written by well-remunerated poets: 'Gewiß, Homer und Hesiod, die repräsentabelsten Dichter unseres Jahrhunderts, konnten wir uns nicht leisten' (181). They had to underplay the true course of events in Elis, otherwise Herkules's reputation would have been ruined! Herkules had taken on Augias's insulting request to cleanse these filthy stables of dung because he was deeply in debt, and Dürrenmatt then cleverly indicates *i*) that Elis is a thinly-disguised Switzerland, *ii*) that its inhabitants are peasants who can only count up to three, and *iii*) that the dung, 'der Mist', is actually all the cultural treasures of the past – Dürrenmatt is thinking here of the 'classics', both Greek and Germanic, which *are* treasured in Germanic lands but, alas, as museum pieces. There is little doubt that the satire was meant to reach the Swiss: Elis is governed by a Swiss-sounding 'Großen Rat', whose members bear Swiss–Greek names such as Adrast von Ankenboden, Pentheus vom Säuliboden, Kadmos von Käsingen, Tydeus vom hintern Grütt and Agamemnon vom vordern Grütt. When Herkules finally fails in the task, the reason is given by Kambyses, the swineherd. 'You failed', he says, 'Weil der Mist vor allem in den Köpfen der Elier zu hoch steht' (222), that is, the wall of conservative tradition is too strong to be broken down.

Herkules is then degraded to earning money as a weightlifter in a doubtful circus, and he leaves Elis – and the King's son Phyleus – in a state of despair. The mood of hilarity in the play has suddenly undergone a change. Phyleus goes to console his father Augias, and finds him tending a beautiful garden made fertile by the Elian dung. 'Ich bin Politiker, mein Sohn, kein Held,' Augias says, and shows Phyleus that this is all that we can do in this 'gestaltlosen wüsten Land', literally 'cultiver notre jardin' (225–6). So the individual *can* solve the problems for himself, and he must now try to convince others to work towards a similar solution for themselves and their country.

Opinions will vary, of course, about this sudden artistic 'change of gear' from comedy to philosophy. Wolff-Windegg, among many others, found it 'ein bißchen Gratiserbauung', and Dürrenmatt later provided a second ending, in the 1963 play, where Phyleus marches off 'heroically' to meet and, we know, to be killed by Herkules.

The first ending does seem to have been the correct one for 1954, when Dürrenmatt was working out his theory of the man who, despite buffets, will stand up and fight for what he believes to be right and, in so doing, might convince others to do likewise – however modest his contribution might be. It was a moral lesson for his complacent, comfortable fellow-countrymen and women, and they did not like it. But for any non-Swiss, the play is a hilarious experience. (How Bänziger could write in connection with this work, 'Er [Dürrenmatt] ist ein schlechter Brecht-Schüler, und der politische Witz ist nicht seine Stärke', is quite inconceivable (C7, 194).)

But a question does remain: if, in 1954, the moral answer to the world's problems was for each to cultivate his own garden – 'Es kehre jeder vor seiner Tür/Und rein ist jedes Stadtquartier', wrote Goethe too – why, in 1962, did Dürrenmatt write as *Punkt* 18 to *Die Physiker*, 'Jeder Versuch eines Einzelnen, für sich zu lösen, was alle angeht, muß scheitern'? I shall try to answer that question when we come to consider the plays in Chapter 6.

* * *

The least interesting of the *Hörspiele* is, in my opinion, *Das Unternehmen der Wega*, also written in 1954, and first broadcast by a consortium of German radio companies. It was extended in 1969, and is now in WA17, 77–124. This is Dürrenmatt's first attempt at 'sci-fi', and a weak attempt it is too. The year is 2255, the earth, after 310 years of peace, is about to break out into war again – still West versus East – and the Earth-dwellers need to take over the planet Venus, now the world's penal colony, as a new haven. The European diplomats in the spaceship *Wega* meet, however, a surprisingly civilised society when they arrive. John Smith(!), the son of an American communist, receives the group in the name of Mr Petrov, the present leader of the colony. The Venusians want nothing to do with war, but wish to live their own lives in their own peace. The commission from Earth comprises, of course, typical pompous, twentieth-century diplomats, who believe that their earthly underhand policies will work on Venus and its simple, 'uncivilised' race. 'Wir haben es mit Menschen zu tun,' says the leader of the delegation, Sir Horace Wood, a lover of the arts and *belles-lettres*. 'Sie sind nicht anders als wir und ebenso leicht zu verführen wie [*sic*] wir' (100). His colleagues, Mannerheim, Oberst Camille Roi, the pilot Kapitän Lee, plus three Ministers, all agree. But no deal is made, for they now have to bargain with a powerful woman (Irene), a Dr Edith Marlok-type nurse (and a former prostitute), who now leads the Venusian delegation. Wood decides on a typical earthly solution: blow the planet up with nuclear weapons to prevent their making a deal with the Soviets. A final conversation between Wood and a former fellow student Bonstetten – they studied Philosophy together in Oxford and Heidelberg (Dürrenmatt's two 'top' foreign universities in these days!) – reveals the philosophical message of the play, when Bonstetten says of the Venusians, 'Der Mensch ist etwas Kostbares und sein Leben eine Gnade' (115), which Earth-people had forgotten, he claims. But Wood's decision has been made, Bonstetten mourns for Venus in the words to be echoed in *Die Physiker*, 'Du kannst die Tat nicht zurücknehmen, die du denken konntest' (119), and Venus is destroyed.

It is perhaps a personal aversion to science fiction stories that leads me to rate this *Hörspiel* as Dürrenmatt's poorest; he seems, however, to have taken a leaden and rather obvious approach to the theme, to have jumped on to a rolling bandwagon, but not to have had the fantasy of an Asimov, or a Bradbury, to have made a success of it. Of course, a good deal of his specialist and considerable knowledge of the stars and the planets is conveyed (cf. 87–8), and the conclusion forms a chilling contrast to what Germans call the naïve 'Fortschrittsglauben' of those who believed that the grass would be greener on the other side of the fence. The author castigates again the short-sighted stupidity of 'those in power' and, as in *Herkules*, suggests that only the individual or, as here, a group of individuals acting *as one*, can show the true way.[3]

* * *

We come finally to the two most important radio-plays, Dürrenmatt's last two to date, written when he had clearly reached maturity as a writer. I am slightly suspicious of dividing any author's (or musician's or painter's) life into the traditional 'three phases' – and *Zufall* plays too great a part to attempt to do this with the career of a living author. (Dürrenmatt vowed to me in 1969 that he would never write another play!) But it does seem that the success of *Der Besuch der alten Dame* (1956) with its consequent fame, popularity and emoluments, marked a watershed in Dürrenmatt's career, and that thereafter he wrote with more flair and confidence. *Die Panne* and *Abendstunde im Spätherbst* were written at the same time as the *Alte Dame*, and both bear witness to this increased maturity.

As we have already established (above, 49–50), the radio-play *Die Panne* was written in 1955 *before* the *Erzählung*, although the latter was published first in 1956; the *Hörspiel* was first broadcast on

17 January 1956 on Bavarian Radio, then repeated on Radio Bern on 26 April. (*Der Besuch der alten Dame* had its première on 29 January 1956 in Zurich, and *Die Panne* certainly did not harm Dürrenmatt's growing reputation.)

In an interview with Jean-Paul Weber in 1960 (in French in the printed version (F21), although Dürrenmatt spoke in German), Dürrenmatt said that the idea for *Die Panne* came partly from a little *conte* by Guy de Maupassant (possibly *Le voleur?*) where three drunken artists catch a thief and hold him to a mock trial, but that it came mainly from an Austrian anecdote about a little post-First World War clerk in Vienna, typically cleaning out a massive pile of old papers when an ex-judge enters and asks where the papers came from. 'They are old legal documents,' says the clerk, who is enjoying himself copying and completing some of the forms. 'Fine,' says the judge. 'When you are finished, bring them to me and I'll sign them.' Weber's ironic comment on the anecdote is 'Nous rions poliment tous les deux'! But then he puts to Dürrenmatt a question which we shall have to ask at the end of our discussion of *Die Panne*, the radio-play, because there is one significant alteration in the plot between the *Erzählung* and the radio-play which demands an explanation.

The general story-line (now in WA16, 9–56) is similar to that of the *Erzählung* but, because of the different media, not the same. The listener cannot go back to check up confusing points, of which there are more than a few, so the plot has to be less complex or made more obvious with sound-effects: motor-car music, doors slamming, corks popping and the like. Traps is also, it seems to me, more of a caricature of a salesman than in the story. His very first words are 'Dieser Wildholz! Der soll was erleben. Junge! Rücksichtslos gehe ich nun vor, rücksichtslos. Dem drehe ich mal den Hals um . . . Fünf Prozent will er mir abkippen' (11). He is much more of a businessman here than in the story, where he is generally cooler and 'distanziert' (Dürrenmatt says so too), more civilised. In the radio-play too, Traps displays a petulance towards the four old men caused not a little by his own humble upbringing: 'Mein Vater war Fabrikarbeiter, ein Proletarier, den Irrlehren von Marx und Engels verfallen' (22). He only had a primary school education which 'makes him what he is' – a man with money, but also with a huge cultural inferiority complex which explains, in part, his immense pleasure at being taken note of by four representatives of a profession perhaps more highly regarded in Germanic countries than in Britain or North America, the Law.

Thus, with the force of the spoken word behind it, its vulgarisms and colloquialisms, the *Hörspiel* paints a more exaggerated picture. To hear Traps discuss his seduction of Frau Gygax, 'da mußte ich hin und wieder den Tröster abgeben auf dem Kanapee in Gygaxens Wohnstube' (31), along with a lecherous laugh, gives a greater impression of a careless, driving, ambitious man than the equivalent scene in the *Erzählung*. It also helps to explain the greatest difference between the two plots; after the 'trial' in the radio–play, Traps is taken – drunk – upstairs by Pilet, the executioner, and shown the guillotine, part of a collection of antiques, torture instruments, etc. Traps 'protests' that he has to be executed as a 'murderer', but he falls asleep like a child: 'ich bin doch müde, alles ist ja schließlich nur ein Spiel, ein Spiel, ein Spiel!' (54) The next morning, without breakfast, he races off in his big Studebaker ready to extract his '5 per cent', a typical twentieth-century businessman who shrugs off a hungover nightmare in the rush to cash in his next profit.

Clearly, the radio-play has neither the psychological depth nor the authorial skill of the story. The writers of radio-plays played on the imagination of the listener for *effects* rather than for intellectual cogitation; the possibilities of the medium were perhaps not yet fully explored. Dürrenmatt himself wrote, 'Sieht man im Film, wie im Fernsehen, durch ein Schlüsselloch, im Theater wie in einen Guckkasten, so lauscht man im Hörspiel an einer verschlossenen Tür ohne Schlüsselloch' (in 'Vom Sinn der Dichtung in unserer Zeit', in WA26, 65). When he came to write the story, his growing mastery of the art of the written word, and the knowledge that a reader has much more time to consider subtleties and nuances, encouraged him to make of this work something of a 'philosophical thriller'. The 'murder' is no 'murder', the 'accused' is not an 'accused', and the 'trial' is not a 'trial'; it is all philosophical speculation, which, however, does end in a true atonement of 'guilt'. The murder was truly 'in the mind', and Traps remains baffled by it all. In his 'Ansprache anläßlich der Verleihung des Kriegsblindenpreises' awarded for this radio-play in 1957, Dürrenmatt said of his play, which he called 'eine Prothese für den Blinden'(!), 'Die Welt des Einzelnen dagegen ist noch zu bewältigen, hier gibt es noch Schuld und Sühne. Wie der Einzelne die Welt besteht oder wie er untergeht, ist das Thema auch meines Hörspiels . . . auch wenn der Hauptheld, der Textilreisende Alfredo Traps, nicht sehr viel von dem, was vorfiel, kapierte' (in WA16, 179).

Jean-Paul Weber asked Dürrenmatt in the interview mentioned above: Why did Traps commit suicide? The answer: 'S'il se pend,

c'est dans un paroxysme d'allégresse, dans un spasme de re-
connaissance . . . En se tuant, il signifait tangiblement son admission définitive dans une société qui l'avait traité avec tant de
sollicitude et d'amour', but he added that he was also thinking of
the great Soviet show trials with their prepared confessions.

Yet, both versions of 1955–6 present a theme which must have
been uppermost in the author's mind at the time: his dislike of the
complacency of his fellow Swiss wallowing in the *Hochkonjunktur*,
the boom, of their and Europe's growing *Wirtschaftswunder* created
by Ludwig Erhard's economic policies in the Federal Republic,
which then had their effects on the whole of Europe. The Swiss,
however, untouched by war, had never really known anything
else. As the rest of Europe caught up with their high living
standards, one heard less of this anti-Swiss motif from Dürrenmatt.
Perhaps, too, the attacks of those critics who persisted in pointing
out to him that he was himself part – and a very successful part – of
the *Kulturbetrieb* had their effects. Siegried Melchinger's 1968 article, for example, with its witty title 'Wie schreibt man böse, wenn
man gut lebt?', summed up this later criticism (E32).

In 1956, however, his *Alte Dame*, this *Komödie der Hochkonjunktur*, found an echo in the ruthless, vulgar behaviour of an Alfredo
Traps who must be a second cousin to Alfred Ill, and to whom (in
the story, anyway) justice comes likewise out of the past as retribution for unwitting sins.

* * *

Abendstunde im Spätherbst was written in 1956 and broadcast by
NDR under the title *Ein Abend im Spätherbst* on 20 March 1958.
Radio Bern broadcast it with the title *Herr Korbes empfängt*, and in
November 1959 Rudolf Noelte directed a stage version for the
Berliner Theater am Kurfürstendamm. There have also been sev-
eral television versions, while the *Hörspiel* itself was awarded the
most prestigious prize for radio drama in Europe, the *Prix d'Italia*,
in 1958.

The charge mentioned above, that some writers who criticise the
society in which they live do, in fact, live very well at its expense, is
one with which every successful writer has to contend. The writer
is only too well aware of the well-founded nature of the criticism
and counters that he or she really wants to write works of art, but
that the *Kulturbetrieb* demands its profits, and that these profits
allow more authors' works to be accepted and published – and so
on and on turns the vicious circle. 'Man kann halt nix dafür.' It was

in *Schriftstellerei als Beruf*, broadcast on Radio Bern just at this time (25 April 1956, and now in WA26, 54–9), that Dürrenmatt attacked those of the 'Betrieb' who claim to be 'Dichter' when they are in fact usually only 'schlechte Schriftsteller', who 'zwar dichten, aber nicht schreiben können, eine in der deutschsprachigen Literatur nicht allzu seltene Erscheinung' (54). The artist in Switzerland, he went on, had to sell his wares according to market forces: 'Die Musen haben bei ihm [i.e. the Swiss public] nicht zu lachen, sondern seiner Forderung nach solider Qualität zu entsprechen und ewig zu halten' (55–6). And the celebrated *bon mot* from his play *Der Meteor* did not exactly settle the matter: 'Ein Schriftsteller, den unsere heutige Gesellschaft an den Busen drückt, ist für alle Zeiten korrumpiert' (WA9, 46)!

Three times, Dürrenmatt has shown his distaste of this 'culture industry', each time in an only lightly veiled autobiographical manner: in 1965–6 in his play *Der Meteor*; in its extension, *Dichterdämmerung* (1980) (both in WA9); and, in 1956, in what now reads like a preparation for these works, *Abendstunde im Spätherbst* (WA9, 169–96).

At the beginning of the radio-play, the author, Maximilian Friedrich(!) Korbes introduces himself with the promise that he is going to tell a true story, indeed that he *only* tells true stories. He describes his house, and those who know Dürrenmatt's house in Neuchâtel realise that Korbes' house resembles it to a T. His life-style, Korbes goes on, is 'verlottert, konfus, wild, skandalumwittert' (172), and his description of himself as 'dick, braungebrannt, unrasiert, kahler Riesenschädel' does remind older readers of the 'wild' Dürrenmatt of the early 1950s. Unlike Dürrenmatt, however, Korbes is a Nobel Prize winner (for Literature), but of an unusual type since his pride in telling only 'true' stories means that the many murders described in his novels actually took place – and that he himself must have done the murdering.

A late-evening visitor, a Swiss, Fürchtegott Hofer – one has learned by this time to look 'behind' Dürrenmattian names – addresses Korbes in the true German(ic) reverential and pedantic manner: 'Verehrter Meister!' (174). ('Den verehrten Meister sparen Sie sich,' grunts Korbes (174), as he also corrects the Weimarian-flavoured appellation 'Dichter' to the Brechtian 'Schriftsteller'.) Hofer is a retired bookkeeper turned private detective ('etwa . . . auf dem religiösen Gebiet'), who had begun to examine the role of the murderer in Korbes' novels – Korbes' nickname is 'Old Mord und Totschlag' (à la Hemingway) – and discovered that the murderer is *always* able to escape detection. In answer, Korbes introduces the theme which was to reappear in *Der Meteor* and was then later to follow Dürrenmatt throughout his career. Korbes asks, 'Sie nahmen an, es existiere zwischen meinen Romanen und der Wirklichkeit ein Zusammenhang?' (178)

Hofer illustrates his point by relating two of the stories, both of which are clearly based on episodes in Korbes's life, and where 'suicides' were, in his opinion, obviously 'murders': 'Alle diese Selbstmorde und Unglücksfälle spielten sich an Orten ab, in denen Sie – verehrter Herr Korbes – auch weilten' (183). He declares that Korbes himself must be the murderer described in his own novels. When Hofer then proposes a little 'pocket-money' ('so sechshundert oder siebenhundert Schweizerfranken im Monat') to allow him to continue to observe Korbes, it is meant, of course, to buy his silence.

But Hofer has to learn, as a pedantic, scholarly, out-of-touch-with-reality Swiss, that the boulevard press has known for a long time that Korbes is his own murderer-hero – 'die Gesellschaft hat uns nicht nur akzeptiert, sie interessiert sich auch fast nur noch für unseren Lebenswandel' (190) – and that *that* is the only way to become truly popular: 'Ich ließ meinen Stil fallen, um ohne Stil zu schreiben, und siehe, da besaß ich auf einmal Stil' (192). Dürrenmatt had already pointed out in 'Theaterprobleme' that this age has no style, only *styles*, part of his attack on the pedantry of Germanisten, classical scholars and philosophers who are more concerned with the 'Wie' than the 'Was' of writing.

Thus, for Korbes to be able to write yet another successful work – this time, significantly, a *Hörspiel!* – Hofer must be done away with too, so there follows the twenty-third (or twenty-second? one is not sure) death, although also disguised here as a suicide!

Dürrenmatt has published the 1978 version of *Der Meteor* as volume 9 of the *Werkausgabe* along with *Dichterdämmerung*, written in May–June 1980. The latter is, in essence, an extended stage version of *Abendstunde*. Together he has given them the title *Nobelpreisträgerstücke* (WA9, 97–156).[4] Whether there is a hint of sour grapes here is a matter of opinion, but certainly *Dichterdämmerung* is an even more authentic autobiographical description, while the title *Dichterdämmerung* is a wicked parody of *Götterdämmerung* by Wagner, the most German of reverential Germans' 'Meister'. (Dürrenmatt prints there Wagner's long scenic instructions for Act III, Scene 3 about Hagen's suicide – and his three words of dialogue, 'Zurück vom Ring!', as Valhalla goes up in flames (WA9, 197–8)!). Thus, this is a further attack on the Staigerian cult of the 'classics' which, as we shall see, had become almost an *idée fixe* in Dürrenmatt's plays – and, like all *idées fixes*, was also to become almost comical!

There is a good deal of hurt pride too in the swingeing attack on the critics in *Dichterdämmerung*, and here and there a sly nudge at himself, as when the visitor, Fürchtegott Hofer, says *à propos* a theatre director's whereabouts, 'Ach wo! Der inszeniert doch in irgendeinem Nest einen Dürrenmatt', and the author asks, 'Wird Dürrenmatt denn noch gespielt?' (116). After Hofer's 'suicide', Korbes dictates one of Dürrenmatt's most fantastic stories which has as its main character a most unlikely Scot, 'Major Sir John Harold Macfire' (with obligatory kilt!), who comes to the front of the stage and declares himself to be the 'Autor des Autors der Dichterdämmerung'. He promptly disappears into the twentieth-century scientists' equivalent of the 'twilight of the gods', the 'black hole' where authors and critics are swallowed up in the flames which cannot be put out: 'Kein Mensch in dieser Stadt weiß mehr, wo das Theater ist!' are the anguished final words (156). (Many of Dürrenmatt's satirical sketches concern his continual battles with his critics (cf. in *Rollenspiele* 'Assoziationen mit einem dicken Filzstift' (A4, 155–96) and on many of his dust-jackets)).

This Rolf Kieser called 'Dürrenmatts Hausmischung von Pennä-ler-Humor and metaphysischem Tiefsinn' (E22, 134). The jokes certainly creak and the 'metaphysics' seem to be only the self-defence of a wounded playwright. It proved to be, in retrospect, and to all extents and purposes, Dürrenmatt's leave-taking as a serious writer for the theatre.[5]

* * *

Like the short stories and the novels, the radio-plays are an essential part of the Dürrenmatt *oeuvre*. At this early stage of his career, they show his growing mastery of scenic details, of dialogue and of plot construction. For his own career, they brought in, firstly, much-needed money for his growing family, and gave him an *entrée* to directors and producers and the theatre in general; artistically and creatively, they show the way in which his fecund imagination would play on and with some of these *Urmotive* for the rest of his career. Renate Usmiani's claim that he created here 'echte Kunst-werke moderner Dramatik' need not be dismissed as exaggeration or hagiography (E44, 144).

-5-

The Later Narrative Works

The Stories of the 1960s and 1970s

After the enormous success of the *Der Besuch der alten Dame* in 1956, Dürrenmatt could no longer rest in his comfortable house(s) up above Neuchâtel, but had to accept the many invitations to lecture, to receive prizes and awards and to attend prestigious functions. Not a well man at the best of times, these journeys proved to be extremely tiring, and at times dangerous, as British colleagues discovered when, having been invited to receive the Welsh Arts Council International Writers' Prize in Wales in 1976, Dürrenmatt took ill and had to return home. Nevertheless, he has continued to travel widely; the works discussed in this chapter were written mainly as a direct result of travels and impressions gained from travel, and are books which finally dispelled any notions that Dürrenmatt was a cosy regional author closeted in a neutral Switzerland.

The author has made two long visits, in 1964 and 1967, to the Soviet Union where his 1962 play *Die Physiker* has usually been taken as an anti-capitalist work, since Dr von Zahnd's sanatorium houses 'die ganze geistig verwirrte Elite des halben Abendlandes' (WA7, 12). Madame Furceva of the Soviet Ministry of Culture wrote in June 1963, however, that the characters were 'unworthy representations of the relationships between the sexes, and the denial of any sort of healthy mentality' (cf. B23, 148, note 38), and the play was not performed again until Dürrenmatt's 1964 visit. No doubt it was banned because of the implied criticism of the KGB in the character of Ernesti.

In 1964 Dürrenmatt and his wife stayed for a month in the USSR to participate in the memorial ceremonies for the Ukrainian poet Shevchenko (1814–61). On his return, Dürrenmatt's views 'Meine Rußlandreise' appeared in the *Zürcher Woche* on 10, 17 and 24 July 1964 and, in the light of what has happened since, they read like a remarkable piece of prophecy. Dürrenmatt's main (positive) impressions were that the old communism was dead and that 'man [kann] – mit allem Vorbehalt und auf lange Sicht gesagt – darin sogar den Ansatz zu einer Demokratisierung Rußlands erblicken', but he warned that the USSR was still 'ein Machtzentrum'. Moreover, the results of his important second visit in May 1967 when he attended the IVth Soviet Writers' Congress in Moscow, thereby incurring the displeasure of some Western colleagues, were much less positive. His own highly critical thoughts were reserved for *Stoffe*, but it was in this visit, and in these thoughts, that his next work originated.

What distressed Dürrenmatt most about the literary reports made by Soviet authors at this conference in pre-*glasnost* times was that they were not discussing literature but 'politische Glaubensbekenntnisse', and that it was plain to see that they only needed to '*confess*' this 'faith', not actually *believe* in it. Power was with the Politburo, seated a few metres away from Dürrenmatt, 'steinern, götzenhaft' as he described them in *Stoffe*, and he realised that 'Der Zahl Eins [kommt] alle Bedeutung zu' (A2, 148); if 'No. 1' falls, then 'No. 7' or 'No. 5' will become 'No. 1'. Thus, after a 'aufgeregte Diskussion über die Sitzordnung des Politbüros', Dürrenmatt returned to his hotel room with the idea for his next story, 'Der Sturz', in his head.

Between the conception and the publication of the story lay some four years, 1967–71, during which Dürrenmatt went through the most difficult period of his life, personally, publicly and politically. His 'political' difficulties were caused by his enthusiastic support of the Israeli cause in the Six-Day War in 1967 and thereafter. As he wrote in *Stoffe, II–III*, 'die Juden galten auch bei meinen russischen Freunden als Faschisten' (A2, 150), whereas Dürrenmatt had long believed that the Israeli way of life was historically founded on what he was later to call 'Israels Lebensrecht' (cf. below, 174). Rudolf Kassner, on the other hand, Dürrenmatt wrote, depicted the Soviet system thus: 'Ordnung ist, daß Einer vollkommen sei; dieser Eine macht dann, daß Ordnung sei' (A2, 151). It was this tendency which Dürrenmatt saw for a socialist philosophy to harden into a 'system' which he disliked so much about the Soviet state. There will be a good deal more to say on this subject later, but for the moment let us look at 'Der Sturz' in the light of these thoughts.

'Der Sturz' (in WA23, 9–64) is the 'report' of a meeting of a 'Politisches Sekretariat' in a nameless country whose economy is going to the dogs; it is a cool, somewhat cynical look at intrigues in high places – and not just in the Eastern bloc countries. There are fifteen places at a long rectangular table for characters identified only by letters of the alphabet thus:

```
        A
   B    C
   D    E
   F    G
   H    I
   K    L
   M    N
   O    P
```

The Chief, A, sits at the head of the table and P (the 'Chef der Jugendgruppen') is at the foot. Each has an official title, and therefore Heinrich Goertz's suggestion is a good one: 'Der Leser tut gut daran, hinter jedem Buchstaben das betreffende Amt zu notieren' (C18, 103)! Otherwise a sentence such as 'Ein Blick auf A genügte N: A erkannte die Falle, in die ihn G gelockt hatte' (51) would be incomprehensible.

The wit in the story – and it is very witty – lies in the secrets revealed behind each of the Ministers' back. The reader is privy already to some of them because of the nicknames given: thus, B (the Foreign Minister) is the 'Eunuch', H (the Defence Minister) is '*Gin*-gis-Khan' (his weakness is obvious), M (a woman) (Minister for Education) is the 'Parteimuse', and so on. But one Minister has not yet appeared: O, the Minister for Atomic Energy.[1]

Dürrenmatt told Urs Jenny in 1966 about his new work, 'Dreizehn [*sic*] Personen in einem geschlossenen Raum, die Mächtigsten eines Landes, wie sie mit einander konspirieren, einander bekämpfen, bis der Mächtigste liquidiert wird' (F8, 2). 'Der Mächtigste' is A who, a peasant-type like Stalin, would love to dispense with the whole body. They, in turn, are highly suspicious of him and, of course, of each other. But . . . O? Where is O? Fear spreads through the group as suspicion mounts. They all know that 'there is a little list' with names of marked colleagues on it and kept by C, the Head of the Secret Police, but cruelly nicknamed 'die Staatstante'!

Dürrenmatt skilfully allows each character to put his or her point of view. We see that their main concern, as in *König Johann* (q.v.), is saving their own skin and their perquisites, a damning indictment of the 'Mächtigen' in *any* country, we must understand. But 'sie besaßen Villen, Wagen, Chauffeure, kauften in Läden, die nur für sie bestimmt waren' (55) shows that Dürrenmatt had remembered well his visits to socialist lands!

But then, as must always happen, as Dürrenmatt would say, with 'Mächtigen', the worm turns. Certain that O has been arrested by A, G (the 'Chefideologe') begins to query the progress of the state since the revolution and claims that it is the Party which has held progress back. 'Die Revolution sei ein dynamischer Vorgang, die Partei ein mehr statisches Gebilde' (49), and the revolution will swallow all its enemies. Therefore, the Politisches Sekretariat must be liquidated, either by itself or by others. They all realise that A has kept his popularity by the device of 'divide et impera', by letting the members fight among themselves; but now their hate and fear have united them – and A is finally removed, strangled by their own hands. 'Nieder mit den Feinden im Schoße der Partei, es lebe unser großer Staatsmann A', cries the Minister of Defence – alas, not for the first time (62–3)!

But in the last paragraph the door opens and O enters, to explain that he had simply mistaken the date of the meeting! *Zufall* has played its part again and 'die schlimmstmögliche Wendung' – Death – leads to a ridiculous conclusion. So, the order of chairs is rearranged, and *plus ça change, plus c'est la même chose*. The new sitting commences. The chilling, and no doubt significant, last sentence reads, 'Draußen begann es zu schneien', as the 'new order' sets about its 'new business', thus:

```
        D
    B   C
    F   E
    M   N
    H   G
    K   I
    O   L
        P
```

It probably depends on one's political stance how this tale will be taken: those on the Right will nod their approval of Dürrenmatt's biting portrayal of socialist oligarchs posing as democrats; those on the Left will find it vastly exaggerated, too far-fetched even to be worthy of a laugh.[2] Neutrals will spot Dürrenmatt's 'fingerprints', the already familiar motifs: the *Richter–Henker, Schuld–Gerechtigkeit, Mächtige–Opfer* themes, with *Zufall* bringing the denouement. There is a flavour, too, of the 'gangster-democracy' of his play *Frank V* (below, 118).

During the denouement, there is a fair sprinkling of grotesque obscenities, as for example when the ageing Marschall, in his fear, urinates over the feet of the female Minister of Education. And, of course, there are the usual Dürrenmattian 'Kalauer', jokes which raise a groan rather than a laugh: the suggestion, for example, that D should order a female octet to play Schubert's Octet before A, naked. But, all in all, this story is highly amusing and among the best that Dürrenmatt has written.

* * *

'Alles, was ich schreibe, ist mehr oder weniger politisch', Dürrenmatt said to me in 1969. If that was not how critics saw his work in the early years, stories like 'Der Sturz' must have encouraged them to change their view. In the 1970s Dürrenmatt was clearly what some of us had believed him always to have been, a *zōon politikon*, and the burgeoning conflict in the Middle East, from 1967 on, began to attract his attention. It may have been Israel's size, a Swiss-like pygmy among the neighbouring Arab giants, or his memories of the Old Testament stories told him by his father and mother, or the exciting adventure of a new type of existence in the kibbutzim, but whatever the reason, Dürrenmatt began to write and lecture in defence of the small Jewish state. We shall look at these essays later in Chapter 7, but here we are concerned at the moment with a short story, which deals with, and illustrates in symbolic fashion, the conflict between Arab and Jew. (It appeared first of all in *Zusammenhänge* (below, 188), a series of essays 'über Israel', written in gratitude for the award of an Honorary Fellowship of the Ben-Gurion University of Beersheba in 1974 (now in WA29)).

'Abu Chanifa und Anan ben David' (WA23, 65–86) (1975, revised 1978) is a parable of this conflict. Abu Chanifa, the Arab, and Anan ben David, the Rabbi, were arrested by the Abbaside al-Mansur in AD 760 and thrown into gaol together. The description of the gaol reminds us forcibly of the labyrinthine caves in 'Die Stadt' and in 'Aus den Papieren eines Wärters'. In their conversations, they discover to their mutual amazement that God is the same God for both of them – only in the Bible He is 'dunkler, unvorausberechenbar in seiner Gnade und in seinem Zorn', while in the Quran, He is 'dichterischer, hymnischer, auch etwas praktischer in seinen Geboten' (71)! The years pass and they remain crouched opposite one another in their dark dungeon until, one night, a Kalif enjoys a sexual encounter with a girl with 'zinnoberroten Haaren' – clearly Dürrenmatt's favourite colour! – and called 'Amanda, Anunciata oder Annabella' (74), as a result of which all prisoners whose names begin with 'A' are released! Two hundred years later(!) the order reached the dungeons, but only Anan ben David is freed since the warder, 'schadenfroh', calls the Arab '*Chanifa*'.

There then follows a 'Wandering Jew' episode which takes the Rabbi through all countries and all ages, including the Nazi Holocaust – rather like the character in 'Die Falle' – until a longing for 'das Gelobte Land' drives him back to the holy place. He has quite forgotten Abu Chanifa, of course, who has been kept alive by friendly rats who have given him of their food, and who is waiting for a sign from Allah: 'Was ihn erfüllt, ist die Gewißheit, sich an einem heiligen Ort aufzuhalten' (82). Anan ben David reaches Istanbul where a drunken Swiss sculptor takes him in a Volkswagen to Baghdad (where the sculptor perishes in a ridiculous, absurd accident!), and leaves Anan to find his way back through the labyrinth with the help of a strange, hairless, white dog.

There the two very old men meet up again in their dungeon and fight murderously: 'jeder verteidigt mit seiner Freiheit die Freiheit seines Gottes, einen Ort für den zu bestimmen, der an ihn glaubt' (85). But then, staring at each other, they utter their first and only word, 'Du'. 'Jahwe ist Abu Chanifa und Allah Anan ben David gewesen, ihr Kampf um die Freiheit war eine Sinnlosigkeit' and they agree that their prison is 'die Freiheit des einen und die Freiheit des anderen' (86).

Such an agreement, that not only *one* 'Truth' was possible, admissible or valid, had appeared in German literature before, so it was not surprising to hear Dürrenmatt admit in Charlotte Kerr's film in 1984 that Lessing was one of his favourite classical authors. In Act III of Lessing's *Nathan der Weise* (1779), Nathan, the rich Jew, tells how a man once owned a ring with magic properties and all who believed in its virtue were 'pleasing to both God and man'. He had three sons whom he loved equally well, so he had another two identical rings made to avoid squabbles after his death. But the sons *did* dispute which one had the 'true' ring, and the court judge at the end of the hearing advises them each to believe that *he* has the true ring. The parable is then applied to the Christian, Jewish and Mohammedan religions in the play: 'Es eifre jeder seiner unbestochenen/Von Vorurteilen freien Liebe nach!' proclaims the judge (Act III, Scene 7).

Lessing's 'enlightened' appeal for tolerance in 1779 might sound as utopian as Dürrenmatt's two hundred years later, but certainly no one who wrote in this vein could be called 'nihilistic' or even 'pessimistic'. Dürrenmatt's views are very much those of the *Aufklärer* Lessing, and he wrote in *Zusammenhänge*: 'Erst die Aufklärung machte die wirkliche Toleranz zwischen den Religionen möglich, weil der Abstand von Subjekt zu Subjekt unendlich wurde, erst in diesem Unendlichen vermochten sich Jude und Christ zu begegnen' (WA29, 37). The topic will recur in our study.

* * *

Many of Dürrenmatt's imaginative prose writings in this later period are to be found embedded in essays or critical writings in the form of parables or exemplars. The third of our stories now contained in volume 23 is 'Smithy', originally included in the volume *Der Mitmacher. Ein Komplex* (Arche 1976) published after the failure of his play *Der Mitmacher* (première on 8 March 1973 in Zurich). 'Smithy' (87–115), termed a *Novelle*, is obviously one of Dürrenmatt's favourite *Urmotive* since it is mentioned so often in his writings, speeches and interviews, but there is another reason for its continuing reappearance. *Der Mitmacher*, a confused and confusing play, was a resounding flop in German-speaking lands (cf. in Zurich and Mannheim in 1973), whereas in Warsaw (1973), Athens (1974) and, surprisingly perhaps, in Genoa (1977) it enjoyed considerable success. The reason was almost certainly linguistic: Dürrenmatt's 'Kalauer' in German were too much for German-speaking audiences (cf. below, 147). Dürrenmatt took the failure very badly indeed and, although the 'Nachwort' to the *Komplex* contains in an early sentence the assertion 'Das Folgende ist daher nicht als eine Verteidigung eines durchgefallenen Stücks konzipiert' (WA14, 98), 124 pages of 'Nachwort' and 103 pages of 'Nachwort zum Nachwort' do little to convince the reader that he was *not* hurt.

'Wir machen mit, weil wir *sind*,' declares Dürrenmatt in the 'Nachwort' to WA14. His main character, Doc, however, is seen as a *negative* character: 'Aber der eigentlich negative Mitmacher in seiner bedenklichsten Form ist der Intellektuelle, der trotzdem mitmacht' (107). To explain this character Doc, Dürrenmatt goes back to a hot, steamy day – 'die Straße kochte' – in Manhattan in May 1959 during his first visit to the USA. Here he thought up the story of J.G. Smith, 'Smithy', whom he then later turned into 'Doc'. He wrote the story in 1961; it remained a fragment, but an *Urmotif* nevertheless, and it blossomed in the writing of the *Komplex* during 1974–6 after his second visit to the States in 1969–70.

The macabre side of death and dying, the dissecting and the disembowelling, seems always to have appealed to Dürrenmatt, perhaps because, as he once wrote, 'es ist nicht zu leugnen, das Makabre ist dem Lächerlichen benachbart' (*Der Mitmacher. Ein Komplex*, WA14, 102). (He describes such a scene with great vividness in *Stoffe I* (A1, 29–31).) In this story, too, there is much talk of death scenes, of dissecting and of the *absurdity* of dying. The story begins on 3 May, a very hot day for the time of year. Smithy is a scientist who has been working for four years with Dr Leibnitz (!), a surgeon struck off for performing illegal abortions. They dissect 'unwanted' corpses and dissolve them in their 'Nekro-dialysator', their own invention. The corpses are, of course, victims of gangland killings, and the profits are enormous. (For those who have experienced the stinking heat of a New York summer day, Dürrenmatt's description of the hot, smelly apartment block and the 'Sezierraum' under the Triboro Bridge heightens the gruesomeness of these descriptions: 'der Geruch der Stadt machte ihn rasend, dieser Geruch, den er haßte, der allen Dingen anhaftete, glühend und klebrig, verpappt mit unendlichen Staub- und Kohlemolekülen, Ölpartikelchen' (WA23, 91). How Dürrenmatt must have longed for the clean, fresh Alpine air of Neuchâtel!).

Smithy then experiences a Dürrenmattian 'miracle' when a beautiful woman offers herself to him, 'Gratis'. 'Sie wollte einfach bestiegen werden wie ein Tier von einem Tier' (99), one of those obscenities encountered increasingly in Dürrenmatt's later works. Later, Smithy has to agree to dispense with a corpse for the Police Chief (Nick) and his gangster friend Holy van der Seelen, who wears a priest's cassock, is said to be a Russian or a Pole – but is probably an Italian or a Greek – and is a homosexual to boot! They will earn 500,000 dollars for this, of which Smithy is promised 10 per cent. But we discover that the corpse is Smithy's 'generous' lady-friend who has been killed by her jealous husband, a famous politician whom Smithy addresses variously as 'Herr-o-mein Gott' or 'Herr der Heerscharen', but whom he thinks of as a 'Laus'. When Smithy sees the corpse, he rebels and refuses the money. 'Ihre Frau lasse ich gratis verschwinden,' he says, thus repaying the woman's favours and, in a little way, 'standing up and saying: No!' to at least one part of the whole revolting business. But, says Holy to Doc, 'Du hast das Geschäft deines Lebens vermasselt', and Doc, knowing that he is about to pay the penalty for failure and to be shot, murmurs, 'Schade um meine Prozente' (114–15).

Looking back over fifteen years to that day in Manhattan, Dürrenmatt felt 'als sei ich durch ein Labyrinth gegangen und durch dieselbe Pforte, in die ich eingedrungen war' (WA14, 261), a coming-together of two important motifs. 'Von Smithy führt ein dialektischer Weg zu Doc', he writes (261) and there is clearly something of the old 'mutigen Menschen' in Smithy: like Alfred Ill in the *Alte Dame*, he makes some sort of atonement for his guilt by an action which will certainly cause his death. (Later, Dürrenmatt will call one of the other characters in the play 'einen ironischen Helden'. We shall have to query whether this is a development of the 'mutigen Menschen'-theme, or the same by another name.)

* * *

The fourth story in volume 23, 'Das Sterben der Pythia' (1976) (117–58), appeared shortly after a discussion in the *Komplex*, on an old Dürrenmattian theme: Fate (*Schicksal*) versus Chance (*Zufall*). He had discussed the role of Fate in Athenian tragedy, of the Greeks' acceptance of the role of the gods and of the certainty of their truths: 'Was uns stört, ist das Orakel, eine Instanz, die fähig ist vorauszusagen. Eine voraussagbare Handlung läßt den Zufall nicht zu' (WA14, 273). He cites the Oedipus myth as one inseparable from the idea of Fate, but what if the proclamation of the Delphic Oracle were dependent on the person who proclaimed it, namely the Pythia, 'Pannychis XI', the priestess of Apollo? And what if she happened to be in a bad mood on the day that Oedipus came to her for her advice . . .?!

And that is the kernel of the story. The priestess is about to go 'off duty' – the language is suitably 'office' German, it was after five o'clock after all – when 'der bleiche Jüngling angehumpelt kam' (119) to ask if his parents really were his parents. So, to get rid of him as quickly as possible, she 'oracled' ('orakelte'!) that he would kill his father and sleep with his mother. No one bothered about oracles, the priestess felt, since 'das Prophezeite nur selten eintraf und, traf es doch einmal ein, auch gar nicht anders hätte eintreffen können' (121). Dürrenmatt then leads us hilariously through a maze of not quite accurate Greek mythology where all the oracles are blackmailing swindles. Jocasta has slept with a guards' officer, Polyphontes, who is *really* Oedipus's father and drives Laius's coach. Oedipus kills both of them and thus makes the oracle come true. Then we find that Oedipus is not Jocasta's son but the Sphinx's – she had exchanged Jocasta's children with her own. So Oedipus sleeps with the Sphinx, and again the oracle is proved to have been accurate, albeit by 'Chance'.

Not even the soundest knowledge of Greek mythology would guide the reader through this immensely complicated tale which is meant only to show that the Greeks too were led by greed, impatience, lechery and ambition. Their lives were dominated not by iron laws handed down by the gods, but by chance happenings dependent on human failings. As the 'blind' seer Teiresias says to the priestess Pannychis XI, 'ich glaube auch nicht an die Götter, aber ich glaube an die Vernunft, und weil ich an die Vernunft glaube, bin ich überzeugt, daß der unvernünftige Glaube an die Götter vernünftig anzuwenden ist. Ich bin Demokrat' (141) – and he, of course, in keeping with the other 'swindles' in the story, can see perfectly well!

One often wonders how deep Dürrenmatt's knowledge of Greek mythology really is. We know of his love for Gustav Schwab's *Die schönsten Sagen des klassischen Altertums*, and in *Rollenspiele* he continually breaks off conversations to look up references in various books. One wonders, therefore, if this knowledge comes largely from these reference books rather than from a reading of the originals. Certainly, he reveals that his knowledge of the Bible is refreshed by his father's 1893 *Calwer Bibelkonkordanz* (cf. in *Rollenspiele*, A4, 84). Charlotte Kerr calls these books his 'Koordinaten für sein Denkuniversum' (103).

No matter. For me, 'Das Sterben der Pythia' is a major representation of a Dürrenmattian motif that there is no certainty in life, that it is dangerous to 'believe' implicitly in a religion or an ideology: 'Denn wer glauben will, muß seine Zweifel unterdrücken, und wer seine Zweifel unterdrückt, muß sich belügen', he wrote in *Der Mitmacher* (WA14, 326). He would claim that this is neither nihilism nor pessimism, but *realism*.

The Stories in *Stoffe I–III* (1981)

It would seem that sixty is the age when famous people – writers, actors, musicians, politicians – begin to want to look back on their lives and careers, to ponder on what they have achieved and how they have achieved it, to try to draw up some sort of balance sheet: the most humble, to show people from a similar unprivileged background what can be achieved with hard work, ambition and, all would admit, a portion of good fortune too; and the most conceited, to establish a chart of success, of people known, places visited, money earned and fortunes won and lost.

In his sixtieth year, 1981, Dürrenmatt published *Stoffe I–III* (now A 1/2), just a year after the appearance of the *Werkausgabe* in thirty volumes in the Diogenes Verlag, Zurich, under whose imprint his works had been appearing from 1979. He had started to work on the book, *Stoffe: Geschichte meiner Schriftstellerei*, around 1973, that is, the year of the première of the ill-fated *Der Mitmacher* and the beginning of his disenchantment with the theatre. It is not difficult to make a collection of quotations to 'prove' that, although the theatre has always *attracted* Dürrenmatt, he has never really enjoyed either attending it or writing for it.[3] My contention is that the drawing-up of a balance-sheet of his career would show that his one true love is painting, and that his pleasure comes more from the construction of stories and, increasingly, of parables or essays, rather than from writing for the stage. This is indeed the major reason for undertaking a 'reinterpretation' since, like most critics, I had previously approached Dürrenmatt as a 'Theatermann' who wrote prose as a 'Nebenprodukt', as it were. I now believe that I, like others, was wrong.

Stoffe is divided into three major sections: 'Winterkrieg in Tibet' (9–190) (now *Stoffe I*), 'Mondfinsternis' (now *Stoffe II*, 7–118) and 'Der Rebell' (*Stoffe III*, 121–73), the last section in each case being the *Erzählung*. We shall look at the other sections later (below, 203); however, it might be interesting, having discussed Dürrenmatt's later prose, to continue to examine the narrative work of these later years in their own right *qua* stories, even though they are embedded in more philosophical and reflective material. They will allow us to pick up and underline the basic themes which we have been following.

Readers might recall that the 'Winterkrieg' was mentioned in the discussions of both 'Die Stadt' (above, 19ff.) and 'Aus den Papieren eines Wärters' (above, 20ff.). In the 'Anmerkung II' after the latter story, the author writes, 'In einem neuen Anlauf vollendete ich den *Stadt*-Stoff zwanzig Jahre später in einem Werk, das unter dem Titel *Stoffe* erscheinen wird: erst dann war ich ihm denkerisch gewachsen. Daß er in der *Frühen Prosa* erscheint, bin ich ihm und mir schuldig' (WA18, 198). This was written in 1980.

The Winterkrieg-theme goes back a long way, probably to Dürrenmatt's undistinguished military service in the summer of 1941. 'Ein linkischer Rekrut', Dürrenmatt nevertheless found that the experience opened his eyes to the real outside world, as it did to many another. The 'sinnlose Gemetzel' (A1, 70) going on all around Switzerland 'außerhalb der Katastrophe' gave him the idea for a parable, 'ein Gleichnis', which he started to write in La Plaine near Geneva in the winter of 1944. He was then nearly twenty-four and it was an attempt 'die Welt, die ich nicht zu erleben vermochte, wenigstens zu erdenken' (73). This first effort became 'Die Stadt' (also, in part, 'Die Falle'), then, in 1951–2, 'Aus den Papieren eines Wärters' and, finally – I think! – this 'Weltlabyrinth', this *Urmotif*, the 'Winterkrieg in Tibet'.[4]

Later, we shall examine the 'labyrinth'-theme more closely – the *Erzählung* is indeed preceded by the eighteen pages of the 'Dramaturgie des Labyrinths' (77–94) – but for the moment let us consider the continuation of the theme in the latest narrative form. The narrative describes the progress of the winter war in Tibet during the Third World War from the viewpoint of a Swiss soldier (or rather 'Söldner') (No. *FD* 256323) and, since we are to learn shortly that this mercenary was studying the philosophy of Plato just before the outbreak of the war, we may assume an autobiographical connection. As in the 'Wärter' story, the Söldner is in a Nepalese town and is ordered along a long narrow corridor, a labyrinth, where he meets his old Kommandant again and an armless, legless mercenary soldier in a wheelchair. There follows a good deal of gratuitous pornography – in which Dürrenmatt seems much more interested than previously, a fact that he strenuously contested when I brought it up in conversation, incidentally – until 'Hänschen', the soldier-narrator, stabs his Kommandant as he lies with/on a prostitute, and takes over his command.

The second section is the story of our mercenary, now also armless and legless – a Dürrenmatt theme from the Stranitzky days of 1952 – who is scratching his thoughts on the winter war and its consequences with his artificial hand, his 'Prothese', on the wall of the caves into which the whole administrative apparatus has been evacuated. His thoughts turn to the 'Gesetz der großen Zahl', which Rudolf Kassner had revealed to Dürrenmatt during that visit in 1950 (below, 187). That 'law', Dürrenmatt now argues, had only been relevant to mathematics and physics, and not to ethical or aesthetic categories such as justice and injustice to which, we might recall, he had sought to apply it previously. Now he applies it to the formation of the large institutions, which he compares to 'institutions of atoms', which have caused the Third World War. The war 'brach in Wirklichkeit aus, weil es noch keine Verwaltung geben konnte' (113), that is only individuals of good faith could have prevented it. But 'die Macht des Staates stieg an', rearmament panic broke out and (here Dürrenmatt picks up a theme from his 'Monstervortrag über Gerechtigkeit und Recht' (q.v.)) 'der Mensch ist für den Menschen ein Wolf' – what he, in the essay, called *homo homini lupus* – and wants to kill.

The third section transfers the action back to Switzerland and to the narrator's home town of Berne. We now have a satire on Switzerland's useless 'bewaffnete Neutralität' and its first war since 1512, when the Swiss conquered Milan! The narrator, now a Colonel, travels through all the well-known Swiss towns now laid waste by atomic bombs; in the University Seminar he finds *Emilia Galotti* (by Lessing), parts of a *Tragische Literaturgeschichte* and of the introduction to a *Grundbegriffe der Poetik* (works by Walter Muschg and Emil Staiger), and an old bookbinder who still 'prints classics' – Johanna Spyri's *Heidi!*

The mercenary now finds the administration evacuated under the 'Blümlisalp', the 3,671-metre mountain south of Berne in the Bernese Oberland, where a quick coupling with a prostitute, Nora, leads to a meeting with her husband Edinger, a former philosophy student – to whom, incidentally, the narrator reveals that he had been going to write a dissertation on Plato's 'Cave Allegory' in the *Republic*, Book VII. Edinger leads a group of dissidents hoping to re-civilise the world. He offers the mercenary the bait that was offered to him in the 'Wärter' story, namely 'Macht über Menschen', but the narrator refuses, shoots Edinger as a 'Landesverräter' (163) and returns to Tibet to find the adversary that he is certain is waiting for him.[5]

The last section has the narrator, now armless and legless in his invalid chair, scratching his story of the war on the cave wall. It is Plato's 'Cave Allegory' again; the shadows flickering on the wall are the shadows of the 'enemy', but when he fires at them he discovers that the shadow is his own. Man is his own (worst) enemy and is destined to be shackled with this adversary to his death: 'Das Ziel des Menschen ist, sich Feind zu sein – der Mensch und sein Schatten sind eins. Wer diese Wahrheit begreift, dem fällt die Welt zu, der gibt der Verwaltung den Sinn zurück' (176). When the dead mercenary is discovered in the cave, the writings on the wall are deemed to be a collage of Plato's 'Höhlengleichnis', Nietzsche's *Genealogie der Moral* and his *Schopenhauer als Erzieher* – the texts of Dürrenmatt's philosophy seminars in the 1940s!

'Winterkrieg in Tibet', for all its seeming pessimism, even nihilism, does, on close examination, continue the theme of the *Mitmacher* stories, of an individual trapped in a web of fear and incomprehension, but just dimly aware that the way out has to be found by himself. This is Man's right and duty, the author proclaims, no matter how fearsome the predicament. It is his freedom, to act, free from any dogma or ideology, to make his own decisions, to encounter and to come to terms with whatever chance phenomena may occur: 'Wir können dem Labyrinth nicht entgehen' (A1, 190).[6]

The second tale, 'Mondfinsternis' (in A2, 67–118), the source of the plot of *Der Besuch der alten Dame*, is a vastly different theme – at first sight. After describing a long-forgotten holiday in the Bernese Oberland when he was a student, Dürrenmatt goes back to the original story of 1955 which concerns an *Auslandsschweizer*, Walt

Lotcher from Canada, who arrives in the little village of Flötigen in a huge Cadillac. Entering the Hotel Bären, he hears from the locals that one Kläri Zurbrüggen has just married a villager, Döufu Mani – and it was Kläri who had become pregnant by Walt just before he left the village to go to Canada. Lotcher asks how many families now live in the village, and is told fourteen. 'Ich vermache euch vierzehn Millionen,' says Lotcher. 'Einfach so?' 'Nein,' is the answer, 'ihr müßt mir dafür Döufu Mani umbringen' (72).

It is not at first clear why Lotcher wants revenge – or on whom, but he agrees to give the villagers ten days to carry out his wishes while he goes upstairs to enjoy the serving-girls. The villagers then decide to kill Mani under – and with! – the beech-tree (shades of Droste-Hülshoff!) at the next full moon and debate what they will do with the money. In a gloriously comic scene, the deed is eventually done – even though the full moon is covered by a cloud ('Mondfinsternis'!) – and Mani lies killed by the felled tree: 'Mani sehe schon zerquetscht aus, soweit man es sehe, ein einziger Brei' as the text delicately puts it (108)! Lotcher leaves the villagers the promised reward and takes his Kläri away with him, but on the way he suffers a heart-attack and dies in the car, while the villagers prepare to erect a new ski-lift to attract the winter tourists.

Clearly, the story goes back to Dürrenmatt's earlier stories and to that day of his wife's operation in 1955 just before the première of *Ein Engel kommt nach Babylon*. The reason for its inclusion here is Dürrenmatt's belief in 'Zusammenhänge', in connections – 'Only connect!' said E.M. Forster famously – and *Stoffe* was written, in part at least, to attempt to bring together all the associations and connections between theme, play, novel, essay – and Life! Here the causal connection between the 'Winterkrieg' and the 'Mondfinsternis' is the mountain, the Blümlisalp, on which his Konolfingen teacher, Gribi, had written a play in about 1930.

Yet, out of this parochial quasi-*Heimatnovelle*, whose characters – at times comic, at times simple – in their hearty Swiss village ambience remind us vividly of the nineteenth-century *Novellen* of Keller, Meyer and Gotthelf, came one of the most powerful tragi-comedies of the twentieth century. Besides the tale's basic ingredients of sexual immorality, revenge, greed and black humour, it needed only Dürrenmatt's train between Berne and Neuchâtel to stop at the still desolate stations of Ins and Kerzers for Güllen to be invented, and the realisation that the opening scene of the plot of the proposed play demanded a *female*, for Claire Zachanassian to replace Walt Lotcher – of course, via '*Kläri* Zurbrüggen'.

'Mondfinsternis' is now in *Stoffe II*; *Stoffe III* contains the third story, 'Der Rebell' (155–73). This takes us back to Dürrenmatt's early familial experiences, to his arguments with his father on religion and choice of a career, and with his own fundamentalist, yet sincere mother, and to his own physical and mental growing pains as a student. Some of this material – on his time in Zurich 1942–3, his illness in 1943, his visit to Rudolf Kassner in 1950 – has been touched on already, but the point is made strongly here by Dürrenmatt how much his 'life' and his 'literature' are now one: 'so sehr hängt in meinem Leben alles voneinander ab, ist alles miteinander verfilzt, erscheint die Literatur vom Leben und das Leben von der Literatur her gesehen ein einziger Schachtelsatz' (138). Thus, the story was conceived in 1950 under the influence of that visit to Kassner, as was 'Der Sturz' to which its general approach to the theme of 'Authority' corresponds.

The main characters (as in 'Der Sturz') are known by letters of the alphabet. A, the 'Rebell' ('sein Name ist mir entfallen' (155)) grows up with his beautiful mother and her old servant in a bourgeois milieu. When the mother begins to go out each night, A follows her to a rich merchant's villa where she is clearly royally received. One day, A is going through his father's dusty books in the attic when he comes across a grammar book of a strange, unknown language – with verbs only! The present tense 'hasse' equals 'Der Haß', whereas the past tense could equal 'den vergangenen Haß' – or 'Liebe', the 'sogenannte reaktivierte erstarrte Mitvergangenheit' (157).

A then tries in vain to find out more about his father, who had simply left home one day to go abroad. He leaves university – his mother has disappeared in the meantime – travels the world until he reaches a country which reminds him of the drawings in the old book that he had found in the attic and which ('durch Zufall') speaks the strange language, 'die Sprache seines Vaters' (159). The land, he finds, is ruled by a tyrant and makes obeisance to no fewer than six gods: 'an die Einheit Gott des Vaters, Gott des Sohnes, und Gott des Heiligen Geistes' plus 'der Gott der heiligen Energie, der Gott der heiligen Materie und der Gott des heiligen Nichts' (162). The people are waiting for a Messiah to free them from their yoke, and of course A, the stranger, 'der Bote aus der Ferne', as the naturalists would have called him, is taken to be the One, since he 'understands' their language. But the tyrant, 'der Herrscher', who had arrived in the country 'auf einem Maulesel' twenty years previously and is also head of their church, orders the arrest of the stranger. A ends his days, bereft of his senses, in a mirror-filled room: 'Irgendwann krepiert er wie ein Tier . . . wird vergessen'

(173). (The 'mirror-filled room' will occupy our attention later (below, 205–7).)

One imagines that psychoanalysts could have a field-day with this story: the 'Herrscher', with strong theological connections as Dürrenmatt's father; A, the writer, himself 'seeking' a land of his own, as Dürrenmatt; the mother, 'lost' in her own interests, as Dürrenmatt's own mother, and so on. The style is nevertheless powerful and attractive; the story, as it stands now, is clearly a product of Dürrenmatt's maturer years, although the theme is of a piece with those of 'Stadt', 'Wärter' and the 'early prose' stories. That is just the point that Dürrenmatt, and I, would wish to make. In retrospect, Dürrenmatt believes that all that has happened to him, in 'Life' and in 'Literature' 'zusammenhängt', is connected. Speculation on whether he is near to believing that it is all part of some 'Grand Design' will be left until later.

Yet it cannot be denied that one lays down the *Stoffe* volumes with some sadness and regret, for in them there is the over-riding impression of a guilt-ridden writer who, despite all worldly and material successes, is not sure that he has been following the right path. These three *Erzählungen* all tell of 'the past', of a past which might have led to a different future – and despite his oft-expressed philosophical belief in the need to come to terms with *Zufall*, Chance, one does have the impression that Dürrenmatt feels that his own behaviour, particularly in relation to his parents, has conditioned his life and career, so that the 'chance' happenings were, in fact, directly *caused* by his own decisions taken as a young man.

The Stories of the 1980s

We noted earlier that Elisabeth Brock-Sulzer had had intimations of a novel titled *Justiz* as early as the 1960s (cf. C12, 290), and Dürrenmatt told me in 1988 that he had started on the theme after the *Alte Dame* in 1957. It was fairly obvious to most Dürrenmatt commentators that a revulsion against the theatre and the whole 'Theaterbetrieb' had set in in the 1970s. Although Charlotte Kerr in *Rollenspiele* claimed that Dürrenmatt was 'der meistgespielte Autor des deutschsprachigen Theaters 1984/5' (A4, 80), she admitted that only his 'Evergreens' [*sic*], namely *Alte Dame* and *Die Physiker*, were produced, not 'der heutige Dürrenmatt'. It is indeed a far cry from the 'boom years' of, say, 1962–3 when *Die Physiker* had 1,598 performances in fifty-nine theatres (*Theater heute* 10, 1970).

Dürrenmatt could claim, of course, as he did to Hugo Rank in 1981, that 'from writing and producing plays, I have now turned to prose. That is a continuation of the theatre by other means', but the number of bitter jibes about the theatre to be found in his recent writings and interviews (cf. below, 222) surely indicate that the 'turn' did not occur solely for artistic reasons.

My own opinion is that this 'turn' was, in many ways, advantageous to Dürrenmatt's reputation. It not only allowed another side of his Protean nature to be more fully illuminated, but it also displayed the basic earnestness of his thought and purpose, and an intellectual calibre which some critics did not believe that he possessed, and on the seeming absence of which he himself had often ruefully commented. In 'Der Rest ist Dank' (1960) he said, 'Ich bin nun einmal in der Welt der literarischen Erscheinung so ein Witz, und ich weiß, für viele ein schlechter und für manche ein bedenklicher' (WA26, 110), while in *Stoffe* (1981) he wrote, 'Mein Kredit, den ich einmal auf der Bühne besaß, ist durch Lächerlichkeiten verspielt worden' (A1, 38). However, this allowed him also to 'turn' into two fields and not just one, firstly to the philosophical and political essay, and secondly to what he has always done best in my opinion, straightforward story-telling, the presentation of these sometimes brilliant, but always thought-provoking 'Einfälle', on his own terms and not on those of a director or producer.

Justiz, Dürrenmatt tells us in one of his favourite 'Nachworte' (A3, 371) was to have appeared as volume 30 of the *Werkausgabe* in 1980, and was then to have been published as a *Fragment*, but in preparing this Dürrenmatt rewrote the whole novel under the influence of his new wife, Charlotte Kerr, whom he had married on 8 May 1984. The work is now dated '22.9.85'.

When reading *Justiz*, one is tempted to groan, as did Bodo von Überlohe-Zabernsee about his situation in *Die Ehe des Herrn Mississippi*, 'Wenn ich nur einen Bruchteil von dem verstehen würde, was hier vorgeht, wäre es mir gleich besser' (WA3, 67)!

The plot (or plots) divide(s) into three sections. The first begins with the suicidal thoughts in 1984 of one Felix Spät ('Happy but (always) late'?), an unsuccessful drunken lawyer born in 1930, and then flashes back to the murder in March 1955 of the sixty-year-old Vice-Chancellor of Zurich University, Professor Winter, in a Zurich restaurant (Dürrenmatt's own favourite Du Theâtre) by Kantonrat Dr h.c. Izaak Kohler, a Jewish millionaire. Kohler is arrested, confesses to the murder and is sentenced to twenty years. He gives no reason for the murder, which worried his friend, the police superintendent: 'Ein Mord ohne Grund war für ihn nicht ein

Verstoß gegen die Sitte, wohl aber gegen die Logik' (39). We are back in the world of Bärlach and Matthäi. From his prison two years later, where he has been a model prisoner, Kohler commissions firstly a sociologist, Professor Knulpe, to examine what effect his crime has had on Swiss society, and secondly young Felix Spät who is asked 'die Wirklichkeit auszuloten, die Wirkungen einer Tat exakt auszumessen' (86). How should he proceed? 'Sie sollen', says Kohler, 'meinen Fall unter der Annahme untersuchen, ich sei nicht der Mörder gewesen' – what *might be* against what *is*, possibility versus reality. This then is the nub of a story which later becomes so confused as at times to be a farrago, almost beggaring description.

The second and third sections are of some interest to Dürrenmatt researchers since there are memories and even references to former works, particularly *Das Versprechen* when the present narrator recalls having been given a lift back to Zurich after a lecture in Chur by a former police superintendent, Dr H. Dürrenmatt uses the identical text of the former story (cf. *Justiz*, 338–9; *Das Versprechen*, A221, 12). There is something too of *Der Richter und sein Henker* here since we find that Spät has been 'used' by Dr Kohler to cause the death of Dr Benno, an unscrupulous businessman, a rival of Kohler. It transpires that Benno, a crack shot, happened to be in the Zurich restaurant on that same night, and since the murder weapon was never found Kohler managed to have Spät pursue Benno to make him think that he was a wanted man. This eventually drives Benno to commit suicide, allowing Kohler to be freed. Kohler is thus *morally*, but not *legally* guilty of murder, and Benno's death was wished for by many in the community anyway. Dürrenmatt defines the 'moral' punishment as *Gerechtigkeit*, the latter, the legal punishment, as *Justiz*. The law may offer *Justiz*, but not always *Gerechtigkeit*.

Had the construction of the story been tighter, the flashbacks not quite so bewildering and the story-line clearer – I have also omitted all the clinching and coupling! – the novel might have been an interesting successor to the three '*Krimis*' of the 1950s. Many of the themes – guilt, vengeance, retribution, freedom to choose different possibilities à la Max Frisch – are of great interest but, alas, I must support the opinion of *Der Spiegel*, whose review of the novel on 24 December 1985 made Charlotte Kerr write in the diary-like *Rollenspiele*, 'Totalverriß von *Justiz*. Kein Weihnachtsengel schwebt durchs Zimmer' (49)![7]

* * *

Dürrenmatt's next work, *Der Auftrag* (a *Novelle*) (A5), was finished on 4 June 1986 and published in the same year. It bore a fashionably baroque sub-title, *Vom Beobachten des Beobachters der Beobachter*, reminding us a little of Peter Handke's *Die Innenwelt der Außenwelt der Innenwelt* (1969). Prefaced by a typically 'pessimistic' Kierkegaardian motto which ends 'Dieses Leben ist verkehrt und grauenhaft, nicht auszuhalten', *Der Auftrag* tells, in twenty-four 'sentences' – and the sentence here can be four pages long – a Moroccan adventure story. Dürrenmatt visited Egypt in November 1985, and the story was to have been a film, Charlotte Kerr's first non-documentary film. She writes in *Rollenspiele*, 'Dürrenmatt der Beobachtete, ich die Beobachtende, beobachtet vom Beobachteten, beide gefangen im Netz unserer unterschiedlichen Erfahrungen, Schuß und Kette verwoben zu einem neuen Muster' (A4, 94). Instead, Dürrenmatt has made what is really a *Novelle* out of the story and dedicated it to Charlotte, featuring a female maker of films who asks advice of the 'Logiker D., dessen Vorlesung auf der Universität von zwei, drei Studenten besucht wurde' (13), one of Dürrenmatt's typical 'academic' jibes. (As in 'Der Sturz', the main characters and places are identified only by initials.)

The story concerns the finding of the raped and murdered body of Tina von Lambert at the foot of the Al-Hakim ruin. Her husband, Otto von Lambert, a psychiatrist, had just written a book on terrorism which defended the 'Arab freedom–fighters', is now accused of his wife's murder and asks the film-maker F. to go to Egypt and make a film of the reconstructed murder. Tina's diary shows that she had been depressed and that she felt that she was being . . . watched. F.'s advice from D., taken obviously in Dürrenmatt's own house 'in den Bergen', equipped with Dürrenmatt's own favourite telescope with which he watches both stars and nature, is suitably gnomic: 'zu jedem Beobachteten gehöre ein Beobachtendes, das, werde es von jenem Beobachteten beobachtet, selber ein Beobachtetes werde' (19). (In *Versuche*, Dürrenmatt relates how he often turns his telescope on to the sightseers who are watching his house through their binoculars down on the promenade in Neuchâtel, and he follows this up with a disquisition on how we are *all* being watched – as we watch others – in this computer-ridden world.)

F. flies to Casablanca and is soon harried and 'observed' by the secret police of the state. The plot thickens as she encounters Western and Soviet suppliers of arms to those Middle East countries and realises that all this is being controlled by computerised cameras and watching satellites which have taken the place of

'God', who had been 'reines Beobachten', unsullied by his Creation (111). F. discovers that the murdered girl was not Tina von Lambert but a Danish girl, Jytte Sörensen, no doubt to underline the importance of the 'Scandinavian' motto to the story, and of the many subsequent quotations. F. then returns to Europe with her film which, despite all her adventures, is turned down by the television company. Thus she has achieved a Dürrenmattian 'Nichts', but on the last page, as D. reads in his newspaper that the secret service chief in M. (presumably 'Morocco') has been shot as a traitor and that they have denied 'that there are any foreign weapons etc. on our soil', he says to F., 'Donnerwetter, hast du aber Glück gehabt' (133).

There are James Bond-like desert scenes of murder, rape and explosions, with excurses on Middle East politics and on God's place in an empty, senseless world . . . and a labyrinth on page 93. It is a most interesting attempt at something new, at writing a novel in a series of twenty-four sentences, with no full stops but, in consequence, a great number of complicated clauses and subjunctive verbs. Dürrenmatt had wanted to write an epic, prose that could be *spoken*: 'Ich ersetzte den Vers durch den Satz, angeregt durch "Das Wohltemperierte Klavier" von Johann Sebastian Bach, doch erlebte ich ein Abenteuer besonderer Art; Nicht ich trieb die Sätze, wohin ich wollte, die Sätze trieben mich, wohin sie wollten', he writes on the dust-jacket of the book.[8]

The experiment certainly makes a much more satisfying book than *Justiz*. One is carried along by the sheer fecundity of ideas and the explosive language, although there is really no characterisation as such attempted. It is a novelist-philosopher's plaything, constructed for a new friend – and, for the first time, a woman is indubitably No. 1 in a 'philosophical thriller'.

Dürrenmatt's latest work, a novel *Durcheinandertal* (1989)(A17) is set deep in an imaginary Switzerland peopled by extraordinarily-named characters who live an equally extraordinary existence in the little village of Durcheinandertal (Neanderthal? Dürrenmatt's own Konolfingen?). The main character, Moses Melker, is the murderer of two wives – Emilie Lauber, who broke her neck climbing along an oak tree branch sawn off by Melker, and Ottilie Räuchlin, whom Melker pushed into the Nile on their honeymoon – and of a local waitress whom he had raped, strangled and then thrown into the village stream. Moses now lives with his third wife, Ottilie's sister, the gourmande, chocolate-eating Cäcilie whom he eventually murders by stuffing her with truffles (137).

The novel turns on the Knipperdollinckian–Biblical themes: 'It is easier for a camel to go through the eye of a needle, than for a rich man to enter into the kingdom of Heaven' (Matthew xix, 24) and 'Blessed are the poor in spirit, for theirs is the kingdom of heaven' (Matthew v, 3), since Moses will give up his ill-gotten gains – all his wives are millionaires – to found a 'Haus der Armut', a Swiss Society for Morality, for the reformed multi-millionaires of this earth.

Many Dürrenmattian themes are echoed here: the impotence of God ('den Großen Alten'); the impotence of Switzerland and its army; the chain of causal coincidences; the erotic (a milkmaid on permanent heat); a savage dog (cf. 218 below), and, at the end, a bewildering array of exotic New York gangsters operated on by one 'Doc' in *Mitmacher*-style.

The publisher's blurb speaks of the book as a new 'politisch-theologisch brisante(n) Roman', but this intoxicating gallimaufry made me wonder if this were not yet another 'Ulk' played on the public by the 'Alten vom Berg'. In one phrase perhaps does a meaning shimmer through: 'Der Mensch braucht den Menschen und keinen Gott, weil nur der Mensch den Menschen begreift' (173), an *Urmotif* with which we are now familiar, and which has dominated Dürrenmatt's recent thinking.

−6−

The Stage-Plays

The Plays from 1947 to 1956

My previous book, *The theatre of Friedrich Dürrenmatt*, treated Dürrenmatt's stage works in great detail, and the reader will find there a vast number of source references. The thesis was developed that, contrary to the early critical opinions expressed from, say, 1947–60, Dürrenmatt was neither a failed philosopher nor a Christian apologist, nor even a theoretician expounding *ad nauseam* a critical doctrine on tragedy and comedy, but was rather a practical, down-to-earth 'Theatermann' whose very first concern as a writer had been to make enough money to keep his wife and three children, hence the *Detektivromane*. But having made the acquaintance of the stage, Dürrenmatt was fascinated by the opportunity, 'möglichst gutes Theater zu machen' as he puts it, and to see his fecund 'Einfälle' become full-blown productions peopled by flesh-and-blood characters. That he could, at the same time, make these characters say something profound or witty or perverse, something that might shock or disturb an audience, appealed on the one hand to his always well-developed sense of the ridiculous, and on the other to his intellectuality, for as he wrote in '*Theaterprobleme*', 'lauter Dummköpfe darzustellen, finde ich nicht interessant' (WA24, 32).

   In considering anew Dürrenmatt's work for the theatre, I do not wish to treat these plays in the same detail as before, but rather to examine some of the major issues in the light of the conclusions reached on other aspects of his *oeuvre*. As I look back over forty years of his writings, I find, in retrospect, that I share his own verdict on his career as a playwright. That verdict has been given, in fact, in many places before, in many of the interviews which have found their way into print – not always with Dürrenmatt's blessing indeed. Hans Bänziger's latest book (1987) lists no fewer than fifty 'Interviews' or 'Diskussionen' with or about Dürrenmatt, and I could add another twenty or so which he omits (C8, 155–7). The titles alone give some idea of the contents: 'Ich bin aus der Mode gekommen' (Ebeling), 'Die größte Gefahr, das ist der Ruhm'

(Lehmann, 1976), 'Das Schweizer Theater ist mir völlig wurscht' (Sonderer, 1979) and 'Das Theater leidet unter Lebensangst' (Bachmann) (cf. Bibliography 'F') – while the scandals about his *Playboy* interview in which he attacked his 'colleagues' (Frisch, Grass, *et al.*) still rumble on and have been neither forgotten nor forgiven (cf. *Der Spiegel* on 5 January 1981, Dürrenmatt's sixtieth birthday).

Dürrenmatt's verdict on his career as a playwright has been mentioned in various places above. It might just be useful here, however, to recall two remarks. 'Das war denn auch mein Schicksal', he said after his disappointment with the première of *Ein Engel kommt nach Babylon*. 'Durch Zufall kam mein Ruhm zustande, durch Zufall der Abbau des Ruhms. Als Dramatiker bin ich ein unvermeidliches Mißverständnis' (A2, 59–60). And to Charlotte Kerr in *Rollenspiele*, 'Theater ist passé, ich bedaure, je ein Theaterstück geschrieben zu haben' (A4, 88): the theatre of today, he feels, has become the theatre of the director rather than of the writer or the actor. (Opera singers make the same complaint; one distinguished singer told me how he rebelled when asked to sing almost the entire role lying on his back.)[1]

It would be idle to pretend that not a little of this criticism of the modern theatre had to do with the comparative failure of most of his stage-plays to register favourably with the audiences or the critics since, say, *Der Meteor* of 1966. The latter group he once called a 'Pack' and he emphasised to Charlotte Kerr that 'Was ich fatal finde, ist die Verbindung von Journalismus und Literatur', what he has (rightly) called 'Kulturjournalismus' (A4, 52). Some academics, too, have sharpened their knives for him of late. Jan Knopf, whose 'knife' is whetted, of course, in the Soviet bloc socialist doctrines, has always critically compared Dürrenmatt's 'late-bourgeois' pessimism with Brecht's proclamation of 'Leben': 'Der Tod ist das Leben der Menschen in Dürrenmatts Welt', he declares roundly in his 1987 book (C32, 9). J.H. Reid however, gives a much more favourable picture of Dürrenmatt's increasing popularity in just those Eastern states: 'Since the late 1960s', Reid writes, 'his star has set in the west only to rise in the east' – although his discussion suggests that Dürrenmatt's work is more appreciated by the critics than by the public (D31).

My aim in this chapter is to 're-view' Dürrenmatt's stage works, to make a critical reassessment of their importance for and in his *oeuvre*, and to suggest which, if any, of them might eventually become 'classics' of modern European literature – not that that would be a 'consummation devoutly to be wished' by Dürrenmatt. When he received Berne's *Literaturpreis* on 19 June 1979, he reminded his audience that some of their 'Literaturpäpste' had already placed him in that category 'bei jenen also, um die man sich ohnehin nicht mehr zu kümmern braucht' (below, 200). He might also have quoted Max Frisch's 1964 comment on Bertolt Brecht's works as now having the 'durchhaltende Wirkungslosigkeit eines Klassikers'. I mean to take the remark in the rather more positive sense of which of Dürrenmatt's works, by common consent, critical and public, will be regularly performed on European stages in the future. (The texts to which I refer are in the *Werkausgabe* unless otherwise specified. Although we are assured by the editor, Thomas Bodmer, that most of the texts are the 'Endfassung 1980', there are, in fact, very few major changes from the last printed book editions.)

Dürrenmatt's first play, *Es steht geschrieben*, had its première in the Zurich Schauspielhaus on 19 April 1947; his last, to date, *Achterloo IV*, in 1988 in Schwetzingen in the Federal Republic. Between these two dates lie productions of thirteen entirely original plays, seven 'reversions' or reworkings of plays either by himself or by others, and various productions in the Dürrenmattian style, a not unworthy total for forty years of involvement with the theatre. In that period, he has been fêted and vilified: fêted in 1969 as a writer who had done enough for him to be listed 'unter die Großen der deutschsprachigen und der Weltliteratur' (Armin Arnold, C2, 91–2); vilified for his first *Achterloo* in 1983, 'das angetreten war, noch einmal die Zuschauer zu narren, schlug, so scheint es, auf Dürrenmatt zurück und wurde sein Waterloo' (Jan Knopf, C32, 183). As critical and public interest in Dürrenmatt and his works has waned in Western Europe in the 1980s, so a vast new 'Dürrenmatt-industry' has grown up in North America, supported by the writings of *émigrés*, Swiss and German, now teaching at North American universities and publishing mainly, though not exclusively, in the German language. But apart from *Der Besuch der alten Dame* and *Die Physiker*, these 'Evergreens', his works are no longer being produced.

In retrospect, it looks as if Dürrenmatt's first two plays, *Es steht geschrieben* and *Der Blinde*, the first written between July 1945 and March 1946 (now in WA1, 9–148), and the second written in the winter of 1947–8 (and in WA1, 149–243) were in the nature of 'false starts'. In the 'Anmerkung II' (248–50) which the author wrote for the 1980 volumes, we can see that *Es steht geschrieben* is indeed a very localised drama. The plot ostensibly concerns the Anabaptist rising in Münster in Germany. The movement began in Zurich in 1525, and in 1534 took over power in Münster ('The New

Jerusalem'), whose Catholic bishop then took sixteen months to break down its resistance. Johann Bockelson, a tailor's apprentice from Leyden, and the mayor of Münster, Bernhard Knipperdollinck, are the main characters: Bockelson, a 'Machtfigur', dictatorial and obscene; Knipperdollinck, a weak man who tries to prove the Biblical word, 'Es ist leichter, daß ein Kamel durch ein Nadelöhr gehe denn daß ein Reicher ins Reich Gottes komme' (Matthew xix, 24), by giving away all his worldly goods (WA1, 30). And what he does not give away, for example his wife, Bockelson steals! The third main character is Jan Matthisson, the Anabaptist leader, who, a passionate defender of his beliefs, sallies out against the enemy with sword raised like a cross, to be killed and decapitated: 'Euch geschehe nach eurem Glauben,' he cries in death (73).

It is not difficult to realise that the 'Welt in ihrem Untergang' which Dürrenmatt described in 'Anmerkung I' (248) is the world of the Third Reich going down in flames in 1945 when the play was being written and that the 'landfremde[n] Schneidergeselle[n] von anrüchiger Vergangenheit' ('Anmerkung II', 249), who becomes King of Zion, has a good deal in common with the failed Austrian painter who became dictator and Führer of Germany in 1933. We could indeed draw, albeit 'vorsichtig', 'die mehr zufälligen Parallelen' which the author invites us to draw in the 'Vorwort' (11). Yet here, and in *Der Blinde*, we have the first appearance of one of those *Urmotive* which we have been tracing: Jan Matthisson, a grotesque Don Quixote-like figure, made up to resemble the medieval Swiss philosopher Niklaus von der Flüe, incorporates that 'beaten-yet-triumphant' figure, of Christian provenance ultimately, who was to be honed into the Dürrenmatt concept of the 'mutigen Menschen', the figure who preserves some scrap of human worth and decency in a senseless, absurd and cruel age. Matthisson has 'das Schwert der Gerechtigkeit in den Händen und Worte der Weisheit auf den Lippen' (57), and recognises that the author who created him is 'ein im weitesten Sinne entwurzelter Protestant, behaftet mit der Beule des Zweifels', suspicious of the Faith that he admires but has lost (58). Matthisson *is* a man of faith who is martyred for his belief, and he dies absurdly defending it, for as the worldly, Catholic Bischof von Waldeck says, looking down at the head of the (true) man of faith, 'der wahre Sieg kommt nur dem Besiegten zu' (80).

Bernhard Knipperdollinck, on the other hand, is a naïve fool who is broken on the wheel, not for his faith, but for his stupidity. Certainly, he seems to expect 'Grace' from God for his self-made despair – 'Die Tiefe meiner Verzweiflung ist nur ein Gleichnis Deiner Gerechtigkeit' (148) – but in fact what he receives is punishment for his witlessness. He is an 'Opfer', exposed and exploited by the 'man of power', 'dem Mächtigen', Johann Bockelson, whose transgressions, political, sexual and religious, are punished also by *his* death on the wheel.

Commentators on these plays have always sought Christian interpretations; it is worthwhile to recall Dürrenmatt's continual protestations that, in these plays, he wanted to set 'the word' against 'the image', to free himself from the overwhelming inner wish (which he *still* has!) to prefer painting to writing. He was seeking a 'vision' – but in words rather than in paint. 'Das Theater', he said in 1981 when 'interviewing himself', 'ist sein [Dürrenmatt's] Ausweg ins Freie' (in WA25, 143). As such, these two first plays are experiments in word–sketches and not Christian exegeses; in consequence, their major interest for scholars should be not the 'Sinn', but the initial appearance of *Urmotive*. Ruth Blum, in 1959, was perceptive enough to remark that Dürrenmatt was no 'Christian author' but rather a 'modern moralist' (E9, 536); Gerhard Marahrens, twenty-four years later, echoed her article in his by stating that 'God is not the central issue any more . . . man himself is responsible for the state of the world' (in B17, 158–9).

* * *

Der Blinde (WA1, 149–243) had its première in the Stadttheater in Basle on 10 January 1948, directed by Ernst Ginsberg. It is an extremely boring work rightly removed from the stage after only nine performances – just as *Es steht geschrieben* was removed by Dürrenmatt himself in 1948 – but it, too, adds to our knowledge of the author's state of mind at this time.

A blind Duke believes that his world is intact, good and peaceful, but all around him rages the Thirty Years War, bringing senseless destruction, looting, pillaging and rape. One of Wallenstein's generals, an Italian named Negro da Ponte, comes to the Duke's castle with a following of 'Mörder, Zauberer, Falschmünzer und Huren' (170), and is appointed 'Statthalter' by the Duke. Deceived as he is, the Duke nevertheless retains his human dignity and faith and sends the tempter on his way, after the usual Dürrenmattian series of grotesqueries and obscenities.

Ostensibly again a Christian-ised drama, it is actually a representation of Dürrenmatt's agonising struggle against an uncomprehending father. 'Ihr seid der Grund meiner Traurigkeit,' (211) says the prince Palamedes to his father, the blind Duke. Dürrenmatt's father too was 'blind' to his son's wishes – and despair – while the bitter, almost nihilistic gloom of the woman, Octavia, reflects the existential guilt of a young Swiss in the cold aftermath of the Second World War. Looked at from the perspective of 1980, Dürrenmatt himself saw *Der Blinde* as the story of a man who (stupidly, like Knipperdollinck in *Es steht geschrieben*) let himself 'believe' and be exploited. But in 1949, he wrote in 1980, no such thoughts were in his mind; this was no 'allegory', but simply an attempt 'das Wort gegen das Bild zu setzen' ('Anmerkung', 256), an attempt to put a good play on the stage, again 'möglichst gutes Theater zu machen'.

The Duke becomes 'ein mutiger Mensch', Dürrenmatt claimed later in 'Theaterprobleme', presumably because he did not 'despair' when he 'saw' 'das Sinnlose, das Hoffnungslose', of this world ('Theaterprobleme', WA24, 63). But his last words echo those of Knipperdollinck on the wheel, 'So liegen wir zerschmettert im Angesicht Gottes, und so leben wir in seiner Wahrheit' (242), and although his arch-enemy and exploiter, the 'tempter' Negro da Ponte, leaves him with the admission that he has failed to 'conquer' the Duke's spirit and that he would therefore become 'ein Engel des Todes' (242), Dürrenmatt made clear in 1980 that the Duke was hardly the 'mutige Mensch', the *positive* figure that he cited in 'Theaterprobleme', but rather one who in his 'blind' belief had actually become inhuman, and therefore foolish and exploited. Yet Dürrenmatt reminded us, again in 1980, that he was writing a stage-play in 1946, not an allegory, and that 'poetic' words like 'God' and 'Nichts' were just that – words – and the more paradoxical he could make them appear, the better. We recall that he wrote *Der Doppelgänger*, 'Die Falle' and 'Pilatus' at this time (1946), all illustrating his Kierkegaardian love of the paradox – perhaps just another, more elevated, way of saying that he enjoyed creating problems for just the type of literary commentator under whom he had 'suffered' at university: 'Auch schleichen sich Mißverständnisse ein', he wrote of his early dramas, 'indem man verzweifelt im Hühnerstall meiner Dramen nach dem Ei der Erklärung sucht, das zu legen ich beharrlich mich weigere' (in 'Theaterprobleme', 48). In the 'Anmerkung' to *Der Doppelgänger* he elaborated, 'Wer die Gerechtigkeit des Himmels unbegreiflich setzt, muß auch dessen Gnade unbegreiflich setzen; wer den christlichen Glauben als paradox hinstellt, muß es mit jedem Glauben tun' (WA1, 326), and he indicated that this remark, and the story itself, should be regarded as part of the 'Motivknäuel' which led to *Der Blinde*.[2]

* * *

These two plays are now followed in the *Werkausgabe* by the 1951 version, *Untergang und neues Leben* (259–94), of his very first play, written in 1943 in Valais. The play was first called *Der Knopf* and then just *Komödie*, and remained unpublished until 1980. Like *Es steht geschrieben*, this too was a *Weltuntergangskomödie*. A stranger comes across an armless, legless, naked soldier hanging from a lantern. He climbs up him to pluck 'the moon from the sky', but the moon is dead. Then a blind whore, Nore (again), appears and begs to be killed, but 'Was soll ich denn Henker sein?' says the stranger who shoots her and goes on his way (268). Next, a drunk, monocled general is watching over a 'Weltuntergangsmaschine' with its deadly 'Knopf' or button. Later the general is executed – as a 'hero', he says – in an electric chair by a 'Henker', who also fries eggs on the chair! Finally, 'Der Fremde' is swept away in the waters singing a Brecht-like chanson. It is a wild, chaotic, disjointed work, useful for our retrospective purposes, however, in underlining those themes which we now recognise from the stories of the period already treated and which were to reappear in various forms in the future: the *Henker* and the *Heldentod*; the thought of world destruction; women as (mere) prostitutes and, overall, the brooding uncertainties of a young 18-year-old doubter fighting against the Christian optimism of a father, and of a mother of whom the son later wrote, 'Sie lebte in einer Welt des sieghaften Glaubens' (A2, 17). What would *they* have thought of Scene 7 where a group of men and women sing:

> Wir Menschen sind arme Kinder,
> Erdenken uns Gott und ewiges Leben,
> Dann recken wir sterbend die Fäuste gen Himmel,
> Und fluchen, daß er keine Gnade ergeben (278).

* * *

Kurt Marti's little book *Die Schweiz und ihre Schriftsteller – die Schriftsteller und ihre Schweiz* (1966) (C34) is an invaluable source of material for the so-called *Verteidigungs-Neurose*, a term conceived by Arnold Künkli, from which so many Swiss seemed to suffer in those early post-war years when, to some, communism offered a greater threat to Switzerland than fascism had ever done. Those who stood in any way to the Left of centre in the country could be – and were – accused of 'Landesverrat'. Some were executed after trial, and when the 'red terror' passed away, the concept of 'geistiger Landesverrat' remained, to be revived incidentally, as the 'Verteidigungs-Neurose' of the 1940s and 1950s gave way to the fear of 'Überfremdung' of the 1960s when, as Max Frisch wrote, 'Wir riefen nach Arbeitskräften und es kamen Menschen.'

Thus, when Dürrenmatt wrote in the 'Programmheft' for the première of his *Romulus der Große* on 25 April 1949, in the Stadttheater in Basle, 'Ich rechtfertige einen Landesverräter' (WA2, 121), he could have anticipated some opposition from his countrymen and -women. The play, which Dürrenmatt conceived from a *Novelle* by Strindberg on the death of Attila the Hun, is an attack on useless heroism, on outdated and anachronistic values, many of which, according to the author, are indeed more relevant to Romulus's age (the fifth century AD) than our own. The critics who attacked the play because of such anachronisms clearly failed to understand this point. But Dürrenmatt was also inspired by the, to him, absurd idea that the Germans who tried to assassinate Hitler on 20 July 1944 were *also* 'Landesverräter' (cf. Chapter 5, note 6, below, 223).

* * *

Romulus Augustulus ('Little Augustus') ironically called Romulus *der Große* by Dürrenmatt, is over fifty, married, with a daughter, Rea, and has ruled the country for twenty years, instead of the historical one year. Sick of imperial power and its consequent blood-letting, Romulus resolves to let the Roman Empire collapse into the hands of the invading Germanii and thus avoid continuing bloodshed. It was, of course, provocative to make the invaders 'Germanii' in 1949 – memories were still very fresh – but even more provocative to imply that, *therefore*, 'Rome equalled Switzerland', and that there was very little point in the neutral Swiss engaging in 'sabre-rattling'. Romulus's passion for hen-breeding was, like Voltaire's gardening, ultimately more 'rational'. That was the point that Dürrenmatt had wanted to make, and of course it could be applied to states which were not neutral: 'Es ist nicht ein Stück gegen den Staat, aber vielleicht eins gegen den Großstaat', he wrote in the 'Anmerkung' (121). But its application was most clearly to Switzerland, the country which had actually considered blowing up the Gotthard and Simplon passes if Hitler had threatened to invade!

Act IV of this 'ungeschichtliche[n] historische[n] Komödie' caused most provocation – and in Germany above all, when the play was produced in Stuttgart by the Basler Theater company. The work was obviously conceived with memories of the Third Reich in mind: the 'troops' of Odoaker, King of the Germanii, who are marching to take over Rome, are described in terms familiar to those who had read so many war reports, and when Odoaker said (in the first version), 'Ich kehre mit meinen hunderttausend Solda-ten im Trauermarsch nach Germanien zurück und klettere mit meinem ganzen Volk wieder auf die Bäume' disapproval was made very plain indeed.[3] Odoaker turns out moreover to be not the barbaric German expected, but a fellow hen-fancier who is dread-ing the rule of his more conventionally 'Germanic' nephew, Theoderich: 'Ein zweites Rom wird entstehen,' Odoaker says, 'ein germanisches Weltreich, ebenso vergänglich wie das römische, ebenso blutig' (WA2, 109).

The original Act IV had Romulus accept a pension and go meekly into retirement, a man who accepts the trick that reality/chance had played on him, and who then 'die Welt besteht'. He is humane and civilised, witty and humorous. The revised 1957 version has a darker, more paradoxical colouring: Romulus will sacrifice himself for Rome's good and so will ask to be killed by the 'brutal' Germanii, but instead he is treated like a helpless 'fool' whose expectations are nullified by the arrival of the friendly Odoaker, and with the bust of the King Romulus who founded Rome under his arm he goes into shameful and absurd retirement. So Romulus is now 'ein mutiger Mensch' and, as Hans Wagener concludes, 'so besehen erweist sich Dürrenmatts *Romulus* nicht nur als ein Beispiel für Zeitkritik in Form einer pseudohistorischen Komödie, sondern als Ausdruck seines auf den einzelnen bezogenen Humanismus und Moralismus' (E46, 206). This is indeed Otto Rommel's 'Bitterkeit der Ohnmacht' (above, 40): 'Es ist alles absurd geworden, was ich getan habe,' says Romulus (109). This tragicomic absurdity is lacking in the first version, and the influence of Dürrenmatt's theoretical writings from 1954 on the second can be clearly seen. 'Spielen wir noch einmal, zum letzten Mal, Komödie,' Romulus says to Odoaker, and we feel that we are reading a *locus classicus* for the author's pronouncement in 'Theater-probleme': 'Wir können das Tragische aus der Komödie heraus erzielen' (cf. WA24, 63). From now, almost all his plays will bear the sub-title 'Komödie' where, in A. Rogge's useful definition, 'der Nachdruck auf der verlachten Schwäche liegt' (C42, 261).

That this 'verlachte Schwäche' referred to Switzerland might be one of the reasons why *Romulus* was not a great initial success, but it was an attitude to his native country which Dürrenmatt was to repeat in his play *Herkules und der Stall des Augias* (1963) and which he had already epitomised in an unpublished poem, 'Schweizer-psalm I' of 1950:

> Deine Sattheit mit Füßen stampfend, höhne ich
> Dich, wo Du schlecht bist. Deine Ahnen
> lassen mich kalt, ich gähne, wenn ich von ihnen
> höre (now printed in WA28, 174–5).

Yet Dürrenmatt himself, in conversation with Heinz Ludwig Arnold, had deplored the fact that he was often taken to be just a cynic. Why will people not take the problems that I treat *seriously*, he asked (F1, 79). In *Romulus*, for example, the issue was clearly 'Haben wir überhaupt noch ein Recht, uns zu wehren und zu verteidigen mit unserer Geschichte?' 'Eine sehr unbequeme Frage' indeed for the Swiss, but one that had to be faced. The theme, I believe, made a very fine and amusing play which should be revived.

* * *

In the introduction to the 'fragment' 'Kaiser und Eunuch' which follows *Romulus* (in WA2, 143–65), Dürrenmatt discusses the difference between Schiller's and his own approach to historical drama. 'Schiller', he writes, 'behandelte die Geschichte als Vorlage, über die er das Netz seiner Dramaturgie warf, ich behandle sie als Stoff, aus dem sich meine Dramaturgie kristallisiert' (148). That is, he uses History as he uses other people's ideas and plots, as material for development. History for Dürrenmatt, then, coincides very much with Karl Popper's view: 'the history of power politics is nothing but the history of international crime and mass murder' (B19, 453) – which is why Dürrenmatt has Romulus say to his wife Julia in Act III, 'Ich bin Roms Richter' (52).

* * *

'Je prends mon bien où je le trouve,' said Molière. Dürrenmatt would agree, and it was this harmless trait which brought Dürrenmatt into the first of his celebrated court cases after the production of his next play, *Die Ehe des Herrn Mississippi – Eine Komödie*, which was written in 1950 but which had to wait for its première until 26 March 1952, in the Münchner Kammerspiele (now in WA3, 9–114). Among other reasons for the delay was the

claim of Tilly Wedekind, Frank Wedekind's widow, that Dürrenmatt
had taken the theme of his play from her husband's work *Schloß
Wetterstein*. Dürrenmatt argued (in *Die Tat* of 9 August 1952) that,
if he had borrowed from anywhere, then it was from Wedekind's
Marquis von Keith from which, he said, he had taken the idea of a
'Dialektik *mit* Personen' and, in any case, what he had really
borrowed from Wedekind was something that no one had yet even
realised about the author, namely that he wrote *Komödien*: 'sie
nehmen ihn ernst, falsch ernst' (cf. 'Bekenntnisse eines Plagiators',
WA3, 216–17). In addition, he has always claimed that this play
was developed out of the scene between Romulus and his wife in
Act III of *Romulus der Große* (cf. WA25, 145).

That, and other incidents, such as Ernst Ginsberg's belief that *he*
was insulted in the play too, clearly made Dürrenmatt dissatisfied
with the work since, as with *Romulus*, there are five distinct stage
versions, and a film scenario. The first version was published in
1952, the second in 1957, the third in 1964, the fourth in 1970 and
the fifth in 1980 (in WA3), where it is called 'eine Art Synthese'
('Anmerkung III', 210). There too Dürrenmatt stresses again – as
he always does – that these 'changes' do not reflect new philosophical or theoretical standpoints, as so many academic studies suggest,
but are simply 'das Resultat einer praktischen Regiearbeit'. (The
film version was directed by Kurt Hoffmann in 1960 and was first
shown in 1961. The libretto is now in WA3, 115–205).

The plot reflects political, and Dürrenmatt's personal, circumstances of 1950–2. Florestan Mississippi is a fanatical worshipper of
'justice', a state prosecutor who already has 350 death sentences to
his 'credit'. Above all, adultery is his No. 1 *bête noire*, which is why
he has poisoned his first unfaithful wife. We meet in succession,
then, three men who, in different ways, want to 'change the
world': Graf Bodo von Übelohe-Zabernsee, as ridiculous as his
name, who will invoke the Christian God's help; Frédéric René
Saint-Claude whose 'god' is Karl Marx; and Florestan Mississippi
whose guide is the Old Testament law of Moses.[4] And directing
their fools' dance is Anastasia who, having accepted poison from
her lover Bodo to kill her husband, is then visited by the state
prosecutor Mississippi to be informed that he had killed *his* wife
because she had slept with Anastasia's husband, and that rather than
arrest Anastasia he had decided to marry her! 'Was *Sie* aus einem
grauenvollen Trieb getan haben, tat *ich* aus sittlicher Einsicht. Sie
haben Ihren Mann hingeschlachtet und ich mein Weib hingerich-
tet,' Mississippi asserts (32). 'Die absolute Gerechtigkeit' demands
that he be 'condemned' to marry Anastasia. This long scene, 'die

Geschichte eines Zimmers' Dürrenmatt calls it in the 'Anmerkung' (209), brilliantly conducted over the drinking of coffee, full of ambiguities and *double-entendres*, must rank as one of Dürrenmatt's cleverest stage set-pieces (17–38).

The typically wild Dürrenmattian plot (and sub-plots) ends with Bodo trying to change the world through Christian charity and loving Anastasia for herself; Saint-Claude trying to change the world through revolution and using Anastasia as a 'secret weapon'; and Mississippi trying to change the world by iron justice, and making Anastasia pay for her sins. The wisest words in the play are uttered paradoxically by the double-dealing, wily politician Diego, who clearly echoes the author when he assures Mississippi, 'Alles in der Welt kann geändert werden, mein lieber Florestan, nur der Mensch nicht' (44). The end is suitably ridiculous: Saint-Claude is shot by his fellow ideologists, and Anastasia and Mississippi poison each other, with coffee! Only the Don Quixote-like, broken, dejected Bodo is left, 'oftmals zusammengehauen, oftmals verlacht/Und dennoch dir trotzend', a 'mutiger Mensch', an 'Einzelner', a 'Besiegter' and not a 'Sieger', whose attempts to retain his human dignity fail with some honour (114). He is Dürrenmatt's real spokesman and, through him, the point of the play – that all fanatical ideologies pursued 'mit einer unerschöpflichen Gier nach Vollkommenheit' (57) *must* fail – is peculiarly, and ludicrously, stated.

As with *Der Blinde*, the early commentators were mainly concerned with Christian interpretations. Later, Gottfried Benn called it an 'existential tragedy' (E7); the Knapps, in 1977, stressed Dürrenmatt's 'zunehmende Konzentration auf den Einzelnen' (E25, 26); while Heinrich Goertz's 1987 book quoted Dürrenmatt's own remarks in the 1967 Zurich 'Programmheft' as a summing-up: this 'Komödienschreibende Protestant' 'bringt seine Helden nicht mit-leidend um, wie die Tragiker, er saß nicht tränenüberströmt an seinem Schreibtisch und schluchzte: Anastasia ist tot! Er mordete sie hohnlachend' (in WA3, 218; C18, 52).[5] In other words, as with most of Dürrenmatt's works, this is a 'joke for, and with the times', an 'Ulk' which, in retrospect, mirrored the prevailing obsession with ideologies and faiths, but also Dürrenmatt's own belief that the 'Age of Tragedy' was 'dead' (to speak with George Steiner) and that 'uns nur noch die Komödie [beikomme]', as he wrote in 'Theaterprobleme' (WA24, 62).

Mississippi is certainly not a great play: the plot is too confused and confusing, although the main thrust is, as we have attempted to indicate, quite clear. That Dürrenmatt himself was aware of this confusion is proved by Bodo's agonising cry, 'Wenn ich nur einen Bruchteil von dem verstehen würde, was hier vorgeht, wäre es mir gleich besser' (67), and this may have caused too the despair that he felt after the première, despite the fact that it was Hans Schweikart's production of *Mississippi* which was generally recognised to have been Dürrenmatt's 'Durchbruch' into European theatrical circles.

* * *

In 1948 Dürrenmatt had begun a drama on one of his favourite themes, the building of the Tower of Babel. This was given to his wife Lotti to burn, but the first act became his next *Komödie*, albeit 'eine fragmentarische Komödie', which was produced as *Ein Engel kommt nach Babylon* (now in WA4, 9–123), again by Schweikart, and again in the Münchner Kammerspiele, on 22 December 1953. If *Mississippi* was his 'breakthrough', then it was *Engel* that decided him, he said later, never again to write for the theatre! He lost, he said, 'meine Naivität dem Theater gegenüber . . . wohl endgültig' (A2, 59). There was a second version in 1957, the *Werkausgabe* version in 1980 which hardly differs from No. 2 and, on 5 June 1977, the première of an opera version by Rudolf Kelterborn in the Zurich opera house. There is also a radio fragment (*Der Uhrenmacher*, now in WA4, 137–140) which Dürrenmatt entitled the 'Vor-Kurrubi-Stoff', also on the theme of 'Gnade'. This was to be the first part of a trilogy; the next part was to be called *Der Mitmacher* – all are against the building of the tower, 'und dennoch kommt er zustande'. (Dürrenmatt's play *Der Mitmacher* had its première on 8 March 1973, cf. below, 144ff.) Why, then, had he been so dissatisfied after the première in 1953? Was it the play, or the production, or . . .?

In an 'ancient-and-modern' Babylon, Akki is the only beggar who has not been 'unionised' by King Nebuchadnezzar. To convince Akki that his individualistic but unrewarded way of life is senseless, the King tells his court that he can 'out-beggar' Akki, 'indem ich, da ich selbst als Bettler vor ihm erscheine, ihm so seine eigene Not vor Augen führe' (20). Thus, disguised as a beggar, he enters into a contest which Akki wins hands down and thereby proves to the King that beggars are not only free and individuals, but 'geheime Lehrer . . . Erzieher der Völker' (39)!

God has promised a cherubim (Kurrubi by name too) the poorest person in Babylon as a prize and, when she arrives on earth accompanied by her 'Engel', she falls in love by chance with the first 'poorest' person she meets – who is now the disguised King, since he has lost the contest. But it is the beggar and not the masked King that she loves and, when the King unmasks and is revealed, she recoils from him and is sentenced to death. When the 'Henker' appears to carry out the sentence – surprise! – it is the disguised Akki, who makes off with the innocent Kurrubi into 'ein neues Land . . . voll neuer Verfolgung, voll neuer Verheißung und voll von neuen Gesängen' (123), leaving the King cursing at his foiled plans and vowing to gather all mankind into a tower which will reach up into the heart of his enemy God, who has abandoned him 'ohne Gnade', to prove which is the more just, 'Meine Gerechtigkeit oder die Ungerechtigkeit Gottes' (122).

The theme is not unlike that of Brecht's *Der gute Mensch von Sezuan* in that, there too, an angel leaves the earth to its own, miserable fate. But Brecht preaches that only a change in social circumstances can 'change this world'; Dürrenmatt's more pessimistic (realistic?) conclusion is that human stupidity will always be with us, and that Akki's individualistic action to save *something* of humanity from the King's all-embracing ideology is as much as one could expect: 'Stelle dich dumm, nur so wirst du alt,' he says (85). 'He who fights and runs away' might well live to fight another day. Also important here, however, is Akki's attack on the uselessness of so much of modern culture and 'civilisation'. Dürrenmatt harks back again to his wasted university years and makes mock of the world of 'Dichter und Denker' by parodying many famous literary quotations: for example, Hölderlin's celebrated 'Was bleibt, stiften die Dichter' becomes Akki's satirical 'Was bleibt, stifte ich den Dichtern', that is, he leaves his few belongings to a rather miserable out-of-work group. Poetry itself is parodied too, since Akki revives an old Arabian prose-verse form, the *maquama*, to deliver his homilies on human behaviour: 'Heldentaten sind sinnlos, sie verraten die Ohnmacht des Schwachen, und seine Verzweiflung bringt die Macht nur zum Lachen' (the 4th *maquama*, 85).

The use above of the word 'satirical' recalls one of the reasons for the author's dissatisfaction with the play's première which he describes so vividly in *Stoffe* (A2, 58–9). Not only was he suffering himself from a 'Stirnhöhlenentzündung', an inflammation of the frontal sinus, but he discovered that Hans Schweikart, the director, wanted to turn the play into a satire on the lines of Wedekind or Sternheim – Schweikart believed that Dürrenmatt was their logical successor. '[W]as heute noch viele glauben', wrote Dürrenmatt, 'vor allem jene, denen Schreiben bloß eine stilistische, sprachliche Angelegenheit ist und nicht ein subjektiver Ausdruck des Denkens' (op. cit., 58). This is a view that he has held for many years, but one with which some critics take issue, and particularly with regard to *Engel* which, perhaps because of its large number of epigrammatic remarks, does appear at times to be a clever satire on modern times: for example, 'Könige denken im Zustand der Erniedrigung stets sozial' (18); 'Verzweiflung macht sich am besten bezahlt' (52); 'Je vollkommener ein Staat ist, desto dümmere Beamte braucht er' (56); 'Beginnt einer zu dichten, schon wird er des Plagiats bezichtigt' (61) – and many, many more.

Thus, whatever the reason, Dürrenmatt felt, after *Engel*, that the stage was 'enemy territory' for him, and he turned to considering the general problems of writing for the theatre in the twentieth century. Thinking about the play years later, and in an 'interview with himself', Dürrenmatt said/wrote, 'Über irgendwen macht sich F.D. in diesem Stück lustig, entweder über den Himmel oder über die Mächtigen oder über die Theologen oder über uns alle oder über sich allein. Es ist mir nicht klar geworden, über wen' (WA25, 148). That confusion could not but have contributed to his general feeling of dissatisfaction!

Finally, over *Engel* hovers again the concept of 'Gnade', grace. But as I have followed Dürrenmatt's work over many years and have been able lately to hear and read his reminiscences and views of these early creative days, I am now convinced that he is writing not of Christian 'Grace', God-given and inclined to dogma, but rather of earthly human love, reason and understanding, of '*Vernunft*', and the ability to withstand with equanimity the 'principalities and powers' of this world, and to enjoy the possibility, 'an die ich glaube, an die ich mich anklammere, die Möglichkeit, ganz ein Einzelner zu werden, die Möglichkeit der Freiheit' (in *Der Mitmacher. Ein Komplex*, WA14, 208). Josef Scherer was therefore quite correct to note how the attack on the *loss* of humanity in our century was becoming more urgent with each new play of Dürrenmatt (E37). It is one of the most important and significant *Urmotive* of our author.

* * *

Salman Rushdie says in his 1988 novel *The Satanic Verses*, 'What follows is tragedy. Or at the least, the echo of tragedy, the full-blooded original being unavailable to modern men and women, so it's said. – A burlesque for our degraded, imitative times' (B20, 424). The *locus classicus* for Dürrenmatt's view of the 'Death of Tragedy' in our times is, of course, the famous passage in 'Theaterprobleme', that lecture given in Germany and Switzerland in 1954 and 1955 and published in 1955 (now in WA24, 31–72):

> Die Tragödie setzt Schuld, Not, Maß, Übersicht, Verantwortung voraus. In der Wurstelei unseres Jahrhunderts, in diesem Kehraus der weißen Rasse, gibt es keine Schuldigen und auch keine Verantwortlichen mehr. Alle können nichts dafür und haben es nicht gewollt. Es geht wirklich ohne jeden. Alles wird mitgerissen und bleibt in irgendeinem Rechen hängen. Wir sind zu kollektiv schuldig, zu kollektiv gebettet in die Sünden unserer Väter und Vorväter. Wir sind nur noch Kindeskinder. Das ist unser Pech, nicht unsere Schuld: Schuld gibt es nur noch als persönliche Leistung, als religiöse Tat, Uns kommt nur noch die Komödie bei.

Then, a few lines further on:

> Doch ist das Tragische immer noch möglich, auch wenn die reine Tragödie nicht mehr möglich ist. Wir können das Tragische aus der Komödie heraus erzielen, hervorbringen als einen schrecklichen Moment, als einen sich öffnenden Abgrund. (62–3)

Many twentieth-century writers, from Sartre to Peter Shaffer, have seized on the ineffable sadness behind so many of the so-called 'comedies' of past ages, racked like ours with wars, pestilences, religious doubts and fear of sudden death. Characters like Cervantes's Don Quixote in particular, an example of Henri Bergson's 'type général de l'absurdité comique', seemed to portray much of what twentieth-century writers found in the world around them too. The two great ideologies of the early twentieth century, Christianity and Marxism, both seemed to *avoid* 'tragedy': where Christianity believed that Man is saved, redeemed by the blood of Christ, Marxism believed that the powers of human reason can defeat the circumstances of the natural world. So, what was to replace tragedy? By and large, modern writers, script writers for television, film and radio, have turned to the 'absurd', the 'grotesque' and to what Susanne Langer called 'averted tragedies' which picture an alienated individual in a world which seems to make little sense. 'Un monde qu'on peut expliquer même avec de mauvaises raisons est un monde familier,' wrote Albert Camus in 1942, 'mais au contraire, dans un univers soudain privé d'illusions et de lumières, l'homme se sent un étranger' (*Le mythe de Sisyphe*, C14, 18).

My previous book dealt with the topic in some detail (cf. B23, 20–41) and my concern here is to consider, in retrospect, how the views expressed might have altered with the passing of the years and the development of Dürrenmatt's art. He has continued to comment on the theme, as we shall see when we come to consider his essays in Chapter 7, and lately, and interestingly, above all in *Rollenspiele* (1986), where he reminded Charlotte Kerr that he writes *Komödien* because only comedies treat the present – the Greek tragedies dealt with the *Vorzeit*. Dürrenmatt's 'present' is the Switzerland in which he has always lived, 'ein untragischer Fall in einer tragischen Zeit' as he was to call it in a 'fragment', 'Zur Dramaturgie der Schweiz' (1968–70) (in WA28, 60–76, 69).

It was very much the 'present age', that is the 1950s, which was the true subject of one of the two plays of Dürrenmatt which, in my opinion, can and will be regarded as international masterpieces, *Der Besuch der alten Dame* (WA5, 9–145) which had its première in the Zurich Schauspielhaus on 29 January 1956, with Therese Giehse as Claire Zachanassian and Gustav Knuth as Alfred Ill. It has since been produced all over the world in many languages and in many versions, as a none-too-successful 20th Century Fox film *The Visit*, directed by Bernhard Wicki in 1964 and starring Ingrid Bergmann and Anthony Quinn, as a successful opera by the Austrian–Swiss composer Gottfried von Einem at the Vienna State Opera on 23 May 1971 and Glyndebourne in 1973, and finally, to date, in a television version for DRS on 28 November 1983.[6] It had not been performed in London since Peter Brook's 1959 production, but the 1988 production at the Almeida by the Théâtre de Complicité moved the *Times* critic Irving Wardle to superlatives: he called it, *inter alia*, a 'piece that sets no limits to human corruptibility' (*The Times*, 11 November 1988).

We traced the genesis of the idea for the play above (88ff.), how it arose out of the short story 'Mondfinsternis', written in 1955 but going back to a Dürrenmatt holiday in the Bernese Oberland in 1943, and written, as so many 'works of art' are – indeed, have to be – to earn money. 'Ich sah darin eine bessere Möglichkeit, Geld zu verdienen, als mit dem Schreiben einer Novelle', Dürrenmatt writes in *Stoffe* (A2, 64) – although he adds that, if you want to make *real* money, you should become a speculator or a gangster! He also describes how the express from Berne to Neuchâtel halted at the decrepit tiny stations of Ins and Kerzers for one or two minutes, and how that gave him the idea for the first scene of the play. He writes, too, that the reason for changing Walt Lotcher in 'Mondfinsternis' into the 'Alte Dame' Claire Zachanassian was not to give Therese Giehse the starring role, as many commentators have continued to assert, but to make the 'premisses' 'bühnenatmosphärisch': Claire's arrival in a sedan chair, the butler and the rest of the strange, eerie and grotesque retinue, her very arrival *in a train* because she had had a car accident, which also then gave him the idea for the false limbs, etc. Giehse, Dürrenmatt feels, despite her great success in the part, was 'eine grandiose Fehlbesetzung' since no one could really believe that such a person would have had such a 'past'! (Hilde Hildebrand, who took the role in a truncated version which Dürrenmatt made for the Atelier-Theater in Basle in 1959, was by far the best Claire that Dürrenmatt has ever seen (cf. 'Friedrich Dürrenmatt interviewt F.D.', WA25, 148–9).[7]

After all this hullabaloo, it comes as a distinct douche to learn that Dürrenmatt dislikes the play – and for a strange variety of reasons. Supreme, I believe, among these is, paradoxically, that it brought him fame. This is clearly expressed in the film made by Charlotte Kerr. He acknowledges, of course, that after the *Alte Dame* he could do and write what he wanted, but he feels that the very success of the play proved that it was both 'schlecht und flach', and that it could not be compared to *Romulus der Große*, *Frank V* or *Der Mitmacher*. He even quotes Eugène Ionesco's remark at the French première in 1960 that, if *he* had written such a play, he would not have bothered to write anything else. It was at the same occasion that he received, Dürrenmatt said, the *worst* compliment that he had ever received: one French critic praised the play as a wonderful 'vraie histoire d'amour').

The plot concerns the arrival in the little Central European town of Güllen ('Die Gülle' is Swiss–German/*Oberdeutsch* for 'fermented cattle urine' or 'liquid manure'), of a monstrous 62-year-old woman, Claire Zachanassian, complete with a retinue of butler, coffin, eunuchs, a black panther *et al*. Her intention is to wreak vengeance on one Alfred Ill, a seedy shopkeeper and Mayor-elect who, as a young man, forty-five years earlier, had made her pregnant and forced her to leave the town, he having denied paternity. Starting from a Hamburg brothel, and after marrying a series of rich men, she has become the richest woman in the world, so that she can promise the townsfolk of Güllen 'eine Milliarde' in an unnamed currency on one condition: that they murder Alfred Ill. Protesting their horror, the citizens nevertheless make clear to themselves, and hypocritically to Alfred, that they intend to claim the money, 'denn wir können nicht leben, wenn wir ein Verbrechen unter uns dulden' (125). They do kill him and live in grandiose comfort afterwards – to be warned by the 'Lehrer', one of the few who have striven to preserve a shred of human dignity, 'Noch weiß ich, daß auch zu uns einmal eine alte Dame kommen wird' (103), a chilling remark clearly directed at Dürrenmatt's own complacent and comfortable citizens living in a Switzerland which, Dürrenmatt often claims, is both 'Privileg und Gefängnis' (WA25, 142).[8]

As so many commentators have observed, the story has something of the simplicity of an Old Testament parable about it, and it is my contention that it is with such plots that Dürrenmatt's *forte* is best displayed – the witty interchange between characters gains in psychological depth, and the characters take on more than one dimension. In so many of his plays before and after *Der Besuch der alten Dame* these qualities are drowned either in the complexities of the plot (*Mississippi!*), or in the referential nature of the witticisms which then appear like raisins in a cake, unintegrated with the rest of the dramatic mixture.

Claire Zachanassian – the name is made up from Zacharoff, Onassis and Gulbenkian, three wealthy men connected with Zurich – is the naturalists' 'Bot[in] aus der Ferne' who suddenly enters a community, wreaks change and just as suddenly leaves – a figure seen countless times in westerns as a black-clothed gunman seeking revenge. Claire is undoubtedly much more than 'just' that – but there is no space here to list the many interpretations of her role. I see her as Everyman's conscience sent late in Life to dislocate his comfortable existence and/or to punish him. Literally 'out of this world', with her 'Prothesen' and her impossible and sinister retinue, she sits above the stage in Act II, slightly altered in the 1980 version, spinning her web over the action and waiting for Ill to be delivered to her in Act III. Irving Wardle in his review already quoted mentions Kathryn Hunter's Clara as an 'awesome figure of maimed glamour', and that is just how she should appear. She is a true 'grotesque', ludicrous *and* demonic, her every action and word directed towards what Dürrenmatt meant the grotesque to achieve: 'Das Groteske ist eine äußerste Stilisierung, ein plötzliches Bildhaftmachen und gerade darum fähig, Zeitfragen, mehr noch, die Gegenwart aufzunehmen, ohne Tendenz oder Reportage zu sein' (in WA24, 24–5).[9]

Dürrenmatt warns in the first 'Anmerkung' to the play (142) that Claire is neither Justice nor the Marshall Plan, nor even the Apocalypse, but simply 'die reichste Frau der Welt'. Yet most commentators see in her some symbolic figure. Although to call her 'Frau Welt' ignores the origin of the character in the author's mind as the '*man* from outside', she is, nevertheless, clearly an avenging figure come to punish a man for his crimes and to tempt a city to sin: 'Denn alle Schuld rächt sich auf Erden.'

If Claire and her name are symbolic, what about 'Alfred Ill'? Dürrenmatt would not give any information when asked. There have been many ingenious suggestions, the most interesting being perhaps Kurt Fickert's that Ill equals il equals Everyman (D17). One wonders why Alfred became 'Anton Schill' in Maurice Valency's American translation, and 'Serge Miller' in Wicki's film? Little seems to have been gained in definition of character or interpretation of his role. (In that 1988 London production, he even became 'Fred' at one stage!)

Alfred does represent, as does his near-namesake Alfredo Traps in *Die Panne*, the 'average man' who has transgressed the moral code in the past, but who has managed to 'live with it'. Now, out of the blue, come Vengeance, Nemesis, Retribution and Redemption, and the character has to meet and accept them all. Alfred, in meeting his retribution and accepting punishment for his 'guilt', becomes one of Dürrenmatt's 'mutigen Menschen' – 'die verlorene Weltordnung wird in [seiner] Brust wiederhergestellt', as 'Theaterprobleme' has it (WA24, 63) – and he has given an 'answer' to the hopelessness of the world in which he lives. 'Für mich ist es die Gerechtigkeit,' he says in Act III to the pompous, hypocritical Bürgermeister, 'was es für euch ist, weiß ich nicht' (109). *We* know that 'it' is money and comfort for them. Their time is yet to come.

The third 'character', as it were, is the townsfolk of Güllen themselves, who can be seen as two blocs: the unthinking 'mass'; and the four named social 'representatives', the Doctor, the Teacher, the Priest and the policeman. They become 'society', 'die bei Sophokles durch den Vollzug der Gerechtigkeit am Einzelnen mit entsühnt wird', in Dürrenmatt's interview with himself (WA25, 149), and which has now become guilty itself after Alfred, the 'individual', 'der Einzelne', has accepted *his* guilt and redeemed himself by his death. As Jenny Hortenbach commented, 'she [Claire] could kill him [Alfred] herself or have him killed. Claire exacts the life of Ill as an atonement from Güllen' (D24, 152).

Dürrenmatt chooses to parody the great Sophoclean chorus 'Ungeheuer ist viel' at the end of the action and, although we are enjoined by the author himself *not* to take the play as a 'Parabel der Konjunktur', it is difficult not to agree with the Knapps' verdict that Claire brings 'Kaufkraft' as temptation to the Güllener, 'und man möchte das Stück in diesem Licht fast als eine Tragikomödie des Wirtschaftswunders verstehen' (E25, 27), particularly as we are told in the 'Randnotizen, alphabetisch geordnet' that the name Güllen '[soll] auf Begehren der stimmfähigen Bürger in Gülden umgewandelt werden' (139) – 'Güllen the Golden', indeed.[10]

If one is to regard the play already as a 'classic', and I believe that one should, what has made it so? Firstly, its timelessness: all of

Dürrenmatt's plays relate in one way or another to their age, and the *Alte Dame* does so too, but in its treatment of age-old motifs, perhaps of the 'seven deadly sins' – pride, covetousness, lust, anger, gluttony, envy and sloth – it touches on what is general to all mankind. Secondly, the language: this too has a strangely timeless quality – the witticisms are integral to the plot and to the relevant character and thus they too become, as in the comedies of Aristophanes, Dürrenmatt's 'model', 'Einfälle, die in die Welt wie Geschosse einfallen . . ., welche . . . die Gegenwart ins Komische umgestalten' ('Anmerkung zur Komödie', WA24, 21). And thirdly, the characters possess both a tragic and a comic value: Alfred has (once) risen to the greatness of the tragic hero – that was his 'persönliche Leistung' (cf. 'Theaterprobleme', WA24, 62) – and his fate was brought about not by *Chance*, but really by *hamartia*, by 'some great error on his part' as Aristotle has it in his *Poetics*. His refusal to accept the Mayor's suggestion to commit suicide, submitting rather to retribution, restores the 'verlorene Weltordnung', but only to him, the individual, the 'Einzelne', who is prepared to accept his responsibility as a *Mensch*, a human being – and this has remained one of Dürrenmatt's abiding themes. The time will come when the Gulleners' Alte Dame visits them (cf. above, 61). These are the 'potential moral contradictions inherent in a society whose institutions are based on the idea of personal freedom' (cf. too Heidsieck in B17, 7–18).

In many ways, *Der Besuch der alten Dame* sums up Dürrenmatt's work and *Weltanschauung*: he is the moralist who warns, who uses comedy 'pour épater le bourgeois' and, in so doing, to 'punish their behaviour' – 'Le rire châtie les moeurs' was the motto above the Opéra Comique – who believes that it is the individual who must take responsibility for his or her actions, and that only when, and if, we all do this will society offer a hope for the future. In 1952 he wrote:

> Ich bin da, um zu warnen. Die Schiffer, meine Damen und Herren, sollen den Lotsen nicht mißachten. Er kennt zwar die Kunst des Steuerns nicht und kann die Schiffahrt nicht finanzieren, aber er kennt die Untiefen und die Strömungen. Noch *ist* das offene Meer, aber einmal werden die Klippen kommen, dann werden die Lotsen zu brauchen sein (in 'Fingerübungen zur Gegenwart', WA26, 32).

Der Besuch der alten Dame is just such a warning. Shortly, we shall be concerned with the other international masterpiece of our author, *Die Physiker*, at the end of which Dürrenmatt appended '21 Punkte', the eighteenth of which reads, 'Jeder Versuch eines

Einzelnen, für sich zu lösen, was alle angeht, muß scheitern', and the seventeenth, 'Was alle angeht, können nur alle lösen.' Thus, Alfred Ill's 'individualistic' action, like Möbius's in *Die Physiker*, will remain useless, *senseless*, unless *all* do as he/they tried to do. To quote Goethe once more:

> Ein jeder kehre vor seiner Tür,
> Und rein ist jedes Stadtquartier.

It is typically paradoxical that Dürrenmatt, the great trumpeter of irrational *Zufall*, Chance, should come to so 'enlightened' a conclusion!

The Plays from 1957 to 1966

Most critics have seen Dürrenmatt's next work, *Frank der Fünfte – Komödie einer Privatbank* (now in WA6, 9–130) written in 1958, either as his 'dünnstes Stück' (Rischbieter, E34, 8) or as 'proof' that the author is simply a Brecht-epigone (Mayer, E31, 488). The title, however, with its hint of the Shakespearean *Henry V* (or 'Hank cinq', as the Americans call it), should have indicated how the play was to be understood, 'Als eine moderne Anknüpfung an Shakespeare und nicht als eine an Brecht' ('Die Richtlinien der Regie', now in WA6, 153). Dürrenmatt explained in an interview with Joachim Werner Preuß that the very idea of the play had a Shakespearean source: he had seen Peter Brook (written 'Pieter Bruck' in the text!) produce *Titus Andronicus* in Paris in 1958, a plot 'die eigentlich nur dazu da ist, gewisse menschliche Grundsituationen zu zeigen' (F16, 13). There is too in this work strong indications of Dürrenmatt's growing interest in the cinema and film techniques – he has sat on several international juries for film awards – although, ironically, unlike so many of his works which have been filmed, this one, *Frank V*, started out as an opera. 'Oper einer Privatbank' was the sub-title, with music by Paul Burkhard, of 'O mein Papa' fame. The première took place in the Schauspielhaus in Zurich on 19 March 1959; Kurt Horwitz played Frank V, and Therese Giehse Ottilie his wife. The book version appeared in 1960.[11]

After the clear, tight, rational plot of the *Alte Dame*, Dürrenmatt 'went wild' again and produced one of his most complicated actions. We have to imagine a (Swiss) family bank, a 'Kollektiv', whose chief, Gottfried Frank, the fifth of the dynasty, pretends to have died in order to enjoy the autumn of his life with his favourite

German authors, Goethe and Mörike, and with his wife Ottilie. We then learn that other members of the bank are indulging in all sorts of shady speculations and transactions which lead to threats from an unknown blackmailer and to the possible liquidation of the concern. All in the leading positions must declare their holdings and *they* will be liquidated should they refuse. Death follows bloody death – until the blackmailers reveal themselves as Herbert (later Frank VI), Frank's son, 'zwanzig Jahre und studiert in Oxford' (66), and his daughter Franziska, nineteen and being educated in Montreux! In the Bochumer Fassung (1964), Frank V is entombed in the bank vault in the cellar and Frank VI takes over the bank; in the 1980 version, the ending seems at first sight to be more humane: the two children take over the bank while the parents go to ground – 'Tauchen wir unter' says Frank V (128) – but Dürrenmatt writes in the 'Anmerkung' that he chose the end of the first version (1958–9) for this new edition because 'der menschlichste Schluß [schien] mir nachträglich der grausamste' (133)!

One can guess at the disappointment felt by Dürrenmatt's well-wishers when this disaster of a work appeared after the brilliant conception of *Der Besuch der alten Dame*. His most faithful hagiographer, Elisabeth Brock-Sulzer, had to write in the 1964 edition of her book, 'Eine "Oper" war ja der *Frank* nie, er hatte sich nur stellenweise als Oper *verkleidet*' (C12, 112) and she could barely excuse the 'harsche Thema' and the 'Kruditäten' of the original. Clearly, those who saw Dürrenmatt as a Brecht-epigone were also influenced by the *Dreigroschenoper*-like verses and Burkhard's music which, alas, sounds like second-class Dessau or Weill. (Therese Giehse has recorded two of the songs on Heliodor 3321011 (1967–8).)

I and others have discussed the Dürrenmatt–Brecht relationship in various articles (cf. my D46; Mayer's E30; Knapp's E23; White's D44), and the major point at issue has always been the philosophical–political one: Can the world be changed? In *Die Maßnahme* (1930), Brecht has his 'Kontrollchor' sing, 'Ändre die Welt; sie braucht es', and one achieves this by altering prevailing social conditions: 'Nur belehrt von der Wirklichkeit, können wir/Die Wirklichkeit ändern'. Dürrenmatt believed, however, that what Brecht (and Marxism) really needed to do to achieve their goal was to change human nature, and that, alas, is impossible. Heinz Ludwig Arnold's conversation with the author dealt with the point *in extenso* (F1, 76–7): 'Jeder Gedanke verändert irgendwo die Welt,' said Dürrenmatt there. 'Nur braucht er nicht mit der Absicht verbunden zu sein, die Welt zu verändern' – *that* would lead 'zur Verkrampfung'.

Frank V remains one of Dürrenmatt's favourite artistic creations: he believes that Emil Böckmann's death-scene (No. 13 Das Weib stößt zu, 91–7) is still one of the best that he has ever written. Certainly, the story 'Der Sturz' (above, 76ff.) reads like a continuation 'by other means' – a 'gangster democracy' following a 'gangster bank'! – and Dürrenmatt demonstrates in both his fondness for the motif of the corrupt 'Mächtigen' and those 'Opfer' who suffer at their hands. Jan Knopf remarks how ironic it was that, in the Soviet bloc, *Frank* was seen 'als konsequente Fortsetzung seiner [Dürrenmatts] Kritik an der "monopolkapitalistischen Gesellschaft"', and was enthusiastically received, yet 'die Kritik des Stücks im Westen ist vernichtend' (C31, 97).

For an author who assured me in 1988 that critics do not worry him and that he rarely reads them, Dürrenmatt is very ready to leap to his own defence when attacked in the press or in person. At the end of WA6, he appends 'An die Kritiker Franks des Fünften' (161–5), his 'Münchner Rede' of 1963 in which he presents himself as his own critic and insists that the central scene of the play is indeed Böckmann's death-scene, because Böckmann demonstrates the freedom of the human spirit which denies that evil *must* happen. We are free, there is 'kein Verbrechen, das getan werden muß' (164), but Dürrenmatt knew that that would not convince the newspaper critics so he ended with Böckmann's own cry 'Gott! Errette mich aus den Händen meiner Freunde!' (165). It is a rather pathetic speech, in both senses, which certainly did his reputation no good. *Frank V* vanished from the general repertoires, although it was given several amateur performances in Wales in 1976 on the occasion of the presentation of the Welsh Arts Council International Writers' Prize in 1976.

* * *

The years between 1956 and 1966 were Dürrenmatt's 'große Zeit', as he calls it: honours, prizes and awards were showered upon him and his plays were produced all over the world. The *Alte Dame*, for example, was performed in Paris, New York (where it opened the Lunt-Fontanne Theatre and received the New York Theatre Critics' prize), in Warsaw, Cracow, Aarhuis, Copenhagen, Oslo, Prague, London, Madrid, Lisbon, Jerusalem, Tokyo and Milan.

It is well known that 1961 was a year of political crisis where the 'finger' never seemed to be far from the infamous 'button' of the nuclear bomb; J.F. Kennedy, 35th President of the United States of

America, had to counter Nikita Khrushchev's moves towards Cuba after the celebrated 'Bay of Pigs' incident; the GDR built the 'Schandmauer', the Berlin Wall, on 13 August; while Yuri Gagarin had conquered space in the spaceship *Vostock* on 12 April. It is therefore not surprising that the amateur astronomer Dürrenmatt, intensely interested in the physical sciences since his early days, as well as in international politics, should turn his thoughts to a play on the theme of the responsibility of the scientist in the twentieth century.

These thoughts were stimulated by his reading of a book by Robert Jungk, *Heller als 1000 Sonnen* (1956), on the making of the first atomic bomb, which Dürrenmatt then reviewed for the Zurich *Weltwoche* on 7 December 1956 (now to be found in WA28, 20–4). He calls this story 'eine Chronik vom Untergang einer Welt der reinen Vernunft' (20), blaming the unscrupulous development of the bomb on an 'internationalen Elite von Wissenschaftern' (22), and pointing out that, once the invention had been made, there was no possibility of 'unmaking' it: 'Auch gibt es keine Möglichkeit, Denkbares geheim zu behalten' (22). Moreover, once it was *there*, they could not prevent the military and the politicians from using it: 'Das Wissen fürchtete sich vor der Macht und lieferte sich deshalb den Mächten aus' (23). He blames the scientists: they *did* give a warning (in the Frank Report), but it fell on the deaf ears of a world 'die gar nicht in der Lage war, diese Forderungen zu realisieren' (24). Thus, scientists and politicians alike let themselves be seduced when each group could have influenced the other. It is a fine piece of trenchant criticism, written with some passion, and it is not surprising that, with his technique at its most mature, he was able to make a first-class play, his second 'international masterpiece', *Die Physiker*, out of it.

Die Physiker – Eine Komödie in zwei Akten had its première on 20 February 1962 in the Zurich Schauspielhaus. Like the *Alte Dame*, the major reason for its success lay, and lies, in its taut, essentially simple construction, its overlying comic and its underlying seriousness. Although the philosophical underpinning of the work relates to Jungk's book, the actual theme of the action harks back to that little satirical sketch which the author wrote for the Zurich Cabaret Cornichon in 1950, 'Der Erfinder' (now in WA17, 136–51), in which the inventor of 'a bomb' allowed his deadly invention to slip into the *décolleté* of a lady-friend, thereby assuring world peace! Dürrenmatt's intention in the more mature work was not all that different: by satirising the aims and procedures of distinguished scientists, he hoped to show that the world, that is 'men in the street', had constantly to be on their guard against those who sought to deprive them of their freedom, indeed of the ultimate freedom, the freedom to live.

The play (now in WA7) had its première, in Zurich, and almost immediately became a world sensation. Dedicated to the actress in the major role, Therese Giehse, who had supported Dürrenmatt so faithfully for so long, it conquered all the German theatres and, after a particularly successful London run by the Royal Shakespeare Company at the Aldwych Theatre in 1963, directed by Peter Brook and starring Irene Worth, Cyril Cusack, Michael Hordern and Alan Webb, it was produced in Amsterdam, Helsinki, Stockholm, Copenhagen, Oslo, Palermo, Warsaw, Buenos Aires and Israel – and, in 1964, in New York. Like the *Alte Dame*, it has never left the repertoires of international professional and amateur companies and has become staple fare for university and school study world-wide. Even the US President Jimmy Carter referred to it in one of his speeches about nuclear disarmament to the United Nations on 4 October 1977, when he quoted one of the most famous passages, Möbius's remark: 'Was einmal gedacht wurde, kann nicht mehr zurückgenommen werden.' (Interestingly enough, there is as yet no film-version.)

There was in Switzerland in 1962 an almost text-book illustration of Point 21 to Dürrenmatt's play. There the author wrote, 'Die Dramatik kann den Zuschauer überlisten, sich der Wirklichkeit auszusetzen, aber nicht zwingen, ihr standzuhalten oder sie gar zu bewältigen' (93). It was a continuation of that argument with, and against, Brecht mentioned above, for in April 1962, after having wildly applauded Dürrenmatt's basic anti-nuclear stance in *Die Physiker*, the Swiss voted in a referendum to share in Europe's nuclear defence programme. One might think that this was *the* answer to what Dürrenmatt calls the modern 'Gretchenfrage': *Can a writer change the world? And his answer?* 'Beruhigen im besten, beeinflussen im seltensten Falle – verändern nie!' (cf. interview with Horst Bienek, 1962, F3).

It was very typical of the Dürrenmatt with whom astute theatre-goers and unbiased critics were slowly coming to terms in the 1960s that he should seek to unite the irrationality of madness with the rationality of atomic scientists. The grounds for constructing a plot around these seemingly polar opposites were rehearsed in my previous book and are discussed in many articles. In the long and interesting introduction to the book version of the play, which, incidentally, faithfully follows the text of the outstanding Schau-spielhaus production with only a few 'grammatical' improvements, the author wrote, 'einer Handlung, die unter Verrückten spielt, kommt nur die klassische Form bei' (12), and thus afforded us yet another paradox, namely an irrational, 'grotesque' plot turning on madness and feigned madness, allied to a strict, rational, classical form where the so-called 'three unities' of time, space and action are strictly observed. The action plays in one room and lies within the actual time-span of the 'actual' play, from 'kurz nach halb fünf nachmittags' in Act I to 'an hour later' in Act II. There is a single plot concerning the activities of the two main characters, Johann Wilhelm Möbius, the physicist who has fled into this asylum ('Les Cerisiers'), and the doctor-in-charge, Frau Dr Mathilde von Zahnd. Möbius has fled society into feigned madness so that his great invention, the 'System aller möglichen Erfindungen' where 'neue, unvorstellbare Energien' could destroy the entire world (69), should not fall into unscrupulous hands. With him in the asylum are two secret agents, one from the East, Joseph Eisler, masquerading as Albert Einstein in madness, and one from the West, Alec Jasper Kilton, posing as Isaac Newton and likewise 'mad'. But in a further Dürrenmattian twist each has also a 'false bourgeois' name: Eisler poses as Ernst Heinrich Ernesti and Kilton as Herbert Georg Beutler – and students of the comic will observe the *three* names!

Möbius, fifteen years a 'patient', is loved by his nurse, Monika Stettler, whom he strangles later in Act I because her love is blind enough to believe his assertion that 'König Salomo' appears to him in a vision – that is *his* 'disguise'. Marriage would, of course, deliver him up to the public and the world's evil politicians. Three months before, Newton-Kilton had murdered *his* nurse, Dorothea Moser – and the play opens with the police inspector examining a second 'Tat', as Frau Doktor von Zahnd delicately insists on calling it, the murder of nurse Irene Straub by Eisler-Einstein.

The tight, economical construction of the plot allows the denouement to burst like a bomb: the announcement by the Doctor that she has seen through their disguises from the outset, that she in fact had photocopied the details of the papers on Möbius's discovery, and that her 'Trust' was now ready to take over the world – that is, she is the real, *true* madwoman. Thus, 'the best-laid schemes o' Mice an' Men gang aft a-gley', and these three representatives of a social group renowned for careful planning and accurate scientific calculations are foiled by an 'alten, buckligen Jungfrau', whose 'hump', like Claire Zachanassian's 'Prothesen', should have been a hint to an audience that all was not what it seemed! 'Die Welt ist in die Hände einer verrückten Irrenärztin gefallen,' says Einstein (85), and the three men prepare to spend their lives, disguised, in the asylum-cum-prison. So, 'die schlimmstmögliche Wendung ist nicht voraussehbar. Sie tritt durch Zufall ein' (Punkt 4).

In retrospect, *Die Physiker* is to be seen as the high-water mark of Dürrenmatt's career as a dramatist, since it dominated the German stages during 1962–3 with 1,589 performances in fifty-nine theatres. Never again was he to be so successful. It was also the most theatrical illustration of his philosophical theory of Chance (cf. Punkt 8: 'Je planmäßiger die Menschen vorgehen, desto wirksamer vermag sie der Zufall zu treffen' (91)), which is, for those who believe with Dürrenmatt that the concept of Chance does rule our lives, the *locus classicus* of his theory. It is a theory which has, of course, a good deal in common with Karl Popper's view that 'science can yield no more than theories that may take us ever closer to the truth, but can never be verified or "justified"; they are falsified by one counter-example' (as quoted by A.M. Wright, cf. D47, 65).

Knapp rightly doubts whether Mayer's often-quoted remark – that *Die Physiker* is a 'Zurücknahme' of Brecht's *Leben des Galilei* – does in fact hold water; like Jan Knopf, Mayer seems blinded at times by Brecht's now fading reputation (cf. Knapp, C29, 78–9; Mayer, E30). *Die Physiker* is not a representation of reality; it is what Dürrenmatt calls a 'model', a model of what could happen if the individual does not make himself aware of the consequences of his actions. Möbius thought that he could solve *for himself* a problem which concerned the whole world. He, like the scientists who made the atomic bomb, should have stood up against those who wanted to use, *mis*use, the invention for destructive purposes; but he, like they, went along a personal track which led to his undoing. Oppenheimer, Einstein *et al.* were delivered up to the military and the politicians who used their invention to maim and to kill; Möbius to a mad doctor whose intentions were similar. 'Was alle angeht, können nur alle lösen,' Dürrenmatt would say to them. Only at first sight has Brecht's Galilei, hale and hearty, acted more sensibly than Möbius: by recanting his beliefs, by not submitting to the tortures of the Inquisition, he has been able to write his *Discorsi*, a work which will serve as the basis for future important scientific research, and have it smuggled out by his pupil, Andrea, whereas Möbius has had to give up everything and remain a prisoner in an asylum while his discovery is exploited by a selfish, late-bourgeois, capitalist madwoman. Yet, at second sight, we see that Galilei too is a prisoner in that his action has made science the slave of authority and, even though we now know that we were supposed to take Galilei to be a criminal in the third (1954) version of Brecht's play, we were also to assume that different social circumstances would have prevented the *need* for his action. Dürrenmatt, the realist, assumes that men will *always* act stupidly and selfishly.

Gerhard Knapp's 1983 article (D26) makes the observation that the 1980 'revised' version of *Die Physiker* contains 'no substantial changes' to the text, only in 'verb tenses, punctuation and minor syntactical points', and he expresses surprise that Dürrenmatt has not altered his 1960s views. His physicists remain 'outsmarted', and Knapp believes that this 'proves' that Dürrenmatt still believes in a 'dramaturgy of victims', when it had looked as if he were moving towards a 'dramaturgy of alternatives'. But we can see now from the vantage point of 1988 that Dürrenmatt has never changed his view that human nature will *never* change: it will always lead some to 'stupidity and cupidity', and all that rational people can do is to limit the extent of the damage (D26, 66). When the first collection of Dürrenmatt's plays was published in the GDR, the editor's opinion of *Die Physiker* in general and of the '21 Punkte' in particular was that they expressed the central paradox of Dürrenmatt's *Weltanschauung*, namely that action is necessary but futile whether on the part of the individual or the collective (cf. Reid, D31).

Considering the date of the production and the prevailing political circumstances – and the dramaturgical mores of the age – it was not surprising that *Die Physiker*, when considered with Dürrenmatt's other great success of six years previously, should have been seen as an anti-bourgeois satire. Pressure on the Right was building up gradually as America's Vietnam commitment became more and more tragic, and more and more certain to be unsuccessful. Brecht's Marxist, alienated plays were still the models for certain European theatres and for a good many of Europe's intellectual youth. Seen, however, from our perspective, post-Vietnam, post-Hungary, post-Czechoslovakia, post-Afghanistan, the age of *perestroika* and *glasnost*, of USSR 'charm offensives' led by Mikhail Gorbachev, one is less likely to take it as an anti-USA, anti-West play than as an attack on *both* sides, a 'plague o' both your houses'. This is consistent with Dürrenmatt's later equilateral boutades 'Sätze aus Amerika' (1970) after his visit to the States in 1969, and with the story 'Der Sturz' (1971) after his visit to the USSR Writers' Congress in May 1967 (cf. 77 and 181).

We begin to sense vaguely by this time in Dürrenmatt's career that we are meeting with a *Grundmotiv* out of what he has called the 'Motivknäuel'. Möbius, the helpless individual, is caught isolated in the labyrinth, a symbol for that inexplicable world with which

the individual must struggle in order to make a rational life possible; a struggle which will and can never be won, but which each
person must undertake to survive, and that is the goal – *just*
survive. And how can he or she be helped to survive this struggle?
'Mit Humor'. Tiusanen's remark that '*The Physicists* does not
conclude with a stalemate between chaos and order. There is an
out-and-out victory for the powers of chaos, one leading to the end
of the world' (B22, 279), makes Dürrenmatt a pitch-black pessimist, leaves his appeal to the 'humanity' out of the game and, above
all, fails to recognise that clarion call to *Humor* which, in the last
resort, makes Dürrenmatt's works worthy of serious study in the
late-twentieth-century 'atomic' society.

*   *   *

Of his next work, the play-version of his *Hörspiel Herkules und der
Stall des Augias*, which had its première in the Zurich Schauspielhaus on 20 March 1963 (now in WA8, 9–117), little need be said on
two counts: firstly, it keeps fairly closely to the radio-play which
we considered in some detail above (65ff.); secondly, the play met
with resounding critical and popular disfavour, was soon withdrawn from regular performance and is unlikely to be revived. The
major point of interest for a retrospective study is that it initiated a
trend in Dürrenmatt's work which was to be continued into the
1970s, what we have elsewhere termed the production of 're-
versions', adaptations of his own or of others' works. In essence, of
course, this procedure is really no different from producing another
version, or other versions, of a play as Dürrenmatt did, as we have
seen, *a fortiori*, with five *Mississippi*s and five *Romulus*es, and was to
do later with four *Die Panne*s.

We ended our discussion of the radio-play with a question (cf.
68) which now demands an answer. The conclusion to the stage-
play has the son Phyleus march off, 'mit gezücktem Schwert', to
confront the 'hero' Herkules with a heroic gesture, *ignoring* his
father Augias's rational and humane injunction: 'Wage jetzt zu
leben und *hier* zu leben, mitten in diesem gestaltlosen, wüsten
Land, nicht als ein Zufriedener, sondern als ein Unzufriedener, der
seine Unzufriedenheit weitergibt und so *mit der Zeit* die Dinge
ändert' (my italics, 114). *That* is the 'heroic deed', all that men can
do in this senseless, inexplicable world, and that was Dürrenmatt's
answer in the post-war world of 1954. In this second (stage) version
(1963), however, Phyleus returns to the age-old way of settling
conflicts – blind aggression – and thus, as 'Die Zehn', the par-

lamentarians, chant at the end, 'Das große Sterben fängt an' (117). Thus, our question – Why in 1962 did Dürrenmatt write, as Punkt 18 to *Die Physiker*, 'Jeder Versuch eines Einzelnen, für sich zu lösen, was alle angeht, muß scheitern', while in 1954 Man was advised to cultivate his garden and *thus* make the world a better place? – is answered. The world has *not* changed for the better, alas, in these eight years. Man still practises inhumanity to man, and it is therefore only realistic for a dramatist to show that stupidity is still abroad and that, as long as it is, 'das große Sterben' will continue. That is no doubt what Ernst Gallati meant when he wrote that the dung, 'der Mist', in the play had a moral dimension: 'Mist ist das, was das "Eigene" behindert' (E16, 122).

* * *

As Dürrenmatt's theatrical works of the 1960s and 1970s met with more and more critical opposition and less and less public acclaim, he seemed to me to have withdrawn into a private world, literally to his eyrie in Neuchâtel and metaphorically to what he now began to apostrophise as 'the labyrinth'. In consequence, I believe, his works have tended to become more autobiographical, almost self-defensive, centring round 'the individual'.

The image of the 'great individual', 'der große Einzelne', is of course nothing more nor less than the age-old image of 'the hero'. In Dürrenmatt's eyes, however, the 'individual' does not launch out on 'derring-do', but tries to act sensibly, to take 'a step back' in order to measure up the possible dangers, whether to fight on, or to run away in order to fight another day. And this image is clearly autobiographical: the *Minotaurus* is the 'great individual' battling against an incomprehensible world, the labyrinth. Dürrenmatt therefore sees himself now either as this wild Minotaur, 'mit dem Kopf eines Stiers und dem Leib eines Menschen', just as he saw himself years ago as an 'etwas verwirrter Naturbursche' ('Anmerkung' to *Der Besuch der alten Dame*, WA5, 142), or, paradoxically – and that too is typical – as the Theseus-figure who enters the labyrinth finally to confront and kill the beast. Dürrenmatt explains himself in his 'Dramaturgie des Labyrinths', an essay in *Stoffe I* (A1, 77–94), where his retrospective view of his life and career centres on his 'Urprotest' against the circumstances of his birth, just as the Minotaur has legitimate complaints about *its* birth: 'der Wurf hatte einen viel zu großen Kopf' (80). As in his 'Theaterprobleme', he confronts the world where he tries 'Distanz zu ihr zu gewinnen, von ihr zurückzutreten, sie ins Auge zu fassen wie ein Dompteur ein wildes Tier' (77). It is both a flight from the real world which frightens him, and an attempt bravely to challenge it by constructing his own counter-world of the imagination. But in addition, as S.G. Donald points out, being 'shrouded in mystery and ambiguity, it admits of many applications and interpretations' (D14, 198), and that is obviously Dürrenmatt's major reason for selecting this myth. And the proof for *that* lies, strangely enough, in his 1980 remark on the next play to be considered, *Der Meteor*, where in one of the postludes, 'Über "Unverbindlichkeit"', he writes proudly 'daß ich mißtrauisch gegen eindeutige Antworten bin' (WA9, 167).

Although, in retrospect, we can find traces of the labyrinth theme in his earliest writings – we noted it in 'Die Stadt' (above, 19) – it is at its most obvious in the next play, *Der Meteor – Eine Komödie in zwei Akten*, which had its première in the Zurich Schauspielhaus on 20 January 1966. Bracketed in volume 9 of the *Werkausgabe* with *Dichterdämmerung* as *Nobelpreisträgerstücke*, *Der Meteor* was written in 1964 and conceived, we learned from his interview 'with himself', at the same time as *Die Physiker* in the Unterengadin in 1960 (WA25, 153). The 1980 version is the text provided for the production in the Theater an der Josefstadt in Vienna in 1978 (WA9, 9–95).

We find at least one 'clue' to Dürrenmatt's intention behind *Der Meteor* in a conversation with Franz Kreuzer in Zurich in 1986: '[*Der Meteor*] ist aber eigentlich meine Auseinandersetzung mit der Welt meines Vaters. Der Stoff geht auch auf groteske Dinge zurück, wie etwa, daß wir immer auf dem Friedhof spielten' (F12, 30). He recalls, as he had done before, how he once fell into an open grave and only managed to clamber out as his father arrived with the cortège to commence the burial service! (We might recall here that Dürrenmatt's father died while he was busy on *Der Meteor*, on 8 February 1965, curiously the day after Dürrenmatt had delivered the funeral oration for his old friend, Ernst Ginsberg, cf. below, 171.)

Wolfgang Schwitter is a feared, outspoken writer, a winner of the Nobel Prize for Literature who, disgusted with the whole 'culture-industry', wishes to die and leave it all behind. Despite his wishes, however, and all his careful, albeit grotesque preparations, he cannot die, or rather he dies, but keeps returning to life. His inability to die leads, directly or indirectly, to the deaths of Pfarrer Lutz, mortally amazed at the sight of a 'miracle', a true resurrection, and of Hugo Nyffenschwander, an amateurish painter for whom Schwitter has nothing but contempt, and whose wife Auguste he has seduced and, in his 'dying' state, seduces again (53).

Nyffenschwander is ironically thrown down the stairs and killed by 'der große Muheim', an eighty-year-old capitalist builder whose wife was also seduced – forty years before – by Schwitter, but who feels that, whereas he is 'erledigt, ausradiert, niedergestampft, verhöhnt, besudelt', it is only Nyffenschwander's silly 'artistic' vanity which is hurt, and one can dispense with that (64). At the end of the play, Schwitter learns the truth about 'Life' from the lavatory attendant, Frau Nomsen, who has brought up her daughters, Olga (whom Schwitter has married) and Inge, as prostitutes and her son Waldemar as a 'spiv', and who shows Schwitter that the 'truth' lies deep down in her 'blaugekachelten, feuchten' underworld, in the avoidance of 'Gefühle', emotions. One should only *pretend* to have feelings, as prostitutes do 'wenn der Kunde es verlangt' (89). Schwitter finds her views sympathetic: Schwitter–Dürrenmatt despises the whole 'artistic' nature of theatrical criticism, academic commentaries, publishers' blurbs and so on. 'Literature' should be like brothel-keeping, just a job: 'Ich beschäftigte die Phantasie derer, die meine Geschichten kauften, und hatte dafür das Recht zu kassieren, und kassierte,' he says (90).

But we then hear that Olga, Frau Nomsen's daughter, had married Schwitter for convention's sake, against her mother's advice, had regretted it, and had poisoned herself. And as Schwitter talks to the mother, herself ailing, tucks her up and brings her pills and a drink, she too dies – the fourth fatal casualty. The play ends with Schwitter, surrounded by Dürrenmatt's favourite religious 'butt', the Salvation Army, groaning four t. .., 'Wann krepiere [N.B. not *sterbe*!] ich denn endlich' (95) – but not before having produced Death No. 5 by strangling the hopelessly Christian-optimist Salvation Army Major Friedli, who accepts Schwitter's 'resurrection' as a Christian miracle. So yet another Dürrenmatt play finishes with the 'grotesque' collection of corpses, the 'Leichenberge' of which one critic wrote years ago.

The confrontation with the world of his father mentioned above is, of course, the confrontation between the 'man of Faith' and the son who has lost it. I have mentioned more than once the deep feelings of guilt still experienced by Dürrenmatt, particularly after the deaths of his parents, and he deals with the theme again in the Kerr film of 1984 when his wife asks, 'Bist du gläubig?' and his answer is 'An was?' He claims that we all need to believe in something, but that he himself cannot believe in a God Whom he cannot see. He needs proof and there is no logical reason that he can find for the existence of a God. *Der Meteor* ist ein Stück über das 'Nicht-glauben-Können' (Punkt 14 to *Der Meteor*) (q.v.). His father could not countenance the thought of there being no life after death, but Dürrenmatt says to his wife, 'Warum sollte man sein?' This attitude, and this play *Der Meteor*, are obviously determined by his own physical experiences with death or dying, with his diabetes illness over a period of thirty years – Renate Usmiani suggested once indeed that the frequent bouts of unconsciousness caused by this debilitating illness might have influenced the choice of theme (cf. D39, 150). His heart attack in 1969, and his serious illness in October 1975, must have confirmed this thought. This aspect of the theme reappears in *Play Strindberg* (below, 136ff.).

Dürrenmatt's principal philosophical point here is that there can be no belief in a 'miracle', in a 'resurrection', no Faith, where there is no confidence, no trust. Schwitter has lost his confidence in his fellow human beings and in God; he is sickened by the hypocrisy of people like his publisher, Carl Konrad Koppe, the literary cant of people like the 'Starkritiker' Friedrich Georgen, the timorous 'artist-ry' of people like Hugo Nyffenschwander and the superficial optimism of 'Christians' like Pfarrer Lutz and Major Friedli. God can prove his existence neither to Schwitter nor, as we have seen, to Dürrenmatt, and this is no doubt what he meant in his comments in 'Sätze über das Theater' (WA24, 176–211): 'Dialektisch ist daher *Der Meteor* nur bei echten Christen und echten Nicht-Christen zu verstehen: Das Faktum des Wunders steht der Unmöglichkeit gegenüber, es zu glauben' (Satz No. 30, 197). Therefore he/they can do without God: 'Glauben kann durch nichts objektiviert werden, Glauben ist rein subjektiv,' he said to Arnold. Thus, he remains one who doubts: 'ich bin ein Zweifler, und ich zweifle und zweifle und zweifle' (F1, 40–1).

Dürrenmatt wrote in an article in December 1963, 'Ich zeige, daß Nihilismus keine Lehre sondern eine Haltung des Menschen ist', and he underlined this in the 'Anhang' to his *Wiedertäufer* drama of 1967 (below, 133): 'Darin, daß viele der heutigen Zuschauer in meinen Stücken nichts als Nihilismus sehen, spiegelt sich nur ihr eigener Nihilismus wieder' (WA10, 134). Nevertheless he, and others, could not have been too surprised when they were taken to task by the High Priest of moral values in Switzerland, Professor Emil Staiger, on 20 September 1966 – not December, as Knopf writes (C31, 149). Their plays and novels, said Staiger, 'wimmeln von Psychopathen, von gemeingefährlichen Existenzen, von Scheußlichkeiten großen Stils und ausgeklügelten Perfidien'. I have written about this 'Zürcher Literaturstreit' elsewhere (D45), but I would mention here Dürrenmatt's riposte a year later, when he claimed (proudly?) that Staiger had only had *him* in mind: 'Ich habe in Frau Nomsen eine Repräsentantin der wahren, ungeschminkten Menschheit [Staiger's own words] geschaffen, die nicht nur Abortfrau ist, sondern auch Kupplerin' (in 'Varlin schweigt', WA26, 166).

Long before that, however, the play itself had caused much consternation in conservative Zwinglian Zurich. The vehement views about the attitude and death of Pfarrer Lutz expressed in the Zurich *Kirchenbote* led to a public discussion in the Kunsthaussaal on 25 February 1966 which, in turn, led to the publication of Dürrenmatt's 'Zwanzig Punkte zum Meteor' in the *Neue Zürcher Zeitung* of 28 February (now in WA9, 159–62). These twenty points follow in the main our discussion above, namely the difficulties of a man who is resurrected but who does not believe in his resurrection because he does not *believe* in the Christian 'Word': 'Er wird zu einem Einzelnen in der Gesellschaft, zu einem totalen Individuum unter den relativ Individuellen' (Punkt 17) – and this makes his world into a labyrinth, Dürrenmatt would add twenty years later. But it also makes his situation paradoxical, and 'ein paradoxer Mensch ist in einem höheren Sinne eine komische Gestalt' (Punkt 11) and also a *tragic* character, where 'comic' and 'tragic' are opposites and must be reconciled by the director of the play on the stage. These are indeed *Urmotive* in a 'Motivknäuel'!

But it is at least questionable whether this play *is* about Christian belief at all. Looking back, I think it much more likely that it is a work written by a disgruntled artist attacking the world of *belles-lettres* which had attacked him. In the 'Notiz zur Dichter-dämmerung', Dürrenmatt wrote in connection with this 'Parodie der Literatur', which had to be enlarged to a 'Parodie des Theaters', that he would be grateful if readers would note 'daß seine Meinung über die Kritik nicht so freundlich ist wie die, welche in diesem Stück geäußert wird'! (168).[12] 'Die Literatur ist hier eine Gegen-Welt,' he said to Urs Jenny about *Der Meteor*, 'ganz einfach das Nicht-Wirkliche. Und an Schwitter zeigt sich, daß sie hinfällig wird, wo es im Ernst auf Leben und Tod geht; die Wirklichkeit des Todes löscht die Erfindungen aus, mit denen Schwitter sich schützend umstellt hat' (F8, 12).

Nevertheless, the play will rank as No. 3 in the Dürrenmatt canon; it was performed by the Royal Shakespeare Company in London, and then in Buenos Aires in 1966, in Paris in 1977 and in Vienna in 1978, but it did not enjoy quite the international renown of the *Alte Dame* and *Die Physiker* and was, in addition, Dürren-matt's last theatrical success of any moment.

The Plays from 1967 to 1973

The 1960s were a time of growing crisis for the Western democracies. The assassination of President Kennedy in Dallas on 22 November 1963 had consequences for the United States and the rest of the world which, I believe, have not yet been fully recognised. The shock to the American political system, the smashing in these years of the dreams of a whole generation which had seen in Jack Kennedy a natural and sympathetic leader, led to an ugly reversion to a looking-inwards and to a suspicion of any authoritarian proclamations. The 1960s mark a steady move to the Left: the Cuban crisis of 1962, Kennedy's death in 1963, the increase in the agony of Vietnam – some 500,000 US troops were in action there in 1968 – the introduction of Mao Tse-Tung's 'Cultural Revolution' in China, the Six-Day War in the Middle East in 1967, and the collapse of the seventeen-year long conservative (CDU/CSU) government in the Federal Republic, leading firstly to the 'Große[n] Koalition' with the FDP, under Kurt Georg Kiesinger in 1966, and then significantly to the first non-conservative coalition government (SDP/FDP) under Willy Brandt in 1969. This was accompanied in the same year by the fall of General de Gaulle in France and the succession of the socialist Georges Pompidou. The great upheaval, the *événements* of May 1968 in Paris and the subsequent student revolts elsewhere in Europe, brought to an end a decade which had seen a dramatic change in political, social, sexual and religious attitudes. And these were reflected in the changes in theatre, film and music too – The Beatles were only one remarkable manifestation!

When we look back at this extraordinary decade, the 'Swinging Sixties', and observe the changes that took place in the theatrical mores, this was the age of documentary theatre, of Hochhuth's *Der Stellvertreter* (1963), of Frisch's *Andorra* (1961), of Walser's *Der schwarze Schwan* (1964), of Kipphardt's *In der Sache J. Robert Oppenheimer* (1964) and, above all perhaps, of Peter Weiss's *Marat-Sade* (1964) and his *Die Ermittlung* (1965) – all of these summed up by Hans Daibler as 'Bühne als Tribüne' (C15, 253) – of actual documents used as theatrical scripts for 'engagierte' (committed) purposes. We can therefore sense how out of touch Dürrenmatt felt himself to be, and why, probably, he made Schwitter's 'swinging' son Jochen, say, 'Die Welt will harte Tatsachen, keine erfundenen Geschichten. Dokumente, keine Legenden. Belehrung, nicht Unterhaltung. Der Schriftsteller engagiert sich oder wird überflüssig' (WA9, 92) and, as a result, 'Es ist aus mit der Schwitterei' (94).

(When *Dichterdämmerung*, written in May–June 1980, was published as a very weak successor to both *Abendstunde im Spätherbst* and *Der Meteor*, we saw that Dürrenmatt had not forgotten these days, for he made a young woman remark in one passage that Dürrenmatt had written a fresh ending for the work: 'Schreibt der immer noch?' asks 'der Autor'. 'Nur noch um' is the self-withering reply (WA9, 143)!)

This 'crisis' in Dürrenmatt's artistic career led him to two decisions: firstly, to look back at some of his works in the light of the prevailing circumstances, and secondly, as we shall shortly see, to take steps to make his more direct contribution to the practical world of theatre. The first step was to take up again his first-born, *Es steht geschrieben* of 1947 (above, 99–101), and to re-think the plot as 'Ein Stück über das Engagement' (cf. 'Friedrich Dürrenmatt interviewt FD', WA25, 154). Now the two committed, 'engagierten' Christians, Knipperdollinck and Matthisson, are confronted by a 'Schauspieler ohne Engagement', as Bockelson now appears, who has been attempting to gain employment in the Bishop's acting troupe. The encirclement of the Anabaptists' town of Münster now becomes a 'play', a 'grausige[s] Schauspiel', in which all the former characters from 1947 participate – but as *actors* playing roles, rather than as kings, politicians and clergy. It becomes a true *theatrum mundi*, a 'Welttheater', a cynical comment on how 'Authority', 'die Mächtigen', once again triumph(s) over the weak, 'die Opfer'. The two Christians die as before, but Bockelson is cynically engaged, 'mit dreifacher Spitzengage', for the Kardinal's troupe.

This 're-version', *Die Wiedertäufer – Eine Komödie in zwei Teilen* 'dedicated to Ernst Schröder' (in WA10, 9–122), bears all the signs of the internal and external conflicts of Dürrenmatt's artistic life of the period, not least in the 'Dramatische[n] Überlegungen' which are appended to the text (127–37), and which, Dürrenmatt told me in 1969, were to be regarded as his most important utterances on the theatre. The most famous remark, and the most-quoted, is certainly, 'Die schlimmstmögliche Wendung, die eine Geschichte nehmen kann, ist die Wendung in die Komödie' (No. 1, 128), which I have always believed must have derived from the notion of the *Wendepunkt*, known to all readers and students of the German *Novellen* of the Swiss Keller, Meyer and Gotthelf and of the North German Storm, and defined by the British academic E.K. Bennett thus: 'Characteristic of its [the *Novelle*'s] construction is a certain turning-point at which the development of the narrative moves unexpectedly in a different direction from that which was anticipated and arrives at a conclusion which surprises, but, at the same time, satisfies logically' (B3, 18–19).

In almost the same way, Dürrenmatt's works 'take a turning' which leads them from the most obvious path to a rational solution on to an absurd, paradoxical, 'comical' ending – the ending which mocks these 'best-laid schemes o' Mice an' Men'. Yet one must bear in mind all the time that these endings, however cynical and pessimistic they may appear to be, must be seen as 'models', indeed 'warnings', about what *might* or *could* happen if . . . I do not therefore share what seems to be a fairly general view that Dürrenmatt is a 'Geschichtspessimist', a cultural pessimist; he is a *realist*, albeit a sceptical one, who has had to take his fair share of Life's buffetings, but who has managed to keep himself on an even keel by maintaining a sense of proportion – and of humour. 'Die Erziehung des Menschengeschlechts zum Humor,' he said to René Sauter in 1966, 'das ist für mich gleichbedeutend mit der Erziehung des Menschengeschlechts zur Humanität. Es gibt keine Humanität ohne Humor' (F19, 1224). Would that some of his critics remember that.

Like all thinking artists, Dürrenmatt wearies sometimes of the stupidity of the world, and just as the ass in the Wieland story *Der Prozeß um des Esels Schatten* raised his head at the end to groan, 'War ich in dieser Geschichte der Esel?', so too Dürrenmatt's Bischof von Waldeck, the 'hilflose Zuschauer', groans at the close of *Die Wiedertäufer*, 'Diese unmenschliche Welt muß menschlicher werden/Aber wie? Aber wie?' (122). This might remind some of Shaw's St Joan, 'How long, o Lord, how long?', in a similar situation.

Dürrenmatt might well have been trying to 'shock' his 'bourgeois' public again by reviving the work that had caused such a scandal in 1947 – but, alas, the critical and public reaction remained cool. Elisabeth Brock-Sulzer noted, 'Dabei ist es beinahe belustigend zu sehen, wie viele Zuschauer das zweite Stück [i.e. after *Es steht geschrieben*] gerade wegen des Fehlens jener Züge anfeinden, die im ersten Stück seinerzeit so heftig angefeindet worden sind' (C12, 171), and that itself is a comment on the mores of the age.

* * *

So much then for Dürrenmatt's first decision; his second was to take up in the autumn of 1968 the invitation of the two Basle theatres to act as 'beratendes Mitglied des Direktoriums'. The then Director was Werner Düggelin, a rather authoritarian figure himself, and the partnership team of 'Dü–Dü' promised to breathe new life into the old company. (Düggelin had produced Dürrenmatt's

Die Wiedertäufer in Zurich, of course). Together they put on versions of Shakespeare's *King John* (*König Johann*, première on 18 September 1968), Strindberg's *Totentanz* (*Play Strindberg*, première on 8 February 1969), *Mississippi 1970* and a new production of Lessing's *Minna von Barnhelm*. It was a disagreement about the latter production which led to Dürrenmatt walking out in October 1969 and causing another theatre scandal. As Dürrenmatt put it himself, however, 'Ich stand nicht vor einem Ozeandampfer, sondern vor einer Rheinfähre, zu der weder die Gallionsfigur Beck [i.e. Kurt Beck, one of Dürrenmatt's favourite actors] noch die Gallionsfigur Dürrenmatt paßten' (in 'Mein Rücktritt von den Basler Theatern', WA24, 158). This made headlines in all the papers: 'Krach mit Dürrenmatt!' cried *Die Zeit* of 25 October 1969; 'Ist das Basler Theater in einer Krise – Dürrenmatt ging – aber warum?' asked the *Basler Nachrichten* of 15 October.[13]

What was achieved by it all? And why did Dürrenmatt renounce work which has always interested him – and still does?

The first joint production in Basle was of *König Johann – Nach Shakespeare* (WA11, 9–113), a reworking of a minor Shakespeare rewriting of a play by John Bales (?) produced at speed as a rival production to a *King John* then running in London in 1591. Dürrenmatt's goal was to produce 'eine Teamarbeit': 'Ich könnte mich also als eine Art Kontrollfaktor in diesem Team nützlich machen,' he told Rainer Litten at the time of his appointment in 1967. In 1969, shortly before his 'departure', he told me in Neuchâtel: '*König Johann* war eine Theatergelegenheitsarbeit. Es war ein ewiger Traum, das zu machen', that is to present a poor Shakespearean play from a modern point of view and to show that it could be made to be relevant. Dürrenmatt achieved this, he believed, by stressing the inhumanity of the rulers ('die Mächtigen') in the play and the neglect of the suffering of 'das Volk' ('die Opfer') which, he said to me, rarely appeared in Shakespeare anyway: 'Das Eigenartige bei Shakespeare', he said, 'ist das Fehlen des Volks' (F22) – an interesting comment on an 'aristocratic' author!

Dürrenmatt had recently shown his political involvement for the world's 'victims' in his speech on 8 September 1968 in Basle against the Soviet invasion of Czechoslovakia (now in WA28, 35–42) and earlier – and more controversially – in his support of Israel in the Six-Day War in 'Israels Lebensrecht' (now in WA28, 29–34). In 1970 he was to join in the anti-British Week protest against Britain's Biafra involvement, and we have seen that he approved his clergyman son Peter's stand later against military service in 1973 which cost Peter four months' imprisonment.

Thus, another paradox: on the one hand, the 'Alte vom Berg', as he was journalistically described, in his Neuchâtel eyrie, 'der große Einzelne'; on the other, the 'team-worker' down in the market-place writing and producing works whose themes bore on contemporary issues. Certainly, *König Johann* was just such a play: 'Daß uns *König Johann* immer noch angeht, weist unsere Problematik auf', he wrote in the 'Prinzipien der Bearbeitung' (WA11, 201–4, here 204). The callous concern for 'Geschäft' (Shakespeare's 'commodity') of all the royal characters, their hypocritical concern for 'national duty' and their 'patriotism' – both feebly dismissed as an excuse either for making 'profits' or for saving their own skins – are castigated: 'durch ihre Macht sind sie von den Menschen und damit von ihren Opfern distanziert, getrennt, unmenschlich', Dürrenmatt wrote in his 'Zwei Dramaturgien' (WA24, 147–9, here 148).[14]

* * *

König Johann was actually quite a popular success, but, true to that 'Zick-Zack' philosophy that we noted above (44), Dürrenmatt changed direction again and produced almost the opposite to a teeming Elizabethan political *Komödie*, namely a 'chamber *Komödie*', with a cast of three, *Play Strindberg*. It was on a theme adumbrated in *König Johann* and elsewhere, inhumanity; this time a marital feud between two grotesque monsters on the lines of the American Edward Albee's *Who's afraid of Virginia Woolf?* (1962). This production, by Dürrenmatt and Erich Hölliger, was both a 'Teamarbeit', in that the artists participated in the production, and a public success. Dürrenmatt told me in 1969 that this was what he loved, 'praktisches Theater', a reworking of a play of a 'Riesenspießer': 'Ich wollte den Schutt wegräumen und ein altes Werk der modernen Zeit [*sic*] geben . . . und den ganzen Plüsch weglassen' (F22).

I wrote twenty years ago that later scholars examining this period of Dürrenmatt's life should bear in mind Wolfgang Kayser's warning, 'der Literaturhistoriker, der bei der Untersuchung eines Dramas nicht die zugehörige Bühne kennt, gerät leicht auf Irrwege' (C25, 196), and that is certainly the case here. Produced as a boxing match under spotlights, with the title a 'play' on the then popular French jazz trio 'Play Bach' (led by Jacques Loussier), this is no 'deathless theatre', no 'work of art', but a piece of stagecraft for the moment, 'eine Komödie über die bürgerlichen Ehetragödien' ('Bericht über *Play Strindberg*' WA12, 193), an alas all too common phenomenon in Switzerland. The text, *Play Strindberg – Totentanz nach August Strindberg* (in WA12, 9–93), is indeed a bitter indictment of unhappy marital life, but its central character, Edgar, is a brother to Wolfgang Schwitter of *Der Meteor*, and both are creations of a writer almost obsessed at this time with the thought of dying. Dürrenmatt's diabetes, and perhaps also the whole ultimately frustrating and certainly unpleasant dealings with the Basle group, led to a heart attack in April 1969.

Play Strindberg had its première in the Basler Komödie on 8 February 1969. Edgar, an impossibly 'heroic' army captain – 'Ich sterbe Knall und Fall wie ein alter Soldat' is only one of his oft-repeated 'heroic' phrases – is married to a shrew, Alice, and lives in an isolated lighthouse where they are visited by a divorced embezzler, Kurt, who in a sense acts as the 'referee' in this 'boxing match' of a marriage. (Gilbert Highet once wrote wisely that you are watching a parody 'if you admire the original a little less' (B12, 68). Strindberg's heated 'soul study' is certainly mocked here.)

These 're-versions' are not truly part of the Dürrenmatt canon, but *Play Strindberg* is particularly interesting because Dürrenmatt's desire here to remove the 'Plüsch x Unendlichkeit' ('Bericht', 193) seems to have resulted in a new theatrical style. He described his intention later: 'Ich versuche dramaturgisch immer einfacher zu zeigen, immer sparsamer zu werden, immer mehr auszulassen, nur noch anzudeuten' ('Programm' of the 'Zürcher Fassung' of *Porträt eines Planeten*, 28 March 1971, now in WA12, 197). What he was really trying to expunge from his theatre was 'das Theaterliterarische, das Rhetorische . . . die schönen Sentenzen und schönen Sätze' (op. cit.).

Play Strindberg had 700 performances on thirty-three stages and was seen by some 220,000 people in 1969–70 according to the *Cultural News* of Germany's *Inter Nationes* (January 1971). Thus a 'popular' success. So maybe Dürrenmatt could quote his own Bockelson in *Die Wiedertäufer* and say, 'Als Schriftsteller bedeutend, bin ich als Regisseur genial'? Werner Düggelin clearly disagreed: his 'interference' in Dürrenmatt's preparations for performances of *Titus Andronicus*, *Minna von Barnhelm* and the fifth version of *Die Ehe des Herrn Mississippi*, plus the 'politicking' among the casts, meant that, when Dürrenmatt returned to Basle after recuperating from his heart attack in Schuls-Tarasp in the Unterengadin, the break between them became more open. Dürrenmatt left in high dudgeon: 'Ich setzte mich für dieses Theater mit allen meinen Kräften ein,' he wrote in his own Zurich *Sonntags Journal* on 18/19 October 1969, 'und muß gestehen, daß ich an diesem Theater der Narren [i.e. the Basler Komödie] der größte Narr war' ('Mein Rücktritt von den Basler Theatern', WA24, 160). Other reports suggest that there were two sides to the coin: 'Es ware höchste Zeit, auch ihm klarzumachen, dass [*sic*] der Schwarze Peter nicht einfach den Basler Theatern zugeschoben werden kann', wrote the *Basler Nachrichten* (15 October 1969). But Dürrenmatt could not leave even this sorry situation without a joke: 'Ich will nicht länger das Havannadeckblatt für Murtenchabis sein,' he told the press. ('Murtenchabis' is a Swiss tobacco.)

* * *

Anyone with an ear for Swiss local politics can imagine what the folk of Basle felt when they read of Dürrenmatt's next move: to take up an almost identical relationship with the director, Harry Buckwitz, at the Zurich Schauspielhaus, which incidentally led to another of Dürrenmatt's court cases when Dürrenmatt attacked the author Hans Habe, who had declared in May 1970 that Buckwitz had a 'Nazi past'. In 1972 Dürrenmatt was eventually pronounced guilty of libel and was fined 100 francs, but gained quite a few friends for his spirited defence. (The case can be followed in WA24, 212–22.)

After a visit to the USA to receive an honorary doctorate from Temple University in Philadelphia, Dürrenmatt's first venture in Zurich was a 're-version' of Goethe's *Urfaust*, première on 22 October 1970, 'ergänzt durch das Buch von Doktor Faustus aus dem Jahr 1589' – 1587? (now in WA13, 9–130). The text reads extraordinarily well, and one has the feeling – after all that has gone before – that Dürrenmatt at least sets out to restore a serious reputation by doing honour to the 'classics', instead of mocking them by parody. But the weight of the 'Bearbeitung' undoubtedly falls on the lust of an old man and the consequent spoiling of a young virginal woman – and both subjects were much in the public's mind at that time. Since Faust was played by the eighty-year-old Attila Hörbiger, and consequently there was no 'rejuven-ation' scene, Mephistopheles' quotation from the *Volksbuch* in Scene 8, that Faust now felt the desire 'eine unschuldige Jungfrau zu verführen und an Leib und Seele zu verderben' (54), met with hostile public reaction. This had really commenced with the first scene where Faust is philosophically preparing to dissect Mephisto on an operating table. Mephisto suddenly rises and introduces himself: 'Mephistopheles.' 'Faust (*ergreift die entgegengestreckte Hand*): Faust.' (25)!

The press criticisms did seem to agree with Heinrich Goertz's summing-up of the production: 'Friedrich Dürrenmatt nutzt jede Gelegenheit, uns das Gewalttätige, Satanische, Sadistische im Menschen vorzuführen. Das ist der Sinn auch seines *Urfaust*' (C18, 99).[15] But was there more to it than that? Certainly, one could claim that Faust is one of the 'great individuals', yet there is little trace of the 'humanity' which Dürrenmatt had been trying to incorporate in his 'flawed heroes'. Faust seems to be single-mindedly selfish, anxious for gratification only and sparing of thoughts for either his equals or his 'victims'. Perhaps we are to feel sorry for Gretgen *as* a victim – but there does not seem to be enough artistic motivation for that – and here Jan Knopf might well be correct to say that 'Faust [ist] reduziert auf den . . . Erzeuger des verhängnisvollen Kindes' (C32, 151); in other words, Goethe's majestic philosophical concept is reduced to the level of a sex-novel with a touch of Grand Guignol.

* * *

Since 1961 Dürrenmatt had been working on a play which would combine the grotesque world of his paintings with the 'sci-fi' world of the planets and stars which he spends long hours studying from his balcony in Neuchâtel. If not quite what Cornelius Schnauber calls him in his eulogistic foreword to *Play Dürrenmatt* (1983), 'one of the outstanding lay astronomers of our time' (B17, 5), he is certainly very knowledgeable on the subject. *Porträt eines Planeten* (originally Portrait . . .) is a work which has puzzled commentators since its appearance, and it certainly puzzled audiences at its performances after the première at the Zurich Schauspielhaus on 8 November 1970, although they applauded vociferously, much to the critics' displeasure. 'Dürrenmatts Debakel' screamed Hans Schwab-Felisch in *Theater Heute* for December 1970; 'En somme, le *Portrait d'une Planète* serait la preuve que les grands succès ne couronnent pas toujours les meilleures pièces' was a more sombre French–Swiss way of saying the same thing (*Gazette de Lausanne*, 28/29 November). When the play was revised – the 'Zürcher Fassung' – and given no fewer than three premières at the Schauspielhaus in Zurich, on 25, 26 and 27 March 1971, criticism was no less fierce: '*Das Porträt eines Planeten* bleibt unscharf, flächig und darum hoffnungslos', wrote Hans Heinz Holz in Basle's *National-Zeitung*.

Who were in the right: the audience who had paid for their seats and applauded, or the critics who had free seats but longer memories? It is hard to disagree, when one *reads* the text in WA12,

95–189, the so-called 'Zürcher Fassung', that it is a very unsatisfactory work indeed as a piece of literature. Dürrenmatt jumps on several bandwagons at once in what seems to be in retrospect a febrile attempt to keep up with the times. If this 'Übungsstück für Schauspieler' is really meant for 'Menschen, die sich noch nicht an die Situation gewöhnt hätten, in der sich die Menschheit befinde' (WA25, 157, his 'interview with himself'), and that 'nur gemeinsame Furcht helfe', then very few would be convinced by this strange piece. So what is the point of it all, all these very peculiar 'set-pieces' – a wounded soldier reciting a prayer, a black man and a white girl in a sort of South African apartheid-situation, a hippy colony with 'fixes' – and all to the accompaniment either of the then popular Peter Hacks-like repeated fractured linguistics, for example 'Das eineckige Gesicht der zweieckigen Erde frißt das dreieckige Loch des runden Kindes' (140), repeated with endless variations, or of the music of Schubert's alienated 'Der Wanderer an den Mond' ('Opus 80, Nummer 1'), a parody on the text's 'Romantic' *Welt- und Ich-Schmerz*:

> O glücklich, wer, wohin er geht,
> doch auf der Heimat Boden steht! (147–8)

What does it all add up to? In the first place, to what Dürrenmatt (according to him) was trying to do in his first period in Basle, namely to write plays for a 'Kollektiv' who would participate in all branches of the production. We see here, perhaps for the first time, what he has latterly attempted in the various versions of his latest play(s) *Achterloo* (I–IV) (below, 153ff.), to write 'role-changes', 'Rollenspiele', as 'Rollentherapie' where the actors are solely 'stereotypes', robot-like humans who with, as Bergson put it, 'du mécanique plaqué sur du vivant', mirror the absurd sides of Life and human nature – and are (as Dürrenmatt would certainly add) or *should be* (as I would say) 'comic'. The word 'banal' begins to creep more and more into critical vocabulary anent Dürrenmatt at this time, and is nowhere more deserved than here. The eight actors in the 'collective', four men and four women, who take on the various roles are playing out, in all their stereotypes, the end of our planet and the collapse of our civilisation 'as we know it' (the journalistic cliché is in place!) The 'action' is supervised, literally, by four men who introduce themselves – and take their leave in *Physiker*-fashion *ad spectatores* – from the very first line: '*Adam*: Ich bin der erste Gott' (97) via Kain and Abel to '*Henoch*: Ich bin der vierte Gott' on page 186. They watch the senseless, inhuman and base behaviour of the various groups as they squander the 'chances' that the Earth affords them. The four women, Eva, Ada, Zilla and Naema, often adopt the then alarmingly modish, feminist, Women's Lib attitude in their parts. All eight come forward towards the end of the 95-minute piece to scream out a psalm 'in höchster Verzweiflung, in unsinniger Hoffnung, daß Gott ihr Schicksal wenden möge' (182). If we do not destroy our Earth by our own mismanagement, the work seems to say, then it will be destroyed anyway by physical causes. The 'Schuld' which is to be 'avenged' here is the 'Urschuld', Man's disobedience of God's natural Law: Ada says as she dies, 'Der Sünder muß ein Ende werden auf Erden und die Gottlosen nicht mehr sein' (185). But if our planet does not perish for *that* reason then it will perish for physical reasons, and the amateur scientist Dürrenmatt tells us that the sun will go 'Hops!' and will spread itself through space on a supernova. Adam's last words as he rids himself and the stage of the human detritus are 'Hops ging sie ohnehin' (189).

The 'Nachwort zu Porträt eines Planeten' (WA12, 194–200) supplies Dürrenmatt's usual 'scientific' underpinning of his literary text. 'Die Wirklichkeit ist die Unwahrscheinlichkeit, die eintritt' is the Popperian beginning, whence the author develops the thesis that he is attempting to show on the stage 'das unermeßliche Feld menschlicher Konflikte' (195) which, Dürrenmatt grants, is easier to illustrate in the visual than in the dramatic arts – as he himself has done indeed. (The Charlotte Kerr film begins with Dürrenmatt's illustrations to and quotations from *Porträt eines Planeten*, accompanied by appropriate 'lunar' music.)

Although he admits that much of the dialogue must sound banal, Dürrenmatt defends his 'new' approach to drama by saying, 'Ich versuche dramaturgisch immer einfacher zu zeigen, immer sparsamer zu werden, immer mehr auszulassen, nur noch anzudeuten' (197), but the anti-Dürrenmatt critical 'mafia' were not convinced of the plausibility of his argument – and, in retrospect, neither am I. *Porträt* remains a banal and disappointing 'exercise for actors' – however valuable the 'message' may be for the world and its citizens. We shall see later that his real merits and talents as a writer were being displayed elsewhere at this time, which only underlined his general disillusionment with the stage and the theatre.

* * *

Porträt eines Planeten should have been produced in Basle, but the upset there in 1969 and Dürrenmatt's heart attack prevented the production, which was then taken over by Dürrenmatt's admirer, Karl-Heinz Stroux in Düsseldorf. Although *Porträt* could not be claimed as a success, Düsseldorf went ahead with another Dürrenmatt production, his version of one of Shakespeare's most bloodthirsty early plays, *Titus Andronicus* (1600), which not all critics accept as being from Shakespeare's own hand. The play is nevertheless celebrated, above all for the fourteen deaths and for the 'pie' which Titus, the Roman general, serves up to Tamora, the Queen of the Goths, and which contains the remains of her two sons, Chiron and Demetrius. In Shakespeare's *Titus Andronicus*, Saturninus, the Roman Emperor, says:

> Go fetch them [the two sons] hither to us presently.
> *Titus*: Why, there they are both, baked in that pie;
> Whereof their mother daintily hath fed,
> Eating the flesh that she herself hath bred. (V. iii. 59–62).

Dürrenmatt kept fairly close to the original text, but typically increased the death toll to twenty, recalling again that critical remark about the 'Leichenberge' at the end of most Dürrenmatt's plays. Those who knew of Dürrenmatt's penchant for good food and drink are reminded of his grotesque sense of humour, when he turned the 'pie' into a 'Fleischpastete' whose 'Soße' is declared 'unbeschreiblich' by the hapless mother, Tamora!

His reasons for choosing the text are given in the 'Materialien zu König Johann und Titus Andronicus' (WA11, 212–23) printed after the text (115–97) of the production in the Schauspielhaus in Düsseldorf on 12 December 1970. The main reason seems to have been that King John and the Titus 'original' Andronikos Komnenos I, the Eastern Roman Emperor 1183–5, were roughly contemporaneous, and the author was fascinated to make the 'connection' between their fates – both brought down by their 'inhumanity', in Dürrenmatt's eyes – and thus both 're-versions' are taken to be 'warnings' of the destruction of our mode of life. Shakespeare's *Titus* ends, despite all bestialities, with some 'optimism': Lucius, Titus's son, says, 'Then, afterwards, to order well the state/that like events may ne'er it ruinate' (V. iii. 203–4). But Dürrenmatt is much less certain. His Alarich, the Goth prince, concludes:

> Der Weltenball, er rollt dahin im Leeren
> Und stirbt so sinnlos, wie wir alle sterben:
> Was war, was ist, was sein wird, muß verderben (197).

Since the play was yet another 'Reinfall', a flop, Dürrenmatt's dark cast of mind was not to be wondered at; perhaps an illustration of something he says in *Rollenspiele*, that his psychological theory is logical, it leads to catastrophe!

* * *

No lighter was his next and, to date, last 're-version', *Büchners Woyzeck*, which had its première in the Zurich Schauspielhaus on 17 February 1972 and is now with the *Urfaust* (above, 138–9) in WA13, 131–89. Georg Büchner (1813–37) was, it may be remembered, one of Dürrenmatt's earliest literary inspirations; indeed, I have claimed (above, 7–10) that it was his acquaintance with Büchner's memorial in Zurich at Christmas 1942 which gave him the idea for his first story, 'Weihnacht' and decided him that he wanted to become a writer.

Woyzeck, which was not published until 1879, had by 1972 attained an almost legendary position in German culture. Büchner was widely regarded as having been a hundred years before his time. His cry, 'Friede den Hütten, Krieg den Palästen' in his *Hessischer Landbote* made that tract the first truly socialist paper of the nineteenth century, while his strongly fatalistic *Weltanschauung* gives the picture of one in the power of uncontrollable historical forces. He wrote to his fiancée in the spring of 1834, 'Ich fühlte mich wie zernichtet unter dem gräßlichen Fatalismus der Geschichte.' Bertolt Brecht saw Büchner as the greatest German dramatist – his *Baal* (1923) is a Woyzeck-like figure – while the composer Alban Berg's opera *Wozzeck* on the theme had its première in Berlin in 1925. As Margaret Jacobs tells us in her outstanding edition (B14), there are four different manuscript phases of the original, and Dürrenmatt's task – like that of all those who wish to make a 'Lese- und Bühnenfassung' – was to decide what to include and what to omit (cf. his 'Anmerkung', WA13, 193–4). He admits that press approval of the production was not 'sonderlich', but attributed that to his being more interested in the 'Dramaturgischen' than in the 'Theaterästhetischen', a comment that we have noted before.

Dürrenmatt eventually chose twenty-three scenes which do not end with Marie's murder and Woyzeck's drowning, as most versions do. Marie's death occurs in Bild 20. Bild 21 has Woyzeck throwing the knife into the pool. In Bild 22 he returns home to find his child dead in the arms of the 'Narr'. The last scene (Bild 23) is the Doktor's look at Marie's corpse: 'Ein guter Mord, ein echter Mord, ein schöner Mord (*steigt über die Leiche*) so schön als man ihn nur verlangen tun kann (*geht zufrieden nach rechts vorn*) wir haben schon lange so keinen gehabt (*Ab. Vorhang*)' (189). (This is the comment of the 'Gerichtsdiener' in the original.) For Dürrenmatt, Büchner's Woyzeck murders without meaning to, but because he *has to*. The key scene is where Woyzeck is shaving the Tambour-major and does not kill him, but rather goes on to kill Marie the prostitute: 'Er tötet jene, die von den Schuldigen ebenso miß-braucht wird wie er' (in *Rollenspiele*, A4, 112), for, as Margaret Jacobs writes, 'primitive justice is to be done in accordance with the voices rising from the earth' (B13, xxviii–xxix). We shall meet the character Woyzeck again later (cf. below, 154ff.).

* * *

Although his plays were still being produced throughout the world – *Die Physiker* in Vancouver in 1972, *Herkules* in Paris and London in the same year, *Porträt* in Yokohama – and the opera based on *Der Besuch der alten Dame* had been staged with some *éclat* at the Vienna State Opera on 23 May 1971, and in September in Zurich, Dürrenmatt's reputation in the theatre was beginning to decline. He still enjoyed an 'international reputation' in the literary field, but I am certain that he refused the offer of the Directorship of the Zurich Schauspielhaus in 1972 because he realised this, and turned away from the theatre to concentrate, or at least to concentrate more, on his essay work. (The congratulations of the Federal German Chancellor, Willy Brandt, on Dürrenmatt's fiftieth birth-day on 5 January 1971 compensated a little perhaps for the icy silence of the Swiss Government!) As he said to Charlotte Kerr after a discussion on the theatre, 'ich freu' mich dann wieder auf Prosa. Das ist dann ganz deins, etwas, was [*sic*] du allein verwirkli-chen kannst' (*Rollenspiele*, A4, 68).

But playwriting is a major element of Dürrenmatt's intellectual make-up, and even then he was already engaged in the writing of a new play – or rather, in keeping with his practice of these years, he had returned to an old motif. I have discussed the motif many times already – *Der Turmbau zu Babel* (1948), *Ein Engel kommt nach Babylon* (1953/1957), the 1977 opera on the same subject, and, of course, in Chapter 5 above (82–4), I treated the story 'Smithy' (and its genesis) which appeared in the 1976 book *Der Mitmacher. Ein Komplex*, whose *raison d'être* will shortly become apparent (now in WA14).

That stinking hot day in Manhattan on 3 May 1959, during Dürrenmatt's very first visit to the United States, a day spent wandering through the maze of narrow, sweating streets, the sun blanketed by the immense skyscrapers on both sides, traffic bumper-to-bumper in the surprisingly narrow streets, steam oozing through the manhole covers, every known accent on every side – this was Dürrenmatt's 'labyrinth' where, with very imperfect English, he lost himself and his individuality, to regain it in the story of Smithy who then became Doc in the play *Der Mitmacher*. The story, 'eine abenteuerliche Prosaarbeit', is told in the bizarre 'Nachwort zum Nachwort' to the play, it will be remembered (cf. *Der Mitmacher. Ein Komplex*, WA14, 223–328), along with many animadversions and digressive philosophical (or sometimes pseudo-philosophical) passages which I shall consider in more detail in Chapter 7.

For the moment, my concern is with the play, one of Dürrenmatt's biggest failures. The seeds of the failure of the play on the Zurich stage lay in the choice of the Polish film director Andrzej Wajda. He had produced *Play Strindberg* brilliantly in Warsaw, but he laboured under two major disadvantages: firstly, most of his work had been in the cinema; and secondly, his knowledge of German was, to say the least, imperfect. For both reasons perhaps, he saw the play as a *scenic* rather than as a *textual* challenge and paid most attention to the setting and the technical details. Dürrenmatt, who by this time had had great experience in the technicalities of a stage production after his long partnership with people like the great set-designer Teo Otto, was not hesitant to offer his co-operation; indeed the 'Nachwort' (95–222) begins with a discussion of these very ideas – how to construct a 'technische Vulva', for example! (Hermann Goertz was not the only critic who felt that Dürrenmatt was committing in these long 'postludes' the sin which he always attributed to his own critics, namely 'sie überinterpretierten ihn, das betreibt er an dieser Stelle selbst' (C18, 112). One should realise that to ninety-three pages of text there are twenty-three pages of 'self-interpretation' and in addition, he wrote yet another *apologia*, his 'Dramaturgie eines Durchfalls' (1976) (now in WA24, 231–49).)

The play suffers, however, from the fault which we have noted time and time again – a good basic idea is allowed to wander, to be side-tracked, eventually to be lost in myriad small details. *Der Mitmacher. Eine Komödie*, written in 1972–3, had its première eventually in the Zurich Schauspielhaus on 8 March 1973; Wajda had left the production in high dudgeon at Dürrenmatt's interference and Dürrenmatt himself had to take over the direction three days before the première. Although German(ic) reception was, and has remained, unfavourable, the play was produced with some success in Warsaw in 1973, in Athens in 1974 and in Genoa in 1977. Dürrenmatt revised the text slightly in 1980, and it is now in WA14, 11–93.

Doc is a failed scientist, abandoned by his wife. After a spell as a taxi-driver he falls into the hands of the New York gangland and is 'persuaded' to misuse his scientific knowledge to invent a 'Nekro-dialysator', a machine which can dissolve corpses supplied by Boss, the gang chief – but also by the 'other side', Cop, the police chief! Bill, Doc's 'unacknowledged' son, is a popular agitator out to murder, if possible, the US President. Ann, a 'hooker', falls in love with Doc, although she is really Boss's 'moll'. Finally, there is Jack, 'eine Nebenfigur des Stückes' (171), who in the book version became the Schwitter-like artist-figure, disgusted with the world's chicaneries.

For Dürrenmatt, 'der eigentlich negative Mitmacher in seiner bedenklichsten Form [ist] der Intellektuelle, der trotzdem mit-macht' (107). Out of fear, but also for profit of course, Doc 'goes along' with both sides and has to sacrifice, like Möbius, his love as well. The 'positive Mitmacher' is Cop, the police chief, who has much to say about 'justice'. He has infiltrated the gangster organ-isation and thus becomes the 'Nicht-Mehr-Mitmacher'. In his long speech before his death, Cop presents the Dürrenmattian phil-osophy again: 'daß ich, ein verkrüppelter Trottel, ein verrotteter Polyp, bevor ich zur Hölle segle, der einzige Schuldige bin, aus dem einfachen Grunde, weil ich als einziger in einer Welt, der die Gerechtigkeit gestohlen werden kann, die Gerechtigkeit suchte, als ob sie nicht die Sache aller, sondern eines Einzelnen wäre' (77).

This character, Cop, sullied but aware of what is right, Dürrenmatt then relates later to his 'dream characters' (the Henker, Romulus, Bodo, Akki, Titus), characters 'in denen immer wieder ein Motiv auftaucht, unerbittlich, ein einziges bloß, die Möglichkeit, an die ich glaube, an die ich mich anklammere, die Möglichkeit, ganz ein Einzelner zu werden, die Möglichkeit der Freiheit', which we shall take to be Dürrenmatt's central statement (in the 'Nach-wort', 208). Thus, we are back *mutatis mutandis* with the 'mutigen Menschen', a 'negative hero' who, a 'positiver Mitmacher', never-theless suffers the slings and arrows of Fate and Chance to restore the ailing world-order. Certainly, few spectators divined this piece of philosophy when their attention was taken up with the aural horrors of a gurgling corpse-dissolving machine in the basement, five storeys down a New York tenement, reachable only by one lift, while above murder after murder takes place in a sweating, stinking New York till, at the end, only Doc, kicked and beaten up

by his putative murderers, is left alive to bear his 'intellectual' guilt
for having 'mitgemacht'. Death, the play seems to say, is the only
honourable way out of the impasse: as Cop says, 'Wer stirbt, macht
nicht mehr mit' (90). We are reminded of Böckmann's death-scene
in *Frank V* which Dürrenmatt has always considered his own best,
and favourite, scene: 'Wer verliert, gewinnt seine Freiheit.' We
shall see in our later discussion of the *Komplex* how Dürrenmatt
attempts to read into his own play, and through the character of
Cop ('ein Rebell'), a general attack on totalitarian states and their
treatment of dissidents – a rather far-fetched 'Zusammenhang'.

Qua play, however, *Der Mitmacher* joins a melancholy gallery of
Dürrenmattian flops. Gerhard Knapp suggests that Dürrenmatt,
and others of his generation, was still writing 'absurd drama' when
the mode was long since past. That is a doubtful thesis when one
thinks of the films and television shows which still depend on the
'absurd' as their model. No, *Der Mitmacher*, with its many 'unintegrated' elements, its 'horror-film' décor, its weird, almost incomprehensible plot, its at times impossible German–American
dialogue is, simply, a bad play.

In the 'Dramaturgie eines Durchfalls' (in WA24, 231–49),
written in 1976 with the *Komplex*, Dürrenmatt describes rather
pitifully his feelings at being excluded from the Schauspielhaus in
1973 twenty-six (although Dürrenmatt writes 'zwanzig') years
after his first production there: 'Doch indem ich mich nicht vom
Ort zu lösen vermochte, wo ich einst etwas bedeutet hatte, wurde
ich ein Gespenst, und so trat der seltene Fall ein, daß einer an
seinem Begräbnis nicht nur passiv, sondern auch aktiv mitmachte'
(234). If, as remarked above, he was already beginning to despair of
the theatre, this 'Müdigkeit, das Gefühl des Sinnlosen, das über
mich hereinfällt, der Zeitverschwendung, des Schreibens in Sand,
über den man nun stampft' (249) could only accentuate the despair.

The Plays from 1974 to 1988

There will be much to be said later about Dürrenmatt's political
activities in the years 1973–7, the years of his fairly individual
support for Israel against its various Arab neighbours which culmi-
nated, one might say, in his long essay *Zusammenhänge: Essay über
Israel* (1974–6)) after he had been awarded the Honorary Fellowship
of the Ben-Gurion University in Beersheba in 1974. Without
wishing to anticipate that discussion, it might be suggested here
that his whole-hearted support of a small state – 'als Kleinstaatler

bin ich nun einmal für Kleinstaaten' (*Zusammenhänge*, WA29, 19) – against greater odds was not incompatible with many of his earlier statements, some of which have been cited already.

These activities, and a fairly serious illness in 1975 which he describes in WA15, (135–47), led to a rather fallow literary period by Dürrenmatt's standards. It was 1976 before published work again appeared. On 6 October 1977, his next play, *Die Frist. Eine Komödie*, had its première in the Corso Cinema in Zurich, the Schauspielhaus being under reconstruction. The text is now in WA15, 9–131 and is accompanied by an essay, 'Wie Die Frist entstand' (135–47), which was written (in one night, the author insists) for the programme of the première.

As had become his unfortunate wont, this essay too became an *apologia pro operibus suis*. We read how Dürrenmatt was taken into hospital in Berne with 'nur zu gut bekannten Schmerzen' on 12 October 1975 – into the very room in which his mother-in-law had died! He returned home too soon, and was taken back into hospital, 'am 29. November, neun Tage nach dem Tode Francos' (136), where he had to lie until the next summer. Then he released himself one afternoon from hospital to wander about the 'labyrinth' of Berne, visiting the university, the artists' quarter, sex-films ('L'histoire d'O'!) to find, on returning towards five p.m., that the idea for a new play had arrived. *Die Frist* was and is, in essence, a protest against his body's failings, against his thirty-year battle with illness, but also 'Was mich faszinierte, war die Assoziation zwischen gewissen Aspekten der modernen Medizin und einem Konzentrationslager' (141). In other words, all the efforts that doctors make to keep us alive are like the tests which concentration camp doctors made on unwilling victims to gauge the limits of their resistance – hardly a generous tribute to the many doctors who had attended him!

Dürrenmatt's first plot concerned an ailing dictator, the 'Generalissimus' (Generalissimo Franco had died on 20 November 1975), operated on by one of his former concentration camp inmates without anaesthetics as the inmate had been operated on in the camp – the theme of *Der Verdacht*, it will be remembered. The second and final plot, however, introduced a Jewish doctor, Goldbaum, who was entreated to keep the dictator alive for three (3, 5, 6?) weeks – 'Die Frist' means the 'waiting period' – so that the succession would be a natural one, 'Damit jene, die sich an der Macht gemästet haben, weiter an der Macht bleiben können' (65). Now Goldbaum must operate on the dictator without anaesthetics – these would have killed him – while two of the dictator's doctors turn out to be the Nazi doctors who operated on Goldbaum in the camp. Finally, Goldbaum, a human rights activist, is elected President. 'Zu menschlich für diese Welt, werden Sie in die Unmenschlichkeit gestoßen' (125), says Exzellenz, the *éminence grise*, before *he* dies.

In '*Wie Die Frist entstand*', Dürrenmatt relates how he used his own drawing of Atlas 'unter der Weltkugel keuchend' as a model to construct the image of a dying Atlas, the dying dictator, who could no longer bear the weight of the old world (cf. Dürrenmatt's drawings in A8, Nos. 23, 91, 92 and 100). This 'old world' is that world of 'sabre-rattling', of Romulus's Rome, Nebuchadnezzar's Babylon, the Switzerland of the 'Old Guard' that Dürrenmatt so castigated in the early post-war years. But the 'new world' is not much better: albeit 'eine humane Vision', communism has now hardened, Marxism is now as institutionalised as Christianity (143). The *éminence grise* behind the dictator, Exzellenz, is a logical intellectual, a mathematician fascinated by prime numbers, the 'Sinnbild einer absolut logisch aufgebauten Welt' (143). While the dictator, attended by thirty doctors (Franco had fifty!) lies audibly and unpleasantly groaning as he is 'kept alive' by the Jew Goldbaum, television cameras relay the European Cup Final between Leeds United and the local team, which then becomes the 'running gag' of the play, of comedy, Bergson's 'diable à ressort'.[16]

An extraordinary cast promenades about the stage, including 'Die Unsterblichen', nine feminist, man-hating centenarians all with names deriving from their leader Rosa – Rosarosa, Rosablanca, Rosanegra, Rosabella, Rosalaura, Rosaflora, Rosaberta and Rosagrande. – Dürrenmatt relates their existence back to that sex-film experience in Berne mentioned above, 'die Frau als glückliches Opfer der männlichen Sexualität', but now they are turned into 'rächende[s] Ungeheuer'. As the 'Mächtigen' perish, Rosagrande ends the play with a Faust-like monologue:

> Was nicht mehr ist, war nur Ereignis,
> Was nicht mehr wird, allein ein Gleichnis,
> Das Weibliche, es hat zum Ziele
> Die Ewigkeit und das Sterile (131).

Although the audience might have dimly perceived what the author was trying to describe – the inhumanity of dictatorships, the growing power of women in the world to prevent men using them as 'Opfer' and, in Goldbaum, the Jewish fight for recognition based in part on its sufferings in the past – the plot was, once again, too diffuse and unclear for any really clear perception to emerge. Both press and public berated it. Martin Esslin, however, once Head of BBC Drama, called it a 'late masterpiece' (D15, 152), and Renate Usmiani's seven-page defence finds the 'Personen der *Frist* [als] echte glaubwürdige Lebewesen', to me an extraordinary statement (E45, 158). I find them inflated and unbelievable, and I long for the day when Dürrenmatt returns to what I believe he does best: a play of taut construction, with few characters and a simple but strong plot representing a strongly-held philosophical belief. The baroque-like tragicomedies, albeit with their new staccato, sparse dialogue, are simply too confusing for modern audiences and readers.

* * *

Apart from the general remarks on his distaste for contemporary theatre which are found scattered throughout his essays, interviews and conversations, such as in *Rollenspiele* and the 1984 film, it is fairly difficult to document with certainty some of the impressions voiced above. Dürrenmatt's decision to turn back to one of his own established 'classic' plots, to *Die Panne*, for his next stage production seems to me, however, substantial proof that he was well aware that, if he were ever to have another theatrical success, the production was going to have to be 'helped' in some way, by the inclusion of a major 'star', or an outstanding stage set – or a plot already popular with the public. We have considered two versions of *Die Panne* already, the radio-play (above, 69) and the *Erzählung* (above, 49), and now comes the *Komödie* (in WA16, 57–173). It had its première on 13 September 1979 in the Komödienhaus, Wilhelms-bad/Hanau, near Frankfurt in the Federal Republic, played by Egon Karter's touring theatre. Karl-Heinz Stroux played the old Richter and Peer Schmidt Traps. They introduced themselves in Brechtian fashion before a flashback to Traps' arrival and the subsequent 'game'. Dürrenmatt directed the production himself. (A Paris première under Oscar Fessler was given in September 1984.)

I had become convinced by this time, 1979–80, that the 'real' Dürrenmatt was to be found – and perhaps should *always* have been found – in the comments that he made in prose on his works, his 'philosophy' and his life. 'Theater ist bloß Theater,' he said to me in 1988 – and his goal, always 'möglichst gutes Theater zu machen', has meant that his ideas, his *Weltanschauung*, have frequently been distorted by his often misguided attempts to provide a 'good evening in the theatre'.

So too with this *Komödie*-version of a favourite theme. The text is prefaced by six pages of comment on *Bühne, Inszenierung, Charaktere, Stück* which are much more revealing than the 106 pages of text! The stage, for example, is to be divided into two, an 'Innenraum' which, seen through the special curtain, will appear 'undeutlich verwaschen, schemenhaft', and 'Draußen', in front of the curtain, 'eine warme Sommernacht' (61). The lighting will achieve these effects as it illuminates or darkens the podium on which the inner action takes place.

The instructions for the *Inszenierung* (61–2) recall the drinking scenes in the two other versions of the plot. All are to become steadily more intoxicated, but on *red* wine, 'immer älteren Bordeaux', while the walls of the room are also in a Freudian red! The red wine, according to the wine connoisseur Dürrenmatt, makes the drinkers 'neigen . . . zur Akrobatik': they stand on chairs and on tables, and hang from chandeliers – in a word, they become Bergsonian 'clowns'. And the greatest clown here is Pilet, the executioner, 'der Henker', who tries to encourage the others to drink as much as he does. Alfredo Traps, alas and significantly, cannot take so much drink, and especially not the cognac on top of the Bordeaux. The *Charaktere* are therefore shown to be not normal but, literally and metaphorically, 'under an influence'. Traps is led on to boast of his relationship with Frau Gygax, but we are fairly sure that he is only boasting. Indeed he says, 'Die stinkfeine Dame behandelte mich wie einen Hund' (155). Still, he is proud to be accused of a crime which makes something special of him. The play itself (*Zum Stück*) is to be treated as a 'Schauprozeß' (Dürrenmatt's original stimulus, it may be remembered), where an innocent man is made to confess 'was es immer wieder gab und immer wieder geben wird' (63). Dürrenmatt admits the difficulty of transposition into other media: now he is faced not just with 'Sprache', as in the other media, but with 'Sprache plus Schauspieler plus Bühne' (64), and once again he allows his imagination free rein.

The by now well-known plot is enlarged to include a series of parodies. Firstly, there is a parody on stage convention. The play begins with Traps' grotesque funeral in the presence of a new character, Justine von Fuhr, the 35-year-old sex-mad granddaughter of Traps' host Wucht (q.v.) who acts in parodistic reality the role of Traps' imagined seducer, Frau Gygax. She becomes the 'galante Mordwaffe', who/which is to cause Traps' death. Secondly, there is a parody on Greek ancient tragedy. The four grotesque old men, now even more grotesquely named – Abraham Gotthold Luis Wucht (ninety years old), Isaak Joachim Friedrich

Zorn (eighty-nine), Jakob August Johann Kummer (eighty-seven) and Roland René Raimond Pilet (eighty-six) – don the masks of the Greek gods, sex-crazed Jupiter, bloodthirsty Mars, cannibalistic Saturn and brothel-keeping Venus, ironically to pronounce Man's sentence on the gods 'welche die Welt regieren' (166), who sent him into the world to suffer. So 'Das Spiel droht in die Wirklichkeit umzukippen', as we read in the *Erzählung* in WA20, 64. The judgement of men (the four) on Man (Traps) was a 'game'; now 'Reality' takes over and the four old men, three of whom bear the names of Old Testament patriarchs, pass parodistic judgement on the Greek gods by 'shooting' them out of the sky. 'Was war die heutige Nacht?' cries old Wucht. 'Ein übermütiger Herrenabend, nichts weiter, eine Parodie auf etwas, was [sic] es nicht gibt und worauf die Welt immer wieder hereinfällt, eine Parodie auf die Gerechtigkeit, auf die grausamste der fixen Ideen, in deren Namen der Mensch Menschen schlachtet' (164–5). This leads then to the third parody, the parody of a 'just death'. As in the other versions, Alfredo claims to have been the chance cause of Gygax's death and, in order to be recognised in life at least, he demands his death sentence. But the 'judges' have discovered that Gygax had, in reality, slept with Alfredo's wife. Thus, *he* is the guilty one, not Traps, and Traps is therefore pronounced innocent – and robbed of his glory. He therefore becomes a true Dürrenmattian character – absurd, laughable, ridiculous – but Dürrenmattian, too, in that he demands to take the guilt upon himself and to be declared morally, if not legally, guilty, that is, as Wucht says, 'durch die Welt, in der du lebst, verurteilt' (163).[17] And Wucht pronounces, 'In einer Welt, in der niemand mehr schuldig sein will, in der die schändlichsten Verbrechen begangen werden, weil sie angeblich entweder unvermeidbar sind, um das Weltgetriebe in Gang zu halten, oder notwendig, um die Veränderung dieses Weltgetriebes herbeizuführen . . . verdient einer, der sich schuldig spricht, belohnt und gefeiert zu werden' (160–1). And Alfredo's death at the end, his suicide, is also a parody.[18] The four drunk old men and Alfredo believe that they are 'shooting' the Greek gods out of the sky with blank cartridges, but Simone, the deaf housekeeper, had loaded the guns this time, and by pure chance, with real bullets. So Alfredo's death by shooting is a true 'accident', 'eine Panne'. 'Traps erleidet kein Schicksal, sondern eine Panne', writes the author in the foreword (65); one could add 'kein griechisches Schicksal', rather 'eine moderne Panne'. The wheel has turned full circle to the 'Theaterprobleme' of 1954–5: 'In der Wurstelei unseres Jahrhunderts . . . gibt es keine Schuldigen, und auch keine Verantwortlichen mehr . . .

Schuld gibt es nur noch als persönliche Leistung, als religiöse Tat' (above, 112).

It is quite difficult to pass an artistic judgement on this new version. When I saw the Berlin production in 1980 it was certainly well received by the audience, but I felt once again that the extra machinery needed to make an 'abendfüllendes Drama' detracted from the powerful effect of the original, brilliant 'Einfall'.

* * *

In his 'Sätze' (formerly 'Gedanken') 'über das Theater' (1970), Dürrenmatt tells the moving story of a car accident in which he was involved in May 1959 to illustrate how many chance events must occur before such an accident can take place. He sums up the incident, 'Die Wirklichkeit ist die Unwahrscheinlichkeit, die eingetreten ist' (WA24, 205), and repeated the remark, with a change of tense, as the first sentence of the 'Nachwort zu Porträt eines Planeten' (WA12, 194) (above, 141).

He must therefore have been deeply moved by the truth of his own comment when his wife Lotti died on 16 January 1983, the 'schlimmstmögliche Wendung' of his own dramatic theory. They had been married for thirty-seven years, during which time she had nursed him through so many illnesses and shared so many triumphs and tragedies on which they could both look back. Dürrenmatt had already begun to 'look back' on his life and career, as I have noted. The *Werkausgabe*, his final thoughts – to date! – on his whole *oeuvre*, had been published in 1980 for his sixtieth birthday on 5 January, and in 1981 appeared his autobiographical *Stoffe I–III*. There had been a great 'Dürrenmatt-Symposium' in Los Angeles in April 1981, he had given two or three exhibitions of his paintings and sketches, and he had received honorary degrees from Neuchâtel and Zurich Universities to add to those from Philadelphia, Beersheba, Nice and Jerusalem in honour of his life's work.

Undaunted, it seemed, by his latest stage-failures and drawn on by this strange love–hate relationship with theatre, Dürrenmatt had started work on a new play written against the background of the political events in Poland on the night of 12–13 December 1981, the conflict between General Jaruzelski's government and the Free Trade Union Solidarność, led by Lech Wałesa. 'Es ist toll, daß der Kommunismus sich in Polen einer Politik bedient hat, die er als faschistisch ablehnte: des Bonapartismus', he says in *Rollenspiele* (40). This was the idea, the crux, of the new play *Achterloo*. It was begun in May 1982, originally called *Der Verräter* and dedicated to his late wife, 'die noch die erste Fassung lesen konnte' (A10).

It was after the Munich production of *Achterloo* (October 1983) – the première had been in the Zurich Schauspielhaus on 6 October 1983 – that Charlotte Kerr, a Munich journalist and film-maker, shortly after meeting Dürrenmatt had discussed the work with him and, when it too proved a failure, had helped him to rewrite it with the aid of a 'Protokoll einer fiktiven Inszenierung', later to be published with the text of the third version *Achterloo III* as *Rollenspiele* in 1986. (The couple were married on 8 May 1984.)

The play was conceived like so many others as 'Rollentherapie für Schauspieler'. The roles were not fixed, but were changeable and interchangeable. 'Theater ist Theater,' Dürrenmatt says again; and it is *never* reality, not even 'vorgetäuschte Wirklichkeit', as Brecht wanted. Thus, the theme seems to be the possible invasion of Poland by the Red Army to crush the Free Trade Union Solidarność's threat of a general strike, the erection then of a military dictatorship and the ensuing possibility of American involvement, which might well lead to the outbreak of the Third World War. Only later, in the first version, do we discover that the play is 'a play within a play': as in Peter Weiss's Charenton, the inmates of a mental home which Dürrenmatt calls 'Sankt Helena' are producing a 'spectacular' to reproduce the political reality outside. (The play is therefore set in 'Achterloo in Acherloo irgendwo bei Waterloo'.)[19] But who are the *dramatis personae*?

It transpires that the government is led by Napoleon Bonaparte (1769–1821) who 'represents' General Jaruzelski; the people ('das Volk') are represented by the downtrodden barber Woyzeck, Georg Büchner's character (who was actually executed in 1824); Jan Hus (1370–1414), the Protestant reformer, represents Lech Wałęsa the Solidarność leader; and Cardinal Richelieu (1585–1642) represents the Roman Catholic Primate of Poland, Cardinal Glemp – although this role was played by a woman, Maria Becker no less, at the première! There are five 'Karl Marxe' ('weil es heute verschiedene kommunistische Führer gibt'!) and a 'Lord Tony' (Snowdon?) who is, in effect, a 'porno' photographer. Thus, 'jede Figur von heute hat ihre Entsprechung in der Geschichte' (*Rollenspiele*, A4, 111).

The plot of the first version is the usual baroque farrago and must have been quite incomprehensible, one would have thought, even with a programme note. Charlotte Kerr says on the first page of *Rollenspiele*, 'Ich kenne den geschichtlichen Hintergrund nicht, wie soll ich die Assoziationen verstehen?' (11), but she also had to admit earlier that 'Das Publikum lacht, applaudiert wie verrückt', not the first time that audiences and critics were at odds after a Dürrenmatt première. There are, of course, reminiscences of the *Urmotive* and *Urstrukturen* from the past: the icy indifference of the 'Mächtigen' to the people (*Richelieu*: 'Nichts schadet der Menschheit mehr als Menschlichkeit' (A10, 35)); justice and grace (*Richelieu*: 'Der Mensch braucht Gerechtigkeit im Diesseits und Gnade im Jenseits' (37)), the one from the 'Party', the other from the church; treason to prevent bloodshed (*Napoleon*: 'Nur Verrat macht Politik noch möglich. Einem Verräter zuliebe löst man keine Weltkatastrophe aus' (80)); and many, many others.[20] The basic plot concept is that people in power can be represented by madmen; we do not realise that these characters *are* madmen in an asylum until far on in the play – page 119 of a 120-page text – a typical Dürrenmattian 'Einfall'.

Dürrenmatt, however, was not satisfied with that project. *Achterloo III* (now in *Rollenspiele*, 198–346) shows many changes as a result of the previous discussions with Frau Kerr (cf. 'Protokoll einer fiktiven Inszenierung', 7–153; 'Assoziationen mit einem dicken Filzstift' (Dürrenmatt's drawings to the text) (155–95); and his characteristic 'Zwischenwort' *before* the text (197–202)). In the latter, he makes mock of his 'scheinbar wirres Unterfangen' to write a *Komödie* on this Polish theme which introduces characters from divers epochs – and then, by the way as it were, introduces a completely new dramaturgical idea, namely that the Age of *Komödie* was now past too, like the Age of Tragedy: 'Nicht mehr die Komödie, nur noch die Posse kommt uns bei' (200). The asylum plot is the only metaphor left for this banal world. And he cites the old 'asylum'-joke: 'I'm writing a letter.' 'Who to?' 'Myself.' 'What's in it?' 'I won't know till I get it'! This mirrors our crazy modern world. 'Jetzt erhalten wir die Briefe, die wir uns selber schreiben' (200).

So we now have characters like those Russian *babushka* dolls, a succession of smaller characters within a larger. Each has a *Spielrolle* (for example, we have Napoleon Bonaparte, Benjamin Franklin and Joan of Arc), a *Wahnrolle* (they become Holofernes, Georg Büchner and Judith) and a *Person* (now they are a Professor, the 'Erbe einer Spanferkelkette and a 'Nazi-Enkelin'). This is all deduced from the Latin word *persona*, the actor's mask, which then became the role that the actor played *under* the mask and finally the role which the actor played in public, in reality – a motif which first saw the light of day in *Die Physiker*. 'Es sind immer Rollen hinter Rollen hinter Rollen', we read in *Rollenspiele* (107). Behind all this stands the figure of Georg Büchner (1813–37), author of *Woyzeck*, which, it will be remembered, Dürrenmatt had adapted for the Zurich stage in 1972, and who, Dürrenmatt claims, had set him on his career as a writer. 'Ohne Woyzeck wäre *Achterloo* nicht entstanden', he wrote, since *Achterloo* is to be considered as a continuation of *Woyzeck*. Indeed, Dürrenmatt's Büchner is presented on the stage as the 'author' of the play: 'Ich schreibe ein neues Stück *Achterloo. Das Stück spielt am 12. und 13. Dezember 1981. Ich spiele darin Benjamin Franklin*' (A4, 210), and Woyzeck has a role too.

It would probably take a book in itself to disentangle the ramifications of the 'plot'. I shall concentrate on the summing-up of the 'Author', Büchner. His interest is not in the 'Zweck der menschlichen Unternehmungen', but in their *causes*. Man is free or unfree, just or unjust – and these are all societal value-judgements. If we examine why men let themselves be influenced by these judgements, we find ourselves confronted by Man's basic nature: 'Darum habe ich *Achterloo* geschrieben, die komische Tragödie eines Aufstands, der unterblieb, weil ein Irrer vernünftig zu sein versuchte und einen Krieg vermied', which would have led to further causes and effects, all conditioned by Chance. And since no one in this madhouse-world will keep to the historical text, Büchner, 'unter Irren der einzige Vernünftige', declares, 'Ich werde von nun an nichts mehr schreiben' (337).

Nevertheless, Dürrenmatt himself *has* produced another play, *Achterloo IV*, which had its première during the Schwetzingen Festival in 1988. On 10 December 1988 the Munich paper, the *Abendzeitung*, carried a short paragraph on Dürrenmatt in which we read, 'Das moderne Weltbild paßt nicht mehr auf die Bühne . . . die heutigen Probleme sind mit dem Theater nicht mehr darstellbar', and the cutting is headed 'Dürrenmatt: Theater ist ohne Zukunft'. Maybe. But he told me in 1988 that he was deeply engaged on his next play, *Der Tod des Sokrates*, and he dilates on the subject in the 1984 film. It would seem to be a play in the old mould, anachronistically employing famous characters from the past to point up the continuing relevance of human stupidity.

Despite his many despairing remarks about his position as a writer and his honest and withering comments on his talent and his methods, I know that he still believes that his is a voice to be heard and to be listened to, a voice that is still there, as it was in 1952, 'um zu warnen'. He will do that by withdrawing from the world and meditating on what he considers modern philosophy has ignored: the discoveries of modern scientific experimentation, their aprioristic and empirical methods which, Dürrenmatt believes, he must now build into his own artistic work, his 'Pech, von der Prosa auf die Bühne und von der Bühne auf die Prose geworfen zu werden, bleibt mir treu' (interview with himself, WA25, 166). And he knows too, 'Wer einmal für die Bühne schrieb, wird immer für sie schreiben' (166).

−7−

The Essays

The Essays from 1947 to 1956

This last major chapter deals with the vast corpus of essays, speeches, criticism and theoretical pronouncements which Dürrenmatt has produced since *circa* 1947.[1] It would need a book twice the length of the present volume to deal with all of these in detail; I have therefore decided to concentrate on those which, in retrospect, seem to me either to have been most significant as an 'explanation' of Dürrenmatt's art, or to have been of particular importance as statements about his position in the intellectual community of the twentieth century. Most studies of Dürrenmatt have referred to these prose works, but more *en passant*, it seems to me, with reference to a particular literary work with which they were obviously connected. Of course I too shall make reference to the literary works conceived contemporaneously with the essays, speeches or whatever. All Dürrenmatt's art is, as we have seen, 'associative': A and B *do* 'connect', and we shall find those *Urmotive* and *Urstrukturen* here too, just as we shall find them in the next chapter on the art-works, for, as he has written about them, 'So stellt denn mein Malen und Zeichnen eine Ergänzung meiner Schriftstellerei dar – für alles, das [*sic*] ich nur bildnerisch ausdrücken kann' (WA26, 216). It is wise to recall that many of his essays, etc. were originally addresses and lectures to a public, thus also 'eine Ergänzung' to his imaginative creations.

It is possible, I believe, to divide Dürrenmatt's essayistic work into four definite phases. His earliest newspaper criticisms, and the essays on general literary and political phenomena which accompanied them, cover the years 1947–56 from *Es steht geschrieben* to *Der Besuch der alten Dame*. The second period saw him dealing with more specific phenomena as his own literary reputation grew and he felt both able and duty-bound to speak on major issues; that covered the years 1959–66, roughly from *Frank V* to *Der Meteor*. Then his growing interest in politics generally, and in the cold war and Middle East politics in particular, led him to a more polemic style when, without ever allowing himself to become a 'committed' writer, he attempted to have a voice on that stage; this period dates between about 1967 and 1975, the beginning of the run of unsuccessful plays. The last phase, 1976 to the present day, picks up many of the basic themes of earlier years as he begins to look back over his life and career and, with his remarriage in 1984, to taste a new life.

Most of the relevant texts are now gathered conveniently in five volumes of the dtb (detebe) edition of the *Werkausgabe* which I have chosen for my references, namely *Theater* (24), *Kritik* (25), *Literatur und Kunst* (26), *Philosophie und Naturwissenschaft* (27) and *Politik* (28). The latest essays are in *Stoffe I–III*, *Rollenspiele* and *Versuche* (q.v.).

Timo Tiusanen was not the only critic who found something 'paradoxical' in 'the whole concept' of 'Dürrenmatt as theoretician' (B22, 203). Dürrenmatt had certainly always inveighed loudly against the 'pedantic Germanist', the 'Theater-als-Doktordissertation'-attitude, and he still rejoices when he can write something that he knows will puzzle the literary world: as he did lately in *Rollenspiele* when, in answer to Charlotte Kerr's question about the reason for Woyzeck's appearance in the play *Achterloo*, Dürrenmatt says 'Um anzudeuten, in welcher Beziehung *Achterloo* in der Literatur steht, da haben die Germanisten Futter' (A4, 111)! But he would not be of Germanic stock if he did not enjoy theorising from time to time. As Elisabeth Brock-Sulzer wrote as the motto to her earlier edition of the *Theaterschriften- und Reden*, 'Wer sich nicht widerspricht, den wird man nie wieder lesen' (1966), and a good deal of Dürrenmatt's 'theorising' should be read with that motto in mind.

* * *

Although Dürrenmatt's concern for the humanity among whom he lived was expressed more strongly later, it first surfaced in his essay 'Zu den Teppichen von Angers' of May 1951 (WA26, 149–150) and in his 'Fingerübungen zur Gegenwart' of 1952 (31–2) both of which I have always regarded as *the* signs of the future internationally acclaimed author whose works clearly held more than regional appeal. The first essay mirrors the child-like faith which had created these works of art in Angers and which, like Dürrenmatt's own faith, had obviously been lost and not replaced in a world of material greed and environmental destruction. It is Dürer's and Bosch's 'wild' pictures which have become our 'reality' – and Dürrenmatt himself was to follow *their* pictorial path and example rather than attempt to regain 'das verlorene Paradies' of the Angers wall-hangings. The same youthful anger was evident in the second essay where Dürrenmatt lays down *his* gauntlet. 'To be a writer nowadays', he writes, 'is like running your head against a brick wall.' 'Meine Damen und Herren,' he continues, 'das tue ich leidenschaftlich gern, und ich bin der Meinung, daß Wände gerade dazu erfunden sind' (WA26, 31). The Angers piece and the little 1952 essay seem to me to sum up the essence even of the later Dürrenmatt. 'Ich bin ein Protestant, und ich protestiere', he writes in 1952, and finishes with the warning which was quoted earlier – that the pilot (the writer) will be needed when the cliffs (the foreseen dangers) heave into sight (above, 117).

From protesting about the world situation, Dürrenmatt began to protest about the state of his own craft of letters. The criticisms which he wrote, mainly for the Berne *Nation* and the Zurich *Weltwoche*, appeared between May 1947 and June 1952 and touch on many of the issues which he was later to develop, firstly in his theoretical writings in this first phase and later in his own theatrical works.

Dürrenmatt was critical from the first about German(ic) stage presentations. 'Die besondere Neigung der Deutschen, pathetisch und sentimental zugleich zu sein' was what he most disliked about the 1951–2 *Die Räuber* of Schiller in Zurich (WA25, 43). '[D]ie heimtückische Gefahr des unfreiwillig Komischen' was his witty and perceptive summing-up of a Swiss audience's greatest problem with their 'Nationaldrama', Schiller's *Wilhelm Tell*, in January 1952 (WA25, 67). All his criticism stresses the importance of taking theatre *as* theatre, there must be no false premises, no hypocritical unthinking worshipping of 'the classics' – and, above all, there must be *humour*, no 'Bierernst', no unwarranted 'Tiefsinn'. (Sartre's *Der Teufel und der liebe Gott* in German translation was sharply attacked for being 'philosophy' and not 'theatre' (WA25, 52–4).)

As Dürrenmatt then began to write for the theatre himself, the 'poacher' turned 'gamekeeper'. He had himself to observe the 'rules' that he had drawn up, for after his first early experience with the theatre he wrote a series of theoretical essays which, one must say, have remained the basis of his theatrical philosophy. In my earlier book, I tried to develop the thesis that Dürrenmatt was indeed what many people besides Siegfried Melchinger have called him, a 'Helvetic Aristophanes', and tried to show how his *Komödien*-technique derived from the 'grotesque' wit of the fifth-century Greek. Some critics have disagreed, of course, but I remain convinced that Dürrenmatt's early confession of a kinship with Aristophanes – he called himself one of the Greek's willing 'Lanzknechte' in the Zurich Schauspielhaus programme for 1953–4 – remained one of his abiding truths. This kinship is seen most clearly in the two essays on the *Komödie* in the Zurich *Weltwoche*: 'Anmerkung zur Komödie' on 22 February 1952 (now in WA24, 20–5) and 'Die alte Wiener Volkskomödie' on 2 April 1953 (now in WA24, 26–30). Both of these lead to the lengthy and important 'Theaterprobleme' of 1954–55. Dürrenmatt began to use the term *Komödie* for his plays from *Romulus der Große* on, and it is plain to see from these essays that he did this because of what he had found in these earlier models. In the first essay, Dürrenmatt points out that Aristophanes' comedies play in the present, whereas the great Greek tragedies tell of past myths: 'Diese Komödien sind Eingriffe in die Wirklichkeit', he writes (21), 'so real, so aktuell', that Socrates was arguably done to death because of the ridicule first heaped upon him in Aristophanes' play *The Clouds*. These are political comedies which treat themes of the day in a coarse and grotesque fashion. For that reason, they are 'Komödien als Ausdruck einer letzten geistigen Freiheit' (23), and are what Dürrenmatt ever after claimed that he himself was writing, namely 'Gleichnisse der menschlichen Situation' (23). It is in this essay that Dürrenmatt first deals with the theme which was then to produce most of the early articles and doctoral dissertations on him: the grotesque. He points out here that there are two types of 'grotesque': a 'romanticising' grotesque which awakens 'Furcht oder absonderliche Gefühle' (as in *Hamlet*); and a 'distancing' grotesque which allows the author to treat serious, everyday themes without making tragedies of them – we are still too near them for that. (He cites the Second World War as such a theme.) 'Diese Kunst will nicht mitleiden wie die Tragödie, sie will darstellen' (25). And with the grotesque comes the cruelty of objectivity, the art of the moralist, salty wit and intellectual acuity. This art is 'unbequem, aber nötig' (25).

This was the grotesque observed in the obscene, cavorting 'Tanz auf dem Dach'-scene in *Es steht geschrieben* in 1947, which distanced the audience in more senses than one, and the 'Grausamkeit der Objektivität' which made *Der Blinde* such a cold, cruel play. But by the time that he wrote these essays, Dürrenmatt had found a new style – the witty, epigrammatic yet sharp tone first struck in *Romulus der Große* in 1949 – and the combination of the old and the new styles is best seen in his musing essay on the 'Alte Wiener Volkskomödie'. This, felt Dürrenmatt, was a theatre relevant to its age and to its public. The essay is, in essence, a review of Otto Rommel's marvellous *Die Alt-Wiener Volkskomödie* (1953), and it celebrates one type of character above all, the one who 'zwar immer Pech hat, aber immer gerade noch einmal davonkommt' (27), Brecht's 'verprügelter Held' and the 'anti-hero' whom Walter Starkie had so christened in his 1926 book on Pirandello. (It was also no coincidence that Thornton Wilder's *By the skin of our teeth* (German: *Wir sind noch einmal davongekommen*) had been playing in Germany since 1947.) Dürrenmatt was to take over the type and make out of it his 'mutiger Mensch', albeit with some 'adjustments'. Again in this essay, the author stresses how important it is for theatre to be relevant, 'Wie bei Aristophanes die Athener, sahen sich die Wiener in der Komödie wieder' (29), and not only relevant, but humorously so: 'es ist nicht immer gut, wenn die Dichter gezwungen werden, tief zu sein' (29). (It is an interesting thought that in 1989 Dürrenmatt, having eschewed 'Tiefsinn' throughout his career, has now had to present himself as a 'Denker', perhaps in order to retrieve his somewhat battered reputation as a dramatist!)

All these thoughts, and his experience of having written five plays, were the foundation for Dürrenmatt's most successful lecture-essay, 'Theaterprobleme' (in WA24, 31–72), the essay for which he is deservedly famed, and which is often cited as a seminal work for and on the theatre of the twentieth century. It is, of course, also often taken as Dürrenmatt's last and final word on dramaturgical theory, just as he is often still represented in histories of literature as the 'author of *Der Besuch der alten Dame*'. I hope that this chapter will show, if nothing else, that both statements are far from the whole truth.

It is perhaps unnecessary to deal with 'Theaterprobleme' here in great detail since I have already mentioned its major points in several of the earlier chapters, and in my previous book. It need only be noted here how the major *Urthemen*, of the 'Death of Tragedy', the 'grotesque' and the 'anti-hero', Dürrenmatt's 'mutiger Mensch' and others, grow out of the earlier essays towards their practical apogee in his masterpiece, the *Alte Dame*. The essay finished, readers will recall, with the rather off-hand remark that perhaps writers should only write 'Trivialliteratur': 'Die Literatur muß so leicht werden, daß sie auf der Waage der heutigen Literaturkritik nichts mehr wiegt: nur so wird sie wieder gewichtig' (72) – a provocative remark which was directed against the 'Tiefsinn' required of all Germanic authors by their local critics, but which, as we saw in Chapter 3, has turned out to be quite prophetic in that this 'Trivialliteratur' has now become an academically recognised genre.

The thought was repeated in 'Schriftsteller als Beruf', a talk given on Radio Bern on 25 April 1956 and enlarged in April 1965 into an essay (now in WA26, 54–9). Speaking of course to a 'native' audience, Dürrenmatt wittily deplored the Swiss public's attitude to writers: 'Die Künstler sind nun einmal in der Schweiz immer noch etwas Dubioses, Lebensuntüchtiges und Trinkgeldbedürftiges, wohnhaft in jenem stillen Kämmerlein, das bei jeder offiziellen Dichterehrung vorkommt' (55). He had, of course, already pictured just such a writer, firstly the 'Schriftsteller' in *Der Richter und sein Henker* and then Fortschig, the writer in *Der Verdacht*, both withering critics of Swiss complacency and earnestness. 'Der Schweizer verträgt an sich in dem, was er treibt, keinen Spaß', Dürrenmatt writes here. 'Die Musen haben bei ihm nichts zu lachen' (55). So he pleads in this talk/essay for the author to be given freedom and respect, reminding his audience that a Swiss author has no chance anyway of living off Switzerland, 'die Schweiz ist zwar sein Arbeitsplatz, doch nicht sein Absatzgebiet' (58), and we have noted Dürrenmatt's early dependence on the Federal German radio stations. Such practical considerations have been more important to Dürrenmatt than he at times concedes; certainly only the enormous success of the *Alte Dame*, in particular, freed him from the financial constraints which he so graphically describes here – although he never seems to be sure whether or not he is the happier for that!

The writer's role in this uncertain world was perhaps best summed up in the essay 'Vom Sinn der Dichtung in unserer Zeit', a lecture held at a conference of the Evangelische Akademie für Rundfunk und Fernsehen in Munich in September 1956 (the essay is now in WA26, 60–9). Dürrenmatt began with his favourite lecturing ploy, to deny that he was entitled to talk about what he was going to talk about: 'Ich lehne es deshalb ab, als Denker aufzutreten' (60). He then proceeded to hold a philosophical discourse on the relationship between physics and mathematics. It does not do to underestimate Dürrenmatt's competence in these fields, and I am certainly not in a position to do so, but all his writings on these subjects, and they are many, smack somewhat of the autodidact, of the reference book and the helpful pre-lecture discussion with an 'authority' – like his 'nächtliches Telefongespräch' with Professor Jost of Zurich before his lecture on Albert Einstein (cf. below, 198). The burden of this lecture, however, is a theme which in one way or another has occupied him for nearly forty years. It is what he describes in *Stoffe I–III* as the 'Gesetz der großen Zahl', Rudolf Kassner's 'Zahlenwesen', which is the theme of Kassner's book *Zahl und Gesicht* and which Dürrenmatt clearly takes to be one of the most important scientific works of this century. It is a work which combines physics and aesthetics, science and literature, in a way not unknown to British readers from the essays of C.P. Snow.

Dürrenmatt had visited Kassner in Valais in 1950, and in this essay he uses Kassner's concept to show how uncertain Mankind had become in the new immensity of the universe: 'Der Mensch sieht sich immer gewaltiger von Dingen umstellt, die er zwar handhabt, aber nicht mehr begreift' (63); he seems to have become a 'Spielball der Mächte' (64) – we are with Camus again where 'l'homme se sent un étranger' (cf. above, 112). From this picture of a humanity bereft of explanation of its surroundings, Dürrenmatt turns to the writer who will be called upon to *try* to explain the universe. He cites three media to be called upon, film, radio and theatre, each with its own possibilities of representing the world. But the greatest difficulty for the author in any medium nowadays is that he has to replace the religion which has been lost – and he himself is therefore often seen as a substitute prophet. How does the writer come to terms with this task? Dürrenmatt's rather confused thought here produces his by this time well-known formula: 'Die Chance liegt allein noch beim Einzelnen. Der Einzelne hat die Welt zu bestehen' (67). The writer must give up any grandiose ideas of 'saving the world', he must simply present a '*Bild* unserer Welt'. He will best do this just by being a 'worker' like any other, and by either 'thinking' about the world, as Science presents it to us, or creating a new world of the imagination, as the artist does, he will either 'denken' or 'sehen'. Science presents us with a unity of ideas about the world, Art its multitudinous problems. All that Mankind can do therefore is – hold on! One would have thought that his listeners of 1956, surrounded on all sides by 'solutions' to Life's problems of more or less practicality, would have found this neither a very enlightening nor a very exhilarating conclusion. It was, however, a note of sceptical resignation which Dürrenmatt was to strike frequently from 1956 on.

The Essays from 1957 to 1966

Although by the beginning of what we have termed Dürrenmatt's 'second phase' he was a famous, established international author, two of his favourite conversational ploys were still to be heard, namely that he 'made' literature and did not 'discuss' it, and that he wrote to maintain his family and not to create 'art'. In a lecture for a reading in Munich in 1959, for example 'Vom Schreiben', (WA26,

74–81), he said, 'Als Schriftsteller mache ich zwar Literatur, aber kenne mich immer weniger darin aus' (75) and later, 'Ich schreibe, um mich und meine Familie durchzubringen' (76), which, he claims, would be a respectable answer to the eternal question: 'Warum eigentlich schreibst du?'

Nevertheless, this period saw Dürrenmatt pronounce on a wide number of topics which could fairly be included under the rubric of 'Literaturwissenschaft', the most important of which were undoubtedly his comments on one of the two great obstacles for all post-classic authors writing in German, Friedrich Schiller (1759–1805). We have already noted Dürrenmatt's distaste for an uncritical worshipping of 'the classics', represented for him by Professor Emil Staiger of Zurich, and a Swiss writer's particular worries about the acceptance of *Wilhelm Tell* (cf. above, 160). He was therefore very agreeably surprised to be awarded the bicentennial *Schillerpreis* in the Nationaltheater in Mannheim on 9 November 1959. His acceptance address (now in WA26, 82–102) turned out to be on a par with the interest and importance of his 'Theaterprobleme', largely because of his clever juxtaposition of the relevant skills and merits of Schiller and Brecht. (One recalls that Dürrenmatt's much-berated Brecht-like opera *Frank V* had just been performed in Zurich on 19 March 1959.)

Having established at least one (comic) right to speak on Schiller, 'daß ich ebenso schweizere, wie Schiller, wir sind unterrichtet, schwäbelte' (82), he then took up again his familiar cudgel against the German classic writer, to resent the 'Absolute, Endgültige, Vorbildliche' of the German classics as 'die heiligsten Güter der Nation' (83) and to suggest that Schiller's philosophising is now 'versteinert', 'moralisierend, kaum zu widerlegen, aber isoliert, bedeutungslos für die Gegenwart, erhaben, doch unfruchtbar' (85) – and that it is therefore no surprise that he is 'der Dramatiker der Schulmeister' (86)![2]

In 'Theaterprobleme' he had suggested that one could present Schiller's answer to the question, How does a writer represent *his* world on the stage? thus: 'Schiller schrieb so, wie er schrieb, weil die Welt, in der er lebte, sich noch in der Welt, die er schrieb, die er sich als Historiker erschuf, spiegeln konnte' (WA24, 59). This meant, incidentally, that Napoleon was the last *true* hero: 'Aus Hitler und Stalin lassen sich keine Wallensteine mehr machen' (op. cit., 59). Schiller's world was a visible one, ours is like an iceberg, mostly hidden under the surface, faceless, anonymous: 'Zwei Spiegel, die sich ineinander spiegeln, bleiben leer' (op. cit., 60).

That thought underpins Dürrenmatt's consequent discussion in this essay – his handling of the familiar Schillerian division of writers into 'naiv' and 'sentimental' – for he skilfully compares the eighteenth-century 'sentimental' writer, Schiller, with the most celebrated twentieth-century example, Brecht. The sentimental writer's eighteenth-century stage, Dürrenmatt suggests, became a tribunal to judge injustice: the writer becomes a 'rebel'. (*In tyrannos* was Schiller's motto for his youthful, rebellious play *Die Räuber* of 1782.) But the twentieth-century writer must go further, he cannot just describe the world as unjust, he must do something about it: 'Sie muß dann als eine veränderbare Welt beschrieben werden, die wieder in Ordnung kommen kann und in welcher der Mensch nicht mehr ein Opfer zu sein braucht. Ist dies aber so, verwandelt sich der Schriftsteller aus einem Rebellen in einen Revolutionär' (91–2). This brings him to Brecht. Dürrenmatt grants the Marxist author all his merits, but reiterates his dislike and suspicion of all doctrinaire, albeit 'revolutionary', solutions to the world's problems: 'Der alte Glaubenssatz der Revolutionäre, daß der Mensch die Welt verändern könne und müsse, ist für den einzelnen unrealisierbar geworden, außer Kurs gesetzt, der Satz ist nur noch für die Menge brauchbar, als Schlagwort, als politisches Dynamit' (96) – which now reads prophetically in our post-Brechtian age of *glasnost* and *perestroika*. Thus, the philosophical 'worlds' of both writers have their merits *and* demerits, 'Ahnen wir in der einen unseren Untergang, wittern wir in der anderen unsere Unterdrückung' (98), for both essentially rob us of our freedom. Authors of today should therefore regard them not as the *judges* of their actions, but as their *consciences* which should encourage them to find new 'models', new ways of presenting their own world on the stage.

The literary reactions to the speech are well documented in all the works on Dürrenmatt. One of the most interesting recent reflections is that of the GDR specialist Jan Knopf who adds an excursus 'Das "verfluchte Altern" oder Dürrenmatt und Brecht', to his 1987 book *Der Dramatiker Friedrich Dürrenmatt* (C32, 184–9). It is, alas, all very obvious: Dürrenmatt's characters are 'Opfer', Brecht's are 'Täter', and he suggests that Dürrenmatt still does not understand Brecht, that he is still exhibiting his 'Zweifel an der Geschichte', namely that it will always produce the same 'menschenmorden-de[n] Wahnsinn', whereas Brecht (and presumably other 'optimistic' communist writers) will see the world as 'changeable'. He ends, 'wo bei Dürrenmatt der Tod nistet, beginnt bei Brecht das Leben – und zwar immer wieder und stets neu' (op. cit., 189), an astoundingly naïve comment in the light of recent political events. I prefer Dürrenmatt's more realistic view of human nature and its frailties.[3]

Dürrenmatt was to return to thoughts on Schiller when he was awarded in 1960 the *Großen Preis der Schweizerischen Schillerstiftung* and, once again, had to deliver an acceptance address on 4 December in the Zurich Schauspielhaus. He entitled it 'Der Rest ist Dank' and began, once again, in comic vein by admitting that it would have been more appropriate for him who writes *Komödien* to have been awarded the *Großen Nestroypreis* – 'aber den gibt es wohl nicht', and his reason was a typical one: 'Ich bin beunruhigt. Nicht eigentlich darüber, daß man mich ernst, sondern daß man mich bierernst nehmen . . . könnte' (in WA26, 109–112, 110). This was a Dürrenmattian flippancy that audiences had come to expect, but when he went on to say, 'Ich bin nun einmal in der Welt der literarischen Erscheinung so ein Witz, und ich weiß, für viele ein schlechter und für manche ein bedenklicher' (110), one realised how wounded he had been by recent savage press criticisms, particularly of *Frank V*. His lecture is therefore directed towards a justification of *Komödie* against the (Germanic) 'falschen Ernst, das falsche Pathos. Der wahre Nihilismus ist immer feierlich wie das Theater der Nazis' (110). It is humour which speaks of Freedom – even though it be 'gallows humour' nowadays, the *comédie noire* of the 1950s and 1960s. So, Dürrenmatt suggests, we must move away from the suspect seriousness of the classics of the past, with their 'tierischen Ernst' and their moralising missions: 'das Komödiantische ist das Medium, in welchem er [der Dramatiker] sich bewegen muß, aus welchem er, das ist sein Gesetz, sowohl das Tragische wie auch das Komische zu erzielen hat' (111). It is all clearly directed against Schiller's doctrine of the theatre as a 'moralische Anstalt' – did not Otto Ludwig sneeringly call Schiller 'den Moraltrompeter von Säckingen'?! The moral of the theatre, Dürrenmatt suggests, lies in its 'unwillkürlichen', not in its 'erstrebten Moralität', because, once again, theatre is theatre – and nothing else. He could not forgo one last boutade, however, in his concluding words of gratitude: 'nach den vielen Verrissen ist man ja ganz gern auch wieder etwas gepriesen'! (112). (We looked at the more direct response to these criticisms, 'An die Kritiker Frank des Fünftens' (now in WA6, 161–5), above (120).)

* * *

Many of Dürrenmatt's most interesting addresses and essays arose out of the need to celebrate friends' and colleagues' anniversaries, birthdays or deaths. He has remained very loyal to that small band who helped him in his early days as a writer, people like Ernst

Ginsberg, Kurt Horwitz, Kurt Hirschfeld, Leonhard Steckel, Therese Giehse, Peter Schifferli, Maria Becker, Teo Otto and Elisabeth Brock-Sulzer. Kurt Hirschfeld, who was Deputy Director of the Zurich Schauspielhaus, is one of those to whom Dürrenmatt felt particularly indebted since he was one of those who 'believed in him'. His moving tribute to Hirschfeld after the latter's death in 1964 proves that (in WA24, 121–3). Interestingly enough, Dürrenmatt called him 'einen mutigen Menschen'. Earlier, in 1962, the author had been asked to contribute to a *Freundesgabe* for Hirschfeld's sixtieth birthday; Dürrenmatt gave the contribution the title 'Literatur nicht aus Literatur' (in WA24, 84–92), and in it we read again of some of those basic beliefs that were to reappear, in practical terms, on the stage. His title gives the general thrust of the article: authors are expected to produce literature, not to read it or to comment upon it. It is his world around him which should attract his attention and vitality, not other (great) men's books: 'Weihrauch vernebelt die Köpfe, klärt nicht. Die Zeit macht beinahe alle fertig, nicht durch Boshaftigkeit, sondern durch ihr Verlangen nach Tiefsinn' – that word again! (85). Again he asks: Why write? Various reasons suggest themselves: out of anger, fear, love of order, or enthusiasm, to change the world or to preserve the world, to follow a party doctrine; but, Dürrenmatt reminds us, writing is a job, 'ein Geschäft', and if it is, how can a writer avoid the sordid task of (merely) writing for a living? '[I]ndem er sich nämlich entschlossen weigert, geistige Werte zu liefern, indem er Stoffe, aber keinen Trost fabriziert, Sprengstoff, aber keine Tranquillizer. Auf die Ware kommt es an' (88), which reminds us of Dürrenmatt's greatest 'fear' – ever to see a book with the title *Trost bei Dürrenmatt!*

His continuing belief that theatre can only be theatre, not a place for doctrines, dogmas or philosophies, is underlined here too in his comments on theatrical productions. He grants critics the right to ask what the play is about, but reserves to authors the right to reply that there is no answer to the question: 'Er [the author] stellt den Stoff zur Interpretation her, nicht die Interpretation selbst' (89) – and he has often likened a play to a musical score whose 'meaning' will/might vary with the interpretation. (No two singers, for example, will ever present, say, Schubert's *Winterreise* in exactly the same way, although the notes remain the same.) 'Kunst beweist überhaupt nie etwas. Sie kann in sich stimmen, das ist alles' (90). That makes its relationship to the audience a difficult one. Dürrenmatt recommends authors not to try to force a thesis on to an audience, 'Dem Publikum wohnt eine hartnäckige Kraft inne, zu hören, was es will und wie es will' (91), and it is therefore wise to avoid a conflict with it.

Finally, he grants that there *is* a place in the theatre for the 'Dramaturgie von der Aussage her', but still feels that that demands extra-theatrical involvement which, he believes, would be out of place in a theatre. Once again, then, he denies the possibility of a theatrical piece bearing one dogmatic meaning only: the art and charm of the theatre lies in its 'Mehrdeutigkeit'.

The essay appeared on 10 March 1962, three weeks after the Zurich première of *Die Physiker*, and underlines the paradox that Dürrenmatt finds the greatest personal satisfaction constructing plots of 'Mehrdeutigkeit' yet has achieved the greatest public successes with plots of 'Eindeutigkeit' – of construction, at least. As we have seen, all his most 'complicated' plots have failed on the stage; his forte has clearly been the construction of 'simple' plots bearing 'complicated' meanings!

The Hirschfeld essay was built up on a lecture-pattern, indeed with paragraph sub-titles: 'Literatur nicht aus Literatur', 'Schwierigkeiten der Schriftstellerei', 'Schriftstellerei als Geschäft', and so on. As the 1960s progressed, and Dürrenmatt felt more at ease and assured of the rightness of his dramaturgical thinking, he turned more and more to the essay form (paradoxically, of course) to clarify his ideas and to explain what he was doing in the theatre.

Such an essay, albeit 'ein Fragment', was his 'Aspekte des dramaturgischen Denkens', a manuscript dated 1964 which first appeared in the 1972 collection *Dramaturgisches und Kritisches* (A14, 201–31) and is now in WA24, 104–20. Here, too, the paragraphs are titled; the result is a number of short 'essayettes' on ways of looking at writing for the theatre. The section 'Vom Erzählen' insists that drama is born out of the epic and is therefore meant to tell a story, or at least *was* meant to. Dürrenmatt 'blames' writers like Proust and Frisch for inventing a literature which 'zwischen Fiktion und Wirklichkeit schwebt und mit diesem Gegensatz spielt' (105). He cites Frisch's *Gantenbein* as an example of what we might now call 'faction', with an 'Erzähler-Ich'. The paragraph 'Von der Dramatik' denies the possibility of 'faction': 'Die Bühne kennt kein Ich'; the author as self on the stage is no 'Ich, sondern ein Gegenüber' (105). Dürrenmatt demonstrates this with the failure of the staging of Kafka's *Der Prozeß*. The character *K.* had to be shown on the stage, but *K.* is the result of very complicated thought-processes; the novel can really only be filmed, with the camera doing an 'I-am-a-camera', representing *K*'s eyes.

The section 'Dramaturgie vom Zweck' brings us again to

Dürrenmatt's almost obsessive involvement in this period with Friedrich Schiller and Bertolt Brecht. Did he really think of them as his two premier rivals to supremacy on the German stage of the 1960s? The statistics would certainly seem to support that view!

The point at issue here is the *Verfremdungstechnik* employed by these two authors: Schiller's chorus in *Die Braut von Messina* and the *Songs* of Brecht's Epic Theatre. Once again, Dürrenmatt denies the relevance of the 'classics' by fairly long quotations from Schiller's own denial of the validity of the eighteenth-century French way of presenting the unities: 'Der Tag selbst auf dem Theater ist nur ein künstlicher', Schiller wrote. Schiller's reason for re-employing the Chorus, to transmute the modern, ordinary world into the old, poetic one, was a failure, Dürrenmatt claims (as do many others, of course), and his iambics in *Wallenstein* also failed to present the Thirty Years War as successfully as did Brecht's prose in *Mutter Courage*.

Dürrenmatt returns now to his early belief that the classical tragedies could not represent the present – we are reminded of his remarks on Aristophanes' comedies (above, 161–2) – and that Schiller had to use the Chorus to try to achieve this. Nor is Brecht's contemporary world able to be represented on *his* stage; it only can be, Brecht claimed, 'wenn sie als veränderbar beschrieben wird', writing, as he did, for a scientific age.

The question of the point, or the goal, of Art, now arises. Brecht believed, says Dürrenmatt, that it has a *general* function, that is, one which affects the generality of society. 'Theater besteht darin,' wrote Brecht, 'daß lebende Abbildungen von überlieferten oder erdachten Geschehnissen zwischen Menschen hergestellt werden, und zwar zur Unterhaltung' (in the first section of his 1948 'Kleines Organon für das Theater'), and this was used later in his career anyway when he realised that his audiences came to the theatre to be entertained, not to be lectured at. Dürrenmatt maliciously wonders whether finance does not play the biggest role in a theatrical production: 'Daß Kunst auch Unterhaltung sein kann, ist vielleicht nur ihr Unterhalt' (113).

The author then turns to the man who most disliked Brecht, Eugène Ionesco (he had called Brecht, famously, 'le boy scout'). Dürrenmatt obviously approves of a man who had held Brecht's Marxist dogmas up to ridicule. He approved of Ionesco's 'Identitätssatz', namely, 'Theater kann nur Theater sein' (113), that it should therefore be free of all that is not 'reines Theater'. But, writes Dürrenmatt, that leads to a contradiction because, again, theatre is not that reality either, but only imagined reality, 'gespielte Wirklichkeit', which therefore can be suborned for any purpose. Ionesco's theatre leads to 'Endmenschen in Endsituationen', to the *clown*, 'den Urpechvogel, der alles ungeschickt unternimmt, an dem sich die toten Dinge rächen' (Harlequin to Chaplin) (115). Here we must recall that in 1964 Dürrenmatt was in the middle of his work on *Der Meteor*, where he had seen his Schwitter as 'den großen Einzelnen', 'er wird zu einem Einzelnen in der Gesellschaft, zu einem totalen Individuum unter den relativ Individuellen' (*Punkt* 17 on *Der Meteor*, WA9, 162) (cf. above, 131). This individual could represent, Ionesco claimed, not only the fall of such characters, but all of our 'abgebrauchten Ansichten, Werte und Wahrheiten, die gestürzten Kulturen, das Schicksal', that is, of modern European culture (116). (In a type of footnote, Dürrenmatt cheerfully agrees that his argument here might be quite incomprehensible to certain critics. So, he writes, 'Gib deine Dramaturgie nicht preis, sonst wirst du dich einmal an sie halten müssen' (117–18)!)

The most important feature of these 'Aspekte' is the emphasis on the individual ('den Einzelnen'). We begin to realise here when we look back at these essays that this individual-type is Dürrenmatt's answer to the fear of the environmentalists that the world is growing too large, too impersonal for the individual to have a voice anymore. He must try to preserve his own integrity by 'surviving' as best he can, by fighting for *his* freedom and for justice for those who are oppressed. It is a philosophy which moves between realism and pessimism, scepticism and cynicism, but which has the saving grace of humour to keep its movements in perspective.

* * *

Another of Dürrenmatt's oldest friends, Ernst Ginsberg, died on 3 December 1964. Dürrenmatt gave an address in the Schauspielhaus in Zurich, where both had worked for many years, on 7 February 1965 (now in WA24, 124–39). The address is interesting for the light that it throws on the playwright's perception of the art and craft of acting. We see that he is well aware of the actors' problems and grateful to one like Ginsberg who honestly strove to realise on the stage what the author was trying to say in the text. With Kurt Horwitz, Ginsberg had in 1946 helped the young Dürrenmatt to clear his mind of 'philosophical theorising' and to write for, and with, the stage. It was Horwitz's Hamlet, says Dürrenmatt, a Hamlet who sought justice, which influenced

Dürrenmatt's Romulus who also wanted to bring justice into an unjust world.

From these personal reminiscences Dürrenmatt turns to the question of dramaturgical theory, to the position of 'the theatre in a scientific age', the Brechtian question. Man lives in a world of conflicts, he suggests, and the question is whether the theatre is a suitable place 'die Welt der Konflikte vom Problem her zu ändern' (137); indeed, whether the dramatist should start his play with the problem or with the conflict. Dürrenmatt's answer is not only clear, but practical: if you start with the problem, then you have to solve it for the audience; the plot then becomes the conflict. You have to be positive, your answer will be either moral or doctrinal. If you start with the conflict, however, all you need then is a conclusion, no solution; the plot will just show the various problems presented by the conflict, and an answer as such will not be needed. 'Beim Dramatiker vom Problem her ist die Frage nach Positiv oder Negativ sinnvoll, beim andern ist sie sinnlos, denn die Frage, ob Coriolan, König Lear, Tartuffe oder der Dorfrichter Adam positive oder negative Helden seien, ist Stumpfsinn' (138). It was Ginsberg's Hamlet which made Dürrenmatt realise that everything in that play was connected with a conflict, and not with a problem. That was how he, Dürrenmatt, decided to write in future. The author and the actor are there to show Man in his conflicts; the thinker, 'der Denker', the philosopher, is there to determine Mankind's problems and, if possible, to solve them. The world needs both types, 'die denkerische als Vorschlag zur Lösung ihrer Konflikte, die künstlerische als Warnung, in ihren Lösungsversuchen nicht unmenschlich zu werden' (138).

(The next day, 8 February 1965, Dürrenmatt's father died in an old people's home, aged eighty-four. He describes his own feelings of 'Unmenschlichkeit' in *Stoffe* A2, 9–25.)

The last important piece of this period concerns Dürrenmatt's untiring and lasting battle with the press and the critics. Significantly, he did not distinguish it with the title of 'Rede' or 'Vortrag', but simply called it 'Plauderei über Kritik vor der Presse' (now in WA25, 90–7). I feel that this was important because it was, in the main, the heavy and continual press criticism – in this case, just after the production of *Der Meteor* in 1966 – that determined Dürrenmatt eventually to leave the theatre and, in his third and fourth 'phases', to concentrate on lectures, essays and, above all, painting. His sallies into the theatre from about 1973 on were more in the nature of aggressive personal crusades.

'Ich stehe mit vielen von ihnen auf dem Kriegsfuß und gehe

ihnen mit Vorliebe aus dem Wege', Dürrenmatt admits early on in this manuscript, but he then continues to insult his critics roundly. There are four classes of critic, he writes: 'Die erste kann weder schreiben noch kritisieren, die zweite kann schreiben, aber nicht kritisieren, die dritte kann nicht schreiben, aber kritisieren, die vierte endlich schreiben und kritisieren' (92). Most critics are in Class I, the most famous are in Class II and those who understand theatre are in Class IV. There are none in Class III!

Again, the burden of his complaint is against those who cannot tolerate anything new in the theatre: 'Es gibt Kritiker, die halten jede neue Dramatik für einen Schwindel' (93) – and the 'Literaturpäpste' are no better, he writes, citing one who had told him that a 'certain German dramatist' [Frank Wedekind?] had ruined German drama with his slovenly language! He also takes issue with those critics who believe that characters in plays echo, of necessity, the sentiments of the author, 'Ein Theaterstück kann heute eine Eigenwelt darstellen, eine in sich geschlossene Fiktion, deren Sinn nur im Ganzen liegt' (95), and he claims that Schwitter's perhaps peculiar 'Ausspruch' can only be understood in, and through, the action of the play (that is, *Der Meteor*). It has no meaning *outside* the play. So again, 'Der bewußte Dramatiker weiß, daß Theater nichts anderes sein kann als Theater, ein brüchiges Gleichnis' (96), and critics should be prepared to understand and appreciate this dramatic irony.

It is an old and well-tried argument, going back to the days when he was taken for a 'nihilist' and there is probably no answer to the critics' individual point of view. If you believe that the author shares the views of his characters, nothing on earth will convince you otherwise. In Dürrenmatt's case, it depends on whether you believe that the characters' views are to be taken as a warning to others, or as a representation of reality! The words were well said and timely and asked to be taken 'mit Humor', but clearly they came 'from the heart'. Whether they 'went to the heart' remains to be seen.

The Essays from 1967 to 1973

The years between 1966 and 1970 were fateful not only for Dürrenmatt, but also for the world, and for Europe in particular. There was a massive swing to the Left in political life, and among the young, popular support for the USSR and China and their policies against the most unpopular of recent conflicts, the Vietnam

War, as well as resentment of right-wing, 'fascist', authoritarian institutions and bodies – university, school, political or media. Dürrenmatt was heavily engaged at the time in his own personal battles: with illness (as always), with critics (as we have just seen) and also with a new political alignment, a support for the state of Israel in its constant struggle for existence against its larger Arab neighbours. Dürrenmatt's sympathies for Jews and Judaism go back to his childhood experiences and particularly, he says, to his mother's accounts of the historical Jews of the Old Testament – Freudians might say, to his fellow-feeling for an 'outsider', 'einen Einzelnen', what was later to become the symbol of the trapped *Minotaurus* facing up to its enemies in its lonely labyrinth. To that, one would add his citizenship of a similarly small country, one whose religious brethren had, in addition, been tortured and tormented by those who spoke Dürrenmatt's own language. It now seems certain that all this added to his personal feelings of guilt just at this time.

The 'Six-Day War', 5–10 June 1967, was seen by Dürrenmatt as the inevitable consequence of the struggle for oil which had been waged by the Arab countries since the Second World War, but also of the greed for material wealth of the countries of the Western world, and of Switzerland in particular, whom he has always charged with 'seeming neutrality' both in war and in peace. The outbreak of hostilities in the Middle East led him to a polemic in *Die Weltwoche* in Zurich on 23 June 1967 ('Israels Lebensrecht', now in WA28, 29–34). It is a fascinating résumé of his independent views. A man who was often charged in Switzerland with being a 'fellow-traveller' in his early years, particularly because of his anti-Swiss sentiments in plays like *Romulus der Große* (1949), is now clearly disenchanted with *both* blocs – with the USA for its 'inhuman' war against the Vietnamese, and with the USSR for its 'inhuman' support of the Arab countries against their tiny neighbour.

The essay starts boldly, 'Es gibt den jüdischen Staat, weil es Hitler gab' (29) – an often-repeated assertion – but then Dürrenmatt defends Israel's existence as an 'Axiom der Menschlichkeit', a 'Naturrecht', and indeed blames the great powers, rather than the Arabs, for having made this inevitable by driving both Middle East groups, which are themselves closely related, into a tribal rivalry. Although Israel 'won' the senseless war, Dürrenmatt believed that the true result was the consequent ideological *idée fixe* of the Arab world to destroy Israel. The major thrust of the essay is to plead with the United Nations not to pass a vote of censure on Israel; if it does, 'so stimmt sie einer Ermordung zu' (33). Dürrenmatt asks all those 1960s intellectuals who were writing about, and seeking, 'commitment' to commit themselves to Israel's cause, in the hope that 'wie aus seinem Lande, aus unserem Planeten ein Garten werde und keine Wüste' (33), an interesting repetition of his words at the end of his *Herkules und der Stall des Augias* (1962–3) (above, 67). This fervent plea ends with the well-known lines from the Brecht play, *Der kaukasische Kreidekreis* (written 1944–5): 'Daß da gehören soll, was da ist, denen, die für es gut sind' – but with barbed side-comments that the lines came from a man who chose to live in the GDR, a country now scandalously attacking Israel (34)!

Dürrenmatt's distaste for ideological dogmatism reappeared the next year, 1968, when yet another small country had to protest against the encroachment of a larger neighbour. Alexander Dubček's 'Prague Spring' was soon deflowered by Soviet tanks on 21 August 1968; Dürrenmatt, along with other German-speaking writers, Günter Grass, Heinrich Böll, Peter Bichsel, Max Frisch and others, spoke out against the invasion in the Stadttheater in Basle on 8 September. In many ways, 'Tschechoslowakei 1968' (now in WA28, 35–42) is a typical intellectuals' tirade, full of fine words which achieved very little. Dürrenmatt even introduced the persona of his favourite communist, the much-maligned Swiss, Konrad Farner, to show that not all communists were 'evil', 'Kommunist ist ein Ehrenname, nicht ein Schimpfwort' (35), and he tried to prove too that his interest in the affair was dramaturgical, not political: 'ich denke über die Welt nach'. But he went on to stamp the twentieth century as the age of the political criminal, agreeing in effect with Jean-Paul Sartre's renowned definition. Stating the paradox that the very system which had fought for 'die Freiheit des Geistes' was now preventing its attainment, he pointed out again that 'thinking' and 'doing' are entirely separate actions: 'Die vernünftige Veränderung der Welt kann nicht durch reines Denken geschehen' (39). The Communist Party had become ossified, it was now a 'bewußte Fiktion', orthodox and even criminal (40). Yet 'das Schicksal des Kommunismus ist das unsrige' (41) – the West's practices are not much better nor less criminal. He cites the USA's support of dictatorships, its economic blackmailing in order (supposedly) to save the relevant country from communism. He knows 'daß auch wir den Menschen mißachten, indem wir ihn manipulieren' (41), and pleads once again for a more human face, not a mask, to be shown by *both* sides. He ends, prophetically, that Czechoslovakia 'durch seinen gewaltlosen Widerstand ein Machtsystem erschüttert, tödlicher vielleicht, als wir zu ahnen vermögen'

(42). The sentence reads well as I write in the winter of 1988, with Poland, Latvia, Estonia, Lithuania, Armenia and Azerbaijan rising up against the too rigid communist system.

In this phase of his career, Dürrenmatt had therefore obviously become intensely interested in the fate of smaller nations and 'der kleinen Leute'. His reworking of his 1947 play *Es steht geschrieben* as *Die Wiedertäufer* (1968) and his 're-version' of Shakespeare's *König Johann* (1968) could both be said to centre round the theme of the powerful, 'Die Mächtigen' versus the victims, 'Die Opfer' – Israel and Czechoslovakia in this context being seen as the latter. His move to the Basle theatre post in 1969 allowed him the space in the Basle theatre programmes to expatiate on these themes. One of his most interesting contributions was the elaboration of one of his *Urmotive*, the relationship between Tragedy and Comedy, by bonding it on to his new intellectual and political outlook. 'Zwei Dramaturgien' (now in WA24, 147–9) appeared in the Basle theatre programme for August 1968 and put forward the Bergsonian proposition, 'Der Mensch lacht über den Menschen, wenn er ihm als Clown erscheint; der Clown ist der vom Menschen distanzierte Mensch, der unmenschliche Mensch' (148) (and cf. my B23, 22–3), from which premiss he deduced that 'Das Tragische ist das Menschliche, das Komische das Unmenschliche' (148). The argument – *Mächtige/Opfer* – was, of course, particularly relevant in the late 1960s, both dramaturgically and politically, as we have seen. Dürrenmatt's analysis is interesting and competent because it is closely linked to others of his great motifs: Freedom, Justice, Guilt, Retribution. 'Die Opfer', the victims, are 'comic' precisely because they are 'unfree', that is they are not respected as human beings, but are treated as political fodder, in East *and* West. In classical tragedy – Dürrenmatt cites Schiller's *Don Carlos* – the powerful men are supposed to be tragic and we identify with them. Dürrenmatt however will see them, the kings, princes, and politicians, as clowns, albeit 'schreckliche Clowns': 'durch ihre Macht sind sie von den Menschen und damit von ihren Opfern distanziert, getrennt, unmenschlich' (148). He sums up his argument with one of his best epigrams: 'Der Königsmantel ist das erhebendste Clownkostüm, das wir kennen' (148). So we are back with 'Theaterprobleme', the empathy of tragedy, the distancing of comedy.

He ends the piece with a plea for freedom for the 'victims' of Life – freedom from the 'Unmenschlichkeit' which makes them victims but also 'comic' – and, as in 'Theaterprobleme', his conclusion is 'Darum gibt es heute vielleicht doch nur eine Dramaturgie: jene der Komödie. Leider' (149). His view is, of course, not too far from the classic absurdist view – Estragon and Vladimir waiting for a Godot in a world 'privé d'illusions et de lumières', in Camus's words. But Dürrenmatt employs a more worldly, politically oriented drama-turgy, with a more grotesque and at times savage, even obscene, stage realisation to make his point.

The major theme of 'men in power' and their 'victims' was continually in Dürrenmatt's thoughts at this time and, in retro-spect, must have been connected with his growing disaffection from the Basle theatrical experiment which then grew into a general disenchantment with Swiss life, politics and culture. All of these must have been contributory factors to the severe heart attack which he suffered shortly after my first visit to him at Easter 1969. There is a personal bitterness in his essayistic writings of this period which had not been so clearly noticeable before. 'Zur Dramaturgie der Schweiz', a manuscript only published in 1980, dated 1968–70 (now in WA28, 60–76), is a savage indictment of Swiss moral values. He had already indicted his country's moral stand in a short essay at the time of the student revolts in 1968 (cf. 'Zu den Zürcher Globus-Krawallen', now in WA28, 43–5) where he summed up: 'Doch eine Gesellschaft, die nur noch Waren und keine Werte mehr zu produzieren weiß, wirkt unglaubwürdig, appelliert sie an Werte' (44). Now he launched a full-scale attack on Switzerland's shady past, not its 'unbewältigte Vergangenheit' (Switzerland had been too skilful to have one!) but its doubtful neutrality: 'Neutralität ist die Kunst, sich möglichst nützlich und möglichst ungefährlich zu verhalten' (63). Yet it had unquestionably allowed Hitler's trains to run over its borders, it shot its 'Landesverräter', and now it feared communism much more than it ever feared Nazism. His *point de départ*, we see, is the question of why there is as yet no 'Drama-turgie der Schweiz', no drama on Switzerland's role in the Second World War. His answer: 'Die Schweiz (wie etwa auch Schweden) ist der Tragik aus dem Wege gegangen, darum ist sie kein tragi-scher Gegenstand, sondern ein untragischer Fall in einer tragischen Zeit. Tragisch sind nur ihre Opfer' (69). The connection with the earlier essays is perhaps clear: Switzerland is what Dürrenmatt had of course already called it in the first of his 'Schweizerpsalme' in 1950,

> Da liegst Du nun, ein Land, *lächerlich*, mit
> zwei, drei Schritten zu durchmessen (my italics, WA28, 174),

impotent in world affairs and often 'inhuman' in its treatment of its unwanted – its communists, its *Gastarbeiter*, its writers who do not conform. This then permits Dürrenmatt to end the essay with, for most readers, a rather parochial delineation of the Swiss 'separatist' problem, the 'Jurafrage': Should the canton of Jura, French-speaking Switzerland, 'Welschschweiz', become independent (a controversy on the lines of Spain's Basque problem, or Austria's Südtirol)? Dürrenmatt, living as a 'Deutschschweizer' in Neuchâtel, but with little or no interest in the cultural activities of the region, finds the whole debate senseless, trivial and all too typical of Switzerland's increasing impotence on the European scene. For our purposes, the essay shows his dramaturgical interest in this major theme but also, perhaps more importantly, the effect of the Basle débâcle on his personal career. We noted in which direction that was then led (above, 134ff.).

* * *

'Das Verhältnis der Autors Friedrich Dürrenmatt zu den Begriffen *Recht* und *Gerechtigkeit* ist von Anfang an ein dialektisches', declare the joint authors, Mona and Gerhard Knapp, of an article 'Recht – Gerechtigkeit – Politik' (E25, 23–40, 23). Densely written, and at times obscure, it nevertheless treats the theme very competently, leaving few stones unturned with its forty-six almost illegible footnotes in tiny print. It deals *inter alia* with the theme found in its 'purest' form in the book version (1969) of a lecture given in 1968 in the University of Mainz as part of the *studium generale*s courses: 'Monstervortrag über Gerechtigkeit und Recht, nebst einem hel-vetischen Zwischenspiel (Eine kleine Dramaturgie der Politik')' (WA27, 36–107). This long, rambling, discursive essay was plainly meant to present the author as a 'philosopher who writes plays': 'ich nahm in meiner Blindheit an, ich sei fähig, über ein Thema zu reden, mit dem ich nichts zu tun habe' (36). Hardly, one would say, since we have seen how all of his works to that date had had some connection with, or relevance to, the theme. His further seeming disclaimer that he had 'only' studied ten *Semester* of philosophy, but 'ohne akademischen Abschluß', would sound more impressive to *Erstsemestern* in 1968 than it now does in 1988, when we know what he did during those ten *Semester*! Nevertheless, the essay is an interesting example, firstly, of Dürrenmatt's ability to philosophise in story-form and, secondly, of his avowed dramaturgical intent of writing of conflicts that can be presented, rather than of problems that can be solved. Little is 'solved' here.

Set between two Middle East 'parables', the essay seemed to be his contribution to the anti-authoritarian debates of the late 1960s.

He takes up Thomas Hobbes's twin categories of the 'wolf' and the 'lamb' and turns the one into the 'Wolfsspiel', where the doctrine *homo homini lupus*, is predominant and the other into the 'Gute-Hirte-Spiel', where *homo homini agnus* rules. The first is typical, then, of modern capitalist society; the second of socialist-communist régimes. 'Glaubt der klassische Bürger, der Mensch sei ein intelligenter Wolf, glaubt der Sozialist, der Mensch sei ein intelligentes Lamm' (50). In both camps, however, injustice rules: 'Die Welt ist in Unordnung, und weil sie sich in Unordnung befindet, ist sie ungerecht' (55). But there are two concepts of justice: a general one, the 'logical' idea, and the individual one, the 'existential' idea. The 'existential' concept is the individual's right to be himself – that we call Freedom. But the right of society is to guarantee each person's freedom, which it can do only by para-doxically *limiting* each person's freedom for the good of society. That is the general idea of justice, a 'logical' concept. The reader will perhaps have already applied these philosophical categories to the antinomies which Dürrenmatt had already set up in the earlier lectures of this period: the 'existential' concept is that of the capital-ist state, of the 'Wolfsspiel'; the 'general' concept, that of the socialist state, the 'Gute-Hirte-Spiel'. Following Marx's division of the class-structure into an 'exploiting' and an 'exploited' class, Dürrenmatt sees the exploiting class as his 'freie, aber ungerechte Wolfsgemeinschaft', the exploited class as 'unfrei und ungerecht behandelt' (83). We are then returned to the theme of these earlier essays, the contrast between capitalist and socialist societies. In both cases, quasi-religious dogmas prevent *true* freedom: in the capitalist state, 'der Faschismus [ist] das zu Ende geführte Wolfs-spiel, sein Schachmatt' (80); while 'die kommunistische Partei [ist] eine zur "Theologie" gewordene Politik' (84), a 'kommunistische Kirche' or 'ein faschistischer Staat mit einer sozialistischen Struk-tur' (85–6). Both conclusions may sound hyperbolical at first hearing, but Dürrenmatt's dramaturgical representations of them in 'Der Sturz' and *Der Mitmacher* did not seem too far-fetched to anyone who, like him, says 'a plague o' both your houses'.

Is there a solution? A middle way? Can computers save us perhaps? *Sonntagsmalerei*? *Protestmärsche*? *Neue Sekte*? *Blutige Glaubenskämpfe*? Will football hooligans tear each other and the world apart? No. His 'solution' is a Kantian one, the practice of pure Reason: 'Nicht der Einzelne verändert die Wirklichkeit, die Wirklichkeit wird von allen verändert. Die Wirklichkeit sind wir alle, und wir sind immer nur Einzelne' (96). But he warns the young student audience that, as the world and its organisations grow, ('Das Gesetz der großen Zahl'), so they must learn to handle them, to control them – and, to do so, they must remain *free*, free from doctrines and dogmas. 'Die Freiheit des Geistes ist die noch mögliche Freiheit, die dem Menschen bleibt' (101). Dürrenmatt's hope is that the precarious situation will *force* Mankind into such rational behaviour, but 'Das Verfluchte dabei ist nur, daß uns vielleicht verdammt wenig Zeit dazu übrigbleibt' (102).[4]

* * *

These years saw Dürrenmatt, paradoxically as always, attacking his Swiss countrymen on the one hand and receiving official plaudits from them on the other – the Swiss Schiller Prize in 1960, the Berne Literature Prize in 1969 – and, in his addresses of acceptance, he never failed to rail at their complacency and small-mindedness. Such an address was his 'Über Kulturpolitik' on the receipt of the Berne prize, the *Große Literaturpreis des Kantons Bern*, on 25 October 1969. It will be recalled that Dürrenmatt had by this time given up his post at the Basle Stadttheater and was recovering from a heart attack – and from the critical broadsides received after his disputed departure. The speech (now in WA28, 46–59) is deliberately provocative, and is directed this time mainly against the well-known rivalries of the various Swiss cantons, viewed here particularly as arts-supporting institutions. Arguing that theatre is no longer a 'Massenmedium', as it was in Greek times, but is now 'ein exklusiver Ort' (49) hailing from the days of kings' and princes' private theatre-houses, he refers to the Maoist 'Kulturrevolution', then proceeding in China, and pleads for a 'Kultur*e*volution' (51). By this term he means a new attitude to culture, which can no longer just be art or literature, music or architecture – but must include science, which he claimed had always been more important for European culture than those other forms. 'Das Denken Europas, das die Welt veränderte, ist das wissenschaftliche Denken' (51), and that is what is needed to revive Switzerland. Here, he returns to his old charge against a 'passive Kunst' which tried to present the Staigerian 'heile Welt', and posits an active art-form which will not abandon 'the classics', but rethink them – critically. 'Das Theater kann nichts anderes sein als Theater. Daß es sich dessen bewußt wird, macht es zum kritischen Theater' (53). The main attack on his Swiss countrymen and his literary critics is that they will not accept anything new, 'daß jede Art von Kritik in der Schweiz als destruktiv empfunden wird, liegt an uns' (54). Every critic of Swiss society is regarded as being unpatriotic, he adds.

Only a few (q.v.), it seemed, enjoyed the speech and approved its conclusion when Dürrenmatt, admitting, again provocatively, that he lived in Switzerland 'aber ich lebe nicht von der Schweiz', and hinting that he would have welcomed some financial help from the Berne authorities in his younger days as an author, announced that he intended to divide the prize money of 15,000 francs among the writer Sergius Golowin, who had written an 'unofficial' history of Berne, the journalist Ignaz Vogel, author of a periodical *Neutralität*, and most controversially, Arthur Villard, a Berne politician who had fought for the highly unpopular introduction of 'Zivildienst', as opposed to the well-known compulsory Swiss Army service. All three men were widely regarded as the type of men for whom Switzerland had coined the term 'Landesverräter', but Dürrenmatt saw them rather as the type for whom Switzerland had always found sanctuary, men like Calvin, Zwingli, Haller, Pestalozzi, Henri Dunant and Karl Barth – and Rousseau, Büchner and Lenin had also sought sanctuary there. These three men were living proof 'daß unter ihrer konservativen Bettdecke die revolutionäre Schweiz zwar bisweilen schläft, aber immer wieder wach wird, unbequem und hartnäckig für uns alle' (58–9). With that he invited some of the APO 'rockers' in the audience to the official reception in the posh restaurant, saying 'Ich liebe junge Leute, die Trachten tragen'!

Almost all the audience listening to Dürrenmatt in Berne that day would have read his article the previous weekend (18/19 October 1969) in his own journal, the Zurich *Sonntags Journal*, when he had explained his reasons for leaving his post in Basle (cf. 'Mein Rücktritt von den Basler Theatern' (above, 135; WA24, 155–61)). The bitterness barely contained in that article broke out, literally, in a 1969 manuscript entitled 'Wutausbrüche', fifteen excoriating thoughts in Chairman Mao-style, on the débâcle: 'Mit einer korrupten Institution vermag man nicht die Welt zu ändern'; 'Seitdem die Künstler glauben, sich alles erlauben zu lassen, halten sich auch die Regisseure und die Kritiker für Künstler'; 'Meine großte Stümperei bestand darin, daß ich trotz zwanzigjähriger Krankheit nie lernte, zur rechten Zeit krank zu werden' (WA24, 162–3).

But Life must go on – 'Das einzige, das weitergeht' – Dürrenmatt would surely have agreed with Karl Kraus's *bon mot*! Soon, in November, Dürrenmatt left for Philadelphia to receive an honorary degree from Temple University, and followed this with an enjoyable month's holiday via Florida, Yukatan, the Caribbean Islands, Puerto Rico, back to New York.[5] His journey of ten years previously to the States eventually produced *Der Mitmacher*, as we have noted. From the 1969 visit came the exhilarating 'Sätze aus Amerika' (1970) (in WA28, 77–114), ninety-one pungent comments, published originally in his own *Sonntags Journal* from 31 January to 15 March 1970.[6] That Temple is a well-known 'white man's' university is sharply noted, but the excellent student performance of *Der Meteor* reconciled him at least to the place, if not to the idea of 'Universitätstheater' – which prompted him to suggest that all theatre was on the way to becoming 'Theater als Doktordissertation' (79) (The clutch of American academic articles which followed his visit underlined his concern (cf. F11).)

What look at first sight like fairly general, even banal, epigrammatic comments on the States, their people and their life-styles followed: 'In Rußland wird das Volk durch die Partei verdummt, in den Vereinigten Staaten durch die Television. Dagegen protestieren weder Arthur Miller noch ich' (83)! The substantive content, however, was by and large a practical comparison, well-founded on facts, between the societies of the USA and the USSR, which makes interesting reading after the theoretical premises of the 'Monstervortrag'. One congratulates Dürrenmatt on having taken the trouble to visit the two countries about which he has written so much and whose policies determine the way of the world which we inhabit. He is reading the new book of his Marxist friend Konrad Farner, *Theologie des Kommunismus*, during his journey, a book which seeks to bring Marxists and Christians closer together in the hope 'der Mensch werde einmal aus Einsicht zu dem, was er sein sollte', whereas Dürrenmatt's 'unverbesserlicher Pessimismus', as he uncharacteristically calls it, fears 'der Mensch, wolle er nicht untergehen, werde nur aus Not zu dem, was er sein sollte' (86).

(There are a few comic incidents related too. Dürrenmatt writes that he was working on a new novel, *Der Pensionierte*, about a Bärlach-style retired detective, when his watch, his fee-cheque from Temple and his safe-key were stolen. He concluded that he had not only earned his honorary degree, but he had paid for it too!)

The serious comments about America concern the tensions between black and white, particularly noticeable among the Puerto Ricans. But in Dürrenmatt's opinion the major reason for America's feelings of guilt was that 'Die Weißen fürchten die Neger, weil sie ein schlechtes Gewissen haben, und die Neger hassen die Weißen, weil sie kein schlechtes Gewissen zu haben brauchen' – a typically formulated Dürrenmattian epigram (97–8). Both the great Empires, the USA and the USSR, he concludes, have – and should have – feelings of guilt. In neither are the people truly free, in neither does society care enough: 'In der Sowjetunion ist die Gesellschaft für den Staat, in den Vereinigten Staaten der Staat für die Gesellschaft da' (104). Such reach-me-down judgements – what a German might call 'pauschale' judgements – are, of course, just what they are: diary-jottings and lightning impressions of the sort that a casual traveller makes, as we all do. My own impressions of the two countries happen to coincide with Dürrenmatt's: the USA as an 'instabiles Gebilde', the USSR as an 'arteriosclerotic'. Will the USA 'explode' while the USSR 'ossifies', or will the gleam that he sees on the horizon become a beacon? 'In der Sowjetunion ist das Volk gebildet worden, und es mag sein, daß es einmal seine dogmatischen Fesseln sprengt. In den Vereinigten Staaten ist die Selbstkritik nicht zu übersehen' (112). Watergate was on the immediate horizon (1973), Gorbachev (1988) on the distant.

* * *

By 1970 Dürrenmatt had moved over to Zurich to work with Harry Buckwitz at the Schauspielhaus. On 31 May 1970 he held yet another of his addresses, this time in Düsseldorf on the occasion of the twenty-fourth anniversary of the meeting of the Volksbühnen there. The speech, 'Dramaturgie des Publikums' (now in WA24, 164–75), is particularly interesting for his public confession that he rarely went to the theatre! 'Ich gehe nur ins Theater, wenn ich muß, aus dem einfachen Grund, die Naivität nicht zu verlieren, die ich benötige, um Stücke zu schreiben' (165).[7]

The speech is a plea, once more, to make the theatre and theatre-going more relevant: 'Das Theater ist dort für das Publikum der natürliche Ort der Opposition', he writes on the theatre in Poland and the Eastern bloc countries (169). Here, on the other hand, it is the opposite: the theatre is political, the public unpolitical. The subventioned theatres, he feels, have lost contact with their publics. They are trying too hard to put revolutions on the stage when the public does not want 'eine Volkshochschule über Revolutionen', a reflection on the earlier Brecht- and the contemporary APO (*Außerparlamentarische Opposition*)-cult. Thus, directors and producers must produce a play both 'kulinarisch *und* revolutionär' in order not to alienate either wing of the public. In that way, theatre may again play its part in presenting all the possibilities of the world in which we live. Even if it may be unimportant at present, 'so ist es doch eine der Chancen geblieben, die Welt zu erkennen' (175).

The speech suggested, then, that Dürrenmatt had rediscovered his love at least for working in the theatre and thinking about it, if not for actually attending it, and this view is supported by another series of epigrammatic, and sometimes enigmatic, 'sentences' which he published in the *Sonntags Journal* from 18/19 April to 29/30 August 1970. (The WA version slightly amends the text in Heft 50/51 of *Friedrich Dürrenmatt I* (Munich, 1976) (C4)).

These forty-six 'Sätze über das Theater' (in WA24, 176–211), originally, and more appropriately, entitled 'Gedanken über das Theater', can now be seen in retrospect to be central to Dürrenmatt's dramaturgical thinking and some of his most important critical utterances since 'Theaterprobleme'. The last section ends with the now familiar denial that the author is a philosopher, but he admits that drama should only offer material, themes, for philosophy – that is indeed its role – but 'ich halte es für einen Irrtum der heutigen Dramatik, daß sie so oft beides sein will, Dramatik und Philosophie' (No. 46, 211). Nevertheless, the essay reads like a philosophical treatise on the theatre à la Brecht's *Organon* – the theatre and its relation to reality. Dürrenmatt, too, proceeds from a definition, theatre as 'bewußte Nachachmung einer menschlichen Wirklichkeit' (No. 6, 178), and he cites wrestling, imitating a battle with a victor and a vanquished, as the *Urform der Tragödie*, while the clown is the *Urform der Komödie* – a view familiar to us by now. Before examining these concepts further, the author introduces Aristotle's own prescription for the dramatist, not 'zu berichten, was geschehen ist, sondern vielmehr, was geschehen könnte' (No. 17, 183); 'Das Verhältnis der Dramatik zur Wirklichkeit ist laut Aristoteles gleich dem Verhältnis der Möglichkeit zur Wirklichkeit' (No. 17, 184). While condemning the view that 'die großen Dramen der Literatur [seien] zeitlos und damit vollkommen und heilig' – 'Unser Goethe, der du bist im Himmel' (185)! – Dürrenmatt once again examines the basic difference between Greek tragedy and comedy, and once again concludes that tragedy was based on known myths, comedy on arbitrary 'Einfälle'. The comedies of Kratinos and Aristophanes 'ahmten nicht mehr Mythen nach, sie stellten Mythen her. Der erste Schritt vom nachahmenden zum darstellenden Theater war getan' (No. 23, 189–90).

Pursuing next the concept of the representation of what is 'possible' on the stage, Dürrenmatt deals in No. 30 with his own *Der Meteor* and the 'possibility of a miracle', of a non-believer believing in a miracle, his (Schwitter's) own resurrection from the dead. The post-production debate 'proved' that only genuine Christians and genuine non-Christians could understand the play,

'Das Faktum des Wunders steht der Unmöglichkeit gegenüber, es zu glauben' (No. 30, 197), and Dürrenmatt deduced from the fracas 'daß mit der Darstellung des Möglichen die Dramatik nicht befriedigend definiert ist' (No. 30, 198).

A further elaboration of the main theme leads the author to discuss the issue of *Zufall*, Chance: 'Auch das determinierteste Drama kommt, sieht man genau hin, ohne Zufall nicht aus. Der Zufall ist das nicht Voraussehbare. Bei den Alten erschien er als Schicksal' (No. 34, 200). To this concept Dürrenmatt links that of Freedom, the freedom that a dramatist (or his characters) has to choose a course of action, and both freedom of choice and chance belong to the 'immanent logic' of a play. A character's 'fate' need not be determined – Dürrenmatt cites Claire Zachanassian's 'choice' to leave Güllen and go into a Hamburg brothel as an example. Critics thought that it was not a 'compelling' reason; Dürrenmatt counters that it was her choice, it lay in her character.

He then presents the reader with a problem: there is only one 'reality' to be presented on the stage, but many possibilities. Reality is, after all, 'die Möglichkeit, die eben wirklich wird' (No. 35, 201), and he refers to Max Frisch's 'Dramaturgie der Fügung, Dramaturgie der Peripetie' mentioned in his correspondence with Walter Höllerer. This denied that a story could only end one way: 'Wir wissen,' wrote Frisch, 'daß Dinge geschehen, nur wenn sie möglich sind; daß aber tausend Dinge, die ebenso möglich sind, nicht geschehen, und alles könnte immer auch ganz anders verlaufen' (C21, 9). This is a view very close to that of Dürrenmatt, one would have thought, but Dürrenmatt suggests that Frisch's stage representation of this sentence, his play *Biografie*, where the character Kürmann has a chance to re-play his life's course, actually 'collides' with reality, which Dürrenmatt would claim 'obwohl sie unwahrscheinlich ist, kausal ist'. This makes Frisch's play according to Dürrenmatt, a 'Märchenspiel' (No. 41, 206).

'Wirklich ist die Möglichkeit, die sich verwirklicht hat', writes Dürrenmatt earlier, 'die Möglichkeit ist die Möglichkeit, die sich verwirklichen könnte', (No. 37, 202), and he illustrates this with the remarkable story of the car crash in May 1959 which I have already mentioned (above, 153). From the chain of possibilities which might have prevented the crash and those which necessary for it to have happened, he concludes 'Die Wirklichkeit ist die Unwahrscheinlichkeit, die eingetreten ist' (No, 39, 205), and suggests that Frisch did not take enough account of this improbability.

Dürrenmatt finishes this fascinating exercise in philosophical criticism with a glance at his own concept of the 'schlimmst-möglichen Wendung', a logical consequence of a 'Dramaturgie des Unfalls'. An accident starts with being improbable, then becomes ever more probable, until it finally becomes reality, that is all the chance occurrences have taken the 'worst possible turn'. In a drama the worst possible turn, claims Dürrenmatt, justifies the fictional story existentially because it represents reality; in other words, this is how it happened, not how it *might have* happened. Thus, 'Durch die schlimmstmögliche Wendung, die ich einer dramatischen Fiktion gebe, erreiche ich auf einem merkwürdigen Umweg über das Negative das Ethische: Die Konfrontierung einer gedanklichen Fiktion mit dem Existentiellen' (No. 45, 209).

This important essay brings together many of Dürrenmatt's most celebrated dramaturgical concepts and helps to explain his obsession with them. It is required reading for any young academic coming to grips for the first time with the thought of this provocative dramatist – and should be required reading, too, for any director about to produce a Dürrenmatt play. One sees that these concepts, which have dominated his thinking for forty years, are part and parcel not only of his dramaturgical *Weltanschauung*, but also of his personal view of the world. They dominate his life as they dominate his writing, concepts such as *Zufall*, *Die schlimmstmögliche Wendung*, *Wahrscheinlichkeit–Möglichkeit*, and so on. Undeniably difficult to read, and not always logically composed either, the 'Sätze' do not however deserve Tiusanen's dismissive footnote, 'A still more scattered and unbalanced sketch for a basic dramaturgy' – although, to be fair to the American author, he probably did not have time to consider them in depth before the publication of his book in 1977 (B22, 403, note 22). One sometimes has the uneasy feeling, nevertheless, that the Swiss author of the 'Sätze' is trying so hard, almost *too* hard, to pretend that he is not what he would like to be taken for, a philosopher; and that many of his concepts, and his method of presenting them, are unnecessarily complex, to give the impression indeed of what Dürrenmatt purports to dislike so much – *Tiefsinn*. But we began with his argument that 'philosophy', not drama, is the place for deep thoughts – and the three productions of 1970, *Porträt eines Planeten*, *Urfaust* and *Titus Andronicus*, might have proved his point!

The Essays from 1976 to 1988

Dürrenmatt's fourth and last 'phase' for our purposes, from around

1976 to the present, is by far the most productive for essay-writing. Although still attracted by the theatre – after 1976, we recall, he wrote two plays, *Die Frist* of 1977 and *Achterloo* (1983) (and *Achterloo IV*, 1988) and made a stage-play out of his successful story-cum-radio-play *Die Panne* (1979) – he devotes himself mainly to polemical essay-writing and, of course, more and more to painting as an extension of, or a corollary to, his literary work.[8]

In many ways, Dürrenmatt is a 'self-made' astronomer and physicist – which is not to say that he is not extremely knowledgeable on the subject; he spends a great many of his sleepless nights star-watching on the patio of his house in Neuchâtel, and he has, of course, written many essays on scientific phenomena and occurrences. There is indeed room for a study by a scholar who shares his dual interests to gauge the influence of these activities on Dürrenmatt's literary and philosophical output. One physical concept which keeps recurring, for example, and to which I have alluded several times in this study is the 'Gesetz der großen Zahl'. This was adumbrated to Dürrenmatt in 1950 by Rudolf Kassner, and Dürrenmatt devoted a whole essay, albeit a 'Fragment', to it in 1976–7 (now in WA27, 108–24). The basic premiss of the concept is that certain laws come into operation only when large numbers of people or 'things' are involved. There are now four milliard people on Earth, *ergo* the *Loschmidtsche Konstante* which states that 'bei 0 °C Celsius und einer Atmosphäre Druck enthalten 22 415 cm^3 eines idealen Gases 6.023 . 10^{23} Moleküle', their movement is subject to Chance as are the Earth's inhabitants. With so many people, the law of *Gerechtigkeit* (Justice) comes before that of *Freiheit* (Freedom). Dürrenmatt takes trains as his example. The train served the 'masses', the principle here is of 'justice', but when the car arrived on the scene, it came first to serve the rich individual – and that was the principle of freedom. Now, however, all (i.e. the 'large numbers') have cars – 'Das Gesetz der großen Zahl wird wirksam' – and we now have mass murders and catastrophes on the roads. The 'Law' has taken the *Primat* of Freedom *ad absurdum*. This is why, Dürrenmatt says, he has always written so much about *Zufall*, Chance: 'ich trage nur dem Gesetz der großen Zahl Rechnung' (110). As the world and its dangers grow, the chance of even greater catastrophes increases. The sub-title to the essay is 'Ein Versuch über die Zukunft'.

His argument then turns to Switzerland and its future. A neutral army will certainly not 'save' her: the army is 'verdammt teure Folklore'! Her people, not her rulers, will save her, because the people are 'Ideen, und als Ideen sind sie unverwundbar' (112).

From this thought – which, of course, refers to *all* small nations – Dürrenmatt widens his argument to a more general and not unfamiliar thought: where do we find Freedom and Justice now in the world? He believes that Marx's basic error was to believe (with Hegel, Kierkegaard's and Dürrenmatt's *bête noire*), that Freedom would arrive of itself once Justice was firmly installed. But no – what we have in the USSR, for example, is not a free, classless society, but a controlled state of classes, 'jenen der Verwalter und der Verwalteten' (114). Once again, he avers that the leaders of the USSR are 'Monumente einer eingefrorenen Ideologie' (118), but 'das Gesetz der großen Zahl fordert den Sozialstaat'. And that will be Switzerland's fate too: Justice before Freedom is the result of the 'Law', more 'Staat' from more 'Volk', not 'demokratisch' but 'demokratisiert'.

This most pessimistic of his essays, written, one suspects, under the shadow of his own and his wife's failing health at the time, ends with the gloomy prediction that the 'Gesetz' that he is discussing will turn out to justify the old Malthusian doctrine that the population will increase in geometrical ratio, while the food supply will increase in arithmetical ratio. For good measure, he mentions that scientists believe that the sun's light will last only for another 25,000 years, and that Man has been lucky to have managed two million years on Earth. They 'reichen möglicherweise schon' (123)!

Here we see perhaps most clearly how obsessed Dürrenmatt has been with the growing size of the world's population and with the baleful influence of 'great states'. As far back as his *Romulus der Große*, he wrote that it was directed towards the 'large state', the state which had the power to do evil. The thought had dominated his political thinking and is certainly a contributory factor to his support for the 'small' state of Israel.

I noted above (148) how Dürrenmatt suffered a severe illness in October 1975, the circumstances of which led bizarrely to his play *Die Frist*, and I can only imagine that the dark essay on the 'Gesetz der großen Zahl' arose out of these circumstances too. The ongoing rumblings from the failure of *Der Mitmacher* led, I am sure, to his diving for protection back into the murky depths of Middle East politics, the opportunity being provided by the award of an Honorary Fellowship of the Ben-Gurion University in Beersheba for his literary support of the Israeli cause. His speech of acceptance, given in 1974, was then greatly extended into an essay – a full book indeed – in 1975 and published in 1976 as *Zusammenhänge. Essay über Israel. Eine Konzeption* (WA29, 9–162), yet another 'monster' production. The Yom Kippur War of October 1973 had just settled into an uneasy truce and, as Armin Arnold notes, Dürrenmatt had been the only prominent Swiss writer to stand up and speak out for Israel. 'Es ist still um die Schriftsteller geworden', he wrote in the *Neue Zürcher Zeitung* of 22 October. 'Die großen Unterzeichner unterzeichnen nicht mehr.' (The article 'Ich stelle mich hinter Israel' is, unfortunately, not in the *Werkausgabe* (cf. C3, 20).)

One of the best of the scholarly comments on this important work *Zusammenhänge* came from Jean Améry (in E1, 41–8), who wrote, 'Dürrenmatts Engagement für Israel ist hochachtenswert, weil der Autor gegen den Strom schwimmt, gegen die Macht, gegen die Ideologie, gegen die geläufigen Phraseologien von rechts wie von links' (48). This seems to me to characterise not only this essay, but also Dürrenmatt's character admirably.

By this time, 1974, Dürrenmatt had worked out a number of philosophical positions to which he was to remain fairly faithful. For the 1968 essay on 'Gerechtigkeit und Recht' (above, 178ff.), he had established his two major philosophical categories of Justice and Freedom = Capitalism and Socialism = Individualism and Socialisation = Wolves and Lambs = Existential and Ideological. It was with the latter pair of antinomies that he began Part I of this essay on Israel. Standing on the Golan Heights, he thought of these opposites: it was *existentially* necessary for Israel to defend them (i.e. it was 'Israels Lebensrecht'), just as it was *ideologically* necessary for her enemies to attack them. In this speech/essay are many of the expressions of guilt that we have noted throughout this study. Dürrenmatt feels for this small state, 'als Kleinstaatler bin ich nun einmal für Kleinstaaten' (19), but he admits that this is both a 'Verteidigungs-' as well as an 'Anklagerede', 'daß es dreißig Jahre nach Auschwitz abermals notwendig ist, eine solche Rede zu halten' (19). He supports Israel because he believes Israel's continuing existence to be necessary for the cause of Justice. He then embarks on a history of Judaism based on the fact that the Jewish sect which killed Christ actually, and paradoxically, brought anti-Semitism into the world *with* Judaism (34). It was only in the eighteenth century that the *Aufklärung*, the Enlightenment, attempted to bring Jew and Christian together; its tolerant attitude 'bot ihm [the Jew] die geistige Möglichkeit, aus seiner Isolation zu entweichen' and freed the Christian from the 'Getto seines Glaubens'.

It was Karl Marx, the grandson of a rabbi, who developed out of the tormented and pursued Jewish race the concept of the exploited proletariat, thus creating a new religion, Marxism. This allows Dürrenmatt a *bon mot*: 'Wie die christliche Kirche das Christentum, führt die kommunistische Partei den Kommunismus ad absurdum' (41)! The first part of the essay closes with a repetition of Dürrenmatt's belief that the state of Israel owes its very existence to Hitler, a paradox which seems to please the author greatly.

Part II deals with Israel's historical connection with the Arab states. For the Arabs, Israel is a 'religiöser Konflikt' (49), a concept which Dürrenmatt dislikes since, in his opinion, a state should not be based on a religion, which is an immutable: 'Wir sehen im Staat nicht eine unveränderbare, sondern eine veränderbare Konzeption (51).' Why? Because the state is dependent on people, who are subject to irrational and unforeseen forces – 'das Unberechenbare' again. He now moves to a long proof that Judaism and Islam are, in fact, one Faith, with Abraham as the *Urvater*: 'Denn der Islam ist noch entschiedener eine jüdische Sekte als das Christentum, wenn er auch von diesem die Internationalität übernahm' (54). Since a good deal of this polemic comes from good reference books, it becomes a trifle arid as Dürrenmatt takes us from the emergence of the Koran to the nationalisms of the twentieth century (61–74), ending with impressions gained from his visit in 1974 and justifying, he believes, his remark that this is part of an 'überreichen Geschichte, ohne deren Kenntnis wir vieles nicht verstehen, was heute im Nahen Osten geschieht' (74).

Its *raison d'être*, however, is clearly to bolster his argument about the similarity of these two Semitic faiths for, since they too are Semites, the Arabs cannot be labelled 'anti-Semitic'. Mohammed tried to convert the Jews to Mohammedanism, after all, with the argument that 'der Islam sei mit dem Judentum identisch' (76). 'Geschichtlich', Dürrenmatt adds, 'ist der Araber durchaus nicht der Erbfeind der Juden' (79).

There follows here the little parable, discussed above (80–2), about Abu Chanifa and Anan ben David, which, we recall, Dürrenmatt claimed might be 'eine Hoffnung für heute, vielleicht eine Möglichkeit für morgen' (87), since the point of the story was that, although the two men did not have the same religion, they shared a common culture.

Part III of this long essay deals with the Arabs' insistence that, with Israel, they are dealing with a 'fascist' state, largely because of its connection with, and reliance on the USA. The paradox that Israel was formed as a consequence of the persecution *by* a fascist state, and that the Jews have fled into 'einen Weltwinkel, der wie kein zweiter vom Faschismus bedroht ist' (93), allows Dürrenmatt to return to his first antinomy, 'existentiell' versus 'ideologisch', clothing it in a complex, rather confused grammatical structure which was to become characteristic of much of his later prose-work in the 1970s and 1980s: 'Wo das Existentielle dem Ideologischen gegenübersteht, nimmt der Ideologe gegen das Existentielle Stellung, nicht das, was ist, ist für ihn berechtigt, sondern das, was sein sollte, auch wenn das, was ist, notwendig ist' (94). That is, for the ideological, Marxist-supported Arabs, 'existential' Israel is a fascist state. (Paraphrasing Hegel, Dürrenmatt adds grimly, 'Um so schlimmer für Israel.')

Dürrenmatt's long-seated dislike of ideologies is then paraded for the next twenty pages or so, to culminate in his reason for seeking all those *Zusammenhänge* (connections): 'ist doch die Notwendigkeit des jüdischen Staates im letzten durch nichts als "wahr" nachzuweisen, durch keine Logik, die ja nie das Existentielle erreicht' (107). Now looking ahead, Dürrenmatt suggests that, if the Palestinians contribute to the fall of Israel, they themselves will be the next victims of the Arab states. So, he thinks, there is room for *two* states there, sharing Jerusalem as their capital – admittedly the greatest stumbling-block in the way of any peace settlement. But 'das Zukünftige ist immer utopisch', he grants (112), notwithstanding Arafat-led terrorism. But the Jews will need all the wisdom and patience that is their *sole* inheritance from History.

Part IV gives the justification for this extraordinary piece of prose: Dürrenmatt's mother, aged eighty-eight in 1976, had introduced him to the Old Testament stories, and he admits that he is still visited by the fear that this small state could be liquidated. Once again he argues that Israel's right to live can only be contested 'ideologically', but it is a 'geschichtliches Axiom' which demands 'existence'.

This ends his 'speech', 162 pages long in the first 1976 Arche edition. But we are then launched into another long section on Dürrenmatt's journeys in Israel before he finally comes to one of the real reasons for the essay: the death of his mother nine months later at the age of almost eighty-nine, a woman 'deren Glaube mich störte und oft ärgerte, der wie ein Schwert zwischen ihr und mir lag' (128). We realise that the feelings of guilt which swept over him as he became aware of his sins of commission and omission were clearly mirrored in the Swiss feeling of guilt *vis-à-vis* the people tortured by Switzerland's Germanic brethren, a sombre and chilling example of the influence of a personal fate on a writer's public expression.

The essay, in its enormous and discursive length, is Dürrenmatt's personal retribution for the crimes visited upon Israel, the Jewish people, God's people, who are 'der erste Gesamtbegriff, dem sich der Einzelne unterordnen konnte, der erste Versuch der Versöhnung des Allgemeinen mit dem Besonderen' (147). It is undeniable that, since the general tide has flowed against Israel, Dürrenmatt's views do appear to be what he himself called them – 'utopisch' – and Jean Améry's picture of the 'vereinsamten Dürrenmatt' (45) is no doubt an accurate one. Nevertheless, although our attention flags throughout the reading of this essay, and a good deal of it does seem a little pretentious, we can only praise the courage of his utterance. (In the WA, the essay is followed by the now almost obligatory 'Nachgedanken', written here especially for the 1980 edition. I shall consider it below in its chronological order. I might mention here too that Peter Spycher's commentary on this 'mühselig entstehenden und nicht fertig werdenden Rede' is a valuable contribution to the Dürrenmatt literature (E41, 243–57).

* * *

Apart from a production of *Emilia Galotti* at the Schauspielhaus in Zurich on 5 June 1974, the years 1974–6 were 'theatre-less' years for Friedrich Dürrenmatt; during them, he concentrated on essay-writing, producing after *Zusammenhänge* another huge essay, the *Komplex* on *Der Mitmacher*, in 1976 and working on what was to become *Stoffe I–III* (A1/2). (Knapp believes that these are meant to form a trilogy (C29, 109), a presumption which will be invalidated when *Stoffe IV–VI* (or *VII*) appears.) We have charted the failure of Dürrenmatt's play *Der Mitmacher* which had its première on 8 March 1973 (above, 144ff.). *Der Mitmacher. Ein Komplex* bore the sub-titles, 'Text der Komödie – Dramaturgie – Erfahrungen – Berichte – Erzählungen', all now in WA14, (The original ISBN number for *Zusammenhänge* was 3 7160 1553 9 and for *Der Mitmacher* 3 7160 1566 0, which might indicate that the two works were prepared for the press at about the same time.)

Since my discussion of the play itself and of the short story 'Smithy' which led to the play allowed me to comment on the 'Nachwort' (97–221), it might be wise to concentrate attention in this chapter on the succeeding 'Nachwort zum Nachwort' (225–328), a self-indulgent, rambling collection of ideas, opinions – and vendettas!

To start off such a section with the pessimistic comment, 'Wozu das alles, muß ich mich nun doch fragen, wozu die unmäßige Länge dieses Nachworts' (221), while justifying my remarks above, hardly sets the reader in the right frame of mind to approach the rest! If one perseveres, however, there are many nuts of gold among the dross. As Dürrenmatt himself suggests, 'Nicht brächte eine Philosophie ein Stück, sondern ein Stück eine Philosophie hervor' (226), which would have been a scholarly justification. But shortly afterwards he gives what we feel must surely be the real reason for the 'unmäßige Länge' of the piece, 'Vielleicht ist dieses ganze Nachwort auch nur ein Purzelbaum, den ich schlage, um mich aus einer verfehlten Affäre zu ziehen' (229), and we recall that he also wrote a 'Dramaturgie eines Durchfalls' (WA24, 231–49) (February 1976) (above, 147), of *Der Mitmacher*. Even the banalities sound bitter here: he started writing on 26 August 1974 at 15.35; it is now 22 January 1976, 'nicht ganz achthunderttausend Minuten danach' (231), and it is now another 'Ich' writing – and each 'Ich', each narrator, is a 'Fiktion', a 'Modell': 'So oder so kann die Wahrheit bloß in Märchenform erzählt werden' (232). The 'Ich' which was strolling down Manhattan on that stinking hot day in May 1959 leads Dürrenmatt into the story of 'Smithy' (235–61) and into what he now begins, frequently, to call a 'labyrinth', a place where he is alone and lost and where he contemplates the life that had gone before. Here, he uses his character Bill (in the play, Doc's son) to expatiate on the subject of 'Faith'. Bill, he writes, possesses Faith which Doc (the 'ironic hero') does not and which makes Doc both cynical and despairing. Dürrenmatt's introduction of the theme at this time makes one wonder whether he is becoming more and more conscious as he grows older of the gulf which separates him, 'den Einzelnen', from that far-off world of Konolfingen and the simple faith of his parents. 'Der ironische Held, der absolut Einzelne,' he writes (ostensibly of Cop), 'steht neben der Menschheit' (266). This *Urmotiv*, the individual alone in the world, a hostile world, has never been so stressed before as here: 'Weil der Mensch ein Einzelner ist, ist er ein Geheimnis, und weil er ein Geheimnis ist, geht er aus keinem System hervor' (267).

Animadversions on Turkey, Verdi, Wagner, Brecht and *Zufall* finally lead to the story 'Das Sterben der Pythia' (274–313) (above, 84–5) whose *raison d'être*, we now learn, was typically trivial: 'Hatte ich die Geschichte von Smithy erzählt, um aufzuspüren, wie ich auf einen Stoff gerate, so erzählte ich die Geschichte des Ödipus aus Neugier, was mich an einem Stoff erregt' (314). But this leads nevertheless to a discussion of Fate and Chance which shows that Dürrenmatt's 'obsession' with the *Zufall*-motif is closely connected to his theory of 'victims'. Man, he claims, 'ist dem Zufall gegenüber, als dem Unvorhersehbaren, nur noch ein Opfer', whereas his Fate, his *Schicksal*, determines his Being for ever, it is part of his *character* (314–15).

This hundred-page 'excursus' (in the WA) ends, peculiarly, with a petulant comparison of Brecht's stage successes with his own failures. The latter he blames on poor productions; Beckett and Ionesco, he felt, made their plays 'narrensicher', but 'dieser Eintrittspreis war mir stets zu hoch' (317). He regrets Brecht's attacks on such writers as himself, those who seemed to Brecht to be writing out of a well of deepest pessimism ('den sie zu guten Preisen verkaufen', wrote Brecht). This charge, often made against himself, thought Dürrenmatt, came unfittingly from a man who seemed not to have been particularly moved by the 'Schreie der Vergewaltigten' which, surely, he could hear all around him in the GDR. But to suggest this, or even to criticise Brecht at all, was almost impossible. Günter Grass had done so, of course, with his *Die Plebejer proben den Aufstand* of 1966, but such works as these 'verschwanden von den deutschen Bühnen, man spielte sie lieber nicht; an Brecht wagt man sich nicht heran' (321), a slight overstatement, I am sure. Dürrenmatt obviously believes that Brecht is in an unassailable position in the German theatre – and that that theatre had *needed* someone like Brecht. However, he adds, the theatre 'durch den Dichter Brecht verführt' is now 'auf den Denker Brecht hereingefallen' (322). His final hope is that people will read *his* pronouncements on theatre as they read Brecht's, and particularly the present one – an attempt, Dürrenmatt writes, 'über sich als Schriftsteller ins klare zu kommen' (323).

His final pages deal with the question of his faith, and his answer is as paradoxical as ever: he is 'against' whatever the ruling 'faith' is! And when he is alone? 'Ich kann es dir nicht sagen. Denn ich glaube, je nach dem Augenblick' (326), because Faith means suppressing Doubt – and to do that means lying to yourself.

Thus this long, self-indulgent odyssey, undertaken he writes 'des Reisens wegen', gives us a view of a wounded, bitter, discontented writer who believes that he has failed in the theatre and who seeks to justify his *modus operandi*. This at best, seems to demand tolerance and understanding from all connected with him, but at worst suggests that he would prefer to 'sit on the fence' and to need, like his Bishop in *Die Wiedertäufer*, 'die Täuschung loser Stunden Zuschauer nur zu sein' (WA10, 23).[9]

* * *

Dürrenmatt is as paradoxical in the matter of giving interviews as he is in everything else. Seemingly cut off from the world in his house(s) high up above the Lac de Neuchâtel, he has always shown himself nevertheless to be an approachable and courteous host who never fails to make the guest feel at home, served with good food and even better wines. My two visits in 1969 and 1988 certainly remain most pleasant memories. The bibliographies testify to the number of interviews that he has given: some fifty-two are listed in *Über Friedrich Dürrenmatt* (WA70, 459–60) and others are not included.

Heinz Ludwig Arnold, who had edited the two volumes in the *text + kritik* series on Dürrenmatt (C4 and C5), spoke at length to Dürrenmatt on 7 and 8 March 1975, at the time of the première of *Der Mitmacher*. (The interview did not appear until 1976 (F1, 9–85).) I have already covered a good deal of the ground of their conversation – early influences, memories, events – but want simply to point out here how Dürrenmatt began the defence of his *Der Mitmacher* almost as soon as it appeared. 'Ich weiß, mein letztes Stück ist eine große Niederlage, das ist mir vollständig egal' (42), he says, and goes on to develop the idea of the 'ironic hero' (Cop in the play), a Kierkegaardian concept, to place beside the 'tragic' and the 'comic' hero. The ironic hero does v. .at he does 'um sich selbst noch achten zu können, um sich selber nicht verächtlich sein zu müssen' (43). Everything else – the world, saving the world, changing the world – is ignored, 'er kann sich noch achten', which is why he lets himself be shot. The phrase 'er kann sich noch achten' seems to be very important, for it is immediately after that that Dürrenmatt admits to Arnold ·v·hat I suggested above. He says, 'Ich bin in einer Sackgasse, ich kann nur immer feststellen: In meinem ganzen schriftstellerischen Leben bin ich immer nur in Sackgassen gelandet' (44), and the feeling had come over him that he was too old (he was then fifty-four). He claimed that he had not had the support of managers, critics or the public, yet 'mich kümmert nicht die Kritik, mich kümmert, daß man nicht hinter mir steht, und daß ich das nicht habe, was Brecht hatte, ein Theater, das hinter einem steht' (47). But he denied vehemently that that was 'große Resignation', particularly, he said to Arnold, grunting humorously, I am certain, 'bei diesem Wein, den ich Ihnen jetzt vorsetze'! (48).

The conversation covers many interesting topics on which we have already touched; out of it, one receives the impression of a man combating his own nature and society at the same time. 'Ich kann mir keine Gesellschaft denken,' he says, 'in der der Schriftsteller nicht die Position der Rebellion bezieht' (63), and it is here that he mentions how enraged he would be to see a book with the title *Trost bei Dürrenmatt*. Such comfort is impossible in a world of corruption – he mentions how timely for *Der Mitmacher* the Watergate affair was! – all a writer can do is to present 'die Wirklichkeit . . . in Form von Gegenwelten', to illuminate for the audience a tiny section of Reality (80–1).

There was thus an air of disillusionment about the author when he made the journey to Wales to receive the Welsh Arts Council International Writers' Prize in November 1976. A full programme of visits and academic lectures and seminars had been planned and, although Dürrenmatt always finds it difficult to be polite among academics, his company was enjoyed until, on the evening that he was due to receive the prize (12 November), he was taken seriously ill and was unable to accept the prize personally.

On 6 March of the next year, 1977, Dürrenmatt was the recipient this time of an even more prestigious award, the *Buber-Rosenzweig-Medaille* of the Gesellschaft für Christlich-Jüdische Zusammenarbeit, in the famous Paulskirche in Frankfurt. His address on this occasion bore the Lessing-like title 'Über Toleranz' (now in WA27, 125–49). His 'Nachträgliche Vorbemerkung' (125–8) explains the early interest in philosophy, his regard for Kierkegaard and his dislike of Hegel. He calls the latter's celebrated *Phänomenologie des Geistes* 'ein Herumrasen im Gefängnis der Sprache'! Once again, however, he strives to present himself as a 'Denker'. 'Aber es ist notwendig, die geistige Landschaft anzugeben, der man entstammt, mag noch so viel in ihr unbewältigt oder falsch vorhanden sein' (127) – and, he added that, as the son of a clergyman, he disliked all theological speculation.

The speech/essay avers that religious tolerance has been more or less accepted, political tolerance not, and he picks up an old motif by then asserting that, before nations can be free, there has to be justice. The Federal Republic's CDU's antinomy in the recent elections, 'Freiheit *oder* Sozialismus' (my italics) was an example of this political intolerance. Lessing's *Toleranzgedanke*, displayed above all in *Nathan der Weise*, Kant's *Kritik der reinen Vernunft* and Kierkegaard's philosophical writings, helped to bring about religious tolerance, 'Gott weicht ins Unbeweisbare zurück', and the church had become a fiction. From there, Dürrenmatt begins to build up the case for tolerance for the Jews. He cites Karl Barth who considered 'die Existenz des jüdischen Volkes als den einzig natürlichen Gottesbeweis' (139) – 'Folgerichtig kann denn für Barth der Christ nur durch die Gnade Gottes kein Antisemit sein' (140) is Dürrenmatt's brave assertion.

He now bitterly attacks Karl Marx's assumption of the Hegelian philosophy which led, Dürrenmatt claims, to the 'Diktatur des

Proletariats', the 'Hegelsche[n], Polizeistaat' and the suppression of the individual's freedom; the 'Opfer' of the 'Mächtigen' in bureaucracy, the intolerance of the Gentile majority. We need, he says, a new *Aufklärung*: 'die Freiheit des Einzelnen kann nur die Freiheit aller sein' (144); we must drop our claims on Truth, Justice and Freedom and substitute, as Lessing himself did, the *search* for Truth, Justice and Freedom; and we must do that by the use of *Vernunft*, Reason, rational thinking. And now another old motif appears, 'Das Gesetz der großen Zahl': 'Es wird die Menschen ärmer machen', Dürrenmatt points out (147). It will necessitate the rational rethinking of established views and institutions because 'das Suchen nach der Gerechtigkeit vor dem Suchen nach Freiheit kommen muß' (148), and we recall how in the 'Monstervortrag' *Gerechtigkeit* was paired with *Sozialismus*.

He ends his speech with a warning that all these thoughts could be rendered useless if nations continued to fear one another, 'Wer aber Furcht sät, erntet Waffen' (149), and his audience was in no doubt that he included the more 'hawkish' of Israeli leaders in his condemnation.

It was the type of speech that one might have expected 'from a Swiss'. For those who knew their Dürrenmatt, however, it gave yet another insight into his complex character: Was this continuing support for the Jews and Israel his continuing abjuration of the faith of his father, on the one hand, and an atonement of the guilt felt for his own small country's treatment of the Jews during the Second World War, and of its foreign 'Gastarbeiter' after it, on the other? And was the 'philosophical' atmosphere of the speech an attempt to prove his ability to think, something not proven by the banalities of his latest plays?

That same year, 1977, saw the publication of his '55 Sätze über Kunst und Wirklichkeit' in the *text + kritik* volume II (C5, 20–2), and now in WA28, 157–65. Dürrenmatt is, as we have noted, fond of this aphoristic, epigrammatic style, so reminiscent of the Austrian Karl Kraus (1874–1936) and the satirists between the wars, but also of the great German writers like Georg Christian Lichtenberg (1742–99) whom Dürrenmatt admires so much.

We are on familiar territory: 'Jede politische Struktur läßt sich von zwei Seiten aus darstellen: von jener der Mächtigen und von jener der Ohnmächtigen aus' (No. 11, 158). Numbers 20–8 make interesting reading on 'politische Kunst' as Dürrenmatt develops the theme that all art needs 'distancing' to be understood. 'Ist sein Inhalt Empörung, ist seine Distanz Versöhnung' (No. 21, 159) and vice versa (No. 22). So, if the contents are 'tragic', 'distancing' makes them 'comic' (and again vice versa). The author then turns from 'comedy' to 'happiness', and we read that only individuals ('Menschen') can be happy, not 'people in the mass' ('Menschheit'). The 'Gesetz der großen Zahl' will prevent that; all that men can hope for is to be allowed to live without oppression: 'Wer Ideologien zerstört, zerstört Rechtfertigungen von Gewalt' (No. 49, 162).

Although one could easily prove that Dürrenmatt thinks in slick aphorisms and could make a collection of them from his works for a sort of 'calendar', as one does for Goethe each year, he has striven hard to prove that he is not what he called himself in his earlier years, a 'Kurzstreckenläufer', but that he has the intellectual stamina for longer works of substance. These 'Sätze' might be proof.[10]

* * *

His next, and one of his most important addresses was given on 24 February 1978 on the hundredth anniversary of the birth of Albert Einstein. It took place in the Eidgenössischen Technischen Hochschule in Zurich, where Einstein himself had worked before the First World War. The motto above the printed 'essay' (in WA29, 150–72) is from Job xix, 4: 'And be it indeed that I have erred, mine error remaineth with myself.'

Once more, Dürrenmatt begins as the 'non-expert', who nevertheless proceeds to lecture competently and, indeed, to provide a lecture of the highest order. Once more, too, he is speaking on a Jewish theme, about a Jewish physicist whom Dürrenmatt treats firstly as a theologian, albeit 'ein verkappter Theologe'! Like Dürrenmatt himself, Einstein lost his faith, in his case after reading Kant at the age of twelve, and later in life he turned to the Deist philosophy of Spinoza. Dürrenmatt then imagines that he is playing chess with Einstein and that both are guided by the same rules, those of *Vernunft*. If the world's happenings are thought of as a chess match, there will be two players at the 'table', 'eine deterministische [Partei] und eine kausale'. For the first, 'die Welt [ist] durch Prädestination determiniert, statt des Chaos' herrscht eine unbarmherzige Ordnung' (153); for the second, the chess pieces are the causes of their effects, their mistakes are their own (cf. the motto of the essay). Lover of antinomies as he is, Dürrenmatt then shows by this method how the great question, Why is the world not perfect? has become more and more difficult to answer: 'einerseits herrschten in der Natur die Gesetze, anderseits brach vom freien Geiste her immer wieder das Chaos in die Welt' (155). But Spinoza turned away from the Jewish God; *his* God knows neither good nor evil: 'Diesem Gott schreibt Spinoza eine determi- nistische, nicht eine kausale Welt zu' (156). And this was Einstein's God also, 'der sich in der gesetzlichen Harmonie des Seienden offenbar[t]' (157).

Dürrenmatt charmingly admits that he is now dealing with two of the most difficult thinkers, 'wobei ich nicht weiß, welchen von beiden ich besser mißverstehe . . .' (158), yet he proceeds with the chess match analogy, firstly because chess is a logical game, and secondly because he at least understands the rules of chess. The burden of his argument is that, without a knowledge, however basic, of the development of the natural sciences in the twentieth century, we cannot hope to be able to construct any sort of *Weltanschauung*, whether it be in the Arts or the Sciences, but also that Einstein's deterministic attitude to the sciences and to philos- ophy, his disbelief in a 'Gott, der würfelt', was a Jewish attitude, a 'Rebellion gegen das Chaos'. Here Dürrenmatt repeats himself and says that this was 'ein Denken, das mehr als jedes andere Denken die Welt veränderte' (170), much more than that of Hegel, Marx, Brecht, etc.

He ends on yet another paradox: that this 'new thinking' has not led 'zum Schauen der prästabilierten Harmonie', as Einstein had hoped and expected, but rather 'zur Vision einer prästabilierten Explosion', and that this man, one of the clearest and most rational thinkers of his age, could only see before him 'dieses ungeheuerli- che Labyrinth, in welchem wir immer hilfloser und hoffnungsloser herumtappen' (170–1).[11]

This essay proves, once more, how intensely interested Dürren- matt is in natural phenomena; anyone who has visited his house, noted his array of telescopes, seen his drawings based on such phenomena and read essays like this one, will better understand the thinking behind literary works such as *Die Physiker*, *Der Meteor* and *Porträt eines Planeten*. For Dürrenmatt, human relationships mirror natural phenomena: the 'rottenness' in the state of Denmark lay outside, as well as inside, the walls of Elsinore.

* * *

The label 'Der unbequeme Dürrenmatt', introduced as far back as 1962 in the Basilius Press volume (cf. C19), remained clearly justified with Dürrenmatt, but even throughout these unhappy 1970s honours continued to be heaped upon him: honorary doctor- ates from the universities of Nice and Jerusalem (1977), the *Litera- turpreis der Stadt Bern* (1979), an honorary doctorate from the university of Neuchâtel on his sixtieth birthday (5 January 1981) and an entire 'Dürrenmatt-Symposium' in Los Angeles in the same year (cf. the volume *Play Dürrenmatt*, B17).

The town of Berne prize followed the award ten years previously of the canton of Berne award – and the scandal of the 'hippies' that came after it (above, 180–1). The prize this time, promised Dürrenmatt with a chuckle, 'behalte ich für meine Frau'! Although the address (given an 19 June 1979) has no provocative title either (now in WA28, 164–73), the barbs followed quickly when he reminded his audience that, although his old enemies, the 'Literaturpäpste', put him at the very back of their shelves, some even 'reihen mich . . . bei den Klassikern ein', beside those authors that is, about whom one has no further need to worry!

Many of his favourite topics are rehearsed. His obsession with the natural sciences at this time makes him remind his audience that it is the scientist who changes the world and, above all, the mathematician: 'niemand ist denn auch weniger in unser Bewußt-sein eingedrungen als sie' (167). And the scientists are much more important than the politicians, who forget sometimes that 'sich die Politik nach dem Menschen, und nicht der Mensch sich nach der Politik zu richten hat' (167).

He then turns to another of his *Urmotive*: 'Der Gegensatz zur Freiheit ist die Diktatur, der Gegensatz zum Kapitalismus ist der Sozialismus' (168). Both systems, taken to extremes, lead to tragedy, the one to fascism, the other to communism; 'beide Gebilde pendeln sich endlich um die Achse der Diktatur ein', a comment which must have pleased those in the audience who had feared anti-Swiss fireworks. Dürrenmatt pleaded for Reason to be employed – against nuclear reactors, bureaucracy in high places and over-powerful armies (*inter alia*).

The last section of his essay is personal, and he sets off here on the track of the next great motif that will sound through his writings. Recalling his early days in Berne, he states that his coming to terms with the town produced two great motifs, 'um die mein Denken seitdem kreist: das Labyrinth und die Rebellion: die Motive und Motivationen meines Denkens zugleich' (171). We shall be pursuing these in his later essays shortly.

On 5 January 1981 Dürrenmatt would be sixty, and birthday celebrations were set early in train. The *Werkausgabe* was produced in thirty volumes, in hard- and paperback, there was a grandiose *Festakt* on 10 January in the Zurich Schauspielhaus (with a production of *Romulus der Große*) and Dürrenmatt, having been interviewed so many times by others, decided to interview himself:

'Friedrich Dürrenmatt interviewt F.D.' appeared in *text + kritik* in December 1980 (and is now in WA25, 139–67). I have, of course, already quoted extensively from this most interesting text since Dürrenmatt discusses in it almost all of his works – in a light-hearted, sardonic fashion, it is true, but for those who can read between the lines and know something of the history of the works the interview gives many an insight into the thinking and the circumstances which lay behind them. All who have interviewed Dürrenmatt have come away, I am certain, with the uneasy feeling that they have heard Dürrenmatt's views for *that* hour and *that* day. This is what he says 'to himself': 'Als ich mit ihm sprach, kam es mir vor, als denke er, während er meine Fragen beantwortete, an das, was er denken wolle, wenn ich gegangen sein werde: an etwas ganz anderes, als er jetzt sprach' (141).

After discussing all of his plays, Dürrenmatt turns to the present, admitting that, after 1973, he knew 'daß ich mich im Theater ins Abseits gespielt hatte' (164): for non-soccer players, he meant that he had put himself outside the 'rules' of the 'game'. He still wants to do something new, something different, however, a play *Der Tod des Sokrates*, a 'Lieblingsstück' is in his head, but when his publishers Diogenes are on to him to write a new novel, 'Wen wundert's da, daß ich mich manchmal zur Staffelei schleiche' (167) – and, of course, in that year he had the first exhibition of his art-works in the Loeb-Galerie in Berne, from 2 September to 16 October.

In 1980 too, 'Nachgedanken unter anderem über Freiheit, Gleichheit und Brüderlichkeit in Judentum, Christentum, Islam und Marxismus und über zwei alte Mythen 1980' his 'second thoughts' to his long essay *Zusammenhänge*, were published. Now in WA29, 163–219, they are Dürrenmatt's strongest anti-Marxist views yet on paper: 'Als Ideologie einer Supermacht', he writes, 'wie sie die Sowjetunion ist, erscheint der Marxismus als Parodie seiner selbst, und das nur, weil er seine Ideologie für eine Wahrheit hält' (165) – a far cry, indeed, from the days when he castigated Switzerland for her fear of communism. The 'Vorbemerkung' explains how the 'Nachgedanken' followed *Zusammenhänge*; the thoughts on determinism and causality, also discussed in the Einstein lecture, became thoughts on Islam–Marxism, on rationalism and irrationalism. Following his declaration of the importance of mathematics as a 'deduktives Phänomen' (170), he deduces that all dogmatic pronouncements on religion came from unprovable ideas, and are therefore deductive – the Christian doctrine of redemption, for example. The Jewish dialectic, on the other hand, comes from the exegesis of the Old Testament – God as a *secret*, an uncertainty. Christians were 'certain', Jews 'uncertain', until the dogma of Papal infallibility drove the church into a cul-de-sac. He turns next to Marxism which, he avers, grew out of the Enlightenment and then destroyed it. The comparison is with Islam – both are deterministic philosophies: 'Mit dem Islam steht das alte Mittelalter dem neuen Mittelalter des Marxismus gegenüber' (176).

What Dürrenmatt is trying to prove is that the Western world, the world of capitalism, Judaism (and 'Freedom') is an irrational world, that of Marxism and Islam (and 'Justice'), a rational one: 'Der Rationalismus strebt nach Ordnung und nach Widerspruchsfreiheit, der Irrationalismus nährt sich vom Labyrinthischen und vom Widerspruch' (177). Clearly then, his new-found interest in Israel and Judaism has 'let him see' the unacceptable face of Marxism. He believes that Marxism has concentrated power in the hands of the 'Mächtigen' and has made it more difficult 'diese Macht zu begründen und damit zu legitimieren' (186).

The essay concentrates now on the difference between the dualistic church (*Ideologie* and *Ärgernis*), that is, 'eine Waffe für die Beherrschten' (192), and the monistic Marxism. Both have their faults but 'will das Christentum bekehren, will der Marxismus herrschen'. Since the latter denies this, it has become for Dürrenmatt 'eine permanente Lüge' (196–7). Finally, we turn to the antinomies of the 'Monstervortrag': capitalists (the 'Wölfe') seek Freedom, the Marxists (the 'Lämmer') *Justice*, and if, or where, there is no brotherly love ('Brüderlichkeit'), the 'regulating principle', they will seek to destroy one another. But again, he sees the USSR as a physicist sees an unstable star – near to explosion – and, remarkably prophetically for 1980, he writes: 'Alles deutet darauf hin, daß die Sowjetunion sich der Grenze der Stabilität nähert . . . daß die Sowjetunion nichts so sehr fürchtet wie Veränderungen in ihrem Innern' (201). In the West we circle round these two suns like satellites attached, as it were, by the force of gravity, and influenced by both. The last words are the relevance to Israel: Israel and Palestine are likewise bound to the two great superpowers; neither can at the moment countenance the other as 'state', but Dürrenmatt believes that they must do that, and that they will: 'Sie sind beide aufeinander angewiesen' (214).

This is a thought-provoking essay from a writer who has grown greater in stature as an essayist as he has declined in stature as a playwright. Ironically, paradoxically perhaps, his strengths seem to lie, perhaps in retrospect always have lain, in what he at first strenuously opposed, in 'philosophising', although to be fair he meant, in those days, 'philosophising *on the stage*'. 'Das Ferne rückt erst mit der Zeit näher', he was to write in *Stoffe* – he is now taking his ten *Semester* of Philosophy study to that 'akademischen Abschluß' which he now obviously regrets having failed to achieve.

We are nearing the end of this examination of Dürrenmatt's 'essayistic' work; a worthwhile examination, I hope, of an area of his *oeuvre* largely unknown to a public which thinks of Dürrenmatt either as a playwright or, in the case of young students, as the author of crime stories. His own re-examination of his talents, in the 'interview with himself' for example, revealed that he is now well aware that he has gifts outside theatrical work, but that he will always be drawn back to the theatre – *Die Frist* (1977), *Die Panne* (1979), *Achterloo* (1983) and *Achterloo IV* (1988) prove that. Yet in the theatre, he has been consistently rebuffed by the critics mainly, and by the public partly, and he seems almost to have taken refuge in this other area. Certainly, all these experiences contributed to a work which appeared in 1981, but which had obviously been maturing for many years, *Stoffe I–III*, first in the Diogenes Verlag, 1981, and now in two volumes, 'Winterkrieg in Tibet' (*Stoffe I*) (A1) and 'Mondfinsternis' and 'Der Rebell' (*Stoffe II–III*) (A2) in the detebe format.

There is not much that I wish to add here to what I have written about *Stoffe* in other sections of this study; the reader will recall the discussions of the various stories included in it (above, 85–91), and I took the opportunity in relevant places to relate Dürrenmatt's introspective, and retrospective, musings on his early life to my own thoughts. The deep pessimistic strain found within, and at the end of, the book(s) should not, however, be overlooked, and if the reader is willing to agree that a writer's work is influenced by the quality of his life, it must be realised that this was written by a man sorely tried in his personal and public affairs. In his 'Dramaturgie des Labyrinths' (A1 77–94), the author writes of the reason for this 'labyrinth' in which he finds himself. It is there 'weil . . . jeder Versuch, diese Welt denkend zu bewältigen – und sei es nur mit dem Gleichnis der Schriftsteller – ein Kampf ist, den man mit sich selber führt: Ich bin mein Feind, du bist der deinige' (94), and this battle, which Dürrenmatt began to wage with himself in his earliest writings as we have seen, seemed in 1980–1 to have been lost . The last pages of 'Der Rebell' (which closes *Stoffe II–III*) breathe hopeless resignation: 'Er gibt den Kampf allmählich auf, stiert vor sich hin, tagelang, wochenlang . . . Und irgendwo hinter den Spiegeln verbirgt sich vielleicht . . . der, gegen den er rebellierte . . . vielleicht der Herrscher, vielleicht das Oberhaupt der Kirche, vielleicht sein Vater, es ist ihm gleichgültig. Es ist wirklich gleichgültig' (172–3).

In the light of the intimate reminiscences of *Stoffe*, *Rollenspiele* and, recently, *Versuche*, I can see little reason for not believing that the sentiments expressed in these pages are personal, and not just authorial. All the more so when one considers that on 16 January 1983 Dürrenmatt's wife Lotti died. In that year, he rewrote an essay which had originally appeared in French in the *Revue neuchâteloise* in the winter months of 1980–1, 'Vallon de l'Ermitage', the district of Neuchâtel where Dürrenmatt's street, the Chemin du Pertuis-du-Sault, is situated. It is a retrospective essay, rather like the material of *Stoffe*, meandering through past and present, but beginning: 'Je mehr die Zeit fortschreitet, desto dichter spinnt sie ihr Netz, worin sie uns verstrickt . . .'. (The essay is now in *Versuche* (A6, 9–56, here 9).)

Interestingly, however, the only mention of Dürrenmatt's wife is of her absence when he suffered his severe heart attack in 1969. Otherwise, the theme is Neuchâtel and Dürrenmatt's obvious lack of sympathy for, and in, its welfare. *Versuche* contains generally rather indifferent material; the most interesting piece is probably the address given as Gastdozent für Poetik at the University of Frankfurt on 16 November 1984, with another baroque title, 'Kunst und Wissenschaft oder Platon oder Einfall, Vision und Idee oder Die Schwierigkeit einer Anrede oder Anfang und Ende einer Rede' (70–95).

Dürrenmatt suggested that an attempt should have been made to deal with questions like 'Ist Beuys noch Kunst?' or 'Ist Astrologie Wissenschaft?' In effect, he launched out again on a favourite theme: 'Wie die Erde befindet sich auch der Mensch in einem Sonnensystem, in jenem des menschlichen Geistes' (74). Neither art nor science can exist without 'Einfälle, Visionen und Ideen', and he reminded his audience of the extraordinary vision of the first Greek scientists: Lucippus, *floreat* 440 BC, for example, 'weil er sah, daß Entstehung und Veränderung in den Dingen ohne Aufhören sei' (76).

Plato and his 'ideas' is his next theme – 'Die Idee war Platons Vision' – and the painter Dürrenmatt expatiates on the Platonic concept of a chair 'als Idee, als Möbel und als Nachahmung', but concludes, rather grandiosely, that Plato the philosopher had had as much success with his 'idea' as Dürrenmatt the writer has had with his: 'Wir sind beide gescheitert' (82)! Both had tried too to 'free' language, Plato from its ambivalencies, Dürrenmatt from the 'Floskeln' 'von denen sie heute immer mehr umstellt wird' (82), a brave claim, one would have thought, from a Bernese writer in Germany. The connection between Plato and Dürrenmatt must have seemed tenuous to his audience, but he took up the point again with Charlotte Kerr in *Rollenspiele*, as we shall see.

He had earlier mentioned a favourite *bête noire*, the monstrous growth in technology; Dürrenmatt cites the CERN, the nuclear complex in Geneva, with its 3,000 staff, as the logical conclusion to a vision born thousands of years ago in the mind of Man that one day the atom would be split. Yet another proof for his belief that 'was einmal gedacht und niedergeschrieben wird, und sei es von anderen, geht nie ganz verloren' (78).

His conclusion brings together his abiding interests in the 'Two Cultures', Arts and Sciences. Both have touched his life in many places, both have clearly not only given him great pleasure but have enriched his life and influenced his career as a writer: 'Die Wissenschaft interpretiert, die Kunst stellt dar, die Wissenschaft zielt auf das Eindeutige, die Kunst auf das Mehrdeutige . . . die eine auf die Idee, die andere auf die Vision' (92). He reminded his audience that his very first seminar essay in Philosophy was on that Book VII of Plato's *Politeia* (*The Republic*), the 'Cave Allegory', which is why he became a writer: 'um Weltgleichnisse zu finden' (95). The reader might agree after this journey through Dürrenmatt's career as a teller of tales that he has remained faithful to his early intent.

* * *

It is this 'Cave Allegory', the 'Höhlengleichnis', which allows a retrospective study of Dürrenmatt's essayistic work (up to 1988 anyway) to close naturally, since this theme, which we first noted on page 19 above and then in the short story 'Die Stadt' (20ff.), has never been abandoned over the forty years of his career. It has gone through various transformations but reappears now as the 'labyrinth', still the vision of a lonely man, 'ein Einzelner', enclosed in a mysterious, nebulous 'somewhere', puzzled, unhappy.

I shall be discussing shortly Dürrenmatt's pictorial art-forms, where the 'labyrinth' and the 'Minotaur' bulk large as themes, but should like to close this chapter with a few comments on the theme as it appears in his last major work to date, the mysterious *Ballade*, 'Minotaurus', of 1985 (A11, 7–51).

Sydney Donald's study of the theme (D14, 187–231) claims that 'Dürrenmatt has passed by stages from pessimistic bewilderment in the face of the 'Weltlabyrinth' through self-doubt and identity crises, and has achieved – if not mastery of the Labyrinth . . . – then at least personal reconciliation with its convolutions' (228).

This is rather a case of hedging one's bets, for no one can be certain that Dürrenmatt, or any author, is not going suddenly to find himself in another personal crisis. He is far from having reached his Elysian Fields; a conversation with him produces sparks of petulance and anger at some silly misinterpretation as before. Whether his marriage in 1984 to Charlotte Kerr may have helped him to achieve this 'personal reconciliation' of which Donald writes will clearly depend on that *Zufall*, Chance, which Dürrenmatt has so often depicted.

A reading of 'Minotaurus' must be preceded by a study of the 'Dramaturgie des Labyrinths' which appeared in *Stoffe I* (A1, 77–94). After reminding us there how first the cornfields and the corridors of the houses back in Konolfingen and then the mazy old streets of Berne formed his first 'labyrinth', Dürrenmatt admits that he is not clear why it should have then become such an *Urmotif* in his life and work. Certainly 'Das Labyrinth ist ein Gleichnis und als solches mehrdeutig wie jedes Gleichnis' (79), as we have often noted already. He then proceeds to explain the Minotaur's genesis. A sacrificial sea-bull was sent by Poseidon to Minos to be slaughtered. Minos kept it instead, to his sorrow, for his wife Pasiphae fell in love with the bull, a love which was 'consummated' only with the help of Daedalus who constructed a seductive artificial cow in which Pasiphae could hide. The outcome was the *Minotaurus*, 'eine Ungestalt mit dem Kopf eines Stiers und dem Leib eines Menschen' (79), which made the birth most painful! (The process of 'covering' cows is shown in great detail, and related with even greater relish, by Dürrenmatt in the 1984 film shot by Charlotte Kerr; he enlarges then on the topic of artificial insemination, gleefully imagining a whole range of cut-price Dürrenmatts created in this way. Few episodes could better illuminate his love of the grotesque!)

Now Dürrenmatt gives us an almost idyllic picture of the Minotaur grazing peacefully in a roomy park amidst trees and a lake – a picture much at odds with the traditional one of the savage Minotaur which devours seven youths and seven maidens from Athens every nine years. Dürrenmatt's Minotaur is, typically, a vegetarian! It is also alone: 'gab es doch kein weiteres Exemplar seiner Gattung' (85). Only now and then did its inborn 'Stierhaftigkeit' drive it to 'plötzlicher, unerklärter Wut'.

When the seven youths and the seven maidens did appear, Dürrenmatt's Minotaur *did* attack them and devour them. Dürrenmatt poses the question: Why did it do this? His answer: the Minotaur felt, instinctively, that he was 'etwas Einzigartiges', and 'daß er als dieser Einzigartige für ein Unrecht büßen mußte, welches er nicht begangen hatte' (86). This injustice is obviously the injustice that Dürrenmatt feels about the circumstances of his own birth and early life; exaggerated perhaps, but when one thinks of those autobiographical characters whom he had created, those whom, in my earlier book, I likened to the Plautian *miles gloriosus* – Tiphys (in *Der Prozeß um des Esels Schatten*), Herkules, Schwitter, *et al.* – and recognises the type of the 'absoluten Einzelnen', then the 'Gleichnis' of the Minotaur becomes obvious: 'Die Schuld des Minotaurus besteht darin, Minotaurus zu sein, eine Ungestalt, ein schuldig Unschuldiger' (89), incarcerated in everyone's labyrinth. For years, Dürrenmatt had felt imprisoned within his, to him, unprepossessing body, perpetually, and at times chronically, ill with diabetes: 'vollzog ich', he writes, 'den Urprotest, protestierte ich gegen meine Geburt; denn die Welt, in die ich hineingeboren wurde, war mein Labyrinth' (89). Such 'psychoanalytical' thoughts are not welcomed by Dürrenmatt, we know, but it is he, after all, who suggests them to the reader! Life is an *Urdrama*, be it tragedy or comedy, the confrontation of a human body with its environ-ment, an individual Minotaur in its labyrinth.

But who is telling the story of the Minotaur? Years later, Dürrenmatt realised that this 'fingierte Ich' was not, as he had always assumed, the 'Minotaur', but was in fact Theseus, the Theseus of old who enters the labyrinth to *kill* the Minotaur. We are once again confronted with the typical Dürrenmattian para-doxical situation: Theseus and the Minotaur could be one and the same person, seen at different times in the writer's development, just as he had already identified himself at various times with the young people in the labyrinth – and even with Daedulus, who had created it.

The *Ballade* then tells the story, accompanied by some of Dürrenmatt's expressionistic drawings, in a newish form. We read only the Minotaur's view of the events, and it is a very different creature now from the one in *Stoffe I*. The labyrinth itself is now the traditional small, cramped, narrow area – and with glass walls, so that the Minotaur, instead of feeling alone from the start, believes that it is in 'einer Welt voll kauernden Wesen, ohne zu wissen, daß es selber das Wesen war' (8), so that the beast is, in fact, happy. In its wild dance of happiness, however, it sees the first naked maiden. 'Seine Welt hatte sich verdoppelt' (17) and the inevitable sex-act follows; then there is 'ein unwirklicher Weltschrei' and the girl falls dead at its feet. It devours the remaining young people who come to kill it, by which time suspicion and anger have eaten into it and it destroys the glass walls. When it discovers that the blood-stained reflection in the shattered glass is indeed itself, and that it was now 'der Vereinzelte', it collapses and awakes to find another 'Minotaur' coming towards it. This is no Minotaur, but Theseus, a cowardly Theseus now, disguised in a bull's mask. As the Minotaur dances a 'Tanz der Brüderlichkeit' at finding a 'Du', a friend, Theseus slaughters it and leaves the corpse to the vultures.

We are to take it then, from both the 1972–3 essay and the 1985 *Ballade*, that any personal relationship can be expected to have an unsatisfactory, if not tragic, outcome. The Minotaur, unhappy on its own, kills the first and is killed by the second 'other object' that it meets. Our labyrinth would, on this reading, seem to be nearer to a hell on earth. As he wrote in his 'Persönliche Anmerkung', to the book of his art-works, 'Der Einzelne steht einer Welt gegenüber, die für ihn undurchschaubar ist; Das Labyrinth ist die Welt vom Minotaurus aus gesehen' (WA26, 212; A8).[12]

* * *

I have always maintained that Dürrenmatt is a realist rather than a pessimist, and I was relieved to find in my conversation with him in 1988 that this was still the case. Despite these bleak texts, Dürrenmatt remains a cheerful, relaxed, good-humoured companion, fond of food, wine, his dogs, his house, his paintings and his writing, but I still believe that he writes, as he was writing as early as 1952 in 'Fingerübungen zur Gegenwart', 'um zu warnen'. Such an impression was confirmed by the four-hour film made by Charlotte Kerr and transmitted by SDR III on 26 December 1984. Heinrich Goertz seemed to be surprised at what he saw, 'Der Autor so vieler Weltuntergange ist ein salopp gekleideter Herr heiteren Gemüts' (C18, 123), and by Charlotte Kerr's *Rollenspiele: Protokoll einer fiktiven Inszenierung und Achterloo III* (1986), which is partly a discussion on the dramaturgy and production of *Achterloo* and partly a general discussion of Dürrenmatt's life and career, much of which we have already considered elsewhere. In *Rollenspiele* we come once again on his growing dislike and distrust of authoritarian Marxism – *Achterloo*, it will be recalled, was written as a protest against General Jaruzelski's dictatorship-like methods – and of what we stated above, his desire to warn: 'Beckett schreit, weiß aber, daß es sinnlos ist zu schreien.' 'Und du?' asks Frau Kerr in *Rollenspiele*. 'Why do you write?' 'Um zu warnen. Es gibt nur einen Weg, der Lawine zu entgehen, nicht hineinzugeraten'. Not to get embroiled in the world's affairs, but to give them thought – 'Denken' is his word (46) – a sort of 'recollection in tranquillity'.

Dürrenmatt's essayistic work is, as we have seen, a considerable achievement. Some of it is clearly of its day, some very lightweight indeed; but at its best, and there is a good deal of 'best' here, it is the work of an original and profound thinker who, even when writing out of kilter, out of temper, out of sorts, can produce stimulating and provocative statements worth reading and listening to. Amédée Scholl believes that Dürrenmatt's *oeuvre* brings him into the orbit 'eines Platon, der mittelalterlichen Mystiker, eines Erasmus, eines Montaigne, eines Swift, eines Shakespeare, auch des genialen Blaise Pascal'. Whether this is rather far-fetched, or to the point, Time alone will tell (cf. E39, 203).

–8–

The Art-Works

As I mentioned in the introduction to the chapter on his essays, Dürrenmatt has always considered his drawing and painting activities to be 'associative', an integral part of his work. Indeed, one recalls that his very first major intellectual decision was whether to take up painting or writing: 'Es war die Lösung irgendwie meines Dilemmas zwischen Malen und Schreiben' was his answer to Charlotte Kerr when she asked (in *Rollenspiele*, A4, 86) why he began to write for the theatre.

Dürrenmatt's early interest in painting and sketching is well documented. At the age of six, he turned his passion for 'Sintfluten und Schweizerschlachten' into paintings whose cruelty frightened his God-fearing mother (cf. WA26, 12). In Konolfingen, too, he was introduced to the works of *inter alia* Michelangelo, Böcklin and Rubens, then later, as a student in Zurich, the painter Walter Jonas had a major influence on him as we have seen (above, 5). His first real painting is (significantly?) a *Kreuzigung* of 1939 (A8, No. 1).

The most perfunctory study of Dürrenmatt's art-works reveals his vision of the world: cataclysmic, catastrophic, cruel, grotesque or bizarrely comic. They are at times Bosch-like, at times Lowry-like, at times almost in the style of the British cartoonist, Ronald Searle, for whom Dürrenmatt had significant words of praise in 1952: Searle, 'durch einen Kniff der Groteske', was able to reproduce 'das Bedrohliche, die schreckliche Möglichkeit im Menschen' ('Über Ronald Searle' in WA26, 151–2). This is what seems to me to be the key to Dürrenmatt's paintings and sketches: as in his writings, he puts on to canvas the results of Man's madness, of his vaunting and senseless ambition, of his greed and insensitivity. He put it thus to Charlotte Kerr: 'Jede psychologische Theorie gibt vor, wissenschaftlich zu sein. Meine ist logisch: sie führt zur Katastrophe' (A4, 35). As J.R. von Salis claims to have said to him once, looking at the huge painting of Dürrenmatt's friend Varlin of the Salvation Army which used to hang on one wall of Dürrenmatt's living room in Neuchâtel, 'Deine Kunst ist doch eigentlich gnadenlos' (in *Über Friedrich Dürrenmatt*, WA30, 420; cf. C52).

Most Dürrenmatt scholars would agree with von Salis's comment in *Grenzüberschreitungen* that Dürrenmatt's 'Einfall' starts from the *image*: 'Alles setzt sich bei ihm in Bilder um, er ist von Natur und Begabung primär ein Zeichner, ein Bildermacher' (WA30, 419). Dürrenmatt's art-work accompanies almost all his writings, it comments and enlarges on them, explains them, to Dürrenmatt himself indeed, as he says in the film where he is seen sketching to the 'Minotaurus' story. In *Stoffe*, he explains how he always has a sketching block by his side as he writes, which he will cover with images connected with the written work in hand.

In *Rollenspiele* he presents some twenty-eight drawings to *Achterloo* significantly entitled *Assoziationen mit einem dicken Filzstift*, and those who have the original Arche editions of Dürrenmatt's works from the early years will have a collection of his art-commentaries to his works on the dust-jackets. In 1969 he presented me with a copy of what I still consider to be his wittiest collection of cartoons, *Die Heimat im Plakat* (A7), drawn for his three children in one of those 'losen Stunden': a savage, witty, at times obscene (in the literary sense of 'zotig') commentary on Swiss, particularly Zermatt mores which, along with the biting *Schweizerpsalme*, would well serve as a companion for an essay on Dürrenmatt's fraught relationship with his native country.

Volume 26 of the *Werkausgabe*, *Literatur und Kunst*, conveniently brings together most, but alas not all, of Dürrenmatt's major pronouncements on art matters, and the volume *Über Friedrich Dürrenmatt* (WA30) contains Manuel Gasser's introductory essay, 'Eine Doppelbegabung', which prefaces the book *Bilder und Zeichnungen* which appeared in 1978. (For convenience's sake, I shall quote from WA30 (347–63) since the album pages are unnumbered.)

The most interesting point about the Gasser essay is that he agrees with neither Dürrenmatt nor me! Indeed, he finds it rather surprising that Dürrenmatt's pictures do *not* reproduce the written work at all faithfully. He feels that Dürrenmatt treats the action 'mit auffallender Vernachlässigung der ihnen innewohnenden theatralischen Möglichkeiten', and that, although the pictures are obviously related to the written matter, 'genau besehen, sind die beiden Äußerungen so grundverschieden wie Handeln und Sein' (351). He cites the Minotaur, not in battle with Theseus but alone in its labyrinth (No. 23) – but that, surely, was an integral part of the story? Or the Tower of Babel, shown by Brueghel and others as packed with people, is 'menschenleer' in Dürrenmatt's version (No. 15) – but is that not a metaphor for the 'unermeßliche Wüste' in which Nebuchadnezzar finds himself, deserted by all (just like

Queen Elizabeth in Schiller's *Maria Stuart*) at the end of the *Engel*-play? Or Christus and Pilatus 'blicken stumm aneinander vorbei', Gasser complains (No. 6) – but does it not say in the story 'Pilatus' that at the head of the mob 'der Gott ruhig verharrte, den er [Pilatus] jedoch noch immer anzusehen vermied' and there is hardly an 'Auseinandersetzung' between them that could be pictured (cf. WA18, 99)? Later, however, Gasser does agree that the 'associations' between story and picture are indeed close, quoting Teiresias, the blind seer, in 'Das Sterben der Pythia': 'Es gibt keine nebensächlichen Geschichten. Alles hängt zusammen. Rüttelt man irgendwo, rüttelt man am Ganzen' (WA14, 300).

The book *Bilder und Zeichnungen* (A8) offers representations of all of the *Urmotive* and *Urstrukturen* which I have attempted to illuminate; of particular interest are those paintings and sketches which portray scenes from the plays, since we might deduce from the presentations of the costumes, the representations of the actions and the positions of the characters, how Dürrenmatt himself might have produced the piece. This is a point of some significance because he never fails, nowadays, to base his lack of interest in the modern theatre on the fact that it has become a 'directors' theatre'; Dürrenmatt's theatre was 'ein Theater der Schauspieler'. Drawings relevant to this point would be: *Die Physiker* (Nos. 25 and 43); *Herkules* (Nos. 36 and 37); *Der Meteor* (No. 40); *Porträt eines Planeten* (Nos. 41 and 42); *König Johann* (Nos. 47 and 53); *Die Wiedertäufer* (No. 54) and *Frank V* (Nos. 56 and 57). One recurring theme in the book, an *Urmotiv sans pareil* as it were, is the Tower of Babel, *Der Turmbau* (Nos. 13–17): Dürrenmatt in his 'Persönliche Anmerkung' writes, 'Der Turm zu Babel ist das Sinnbild der menschlichen Hybris' (WA26, 206), and Gasser cleverly points out the connection between this image and the space-travel-motif in *Das Unternehmen der Wega*, for example. For Dürrenmatt, however, the Tower is the image of the self-destroyed world: 'Was die Menschheit hinterlassen wird, sind ihre Ruinen' (206). But if this is the 'schlimmstmögliche Wendung', it is also the underlining of that Goethean line which is the motto of my study: 'Denn alle Schuld rächt sich auf Erden.' 'Daß ich immer wieder die schlimmstmögliche Wendung darstelle,' writes the author, 'hat nichts mit Pessimismus zu tun, auch nichts mit einer fixen Idee.' It is simply 'das dramaturgisch Darstellbare' (209), that is, he would have us believe that all these apocalyptic drawings are just drawings, as theatre can only be 'theatre', not reality. 'Was ich – in meinem Schreiben wie Zeichnen – suche, sind die Bilder und Gleichnisse, die im Zeitalter der Wissenschaft noch möglich sind, einem Zeitalter, dem etwas ge-

lang, was der Philosophie mißlang: die Realität abstrakt zu beschrei-
ben' (215).

* * *

I would take Dürrenmatt's own advice at this point, given in his
excellent essay 'Notizen zu Hans Falk', 'Es ist sinnlos geworden,
ein Bild erzählen zu wollen' (WA26, 185) and point the reader in
the direction of these collections of Dürrenmatt's works already
mentioned: *Bilder und Zeichnungen* (A8, 1978), *Die Heimat im Plakat*
(A7, 1963), *Minotaurus* (A11, 1985) or the *Oeuvres graphiques* (A12,
1985) – or, of course, to his house in Neuchâtel which is an art
gallery in itself with his pictures on every wall!
There are, of course, those few – what Germans would call
'Fachidioten' – who would deny categorically that a person can be
gifted in more than one field and would see Dürrenmatt's works as
'Sonntagsmalerei'. Such people might have been astonished by the
exhibition held in the Neuen Residenz in Bamberg in 1980, which
showed how distinguished some of these 'amateur' painters could
be. Entitled *Künstlerische Doppelbegabungen von E.T.A. Hoffmann bis
Dietrich Fischer-Dieskau*, it included, for the first time in public, a
Dürrenmatt painting. (Unlike Fischer-Dieskau, who held a recital
of Nietzsche-*Lieder* afterwards, Dürrenmatt was unable to display
his major talent!)
One of the greatest influences in the field of art on Dürrenmatt's
pictorial vision was the Swiss Jean Varlin (né Guggenheim).
Dürrenmatt has written several essays on Varlin and has painted
him – and been painted by him – several times. Dürrenmatt
admired Varlin's sturdy independence, both in art and in politics,
and found in his paintings that 'Humor' which he had sought to
impart to his own literary and pictorial creations, that 'Humor'
which, Kierkegaard said, lay above all in Tertullian's brave declaration: *Credo quia absurdum*. And that is why Varlin's paintings are
'Geschöpfe eines Malers, der die Menschen liebt, obwohl er sie so
sieht, wie er sie malt' (in 'Varlin' (1969) in WA26, 174–82, here
182).
Dürrenmatt first met Varlin in 1961 and has some thirty-four of
his paintings in his own work-room in Neuchâtel, plus, of course,
Varlin's huge Salvation Army ('Heilsarmee') painting (on fir-
wood) which has accompanied Dürrenmatt in all his work for
many years and to which he turns again in the film of 1984. His last
appreciative essay, 'Varlin' of 1982 (now in *Versuche*, A6, 121–8),
sums up the author's own attitude to art by letting us appreciate

what he has learned from this 'Kauz', this very individualistic painter. 'Ich lernte durch Varlin beobachten', he says. Varlin was, like Dürrenmatt, a realist, he was 'einer der letzten, die sich über die Wirklichkeit wunderten, daß sie so ist, wie sie ist, und *nicht anders*' (my italics, 123). 'Reality' and 'Possibility' (Wirklichkeit/Möglichkeit) were closely related for Varlin, so that everything that was 'wirklich' was also 'möglich' – which is why he painted a Cinzano bottle on a Japanese tea-tray! His motifs, like Dürrenmatt's, were 'Einfälle' – for example, 'Kasernen, Hotels, Spitäler, Pissoirs, Omnibusse, Telefone, Regenschirme' (125) – one thinks involuntarily of Dürrenmatt's stage-directions for his *Ein Engel kommt nach Babylon* (cf. WA4, 13). But above all it was the paradoxical nature of Varlin's art that fascinated and clearly influenced Dürrenmatt: Varlin's wish 'die Gegenwart festhalten zu wollen, damit das eigentliche Zeitlose' (124).

This we see in Dürrenmatt's own pictures and drawings; he attempts to keep intact what *is* but by seeing it through a paradox. Thus his pictures, abstract though they may at first sight appear to be, do in fact 'describe reality abstractly', they represent his thinking in the same way as his writings do: 'Malerei als eine Kunst, "schöne Bilder" zu machen, interessiert mich nicht, ebenso wie mich die Kunst, "schönes Theater" zu machen, nicht interessiert' (WA26, 216).

So, the absurdity of Life is likewise the subject of Dürrenmatt's art-works; we are invited to scorn the all too obvious misalliances of Life, the 'Mächtigen' who are ludicrous because they have lost contact with normal life and times – they are shown as 'unmenschlich'. And these 'Mächtigen' are not just Kings or Princes or Popes, they can be professors or critics or statesmen. Then we are invited to take pity on the 'Opfer', the victims of Life, the oppressed and the lonely and the tortured who, however, have their own place in the 'Weltenplan' too. Manuel Gasser might well be correct to end his essay with the words, 'durch das Werkganze dröhnt der Choral: 'O, Ewigkeit, du Donnerwort' (WA30, 363)!

Conclusion

This study has attempted to do justice to Friedrich Dürrenmatt's whole *oeuvre* by illuminating more closely than has been the usual practice the corpus of his writings in prose, narrative and essay, and by comparing and contrasting that output with the more familiar stage-plays and the perhaps less familiar art-works to present a more rounded picture of what I termed in Chapter 1 a 'Protean figure' of European culture.

The search for *Urmotive* and *Urstrukturen* has revealed, I believe, that Dürrenmatt, despite all the seeming paradoxicalities and contradictions, has kept returning to themes which, on close inspection, reveal themselves to be basic philosophical tenets. The motto chosen for this study, the Goethean line 'Denn alle Schuld rächt sich auf Erden', has, I hope, been proved to be valid. A strong sense of personal and public guilt has been seen to run through all these works, showing itself now defensively, now accusingly, in various forms: a defence of the 'small' against the 'gargantuan', of small nations against large, of individual rights against mass ideologies, of personal freedoms against state oppression, of 'victims' against 'men in power', all culminating in a belief that Good will eventually triumph over Evil, and that the wages of the sins of the wicked will be – as often as not – death.

Yet the realist Dürrenmatt reminds us that this punishment will not always be immediate: the world may often have to wait with patience and will perhaps have to suffer before retribution is finally dealt out. In his more pessimistic moments, the author might agree with the writer of a letter to *The Times* on 10 January 1989 who, in the wake of the terrible air disasters over Lockerbie in Scotland and on the M1 motorway in England, wrote, 'The distressing and inevitable conclusion to be drawn is that, with ever-increasing speed, size, method and quantity of all forms of transport, there will be a corresponding increase in disasters and, regrettably, in fatalities' – a dramatic example of Kassner's 'Gesetz der großen Zahl' to which I have so often alluded in this study.

It cannot now be denied that any critical assessment of Dürrenmatt's stage-plays can be only a partial one without a consideration of the rest of his *oeuvre* and, in particular, of his essayistic work. There we find the true background to all his fictional output: his obsession with the theme of 'the individual', first as one whose *freedom* must be respected, but then, later, as one who detaches himself defiantly from Life, to fight, like a cornered animal in its lonely labyrinth, against the attacks of a hostile, uncomprehending world.

Yet if we were to except those occasions where personal petulance at some real, or imagined, wrong clouded his better judgement and led him to less than worthy comment, I believe that Dürrenmatt's contribution to the European cultural heritage is a proud one. It could well be that he will be remembered by some only as the author of *Der Besuch der alten Dame* or *Die Physiker*, but by those who have taken the trouble to examine his complete literary legacy he will be seen as one who, often under the cloak of banal persiflage, sardonic wit and humour, and grotesque buffooneries, sought to defend the most precious value of *all* civilisations: Man's inalienable right to be free. Of all the motifs examined and illustrated here, this is, I believe, the *Urmotif*:

> Sie [the characters in his works] sind meine Träume, in denen immer wieder ein Motiv auftaucht, unerbittlich, ein einziges bloß, die Möglichkeit, an die ich glaube, an die ich mich anklammere, die Möglichkeit, ganz ein Einzelner zu werden, die Möglichkeit der Freiheit.

Notes

1. Friedrich Dürrenmatt

1. His antipathy to Professor Emil Staiger and his Weimarian concept of 'die heile Welt' showed itself again during the so-called 'Zürcher Literaturstreit' in 1966–7 (cf. *inter alia* my D45). Spycher quotes from an unpublished letter to Walter Muschg that Dürrenmatt studied philosophy in order 'sich mit dem protestantisch-christlichen Glauben seines Vaters auseinanderzusetzen'. (C46, 17).

2. The embarrassingly candid description of his visit to Rudolf Kassner in Sierre in Valais in 1950 is a good example of how he suffered at this time. He had to eat cheese, which he disliked, while the perspiration poured down his face. In this context, it is not uninteresting to note how often comments about 'sweat', 'perspiring', etc. creep into his work. A few examples: 'Er wischt sich den Schweiß ab' (Saint-Claude in *Die Ehe des Herrn Mississippi*, WA3, 100); 'Newton wischt sich mit der Serviette den Schweiß von der Stirne' (*sic*) (in *Die Physiker*, WA7, 67); Arkanoff's: 'Heiß. (*Wischt sich immer noch den Schweiß ab*)' in *Die Frist* (WA15, 17). These are all signs of anxiety, fear and doubt.

2. The Early Narrative Works

1. We read in *Der Rebell*, however, that the books were simply discussed, not read (A2, 126). The Kafka works were *Vor dem Gesetz* and 'Strafkolonie'. The latter bears only a slight resemblance to the theme of 'Der Folterknecht'. Dürrenmatt read Kafka only after the war when the books became available (A1, 77).

2. Bänziger's latest book (1987) on the 'dioscuri', Frisch and Dürrenmatt, only deals with certain themes in their work and records a certain resentment towards him on the part of both authors (C8).

3. The *Komödie* of the same year, 1943, originally titled *Der Knopf*, appeared in a new form as *Untergang und neues Leben* in 1980 in WA1 (259–94) having been rewritten in 1951.

4. Cf. the discussion in my B23, and Jan Knopf's similar dissatisfaction with the critics' playing with the concept in his *Der Dramatiker Friedrich Dürrenmatt* (1987) (C32, 193, note 29).

5. 'Hochfrequenzstil' would certainly be the Germanisten/academics' description of this prose, but one should not forget Dürrenmatt's own explanation in *Stoffe*: 'doch machte mir das Schreiben meistens Mühe, mein Deutsch hatte ich aus der Literatur übernommen . . . Ich wagte zuerst nur kurze Sätze zu schreiben' (A2, 127).

6. For some reason, Emil Weber omits 'Der Alte' from his 'theological' discussion in the peculiarly titled *Die Welt der frühen Werke, oder vom Einfall des Schrecklichen und von der Kunst, sich recht zu ängstigen* (in E48, 23–41).

7. This is, of course, the last line of Goethe's third 'Harfenspieler' poem from *Wilhelm Meister* (1783–96).

8. In Charlotte Kerr's 1984 film on Dürrenmatt, the author relates how he was once set upon and savaged by an Alsatian which he had taken for a walk in Berne. He was fourteen at the time (1935), and says that he had never hated an animal so much; he goes on to claim that the hatred shown by the Theaterdirektor towards the woman is of a type that he himself has never experienced between people.

9. If Peter Spycher's remark (in C46, 112) that Kurt Horwitz read 'Pilatus' to the Zurich Theaterverein the night after the première of *Es steht geschrieben* (i.e. on 11 April 1947) is correct, it would seem that Knapp's 1947 dating must be wrong (cf. C29, 16). The date in the *Werkausgabe* (WA18, 97) is also 1946.

10. Spycher believed in 1972 that Arnold's 1969 interpretation of the story, namely that Jesus was the 'absolute Gleichgültige' and that the reader finished the story with sympathy for Pilatus, which shows Dürrenmatt's 'pessimistische Weltvision' (C2, 19–20) would only hold water if we shared Pilatus's standpoint. Spycher believed that Dürrenmatt had condemned it (C46, 121–2). Bark's rather complicated article, with many mis-spellings of names and book titles, covers most of the theories on 'Pilatus' (in E6, 53–68).

11. This is, in a sense, 'accepted' Dürrenmatt scholarship, i.e. that he 'believed' until quite late in life. In *Stoffe*, however, we read again and again that his 'belief' had left him very early. Cf. in 'Mondfinsternis', after a bicycle accident when he had prayed for God to save him: 'Die Religion wurde mir peinlich, ich mißtraute ihr und hatte ein schlechtes Gewissen, weil ich ihr, als es ernst wurde, doch nicht gewachsen gewesen war' (A2, 23). The film conversation confirms this. Cf. here, too, Peter Graves's excellent article (D20, 133–142, especially 140) and Diller's D11.

12. This 'Cave Allegory' seems to be a work more quoted from than read. Commentator after German commentator insists upon writing that 'ein' or 'der' Mensch is incarcerated in the cave. Nestle's German translation states clearly, however, 'Stelle dir *Menschen* in einer unterirdischen höhlenartigen Behausung vor' (my italics, C38, 205). In *Versuche*, Dürrenmatt tells us that this was the theme of his very first *Seminararbeit* (A6, 95).

3. *Trivialliteratur* or 'Philosophical Thrillers'?

1. Typical of the 'philosophical investigations'-approach were *Friedrich Dürrenmatt: Studien zu seinem Werk* (1976) (C28) and *Facetten: Studien zum*

60. *Geburtstag Friedrich Dürrenmatts* (1981) (C30). All of the contributors to the first book, and a good proportion of those to the second, live and teach in North America but are, or at least seem to be, almost all of Germanic extraction, which may say something both about Dürrenmatt scholarship generally and about the North American teaching of German.

2. The scandal was all the more surprising since one Swiss writer observed (in 1958) of Zurich that 'die Wohlanständigkeit des Publikums da so weit geht, daß allfällig pfeifende Zuschauer von den immer anwesenden Polizisten schleunigst aus dem Zuschauerraum herausbefördert werden' (E11, 18)!

3. The German version runs, 'Ein Verleger hatte mir nicht genug Vorschuß gegeben. Ich telephonierte also mit fünf oder sechs Verlegern . . . Jedem erzählte ich, daß ich im Begriff sei, einen Roman zu schreiben. Und jeder Verleger war interessiert und wollte Näheres hören. Und jedem mußte ich den Inhalt des vorgeschlagenen Romans erzählen – (es handelte sich nicht sechsmal um denselben Roman, sondern um sechs verschiedene). Und jeder erklärte sich bereit, mir Vorschuß zu schicken. 'He wrote none of the novels, of course, but did later pay back the advances: 'Schließlich leben wir ja in der Schweiz'! (Curt Rieß in F18, 385; D32, 119f.) In his interview with Dieter Fringeli, Dürrenmatt says that he received 1,000 francs for *Der Richter und sein Henker* and 2,000 francs for *Das Versprechen in toto* (E7, 7).

4. Chambers's *Twentieth Century Dictionary* (1983) gives a 'who-*dun*-it' or a 'whodunnit' – Germans, and particularly German–Americans, seem to be uncertain of the correct usage. Armin Arnold writes 'Whodoneit' in E2, 153, and also strives to prove that Dürrenmatt's novels are all actually based on Simenon and others. Quoting Spycher quoting a 1959 article by one Siegfried M. Pistorius, he claims that Dürrenmatt owns 'vollständige Sammlungen der Werke von Edgar Wallace, Agatha Christie und Georges Simenon' (153). Dürrenmatt told me 'categorically' that he had not read Simenon at that time and very rarely since. It is probable that it is Arnold who is 'honoured' in *Rollenspiele* by the remark that this 'Literaturhistoriker ist sicher ein Simenon-Fan und bildet sich ein, jeder, der einen Kriminalroman schreibe, blättere vorher bei Simenon nach, er ist nicht von der Idee abzubringen, und andere Literaturhistoriker glauben den Unsinn, weil sie voneinander abschreiben' (A4, 54)! Dürrenmatt says that Simenon bores him: 'es regnet immer'! Others have claimed the Swiss writer Friedrich Glauser, of *Wachtmeister Stauder* (1936) fame, as the model, but Dürrenmatt told Fringeli with great emphasis that he had never read Glauser then either, and put forward Fontane's *Stechlin* as the major linguistic influence (F7, 5ff.). Gerhard Knapp and other scholars find this difficult to believe (cf. C29, 31).

5. It might just be worthwhile pointing out here that the name 'Tschanz' has no connection with the English word 'chance'. Firstly, Dürrenmatt would not, indeed *could* not, think in English, and secondly,

he assured me in 1969 that the name was a common one in the district. Most of the names, place- as well as family-names, can be easily checked on a map of the area Berne–Neuchâtel. Indeed, Dürrenmatt showed me the map from which he had taken the names.

6. There are, of course, full-scale school studies of the novel. The German series 'Interpretationen zum Deutschunterricht' carries a study by Walter Seifert (C45) with chapter headings such as 'Historische und klassifikatorische Gattungstheorie' and 'Gerechtigkeit und Vernichtungswille in moralischer Deutung'. Unfortunately, the very first line of this scholarly study has Dürrenmatt born in Konnolfingen. Seifert closes with the suggestion that the 'Zentralthematik' leads to a comparison with Kleist's *Der zerbrochene Krug* und Sophocles' *Oedipus Rex* (117). See too E. Neis and H. Bodensieck (C37; E10); the latter supplies a good bibliography for school work on *Der Richter und sein Henker*.

7. Arnold, still convinced that Dürrenmatt could have no independent imaginative ideas, now insists that the Bärlach-novels are modelled on those of Friedrich Glauser – but, in addition, that the Emmenberger-motif 'entspricht' the story in Karl Unselt's 1935 novel *Der Arzt aus Leidenschaft*. The story, as Arnold tells it, seems to me to be very far from the plot of *Der Verdacht* (E3, 190).

8. Professor Subiotto agrees and points out that, like Büchner, Camus and Kafka – who have all been accused of being 'nihilists' – Dürrenmatt is, rather, a 'true realist and moralist' (D38, 182).

9. There is, however, a whole truly fantastic world of '*Krimis*' known to all Germans interested in the genre, the products of the Bastei-Verlag in Cologne and starring, above all, 'G-Man Jerry Cotton', a tough New York FBI-man whose 58–62-page adventures are written by a team of six main German authors and some volunteers, few of whom have ever visited America but who, 'with typical German thoroughness', get all their facts correct. The 'Cotton-Bände' have now reached vast proportions and cost *c*. DM 1.80. Since their first appearance in 1956, they boast a readership in fifty-two countries and nineteen languages. The American actor George Nader starred in the first Cotton-film and two more have followed. Promoted by the millionaire Gustav Heinrich Lübbe, the series offers slick Americanised plots – 'jedes Mädchen ist ein Girl'! – and there is no 'sex' (cf. Klaus Kunkel, E27). It is a far cry from the days when this could be called the 'Lieblingsgenre elitärer Schriftsteller' (Pulver, E33, 43)!

10. Bergson's general theory of laughter in *Le rire* (C10) was enormously helpful in explaining the development of twentieth-century theatre (cf. my B23, 31). His concept of 'raideur', an act of clumsiness which becomes 'un défaut ridicule', can be equated with the 'Hang zum Absoluten' or the *idée fixe* which I mentioned in connection with Dürrenmatt's 'fanatical' characters and is the source of Geoffrey Wagner's comment that 'Matthäi's obsessive logic is likened to that of an automatism' (D42, 325). His obsession is much stronger and has ultimately more

'tragic' consequences than Bärlach's (cf. 40–1).

11. One wonders why Professor Knapp should call the family Sch*roll* in his 1980 book (cf. C29, 35–6)?

12. Cf. note 4 above!

13. 'Wit, with all its brilliance and ingenuity, is sadly wanting in unction, if it takes no-one down' (Bain, B2, 8).

14. Despite Dürrenmatt's sense of 'failure', however, the canton of Berne decided to award him its *Literaturpreis* of 750 francs plus an honorarium of 1,000 francs for the play! And he did not even have to give a speech of acceptance. There is a rather bitter comment on this in the introduction to the book version of *Die Panne* where he wrote ironically, 'welche Stümpereien wurden nicht schon ausgezeichnet' (WA20, 37).

15. It is strange that Tiusanen (in B22) and Schuster (in E40, 160–72) both make such wild guesses about the name Gygax: Tiusanen writes that it 'sounds like' the name of a Greek god (160), while Schuster writes that Dürrenmatt '[wollte] . . . lautmalerisch (gicksen, gacksen) auf "Hahnrei" deuten' (162). It is, however, a common Emmentaler name, Dürrenmatt assured me.

16. The list of 'noble wines' might be worth noting! Campari (45), Neuchâteller (51), Réserve de Maréchaux (53), Pichon-Longueville '33 (57), Château Pavie '21 (64), Château Margaux' 14 (68), the cognac Roffignac '93 (84) and the champagne (92).

4. The Radio-Plays

1. According to Carl Seelig, in 1956, Dürrenmatt received some 5,000 Swiss francs for each of the later radio-plays, which took only two months to write (cf. Arnold, C3, 12). It is worth noting, however, that in these straitened times the Swiss franc and the Deutschmark stood at *c.* 12 to the pound sterling in 1951.

2. Usmiani's article originally appeared in English (D40). There are, one might perhaps be allowed to add, a few 'continentalisms' in this German version: for example, *Mac* Leish and *Mac* Neice (126), and the ubiquitous 'happy end' (129) makes its appearance.

3. Dürrenmatt's scientific knowledge was perhaps displayed in his estimation in 1951 of the speed that a spaceship would need to achieve to go into orbit: he writes '36 000 Km/St' (*c.* 22,500 m.p.h.). In 1988 *Discovery*'s speed was 17,500 m.p.h. *c.* 28,000 Km/St.

4. Rolf Kieser felt that Dürrenmatt's dislike was due to the Nobel Prize money's having come from the fortune of an armaments manufacturer, remembering no doubt Dürrenmatt's dislike of the Zurich armaments manufacturer Bührle, satirised in *Grieche sucht Griechin* as Petit-Paysan (in E22, 125).

5. The two cabaret sketches which Dürrenmatt wrote for the Cabaret Cornichon in Zurich in 1949 are also printed in WA17, but *Der Erfinder*

really belongs to my discussion of *Die Physiker*. *Der Gerettete* (WA17, 127–35) is very weak, although it does contain one line relevant to the Korbes-situation: when the one-legged author Armin Schucker is rescued from the sea through the offices of Dr Matthias Blauhals and tells his fantastic story, it is not believed. 'Die Wahrscheinlichkeit Ihrer Erzählung', says the Herr Doktor, 'macht sie unwahrscheinlich. Ein Betrüger würde keine unwahrscheinliche Geschichte erzählen' (131)! But there are no 'metaphysical depths' here.

5. The Later Narrative Works

1. Speculations about the characters' identities have been frequently made. Professor Adam Ulam from the Russian Research Centre at Harvard has suggested a series of possible Soviet politicians whose characteristics match the Dürrenmattian individuals, but much of his discussion ends in 'either/or' or 'a mixture of —— and ——'. Likewise, Arnold claims that G (the 'Chefideologe') is a bitter caricature of Professor Emil Staiger with whom Dürrenmatt has often crossed swords. 'Wie viele Kritiker, vertrug er keine Kritik', writes Dürrenmatt of G and adds that G ruined the country's literature, 'indem er nach dem Schema der Ideologie die Klassiker für gesund und positiv, die Schriftsteller der Gegenwart für krank und negativ erklärte' (47–8). So, apart from the reminiscences of Goethe's celebrated comparison of Classicism and Romanticism, there are certainly memories here of the *Zürcher Literaturstreit*! (Cf. Arnold, E3, 197–8; Spycher C46, 346; my D45.) (Spycher, with his usual *akribeia*, went through the original 1976 edition and chronicled nearly twenty serious mistakes, either of fact ('B2' instead of 'D', etc.) or of grammar (e.g. 'das Land mit *ihren* Agenten'). Almost all have been corrected in WA23.)

2. I find it difficult to agree with Helbling or Knapp in their assessments of 'Der Sturz', namely 'Er wertet nicht; er wägt nicht; er urteilt nicht.' (E28, 273). That would be true if one did not know the identity of the author; one *knows* what Dürrenmatt is after here!

3. Here are a few recent examples: '. . . ich gehe in Neuchâtel ebenso ungern ins Theater wie in Zürich oder in München. Ich gehe überhaupt nicht gern ins Theater' (*Versuche*, A6, 33); 'It was torture for him to visit theatres, especially if he had to see his own plays', because it was 'the contemporary directors' theatre' (to Hugo Rank); and then recently in *Rollenspiele* he tells Charlotte Kerr that he prefers prose because 'Das ist dann ganz deins, etwas was du allein verwirklichen kannst' (A4, 68), and again, 'Theater ist *passé*, ich bedauere, je ein Theaterstück geschrieben zu haben' (A4, 88).

4. It is interesting that, although the labyrinth theme is clearly in Dürrenmatt's paintings from the earliest days, it is mentioned in his literary works only from the 1980s. I believe that it was only at a more advanced age, and with the bitter experience of 'failure' behind him, that

he began to seek reasons for the traits in his character which had led to these 'failures'.

5. There is room for an article on Dürrenmatt's attitude to the Swiss term 'Landesverräter'. Kurt Marti, of an age with Dürrenmatt, discusses the point in his *Die Schweiz und ihre Schriftsteller – die Schriftsteller und ihre Schweiz* (C34). In the section of *Stoffe II* leading up to 'Mondfinsternis', Dürrenmatt relates the problems that he has with those Swiss who defended Hitler, and defends the 'Landesverräter' who were convinced of Hitler's ultimate victory and proclaimed the fact. Some of these, Dürrenmatt wrote, were in fact patriots who were thinking of Switzerland's fate after the war. The same went for the communists. He writes, 'Unsere Landesverräter starben den einzigen Heldentod, den wir zu verzeichnen haben: Sie wagten den illegalen, nicht den geistigen Verrat – der war legal' (A2, 42).

6. Dürrenmatt said, in an interview for the *Guardian* with Hugo Rank, 'One motif of the narrative is – can we live without the image of an enemy. The labyrinth is an expression of the world in which we live. On the one hand, we believe we can see it in a more lucid light now, but, really, it has become more entangled. The labyrinth is shorthand for today's world. The minotaur *belongs* to the world' (in Arts Guardian, 15 April 1981). Cf. too Michael Butler (D7) and Sydney Donald (D14).

7. Certainly the *thriller* with the same title, *Justice* (Collins, 1988) by the British author Ian St James makes the reading that one would have wished for from Dürrenmatt!

8. Dürrenmatt regularly writes to music. Brahms is by far his favourite composer: 'Meine Vorliebe für Brahms kommt wahrscheinlich daher, weil für mich wie für ihn nach der Exposition und nach dem Kopfteil vor allem das Finale das Wichtigste ist, eigentlich das Allerwichtigste' (*Rollenspiele*, A4, 64).

6. The Stage-Plays

1. Cf. 'The backdrop goes up and we appear to be in an artist's studio 50 miles above the surface of the earth. Through the lop-sided rear window, we see what looks like an astronaut's view of a glacier. Against this, the court of Claudius . . . wear varieties of costumes from the past two centuries. The cornices of the enclosing walls do not meet. Space as well as time is out of joint' (from a review of a London *Hamlet*, in *The Times*, 6 October 1988).

2. Brock-Sulzer's eulogy of *Der Blinde*, 'Man denkt an Shakespeare, man denkt an mittelalterliche Kathedralen, man denkt an barocken Rausch – und doch ist alles Heute' (in *Die Tat*, Zurich), is difficult to take seriously. The play was an abysmal failure. Shortly afterwards, Dürrenmatt had the opportunity of discussing it with Karl Barth and Hans Urs von Balthasar, respectively Protestant and Catholic theologians, along

with Kurt Horwitz and Ernst Ginsberg, both practising Christians and Catholics. Their efforts to convert him obviously failed because, he said, to believe means to *trust* someone, and Dürrenmatt knew – and knows – no transcendent being in whom he can have such trust (and cf. below, 129ff.).

3. Bertolt Brecht, whose Marxism Dürrenmatt had felt was too 'doktrinär', was delighted with Dürrenmatt's portrayal of the 'Germanii' when they met briefly after the performance of *Romulus* in 1949. Dürrenmatt reports his own unease in the discussion otherwise, and was relieved when the conversation turned to cigars (A2, 141–2)!

4. With the best will in the world, I really cannot believe in some of Gerwin Marahren's fanciful sources for the names in the play: 'Mississippi' from '"Mr and Mrs Ippi"', wobei sich ein Wortspiel ergeben würde', namely the Swiss 'hippen' = schmähen, lästern – or 'Diego' from 'die ego'; or Bodo von Übelohe's '"Leiden-schaftlichkeit" loht wirklich übel'! These are the 'wilder shores' of academe surely (E29, 95–6)?

5. Cf. *inter alia* Carew (D9), Heilmann (D21), Benn (E7), Kästner (E21), Marahrens (E29), and my B23, 94–6.

6. Hugo Dittberner's rather carelessly written article in *text + kritik* (E13) compares the play and the film versions, but Mona Knapp's remarks (in E24), comparing the original with the American translation, are much more interesting, although she is perhaps not aware that there is a firm called 'Anton Schill' in the Viennese suburb of Mehring!

7. The literature on this play is, of course, enormous. A selection will be found in the bibliography. A useful summary of the most interesting and useful interpretations is in Gerd Labroisses's article (E28) which contains, alas, a great many of these psychologising jargon-terms so beloved of some modern literary commentators.

8. The 'strangling' of Alfred is carried out by the 'Turner'-character. There is a delightful essay in Hans Bänziger's latest (1987) book, *Turner, Maos Witwe und die Alte Dame* which documents the protest of the Deutschen Turnerverband at this 'Beleidigung der Millionengemeinschaft' of gymnasts (C8, 80–97)!

9. I am not ignoring Robert Helbling's latest article on the grotesque (D22) which is, in part, a reply to some of the points advanced in my book (B23). His contribution to the 'still simmering, if not burning controversy' re. the grotesque is to suggest that characters like Claire are perhaps only 'grotescent' – Lee Jennings himself suggested the term, I understand – that is they are 'on the way' to becoming *true* grotesques! (I still disagree.)

10. It was indeed this aspect of Dürrenmatt that so attracted Eastern commentators and audiences when Dürrenmatt's works were eventually allowed to be produced in the East after about 1973. In 1965–6, *Der Besuch der alten Dame* 'stood in twenty-ninth place in the number of performances of any play staged in the GDR, higher than anything by Brecht or Shakespeare'. Its first performance was in Dresden on 11 May 1963; *Die Physiker* did not have its GDR première until 12 November 1977, in

Balthasar, respectively Protestant and Catholic theologians, along with Magdeburg. The character of the Soviet agent, Eisler, had been the obstacle to performance (cf. J.H. Reid, D31, 356–8).

11. The *Bochumer Fassung* (simply sub-titled *Eine Komödie mit Musik von Paul Burkhard*) should have had *its* première in 1964, but disagreement with the Bochum manager, Hans Schalla, led to its cancellation. This is the book version of 1964; Dürrenmatt also prepared an NDR television version in 1966, broadcast in 1967.

12. In *Rollenspiele*, Dürrenmatt describes the three 'human types', 'Leptosome, Pykniker, Athletiker', and claims that Romulus, Akki, Bockelson and Schwitter are all *Pykniker* ('pykniks'). Charlotte Kerr says, 'Du sagst ja immer, du beschreibst dich endlos selbst'; Dürrenmatt later adds, 'Die Pykniker neigen zum manisch-depressiven Irresein, wenn sie verrückt werden' (A4, 31–2). He seems fascinated by asylums and disturbed people.

13. Hans Bänziger provides as good a summary as any of the events in his chronology in Arnold's C3, 17–18. A very personal series of comments is provided by Dürrenmatt in his bitter 'Wutausbrüche' in WA24, 162–3: 'Im heutigen Theater geht es wie im Rom der Borgias zu: wer nicht schmiert, wird vergiftet' (162)!

14. Dürrenmatt has Philip of France say to Leopold of Austria:

> Um unsere Zwistigkeiten auszufechten,
> Gibt's unsere Völker, gibt's die beiden Heere;
> Doch uns, die wir einander hart bedrängen,
> Trennt nur Geschäft, nicht Haß . . . (27)

The 1980 ending is slightly different from the 1988 version. The Bastard, Philip Faulconbridge, apostrophises:

> Was schert mich England noch, was die Geschichte?
> Ein Ungeheuer starb, es bleiben Wichte. (113)

Dürrenmatt notes (1980) that he altered the former 'patriotic' ending

> Und senke in das Volk die Kraft des Löwen!
> Nur so ist diesem England noch zu helfen

with the rather disillusioned comment: 'Mein Vertrauen in das Volk ist in letzter Zeit zu arg erschüttert worden; schon das Wort "Volk" ist politisch so zweideutig geworden, daß es kaum anständig verwendet werden kann' (223). This is a remark which presumably goes back to the lack of public support at the time of the Basle *débâcle* – but which, he told me in 1988, he now regretted making.

15. Jan Knopf's comment that Dürrenmatt's version was 'Greis und Gretgen' as compared with Eisler's and Brecht's reworking of the theme, namely their 'aktuelle Korrektur des bürgerlich hochfahrenden Geistes

nach dem Faschismus', really does give the flavour of this politically oriented book on Dürrenmatt (C32, 151).

16. Dürrenmatt is still a passionate follower of football on television. I had an interesting discussion with him in 1969 about Leeds United, then a leading team in European football and the team of the city in which I live!

17. Dürrenmatt returned to the theme of 'moral' versus 'legal' guilt, *Gerechtigkeit* versus *Justiz*, in his 1985 novel *Justiz* (above, 91ff.). There Isaak Kohler is in the same situation as Alfredo, morally but not legally guilty of murder.

18. In his 'Friedrich Dürrenmatt interviewt FD', the author makes a curious error when, discussing the *Komödie, Die Panne*, he says that Alfredo 'sich erhängt' (WA25, 163). He too must be confused at times!

19. 'Achterloo' comes from a whole series of associations: Napoleon and Waterloo, *Achter*bahn, and *Acherloo* from C.F. Meyer's poem:

> Liebe Kinder, wißt ihr wo
> Fingerhut zu Hause?
> Tief im Tal von Acherloo
> Hat er Herd und Klause.

This was Dürrenmatt's father's favourite poem (*Rollenspiele*, A4, 98)!

20. The most distinctive addition to the Dürrenmattian style in this play – and it could be noticed too in the text of *Porträt* and *Die Frist* – is the growing emphasis on the obscene remark ('Die Zote') and the sexual innuendo. Jeanne d'Arc is a call-girl (in *Achterloo III*), Woyzeck's Marie a prostitute (who 'deflowers' Richelieu!) and scattered through the text are phrases and words like 'saftige Magazine', 'Scheiße', 'furzen', 'bumsen' ('mit und ohne Pariser') and 'Arsch'. Although Dürrenmatt had, of course, seen the need to use these from time to time in the past, they do seem to me to have been more textually integrated and less gratuitous then than they are now. It is probably another case of a jump on to a bandwagon.

7. The Essays

1. Critical evaluation of these writings has been neither so full nor so interesting as some of the other two thousand or so publications on the author. It would be well worthwhile to make a study of these essays as Peter Spycher did of the narrative prose. Comment is limited to relevant quotation within articles on other topics. Knapp in his 1980 book (C29) only deals in any detail with the essays from 1968 to 1979, Goertz in his little 1987 book (C18) devotes only three pages to 'Theaterprobleme', while Arnold's 1982 collection (C3) does not really deal with them at all.

2. Four years previously, in 1955, Thomas Mann had finished his eulogy on the 150th anniversary of Schiller's death thus: 'Von seinem sanft-gewaltigen Willen gehe durch das Fest seiner Grablegung und Aufer-

stehung etwas in uns ein: von seinem Willen zum Schönen, Wahren und Guten, zur Gesittung, zur inneren Freiheit, zur Kunst, zur Liebe, zum Frieden, zu rettender Ehrfurcht des Menschen vor sich selbst' (*Versuch über Schiller*, Berlin, 1955, 103). There could hardly be a better example of the style that Dürrenmatt disliked so much.

3. In *Stoffe II–III* (A2, 142) Dürrenmatt avers that 'ich mich nicht mehr erinnern kann, die Frage gestellt zu haben, die Brecht dort beantwortet', namely 'ob die heutige Welt überhaupt noch wiedergegeben werden kann' (in volume 4 of the Suhrkamp edition of Brecht's *Schriften zum Theater*), and Dürrenmatt refers to a discussion in Baden-Baden (he thought, in 1955) with Erwin Piscator (he thought!). I believe that Brecht was referring (in the *Fifth Darmstädter Gespräch* of 1955) to 'Theaterprobleme' (cf. my article 'Friedrich Dürrenmatt and the legacy of Bertolt Brecht' (D46, 71)). Brecht died in 1956 and did not see Dürrenmatt's *Frank V.*

4. The uninteresting little 'Helvetisches Zwischenspiel' (70–7) is a needless continuation of his earlier discussion of Switzerland's 'ridiculous neutrality' and was prompted by the call for a 'geistige Landesverteidigung', where Switzerland shows itself to be, in the terminology of the main lecture, a 'wolf in sheep's clothing' which insists on being called a lamb!

5. Dürrenmatt's visit, the ceremony and the performance in his honour of *Der Meteor* are charted in Violet Ketels' account *Friedrich Dürrenmatt at Temple University* (F11).

6. Dürrenmatt shared ownership of the *Sonntags Journal* with Rolf Bigler and J.R. von Salis from April 1969 to 1971. Its independence served him well during these traumatic years.

7. He repeated this even more firmly in 1973 when, in his article in *Die Tat* on Elisabeth Brock-Sulzer's seventieth birthday he wrote that he was not only 'ein leidenschaftlicher Nicht-ins-Theater-Geher', but when he does not go, 'scheint es mir dann, daß ich das Theater hasse' (now in WA25, 98–105, 102).

8. Dürrenmatt's important essay 'Dramaturgie des Labyrinths', closely connected with his painting (1972) and published in *text + kritik 56* (1977), will be considered later since it is most relevant to my closing remarks.

9. Anton Krättli's otherwise valuable article on the *Komplex* (E26), seems to me just a little optimistic in calling it 'wahrscheinlich eines seiner Hauptwerke' (56). There is so much repetition of ideas, so much self-indulgence, so much petulance, that it is difficult to allot it such an important position in the *oeuvre*, notwithstanding its considerable interest. Renata Usmiani reads it as an example *expressis verbis* of the author's 'tiefen Pessimismus', a 'Katastrophismus' (!) *vis-à-vis* the world, but she too praises it highly (E45, 150).

10. An attempt at such a collection has been made by Daniel Keel in his *Denken mit Dürrenmatt*, which reproduces 'paragraphs' containing such

aphorisms (C27). (It was re-issued as *Denkanstöße* in 1989.)

11. Attached to the essay are eleven pages of 'scholarly' footnotes and sixteen pages of a 'Skizze zu einem Nachwort', plus a two-page bibliography – which makes one wonder if Dürrenmatt, despite his protestations to the contrary, is now writing within a good Germanic tradition. Is he seeking academic respectability?

12. Manfred Durzak's article 'Dramaturgie des Labyrinths – Dramaturgie der Phantasie' (E14) suggests that the 'Ungestalt' of the 'Minotaurus' is a legitimation of Dürrenmatt's old definition of the grotesque in 'Theaterprobleme', 'die Gestalt nämlich einer Ungestalt, das Gesicht einer gesichtslosen Welt' and that Theseus is therefore the 'Dichter' who goes into the labyrinth 'die Ungestalt einer unmenschlichen Wirklichkeit zu bezwingen' (178). The suggestion certainly brings together a few more *Urmotive*!

Chronology

1921:   Born in Konolfingen, Canton Berne, 5 January. Parents: Reinhold Dürrenmatt, Protestant clergyman and Hulda (née Zimmermann).

1933:   Secondary school in Großstetten, a neighbouring village.

1933–5:   Family moves to Berne; father now Pfarrer at the Diakonissenhaus. Dürrenmatt attends the Freie Gymnasium (later Humboldtianum).

1941:   *Maturität* (Leaving Certificate). Begins studies at University of Berne, 1941–2 Literature and Philosophy. Zurich, 1942–3, Philosophy. Berne, 1943–5, Philosophy. Studies Aristotle, Plato, Kant, Kierkegaard. Reads Greek tragedies, Aristophanes, Shakespeare. Later Kafka, Jünger, Wedekind. Lessing, his favourite 'classic'.

1943:   First literary efforts: 'Weihnacht', 'Der Folterknecht', 'Die Wurst', 'Der Sohn'; *Komödie* (became *Untergang und neues Leben*, published 1980).

1945:   First published work, 'Der Alte' (in *Der Bund*, Berne). Writes 'Das Bild des Sisyphos', 'Der Theaterdirektor'. Begins *Es steht geschrieben*.

1946:   Marries actress Lotti Geißler, 12 October.

1947:   Moves to Basle. Writes 'Die Falle', 'Pilatus', *Der Doppelgänger*. Première of *Es steht geschrieben*, Schauspielhaus, Zurich, 19 April. Prize of the 'Welti-Stiftung für das Drama'. Son Peter born, 6 August. Works on *Der Blinde* and on a story (which becomes 'Die Stadt', 1952). Writes theatre reviews for *Die Nation*, Berne.

1948:   Première of *Der Blinde*, Stadttheater, Berne, 10 January. Moves to Ligerz on the Bielersee, 17 July. Works on, then destroys, drama *Der Turmbau zu Babel*. Writes sketches for Cabaret Cornichon, Zurich. Works on *Romulus der Große*.

1949:   Première of *Romulus der Große*, Stadttheater, Basle, 25 April. Daughter Barbara born, 19 September. First Dürrenmatt production in the Federal Republic, *Romulus der Große*, in Göttingen. Meets Bertolt Brecht.

1950:   Writes *Der Richter und sein Henker* in instalments for the *Schweizerische Beobachter*. Working on *Die Ehe des Herrn Mississippi*.

1951:   Writes *Der Verdacht* in instalments. Writes *Der Prozeß um des Esels Schatten.* and 'Der Hund'. Writes reviews for the Zurich *Weltwoche* (until 1953). Daughter Ruth born, 6 October.

1952:   Moves to own house in Chemin du Pertuis-du-Sault, Neuchâtel, 1 March. Première *Die Ehe des Herrn Mississippi* in the Munich Kammerspiele, 26 March. 'Die Stadt' published. Writes '*Der Tunnel*', *Stranitzky und der Nationalheld, Nächtliches Gespräch mit einem verachteten Menschen* (produced as play in the Munich Kammerspiele, 26 July.

1953:   Première of *Ein Engel kommt nach Babylon*, Munich Kammerspiele, 22 December.

1954:   *Literaturpreis der Stadt Bern* for *Ein Engel kommt nach Babylon*. Working on *Herkules und der Stall des Augias, Das Unternehmen der Wega*. 'Theaterprobleme' written. Produces *Mississippi* in Stadttheater, Berne.

1955:   Working on *Grieche sucht Griechin* and *Der Besuch der alten Dame*.

1956:   Première of *Der Besuch der alten Dame*, Schauspielhaus, Zurich, 29 January. Writes radio-plays *Die Panne, Abendstunde im Spätherbst*. New version of *Mississippi*. Lecture on 'Vom Sinn der Dichtung in unserer Zeit'.

1957:   *Preis der Kriegsblinden* for *Die Panne*. Writes script for television film of *Der Richter und sein Henker* and for film *Es geschah am hellichten Tag*, (which then becomes *Das Versprechen*). New version of *Ein Engel kommt nach Babylon* and *Romulus der Große*. Writes 'Mister X macht Ferien'. *Der Besuch der alten Dame* produced in Paris.

1958:   *Prix d'Italia* for *Abendstunde im Spätherbst*. *Literaturpreis* of the Tribune de Lausanne for *Die Panne*. *Es geschah am hellichten Tag* shown in Germany. Première of *Der Besuch der alten Dame* in New York at opening of Lunt-Fontanne Theatre (*The Visit*), directed by Peter Brook.

1959:   Première of opera *Frank V*, Schauspielhaus, Zurich, 19 March. New York Theatre Critics' Prize for the *Alte Dame*. To New York in April/May. *Schillerpreis*, Mannheim, 9 November. Lecture: 'Friedrich Schiller'. Produces *Alte Dame* in Ateliertheater, Berne. *Ein Engel* produced in Stockholm, the *Alte Dame* in Prague, London, Madrid, Lisbon, Jerusalem and Tokyo.

1960:   Visit to London. *Alte Dame* (*La visita della vecchia signora*) in Milan. *Mississippi* produced in Paris. *Großer Preis der Schweizerischen Schillerstiftung*, 4 December. Writes script for film of *Mississippi*. New ending for *Frank V*, Munich.

1961:   Visits Berlin. Première of film *Die Ehe des Herrn Mississippi* in Germany. *Alte Dame* produced in la Comédie de l'Est in Paris.

1962:   Première of *Die Physiker*, Schauspielhaus, Zurich, 20 February. *Herkules* developed as *Komödie* from radio-play. *Die Physiker* produced in Santiago, Mexico City and Lima.

1963: Première of *Herkules und der Stall des Augias*, Schauspielhaus, Zurich, 20 March. *Die Heimat im Plakat*, drawings, published. *The Physicists* produced in London by RSC at the Aldwych Theatre, directed by Peter Brook, then in Amsterdam, Helsinki, Stockholm, Copenhagen, Oslo, Palermo, Warsaw, Israel and Buenos Aires.

1964: Première of *Romulus der Große* in the Théâtre National Populaire, Paris. To the USSR for ceremonies for Soviet poet, June. Produces new version of *Frank V* in Bochum, work suspended before première. Première of film of *Alte Dame* in Germany: *The Visit*, with Ingrid Bergman and Anthony Quinn. *Die Physiker* produced in New York.

1965: Working on *Der Meteor*. Father dies, 8 February, aged eighty-four.

1966: Première of *Der Meteor*, Schauspielhaus, Zurich, 20 January. Writes script for television version of *Frank V* and directs performance in Hamburg. *Es steht geschrieben* rewritten as *Die Wiedertäufer*. *Theater-Schriften und Reden* published. *Grieche sucht Griechin* film in Germany. *Der Meteor* produced in London (RSC) and Buenos Aires.

1967: *Frank V* film in Germany, produced by Dürrenmatt, music by Paul Burkhard. Première of *Die Wiedertäufer* in Schauspielhaus, Zürich, 16 March. Visit to Writers' Congress in Moscow, May. Begins work on *Porträt eines Planeten*. Lecture in Zurich Schauspielhaus: 'Israels Lebensrecht', 17 June.

1968: 'Monstervortrag über Gerechtigkeit und Recht', Mainz University, January. Speech: 'Tschechoslowakei 1968', Stadttheater, Basle, 8 September. Begins work at Basle theatres with Werner Düggelin. Première of *König Johann*, Stadttheater, Basle, 18 September. *Grillparzer-Preis der österreichischen Akademie der Wissenschaften*.

1969: Première of *Play Strindberg*, Basler Komödie, 8 February. Dürrenmatt falls ill, Easter. In October, after differences with the management in Basle, Dürrenmatt leaves theatre. *Großer Literaturpreis des Kantons Bern*, 25 October. Honorary doctorate of Temple University, Philadelphia; Dürrenmatt in USA from November till January 1970. Visits Florida, Caribbean Islands, Puerto Rico and New York. Co-publisher of Zurich *Sonntags Journal* till 1971.

1970: Première of *Goethes Urfaust*, Schauspielhaus, Zurich, 22 October. Première of *Porträt eines Planeten*, Schauspielhaus, Düsseldorf, 10 November. Première of *Titus Andronicus*, Schauspielhaus, Düsseldorf, 12 December. 'Sätze aus Amerika' published.

1971: 'Der Sturz' published. New version of *Porträt* produced by

Dürrenmatt for Schauspielhaus, Zurich, 25–7 March. Première of opera *Der Besuch der alten Dame* (by Gottfried von Einem) in Staatsoper, Vienna, 23 May.

1972: Produces *Büchners Woyzeck* in Schauspielhaus, Zurich, 17 February. Turns down offer of Intendant of Schauspielhaus, Zurich. Italian film of *Die Panne* (*La più bella serata della mia vita*). *Die Physiker* in Vancouver; *Herkules* in Paris and London; *Porträt* in Yokohama.

1973: Produces *Die Physiker* for Swiss theatrical tour. Première of *Der Mitmacher*, Schauspielhaus, Zurich, 8 March. Opera of *The Visit* in Glyndebourne. *Play Strindberg* in London, Paris, Copenhagen, Ankara and Rio de Janeiro. *Frank V* in Paris. *Der Mitmacher* in Warsaw.

1974: Honorary Fellowship, Ben-Gurion University, Beersheba, Israel. Lecture (later essay): *Zusammenhänge* (published 1976). Produces Lessing's *Emilia Galotti*, Zurich, 5 June. Working on *Der Mitmacher. Ein Komplex*.

1975: Lecture against anti-Israel resolution at UNO in PEN congress, 14–20 November in Vienna. Working on *Die Frist*.

1976: *Der Mitmacher. Ein Komplex* published. To Wales for the Welsh Arts Council International Writer's Prize, but falls ill before presentation. Films *Der Richter und sein Henker* (directed by Maximilian Schell, with Martin Ritt, Jon Voight and Jacqueline Bisset – and Dürrenmatt).

1977: *Der Meteor* produced in Paris. Awarded the Buber-Rosenzweig medal, Paulskirche, Frankfurt, 6 March. Lecture: 'Über Toleranz'. Première of opera *Ein Engel kommt nach Babylon* (by Rudolf Kelterborn), Opernhaus, Zurich, 5 June. Première of *Die Frist*, Kino Corso, Zurich, 6 October. Honorary doctorates, Université de Nice, 17 November, Hebrew University, Jerusalem, 26 November.

1978: Film of *Der Richter und sein Henker* appears. *Die Frist* in Lodz, Poland. Produces *Der Meteor* (new version) in Theater an der Josefstadt, Vienna, in November. *Bilder und Zeichnungen*, Dürrenmatt's drawings and paintings, published.

1979: Lecture: 'Albert Einstein' in ETH, Zurich, 24 February, then as book. *Großer Literaturpreis der Stadt Bern*, 19 June. Première of *Komödie, Die Panne*, in Wilhelmsbad/Hanau, near Frankfurt, 13 September, directed by Dürrenmatt. *Die Frist* produced in Rostock (GDR)

1980: *Dichterdämmerung* and 'Nachgedanken' (to *Zusammenhänge*) published with the *Werkausgabe* in thirty volumes (Diogenes Verlag, Zurich). *Vallon de l'Ermitage* appears in *La Revue Neuchâteloise*.

1981: Dürrenmatt is sixty on 5 January. Honorary doctorate, Uni-

versity of Neuchâtel. *Festakt* in Schauspielhaus, Zurich,
10 January. *Romulus der Große* staged. Writer-in-residence,
University of Southern California, Los Angeles, March to
June. International Dürrenmatt-Symposium, Los Angeles,
23–5 April. Exhibition of his paintings, Berne, 2 September to
16 October. *Stoffe I–III* published, September. *Weinpreis für
Literatur der edition text + kritik*, Göttingen.

1982: Working on *Achterloo*. *Die Welt als Labyrinth* in ORF discussion with Franz Kreuzer, on *Stoffe I–III*. Television version
of *Alte Dame*, DRS, 28 November.

1983: Wife, Lotti, dies on 16 January. Honorary doctorate, University of Zurich, 29 April. Première *Achterloo*, Schauspielhaus,
Zurich, 6 October. Book published. Visits Greece, November. Visits South America, December to January 1984.

1984: *Carl-Zuckmayer-Medaille des Landes Rheinland-Pfalz*, 28 Febru-
ary. *Österreichischer Staatspreis für Europäische Literatur* 1983.
Marries Charlotte Kerr, 8 May. Writing 'Minotaurus. Eine
Ballade'. New version of *Achterloo*, August to December. *Die
Panne* produced in Théâtre Le Carré, Paris. Lecture: 'Kunst
und Wissenschaft', University of Frankfurt, 16 November.
Charlotte Kerr film: *Portrat eines Planeten* (*Von und mit Friedrich
Dürrenmatt*) SDR III Programme 26 December.

1985: 'Minotaurus' published (Diogenes) in May. Working on *Justiz*, May to October. Introduction to Japanese author Yasushi
Inoue at Berlin Festspiele, 23 June. Exhibition of paintings,
Neuchâtel, September 1985 to January 1986. *Bayrischer Litera
turpreis* (*Jean-Paul-Preis*), 4 October. *Justiz* published (Diogenes Verlag), October. Visits Egypt, November.

1986: *Der Auftrag* published. Awarded *Premio Letterario Internationale
Mondello* for *Justiz* (in Sicily). Awarded *Georg-Büchner-Preis* in
Darmstadt. Awarded the *Schiller-Gedächtnis-Preis des Landes
Baden-Württemberg*, Stuttgart. *Rollenspiele* published (Diogenes).

1987: To Moscow for Friedensforum für eine atomfreie Welt. International prize for *Humor und Satire in der Literatur* 'Hitar Petar'.

1988: *Versuche* published (Diogenes). Television version of *Abendstunde im Spätherbst*. Première of *Achterloo IV* in Schwetzingen
Castle, directed by Dürrenmatt.

1989: Awarded the *Ernst-Robert-Curtius-Preis für Essayistik*. Published *Durcheinandertal* (Diogenes).

Bibliography

1. Bibliographies of Dürrenmatt literature

Hansel, J., *Friedrich-Dürrenmatt-Bibliographie*, Bad-Homburg–Berlin–Zurich, 1976.

Hönes, W., 'Bibliographie zu Friedrich Dürrenmatt', in *text + kritik*, Heft 50/51, 1976, 93–108.

Keel, D. (ed.), 'Bibliographie', in *Über Friedrich Dürrenmatt*, Diogenes Verlag AG, Zurich, 1980 (WA30, 449–96).

Knapp, G.P., 'Bibliographie der wissenschaftlichen Sekundärliteratur', in *Friedrich Dürrenmatt*, Lothar Stiehm Verlag, Heidelberg, 1976, 257–68.

Whitton, K.S., *The theatre of Friedrich Dürrenmatt*, Wolff, London, 1980, 228–42.

2. Primary Literature

The edition worked in this study is the *Werkausgabe* (WA) edited by Thomas Bodmer and Daniel Keel and published in thirty volumes in the dtb (detebe) format by Diogenes Verlag AG, Zurich, 1980. (The WA is also published in hardback edition by the Verlag der Arche, Zurich, 1980.) These volumes are identified in the text as 'WA1', etc. The major items in each volume are:

WA1:   *Es steht geschrieben – Der Blinde – Der Doppelgänger* (*Hörspiel*)
WA2:   *Romulus der Große –* 'Kaiser und Eunuch' (*Fragment*)
WA3:   *Die Ehe des Herrn Mississippi*
WA4:   *Ein Engel kommt nach Babylon –* 'Der Uhrenmacher' (*Fragment*)
WA5:   *Der Besuch der alten Dame*
WA6:   *Frank der Fünfte*
WA7:   *Die Physiker –* '21 Punkte zu den Physikern'
WA8:   *Herkules und der Stall des Augias – Der Prozeß um des Esels Schatten – Herkules und der Stall des Augias* (*Hörspiel*)
WA9:   *Der Meteor – Dichterdämmerung – Abendstunde im Spätherbst* (*Hörspiel*)
WA10: *Die Wiedertäufer*
WA11: *König Johann – Titus Andronicus*
WA12: *Play Strindberg – Porträt eines Planeten*
WA13: *Urfaust – Woyzeck*
WA14: *Der Mitmacher. Ein Komplex – Der Mitmacher* (*Komödie*)
WA15: *Die Frist*
WA16: *Die Panne* (*Hörspiel* and *Komödie*)

WA17: *Nächtliches Gespräch mit einem verachteten Menschen – Stranitzsky und der Nationalheld – Das Unternehmen der Wega – Der Gerettete – Der Erfinder*

WA18: *Aus den Papieren eines Wärters*: – 'Weihnacht' – 'Der Folterknecht' – 'Die Wurst' – 'Der Sohn' – 'Der Alte' – 'Das Bild des Sisyphos' – 'Der Theaterdirektor' – 'Die Falle' – 'Pilatus' – 'Die Stadt' – 'Aus den Papieren eines Wärters'

WA19: *Der Richter und sein Henker – Der Verdacht*

WA20: 'Der Hund' – 'Der Tunnel' – 'Die Panne' (*Erzählung*)

WA21: *Grieche sucht Griechin* – 'Mister X macht Ferien' – 'Nachrichten über den Stand des Zeitungswesens in der Steinzeit'

WA22: *Das Versprechen* – 'Aufenthalt in einer kleinen Stadt'

WA23: 'Der Sturz' – 'Abu Chanifa und Anan ben David' – 'Smithy' – 'Das Sterben der Pythia'

WA24: *Theater*: Essays, Gedichte und Reden

WA25: *Kritik*: Kritiken und Zeichnungen

WA26: *Literatur und Kunst*: Essays, Gedichte und Reden

WA27: *Philosophie und Naturwissenschaft*: Essays, Gedichte und Reden

WA28: *Politik*: Essays, Gedichte und Reden

WA29: *Zusammenhänge. Essay über Israel. Eine Konzeption* – 'Nachgedanken'

WA30: *Über Friedrich Dürrenmatt*: Essays, Aufsätze, Zeugnisse und Rezensionen, Chronologie und Bibliographie (3rd edn 1986, ed. by D. Keel)

A. Dürrenmatt's Works Since 1980

Since 1980 the following works by Friedrich Dürrenmatt have been published (referred to in the text as A1, etc.):

A1: *Stoffe I* ('Der Winterkrieg in Tibet') (Diogenes, Zurich, 1984)

A2: *Stoffe II–III* ('Mondfinsternis' and 'Der Rebell') (Diogenes, Zurich, 1984) (Both volumes were first published as *Stoffe I–III*, Diogenes, Zurich, 1981)

A3: *Justiz* (Roman) (Diogenes, Zurich, 1985)

A4: *Rollenspiele* (*Protokol einer fiktiven Inszenierung, Assoziationen mit einem dicken Filzstift* and *Achterloo III*) (Friedrich Dürrenmatt and Charlotte Kerr) (Diogenes, Zurich, 1986)

A5: *Der Auftrag* (*oder Vom Beobachten des Beobachters der Beobachter*) (Diogenes, Zurich, 1986)

A6: *Versuche* (Diogenes, Zurich, 1988)

In addition, I have referred in the study to the following works which are not in the *Werkausgabe*:

A7:   *Die Heimat im Plakat (Ein Buch für Schweizer Kinder)* (Diogenes, Zurich, 1963)
A8:   *Bilder und Zeichnungen* (ed. by Christian Strich) (Diogenes, Zurich, 1978)
A9:   *Friedrich Dürrenmatt Lesebuch* (Arche, Zurich, 1978)
A10:   *Achterloo. Eine Komödie* (Diogenes, Zurich, 1983)
A11:   'Minotaurus. Eine Ballade' (Diogenes, Zurich, 1985)
A12:   *Oeuvres graphiques*, Catalogue du Musée d'art et d'histoire, Neuchâtel, 1985
A13:   *Theater-Schriften und Reden* (ed. by E. Brock–Sulzer) (Arche, Zurich, 1966)
A14:   *Dramaturgisches und Kritisches (Theater-Schriften und Reden II)* (Arche, Zurich, 1972)
A15:   Excerpts from Dürrenmatt's works have appeared in *Wiederholte Versuche, die Welt auszumisten* (ed. by K. Wagenbach and W. Stephan) (Wagenbachs Taschenbücherei, Berlin, 1988)
A16:   *Friedrich Dürrenmatt: Gesammelte Werke* (ed. by Franz Josef Görtz) (Diogenes, Zurich, 1988)
A17:   *Durcheinandertal* (Diogenes, Zurich, 1989).

3. Secondary Literature

The secondary literature to Friedrich Dürrenmatt and his works has now reached some 2,000 items and it would obviously be both impossible and impracticable to list them all. Students of Dürrenmatt will find these in the listed bibliographies. I have decided to list here only those works which were of value for the present study. My first book *The theatre of Friedrich Dürrenmatt* (London, 1980) presents a very full bibliography of works that I have found generally of value and use.

B. Books in English

B1:   Arnold, A., *Friedrich Dürrenmatt* (New York, 1972)
B2:   Bain, A., *The emotions and the will* (London, 1865)
B3:   Bennett, E.K., *A history of the German Novelle from Goethe to Thomas Mann* (Cambridge 1934, revised and continued by H.M. Waidson, 1965)
B4:   Bullivant, K., *The modern German novel* (Leamington Spa, 1987)
B5:   Bullivant, K., *Realism today* (Oxford, 1987)
B6:   Butler, M., *The novels of Max Frisch* (London, 1976)
B7:   Esslin, M., *Brecht, a choice of evils* (London, 1959)
B8:   Flood, J.L. (ed.), *Modern Swiss literature: Unity and diversity* (London, 1985)
B9:   Forster, L.W. (ed.), *Der Richter und sein Henker* (London, 1962)

B10:   Forster, L.W. (ed.), *Der Verdacht* (London, 1965)
B11:   Forster L.W. (ed.), *Das Versprechen* (London, 1967)
B12:   Highet, G., *The anatomy of satire* (Princeton, 1962)
B13:   Innes, C.D., *Modern German drama* (Cambridge, 1979)
B14:   Jacobs, M. (ed.), *Dantons Tod* and *Woyzeck* (of Georg Büchner) (Manchester, 1954)
B15:   Jennings, L.B., *The ludicrous demon* (Berkeley, Calif., 1963)
B16:   Jenny, U., *Dürrenmatt: A study of his plays* (trans. by K. Hamnett and H. Rorrison, London, 1978)
B17:   Lazar, M. (ed.), *Play Dürrenmatt* (Malibu, 1983)
B18:   Peppard, M., *Friedrich Dürrenmatt* (New York, 1969)
B19:   Popper, K., *The open society and its enemies* (Princeton, 1950)
B20:   Rushdie, S., *The Satanic Verses* (London, 1988)
B21:   Steiner, G., *The death of tragedy* (London, 1961) (1963 edn)
B22:   Tiusanen, T., *Dürrenmatt: A study in plays, prose, theory* (Princeton, 1977)
B23:   Whitton, K.S., *The theatre of Friedrich Dürrenmatt* (London, 1980)

C. Books in German and French

C1:   Angermeyer, H.C., *Zuschauer im Drama: Brecht – Dürrenmatt – Handke* (Frankfurt, 1971)
C2:   Arnold, A., *Friedrich Dürrenmatt* (Berlin, 1969; 4th edn, 1979)
C3:   Arnold, A. (ed.), *Interpretationen – zu Friedrich Dürrenmatt* (Stuttgart, 1982)
C4:   Arnold, H.L. (ed.), *Friedrich Dürrenmatt I* (Vol. 50/51, *text + kritik*, Munich, 1976)
C5:   Arnold, H.L. (ed.), *Friedrich Dürrenmatt II* (Vol. 56, *text + kritik*, Munich, 1977)
C6:   Badertscher, H., *Dramaturgie als Funktion der Ontologie* (Stuttgart, 1979)
C7:   Bänziger, H., *Frisch und Dürrenmatt* (Berne, 1960; 7th edn, 1976)
C8:   Bänziger, H., *Frisch und Dürrenmatt* (Tübingen, 1987)
C9:   Beckmeier, R.W., *Dürrenmatt and the detective novel* (Diss., Univ. of New York, 1973)
C10:   Bergson, H., *Le rire* (Paris, 1901; 233rd edn, 1967)
C11:   Bienek, H., *Werkstattgespräche mit Schriftstellern* (Munich, 1962)
C12:   Brock-Sulzer, E., *Friedrich Dürrenmatt* (Zurich, 1960; 4th edn, 1973)
C13:   Brock-Sulzer, E., *Dürrenmatt in unserer Zeit* (Basle, 1968; 2nd edn, 1971)
C14:   Camus, A., *Le mythe de Sisyphe* (Paris, 1942)
C15:   Daibler, H., *Deutsches Theater* (Stuttgart, 1976)
C16:   Durzak, M., *Dürrenmatt, Frisch, Weiss* (Stuttgart, 1972; 2nd edn, 1978)

Bibliography

C17:   Frisch, M., *Tagebuch 1946–1949* (in *Gesammelte Werke in zeitlicher Folge*, ed. by H. Mayer (Frankfurt, 1976) II, 628–32)

C18:   Goertz, H., *Dürrenmatt* (Hamburg, 1987)

C19:   Grimm, R., Jäggi, W., Oesch H. (eds), *Der unbequeme Dürrenmatt* (Basle–Stuttgart, 1962)

C20:   Hebbel, F., *Sämtliche Werke* (ed. R.M. Werner) (Berlin, 1904)

C21:   Höllerer, W., *Max Frisch: Dramaturgisches. Ein Briefwechsel mit Max Frisch* (Berlin, 1969)

C22:   Howald, J., *Ulrich Dürrenmatt und seine Gedichte* (Meiringen, 1927)

C23:   Jauslin, C., *Friedrich Dürrenmatt* (Zurich, 1964)

C24:   Jenny, U., *Dürrenmatt* (Hannover, 1965; 5th edn, 1973)

C25:   Kayser, W., *Das sprachliche Kunstwerk* (Berne–Munich, 1948; 12th edn, 1967)

C26:   Kayser, W., *Das Groteske* (Oldenburg/Hamburg, 1957; 2nd edn, 1961)

C27:   Keel, D., *Denken mit Dürrenmatt* (Zurich, 1982) (now *Denkanstöße*, Zurich, 1989)

C28:   Knapp, G.P. (ed.), *Friedrich Dürrenmatt: Studien zu seinem Werk* (Heidelberg, 1976)

C29:   Knapp, G.P., *Friedrich Dürrenmatt* (Stuttgart, 1980)

C30:   Knapp, G.P. and Labroisse, G. (eds), *Facetten: Studien zum 60. Geburtstag Friedrich Dürrenmatts* (Berne–Frankfurt, 1981)

C31:   Knopf, J., *Friedrich Dürrenmatt* (Munich, 1976; 3rd edn, 1980)

C32:   Knopf, J., *Der Dramatiker Friedrich Dürrenmatt* (Berlin, 1987)

C33:   Lengborn, T., *Schriftsteller und Gesellschaft in der Schweiz* (Frankfurt, 1972)

C34:   Marti, K., *Die Schweiz und ihre Schriftsteller – die Schriftsteller und ihre Schweiz* (Zurich, 1966)

C35:   Mayer, H., *Dürrenmatt und Frisch* (Pfullingen, 1963)

C36:   Mayer, H., *Über Friedrich Dürrenmatt und Max Frisch* (Pfullingen, 1977)

C37:   Neis, E., *Friedrich Dürrenmatt: Der Richter und sein Henker* (Hallfeld, n.d.)

C38:   Nestle, W. (trans.), *Platon: Hauptwerke* (Stuttgart, 1973)

C39:   Neumann, G., Schröder, J. and Karnick, M., *Dürrenmatt – Frisch – Weiss* (Munich, 1969)

C40:   Profitlich, U., *Friedrich Dürrenmatt* (Stuttgart, 1973)

C41:   Rischbieter, H., *Theater im Umbruch* (Munich, 1970)

C42:   Rogge, A., *Das Problem der dramatischen Gattung im deutschen Lustspiel* (D. Phil, Hamburg University, 1926)

C43:   Schulz-Buschhaus, U., *Formen und Ideologien des Kriminalromans* (Frankfurt 1975)

C44:   Schwab, G., *Die schönsten Sagen des klassischen Altertums* (Freiburg i. Breisgau, 1961)

Bibliography

C45:   Seifert, W., *Der Richter und sein Henker* (Munich, 1975)

C46:   Spycher, P., *Friedrich Dürrenmatt: Das erzählerische Werk* (Frauenfeld–Stuttgart, 1972)

C47:   Staiger, E., *Grundbegriffe der Poetik* (Zurich, 1946)

C48:   Strelka, J., *Brecht – Horváth – Dürrenmatt* (Vienna–Hanover–Berne, 1962)

C49:   Syberberg, H.J., *Interpretationen zum Drama Friedrich Dürrenmatts* (D. Phil, Munich University, 1963; 2nd edn, 1965)

C50:   Vietta, A. (ed.), *5. Darmstädter Gespräch – Theater 1955* (Darmstadt, 1955)

C51:   Von Salis, J.R., *Schwierige Schweiz* (Zurich, 1968)

C52:   Von Salis, J.R., *Grenzüberschreitungen* (2. Teil 1939–78) (Zurich, 1979)

D. Articles in English

D1:   Arnold, A., 'On the sources of Friedrich Dürrenmatt's detective novels' (in B17, 189–202)

D2:   Ashbrook, B., 'Dürrenmatt's detective stories' (*Philosophical Journal*, 4, 1967, 17–29)

D3:   Bänziger, H., 'Wolfgang Schwitter's bed: On one of the requisites in Dürrenmatt's *Meteor*' (in B17, 85–95)

D4:   Boa, E., 'Approaches to an "A" Level text: Dürrenmatt's *Der Richter und sein Henker*' (*Modern Languages*, 67, 1, 1986, 40–6)

D5:   Bond, M., *Das Hörspiel*: Epic, lyric or dramatic? The critical debate about a literary form (*German Life and Letters*, 28, 1, 1974, 45–58)

D6:   Bond, M., 'Some reflections on post-war *Hörspiele*' (*New German Studies*, 4, 2, 1976, 91–100)

D7:   Butler, M., '"Das Labyrinth und die Rebellion": The absurd world of Friedrich Dürrenmatt' (*Modern Languages* 66, 2, 1985, 104–8)

D8:   Butler, M., '"Frische" and "Dürre": Aspects of the contemporary Swiss–German theatre' (in B8, 111–26)

D9:   Carew, R., 'The plays of Friedrich Dürrenmatt' (*Dublin Magazine*, 4, 1965, 57–68)

D10:   Daviau, D., 'The role of *Zufall* in the writings of Friedrich Dürrenmatt' (*Germanic Review*, 47, 1972, 281–93)

D11:   Diller, E., 'Despair and the paradox: Friedrich Dürrenmatt' (Wisconsin Studies in Contemporary Literature 7, 1966, 328–35)

D12:   Diller, E., 'Friedrich Dürrenmatt's "Weihnacht": A short, short, revealing story' (*Studies in short fiction*, 3, 1966, 138–40)

D13:   Diller, E., 'Friedrich Dürrenmatt's Chaos and Calvinism' (*Monatshefte*, 63, 1, 1971, 28–40)

D14:   Donald, S.G., 'Of mazes, men and minotaurs: Friedrich Dürrenmatt and the myth of the labyrinth' (*New German Studies*, 14, 3, 1986–7, 187–231)

D15: Esslin, M., '*Die Frist*, Dürrenmatt's late masterpiece' (in B17, 139–53)

D16: Federico, J.A., 'The hero as playwright in dramas by Frisch, Dürrenmatt and Handke' (*German Life and Letters*, 32, 2, 1979, 166–76)

D17: Fickert, K. 'Dürrenmatt's *The Visit* and *Job*' (*Books abroad*, 41, 1968, 389–92)

D18: Gillis, W., 'Dürrenmatt and the detectives' (*German Quarterly*, 35, 1962, 71–4)

D19: Gontrum, P.B., 'Ritter, Tod und Teufel: Protagonists and antagonists in the prose works of Friedrich Dürrenmatt' (*Seminar*, 1, 1965, 88–98)

D20: Graves, P., 'Disclaimers and paradoxes in Dürrenmatt' (*German Life and Letters*, 27, 2, 1973–4, 133–42)

D21: Heilmann, R., 'The lure of the demonic' (*Comparative Literature*, 12, 1961, 346–57)

D22: Helbling, R., 'Dürrenmatt criticism: Exit the grotesque?' (in B17, 175–88)

D23: Holzapfel, R., 'The divine plan behind the plays of Friedrich Dürrenmatt' (*Modern Drama* 8, 1965, 237–46)

D24: Hortenbach, J.C., 'Biblical echoes in *Der Besuch der alten Dame*' (*Monatshefte*, 57, 4, 1965, 145–61)

D25: Johnson, P., 'Grotesqueness and injustice in Dürrenmatt' (*German Life and Letters*, 15, 4, 1962, 264–73)

D26: Knapp, G.P., 'Dürrenmatt's *Physicists* as a turning-point for the dramatist and his concept of history' (in B17, 55–66)

D27: Leah, G.N., 'Dürrenmatt's detective stories' (*Modern Languages*, 48, 2, 1967, 65–9)

D28: Menhennet, A., 'Dürrenmatt and Goethe: The "classics" in a cold climate' (*Modern Languages*, 61, 1, 1980, 21–7)

D29: Murdoch, B.O., 'Dürrenmatt's *Physicists* and the tragic tradition' (*Modern Drama*, 13, 1970, 270–5)

D30: Pfeiffer, J.R., 'Windows, detectives and justice in Dürrenmatt's detective stories' (*Revue des langues vivantes*, 33, 1967, 451–60)

D31: Reid, J.H. 'Dürrenmatt in the GDR: The dramatist's reception up to 1980' (*Modern Language Review*, 79, 1984, 356–71)

D32: Rieß, C., 'The shocking world of Friedrich Dürrenmatt' (*Esquire*, 55, 5, 1961, 119ff.)

D33: Robinson, G.S., 'The games Dürrenmatt plays' (*Modern Drama*, 18, 1975, 325–35)

D34: Rock, D., 'A wager lost: Some thoughts on the role of Chance in Dürrenmatt' (*Modern Languages*, 68, 1, 1987, 22–7)

Bibliography

D35: Schnauber, C., 'Friedrich Dürrenmatt: *Stoffe*' (in B17, 203–7 and Foreword 1–5)

D36: Spycher, P., 'From *Der Mitmacher* to "Smithy" and "Das Sterben der Pythia"' (in B17, 107–24)

D37: Strelka, J., 'The significance of Friedrich Dürrenmatt's play *The Collaborator (Der Mitmacher)*' (in B17, 97–105)

D38: Subiotto, A., 'The "comedy of politics": Dürrenmatt's *King John*' (in *Affinities*, ed. by R.W. Last, London, 1971, 139–53)

D39: Usmiani, R., 'Friedrich Dürrenmatt as Wolfgang Schwitter' (*Modern Drama*, 11, 2, 1968, 143–50)

D40: Usmiani, R., 'Masterpiece in disguise: the radio plays of Friedrich Dürrenmatt' (*Seminar*, 7, 1971, 42–57)

D41: Usmiani, R., 'Friedrich Dürrenmatt's *The Meteor* and the tradition of Plays with Corpses' (in B17, 67–83)

D42: Wagner, G., 'Dürrenmatt and the *Kriminalroman* (*Commonweal*, 76, 13, 1962, 324–6)

D43: Waidson, H.M., 'Friedrich Dürrenmatt' (in *German Men of Letters*, Vol. III, ed. by A. Nathan, London, 1964, 323–43 and in *Swiss Men of Letters*, ed. by A. Nathan, London, 1970, 259–86)

D44: White, A.D., '*History and its adaptation: Shakespeare, Brecht, Dürrenmatt*' (*Modern Languages*, 58, 4, 1977, 195–200)

D45: Whitton, K.S., 'The Zürcher Literaturstreit' (*German Life and Letters* 27, 2, 1974, 142–50)

D46: Whitton, K.S., 'Friedrich Dürrenmatt and the legacy of Bertolt Brecht' (*Forum for Modern Language Studies*, 12, 1, 1976, 65–81)

D47: Wright, A.M., 'Scientific method and rationality in Dürrenmatt' (*German Life and Letters*, 35, 1, 1981, 64–72)

E. Articles in German

E1: Améry, J., 'Friedrich Dürrenmatts politisches Engagement: Anmerkungen zum Israel-Essay – *Zusammenhänge*' (in C5, 41–8)

E2: Arnold, A., 'Die Quellen von Dürrenmatts *Kriminalromanen*' (in C30, 153–74)

E3: Arnold, A., 'Dürrenmatt als Erzähler' (in C3, 187–203)

E4: Arnold, H.L., 'Theater als Abbild der labyrinthischen Welt' (in C4, 19–29)

E5: Bänziger, H., 'Die Gerichte und das Gericht von Alfredo Traps in einer ländlichen Villa' (in C28, 218–32)

E6: Bark, J., 'Dürrenmatts "Pilatus" und das Etikett des christlichen Dichters' (in C28, 53–68)

E7: Benn, G., '*Die Ehe des Herrn Mississippi*' (in C19, 31–3)

E8: Bloch P.A., '*Die Panne*' (in WA30, 226–40)

E9: Blum, R., 'Ist Friedrich Dürrenmatt ein christlicher Schriftsteller?' (*Reformatio*, 9, 1959, 535–9)

E10:   Bodensieck, H., 'Dürrenmatts Detektivgeschichten' (*Pädagogische Provinz*, 17, 1965, 385–96)

E11:   Brock-Sulzer, E., 'Das deutsch-schweizerische Theater der Gegenwart' (*German Life and Letters*, 12, 1, 1958, 12–23)

E12:   Buri, F., 'Der "Einfall" der Gnade in Dürrenmatts dramatischem Werk' (in C19, 35–69)

E13:   Dittberner, H., 'Dürrenmatt, der Geschichtenerzähler' (in C4, 86–92)

E14:   Durzak, M., 'Dramaturgie des Labyrinths – Dramaturgie der Phantasie. Friedrich Dürrenmatts dramentheoretische Position' (in C3, 173–86)

E15:   Flemming, W., 'Hörspiel als Kunstform' (in *Rundfunk und Fernsehen*, Hörspielheft, 1954)

E16:   Gallati, E., '*Herkules und der Stall des Augias*: Mythos, Parodie und Poesie' (in C3, 110–23)

E17:   Gasser, M., 'Eine Doppelbegabung' (in WA30, 347–63 and in A8, unnumbered pages)

E18:   Grimm, R., 'Parodie und Groteske im Werk Dürrenmatts' (in C19, 71–96)

E19:   Heer, F., 'Politische Tragödie' (in *Die Furche*, 12, 38, 1956, 13)

E20:   Helbling, R., 'Groteskes und Absurdes – Paradox und Ideologie. Versuch einer Bilanz' (in C28, 233–53)

E21:   Kästner, E., 'Dürrenmatts neues Stück' (in *Die Weltwoche*, 20 April 1952) (on *Die Ehe des Herrn Mississippi*)

E22:   Kieser, R., 'In eigener Sache. Friedrich Dürrenmatt und sein *Meteor*' (in C3, 124–35)

E23:   Knapp, G.P., '*Die Physiker*' (in C3, 97–109)

E24:   Knapp, M., 'Die Verjüngung der alten Dame' (in C5, 58–66)

E25:   Knapp, M. and Knapp, G.P., 'Recht – Gerechtigkeit – Politik' (in C5, 23–40)

E26:   Krättli, A., '"Wie soll man es spielen? Mit Humor!" Friedrich Dürrenmatts Selbstkommentar Der Mitmacher – ein Komplex', (in C5, 49–57)

E27:   Kunkel, K., 'Ein artiger James Bond: Jerry Cotton und der Bastei-Verlag' (in *Der Kriminalroman* (ed. by J. Voigt)) (*Fink Verlag*, 2, 1971, 559–78)

E28:   Labroisse, G., 'Die Alibisierung des Handelns in Dürrenmatts *Der Besuch der alten Dame*' (in C30, 207–23)

E29:   Marahrens, G., 'Friedrich Dürrenmatts *Die Ehe des Herrn Mississippi*' (in C28, 93–124)

E30:   Mayer, H., 'Dürrenmatt und Brecht oder Die Zurücknahme' (in C19, 97–116)

E31:   Mayer, H., 'Friedrich Dürrenmatt', (*ZfdPh*, 87, 1968, 482–98)

E32:   Melchinger, S., 'Wie schreibt man böse, wenn man gut lebt?' (*Theater heute*, 9, 1968, 6–8)

E33:   Pulver, E., 'Literaturtheorie und Politik' (in C4, 41–52)

E34:   Rischbieter, H., 'Dürrenmatts dünnstes Stück' (*Theater heute*, 3, 1960, 8–12) (on *Frank V*)

E35:   Rommel, O., 'Die wissenschaftlichen Bemühungen um die Analyse des Komischen' (*DVJS* 21, 1, 1943, 161–95)

E36:   Rommel, O., 'Komik und Lustspieltheorie' (*DVJS* 21, 2, 1943, 252–86)

E37:   Scherer, J., 'Der mutige Mensch' (*Stimmen der Zeit*, 169, 5, 1962, 307–12)

E38:   Schnauber, C., 'Friedrich Dürrenmatt in Los Angeles' (*Welt im Wort*, 15, 1981, 2–41)

E39:   Scholl, A., 'Zeichen und Bezeichnetes im Werk Friedrich Dürrenmatts' (in C28, 203–17)

E40:   Schuster, I., 'Dreimal "Die Panne": Zufall, Schicksal oder "moralisches Resultat"?' (in C3, 160–72)

E41:   Spycher, P., 'Friedrich Dürrenmatts Israel-Essay. Religiöse Konzeption und Glaubensbekenntnis' (in C30, 243–57)

E42:   Spycher, P., 'Friedrich Dürrenmatts "Meteor". Analyse und Dokumentation' (in C28, 145–87)

E43:   Tschimmel, I., 'Kritik am Kriminalroman' (in C30, 175–90)

E44:   Usmiani, R., 'Die Hörspiele Friedrich Dürrenmatts: unerkannte Meisterwerke' (in C28, 125–44)

E45:   Usmiani, R., 'Die späten Stücke: *Porträt eines Planeten, Der Mitmacher, Die Frist*' (in C3, 136–59)

E46:   Wagener, H., 'Heldentum heute? Zum Thema Zeitkritik in Dürrenmatts *Romulus der Große*' (in C30, 191–206)

E47:   Waldmann, G., 'Requiem auf die Vernunft. Dürrenmatts christlicher Kriminalroman' (*Pädagogische Provinz*, 15, 1961, 376–84)

E48:   Weber, E., 'Die Welt der frühen Werke, oder vom Einfall des Schrecklichen und von der Kunst, sich recht zu ängstigen' (in C3, 23–41)

E49:   Wyrsch, P., 'Die Dürrenmatt-Story' (in *Schweizer Illustrierte Zeitung*, 18 and 23 March and 1, 7, 15 and 22 April 1963; all on 23–5 except 15 and 22 April on 37–9)

F. Interviews, etc.

F1:   Arnold, H.L., 'Gespräch mit Heinz Ludwig Arnold' (Zurich, 1976)

F2:   Bachmann, D., 'Das Theater leidet unter Lebensangst' (in *Die Weltwoche*, 20 March 1974)

F3:   Bienek, H., 'Werkstattgespräch mit Friedrich Dürrenmatt' (in *Neue Zürcher Zeitung*, 11 March 1962, and in *Werkstattgespräch mit Schriftstellern*, Munich, 1962, 99–113)

Bibliography

F4: Bloch, P.A., '"Ich bin gegen das Eindeutige"' (in *Basler Zeitung*, 3 January 1982)

F5: Ebeling, R.T., 'Dramatiker Dürrenmatt: "Ich bin aus der Mode gekommen"' (in *Westfälisches Volksblatt*, 9 October 1976)

F6: Esslin, M., 'Dürrenmatt, merciless observer' (in *Plays and Players*, 10, 6, 1963, 15f.)

F7: Fringeli, D., *Nachdenken mit und über Friedrich Dürrenmatt* (Breitenbach, n.d. Conversation held in May 1977)

F8: Jenny, U., 'Lazarus der Fürchterliche' (*Theater heute*, 7, 1966, 10–12)

F9: Jonas, W., 'Friedrich Dürrenmatt und die "abstrakte Bühne"' (in *Zürcher Woche*, 30 June 1961)

F10: Kerr, C., *Porträt eines Planeten: Von und mit Friedrich Dürrenmatt. Die Welt als Labyrinth* (film in SDR III Programme, 26 December 1984)

F11: Ketels, V., 'Friedrich Dürrenmatt at Temple University' (*Journal of Modern Literature*, 1, 1971, 88–108)

F12: Kreuzer, F., *Die Welt als Labyrinth* (in ORF II programme, 10 June 1982 and in Diogenes, Zurich, 1986)

F13: Litten, R., 'Gespräch mit Dürrenmatt' (*Christ und Welt*, 19, 4, 28 January 1966)

F14: Mayer, H., 'Interview mit Dürrenmatt' (*Programmheft des Schauspielhauses Zürich*, 1965/66)

F15: Melchinger, S., 'Wie schreibt man böse, wenn man gut lebt?' (in *Neue Zürcher Zeitung*, 1 September 1968)

F16: Preuß, J.W., 'Wie ein Drama entsteht' (in *Literarische Werkstatt*, Munich 1972, 9–18, interview held in January 1969)

F17: Raddatz, F., '"Ich bin der finsterste Komödienschreiber, den es gibt"' (in *Die Zeit* 16 August 1985)

F18: Rieß, C., 'Dürrenmatt. Eine Welt auf der Bühne' (in *Die Weltwoche*, 23 February 1962)

F19: Sauter, R., 'Gespräch mit Dürrenmatt' (*Sinn und Form*, 18, 4, 1966, 1218–32)

F20: Vietta, E., 5. Darmstädter Gespräch – Theater 1955 (Darmstadt, 1955)

F21: Weber, J.P., 'Friedrich Dürrenmatt ou la quête de l'absurde' (*Le Figaro Littéraire*, 10 September 1960, 3)

F22: Whitton, K.S., 'Afternoon conversation with an uncomfortable person' (interview on 5 April 1969; text in *New German Studies*, 2, 1, 1974, 14–30)

Index to the Works of Friedrich Dürrenmatt

General Index

Radio Bern, 58, 59, 60, 66, 70, 72, 73, 163
Radio Beromünster, 27
Rank, Hugo, 91, 222, 223
Reid, J. Hamish, 98, 125, 225
Rekrutenschule, die, 4, 12, 86
Richelieu, Cardinal Armand-Jean, 154, 155, 226
Richter, der, see judge/executioner (theme)
Rieß, Curt, 28, 219
Rischbieter, Henning, 118
Ritt, Martin, 232
Rock, David, 41
Rogge, A., 105
Rommel, Otto, 40, 105, 161
Rousseau, Jean Jacques, 181
Royal Shakespeare Company, 122, 131, 231
Rubens, Peter Paul, 210
Rühmann, Heinz, 37, 49
Rushdie, Salman, 111

Salis, J.R. von, 210, 227
Sartre, Jean-Paul, 22, 112, 160, 175
Sauter, René, 134
Sayers, Dorothy Leigh, 27, 28, 32
Schalla, Hans, 225
Schauspielhaus Düsseldorf, 142, 231
Schauspielhaus Zürich, *see* Zurich
Schell, Maximilian, 32, 232
Scherer, Josef, 111
Schevchenko, Taras G., 76
Schifferli, Peter, 168
Schill, Anton, 114, 224
Schiller, Johann Christian Friedrich, 106, 165, 166, 167, 170, 226
Braut von Messina, Die, 170
Don Carlos, 176
Maria Stuart, 212
Räuber, Die, 160
Wallenstein, 170
Wilhelm Tell, 160, 165
Schirach, Baldur von, 64
Schmidt, Peer, 150
Schnauber, Cornelius, 139
Scholl, Amédée A., 209
Schopenhauer, Artur, 4
Schröder, Ernst, 133
Schubert, Franz, 58, 80, 140, 168
Schulz-Buschhaus, Ulrich, 37
Schuster, Ingrid, 221
Schwab, Gustav, 66, 85
Schwab-Felisch, Hans, 139

Schweikart, Hans, 45, 62, 109, 110
Schweizerische Beobachter, Der, 28, 32, 33, 229
Schwengeler, Arnold H., 33
Searle, Ronald, 210
Seelig, Carl, 221
Seifert, W., 220
Shaffer, Peter, 112
Shakespeare, William, 10, 59, 118, 136, 209, 223, 224, 229
Coriolanus, 172
Hamlet, 161, 223
Henry V, 118
Henry VI, 59
King John, 135, 142, 176
King Lear, 172
Titus Andronicus, 10, 118, 137, 142, 186
Shaw, G.B., 134
Simenon, Georges, 32, 42, 219
Simon, Michel, 37
Simplon Tunnel, 24, 104
Sisyphus/*Sisyphos*, 13
Six-Day War, 77, 132, 135, 174
Smutny, Jiri, 58, 62
Snow, Charles P., 164
Socrates, 161
Solidarność, 153, 154
Sonderer, R., 98
Sonntags Journal, 137, 181, 182, 184, 227, 231
Sophocles, 116, 200
Spiegel, Der, 93, 98
Spinoza, Benedict (Baruch) de, 198, 199
Spycher, Peter, 7, 14, 28, 31, 42, 192, 217, 218, 219, 222, 226
Spyri, Johanna, 88
St James, Ian, 223
Staiger, Emil, 4, 38, 74, 88, 130, 131, 165, 180, 217, 222
Stalin, Josef, 51, 63, 165
Starkie, Walter, 162
Steckel, Leonhard, 168
Steiner, George, 108
Sternheim, Carl, 45, 110
Stevenson, Robert Louis, 58
Storm, Theodor, 133
Stranitzky, Josef Anton, 64, 87
Strich, Fritz, 4
Strindberg, August, 104, 135
Stroux, Karl-Heinz, 142, 150
Stuttgart (FRG), 62
Subiotto, Arrigo, 220

Süddeutscher Rundfunk, 59, 208
Swift, Jonathan, 209

Tat, Die, 107, 223, 227
Temple University, Philadelphia, 138, 181, 227, 231
Tertullian, 18, 213
theatre of Friedrich Dürrenmatt, The, 7, 14, 20, 97, 224
Theseus, 2, 127, 207, 208, 211, 228
Thiele, Rolf, 49
Times, The, 113, 215, 223
Tiusanen, Timo, 8, 16, 49, 54, 126, 159, 186, 221
Todorav, Tzvetan, 29
Tower of Babel, 45, 109, 110, 211, 212, 229
Trakl, Georg, 5
Tschimmel, Ira, 29, 34

Ulam, Adam B., 222
Unselt, Karl, 220
Usmiani, Renate, 61, 75, 130, 150, 221, 227

Vajda, Ladislao, 37
Valency, Maurice, 116
Varlin, Jean, 210, 213, 214
Verdi, Giuseppe, 193
Vienna,
    Staatsoper, 113, 144, 231, 232
    Theater an der Josefstadt, 128, 232
    Volkstheater, 64
Villard, Arthur, 181
Vogel, Paul Ignaz, 181
Voight, Jon, 232

Wagener, Hans, 105
Wagner, Geoffrey, 220
Wagner, Richard, 74, 193
Wajda, Andrzej, 145
Waldmann, Günter, 30
Walesa, Lech, 153, 154
Wallace, Edgar, 27, 219
Wallenstein, Albrecht von, 165
Walser, Martin, 132
Wardle, Irving, 113, 115
Watergate, 183, 196
Waterloo, 154, 226

Webb, Alan, 122
Weber, Emil, 17, 23, 218
Weber, Jean-Paul, 70, 71
Wechsler, Lazar, 37
Wedekind, Frank, 45, 107, 110, 173, 229
Wedekind, Tilly, 107
Weill, Kurt, 119
Weiss, Peter, 132, 154
Weltwoche, Die, 28, 55, 58, 64, 121, 160, 161, 174, 229
Wessel, Oscar, 57
White, Alfred D., 119
Wicki, Bernhard, 113, 116
Wieland, Christoph Martin, 4, 59, 60, 134
Wilder, Thornton, 162
Wilhelmsbad/Hanau, 50, 150, 232
Winston, Richard and Clara, 49
Wolff-Windegg, Philipp, 67
World War II, 57, 63, 102, 161, 174, 177, 197
Worth, Irene, 122
Wright, A.M., 30, 124
Wyrsch, Peter, 10, 33, 66

Yom Kippur War, 188

Zacharoff, Basil, 115
Zeit, Die, 135
Zürcher Literaturstreit, Der, 130, 217, 222
Zürcher Theaterverein, 218
Zürcher Woche, 76
Zufall, see chance (theme)
Zurich, 4, 6, 7, 8, 12, 13, 15, 23, 24, 26, 27, 35, 36, 38, 42, 44, 45, 60, 65, 70, 82, 85, 90, 92, 93, 99, 122, 128, 131, 135, 143, 145, 153, 160, 165, 169, 183, 210, 219, 222, 229, 232, 233
    Kino Corso, 148, 232
    Opernhaus, 232
    Schauspielhaus, 13, 26, 66, 99, 113, 118, 121, 122, 126, 128, 138, 139, 143, 144, 145, 147, 154, 161, 167, 168, 171, 183, 192, 200, 219, 229, 230, 231, 232, 233
Zwingli, Ulrich, 181